TECHNOLOGICAL POWERS AND THE PERSON

NUCLEAR ENERGY AND REPRODUCTIVE TECHNOLOGIES

The Pope John Center
St. Louis, Missouri

CONTRIBUTORS TO THIS VOLUME

John Ahearne, Ph.D.
Commissioner,
United States Nuclear Regulatory Commission
Washington, D.C.

The Rev. Benedict Ashley, O.P., Ph.D.,
    S.T.M.
Professor of Moral Theology
Aquinas Institute of Theology
St. Louis University
St. Louis, Missouri

The Rev. Terence P. Brinkman, S.T.D.
Lecturer In Moral Theology
University of St. Thomas, School of Theology
Houston, Texas

Frederick S. Carney, PH.D.
Professor of Ethics
Perkins School of Theology
Southern Methodist University
Dallas, Texas

Christopher Derrick
Wallington
Surrey, England

John Deutch, PH.D.
Dean of Science
Massachusetts Institute of Technology
Cambridge, Massachusetts

The Rev. Michael Himes, PH.D.
Professor of Historical Theology
Seminary of the Immaculate Conception
Huntington, New York

Gordon C. Hurlburt, M.E., M.B.A.
President
Westinghouse Power Systems Company
Pittsburgh, Pennsylvania

Sister Margaret John Kelly, D.C., Ph.D.
Vice President, Mission Services
The Catholic Health Association of the U.S.
St. Louis, Missouri

The Honorable Carol Los Mansmann
U.S. District Judge
Western District of Pennsylvania
Pittsburgh, Pennsylvania

The Reverend Francis G. Morrisey, O.M.I.,
J.C.D.
Dean Faculty of Canon Law
St. Paul University
Ottowa, Ontario, Canada

Thomas Nabors, M.D.
Clinical Professor of Obstetrics-Gynecology
University of Texas
Dallas, Texas

The Rev. Donald Senior, C.P., S.T.D.
Professor of Sacred Scripture
Catholic Theological Union
Chicago, Illinois

George Tagatz, M.D.
Chief, Reproduction Endocrinology
and Infertility Clinic
Department of Obstetrics-Gynecology
University of Minnesota
School of Medicine
Minneapolis, Minnesota

Anna-Teresa Tymieniecka, Ph.D.
President
The World Institute for Advanced
Phenomenological Research and Learning
Belmont, Massachusetts

Paul C. Vitz, Ph.D.
Professor of Psychology
New York University
New York City, New York

Edwin Zebroski, Ph.D.
Vice President
Institute of Nuclear Power Operations
Atlanta, Georgia

THE EDITORS

The Pope John Center Staff

The Reverend Albert S. Moraczewski, O.P., Ph.D.
Vice-President for Research

The Reverend Donald G. McCarthy, Ph.D.
Director of Education

The Reverend Edward J. Bayer, S.T.D.
Director of Continuing Education

The Reverend Michael P. McDonough, S.T.D.
Director of Social Ethics

The Reverend Larry D. Lossing
Director of Communications

Nihil Obstat:
  Rev. Robert F. Coerver, C.M., S.T.D.
  Censor Deputatus

Imprimatur:
  The Rev. Monsignor Edward J. O'Donnell, V.G.
  Archdiocese of St. Louis

The Nihil Obstat and Imprimatur are a declaration that a book or pamphlet is considered to be free from doctrinal or moral error. It is not implied that those who have granted the Nihil Obstat and Imprimatur agree with the contents, opinions, or statements expressed.

Library of Congress Cataloging in Publication Data
Main entry under title:

Technological powers and the person.

  Includes index.

  1. Atomic energy—Religious aspects—Catholic Church—Congresses. 2. Man (Christian Theology)—Congresses. 3. Human reproduction—Religious aspects—Catholic Church Congresses. 4. Infertility—Religious Aspects—Catholic Church. Congresses. 5. Catholic Church—Doctrines—Congresses. I. Pope John XXIII Medical-Moral Research and Education Center.
Br115.A83T   1983   261.8   84-1933
ISBN 0-935372-12-1

Contents

Preface

This third workshop conducted for the members of the Catholic Hierarchies of the Central and North American continents by the Pope John Center was funded by the most generous support of a grant from the Knights of Columbus. In it, we have departed in several ways from the first two. It provided simultaneous translation in French and Spanish; it undertook to include a topic which departed from strictly medico-ethical considerations; it recorded the plenary discussions in order to include an edited version of the transcript in this publication; and arrangements were made to provide a Spanish translation of the published work.

The over-arching concern of this Workshop III was to distinguish carefully between the proper *use* of technological power and its *abuse*. The misuse of power has plagued the human race since its beginning. So simple a tool as a knife (presumably) was used by Cain to kill Abel and spill his blood (see *Genesis* 4:8, 11). The constant challenge to humans since they first disobeyed God and inordinately reached out for the power to "be like gods" promised by Satan (see *Genesis* 3:5–6), is to use power in accord with God's law. God has given the human race a delegated dominion over creation and with it the necessary power and skills. The temptation, however, is to misuse that power, to seek to "be like gods" but in a manner contrary to God's law.

In contemporary times, the human race has indeed acquired control, or partial control, over awesome powers: nuclear energy and reproduction. The former is more apparent because of the magnitude and scale of its misuse; the latter, though less dramatic, perhaps, is no less devastating because its abuse can do much to destroy the sacredness surrounding the creation of a new human person.

For these reasons, especially, these topics were selected for treatment in this present workshop. The two topics are united not only in their being manifest examples of how the God-given skills and powers can be readily perverted, but also in their being pressing contemporary problems for the bishops.

To initiate the workshop, the keynote speaker was selected as a person who could view the whole technological enterprise of modern man against the background of the Church's rich theological and humanistic tradition. Historically, the Church not only passed on the Faith as a living and developing heirloom, but also served to preserve through difficult periods of human history the cultural heritage which had painstakingly emerged over many centuries. While the Church stands in the stream of history, it is also altered and shaped by it. Yet at the same time it can have a reciprocal effect on that stream of history. The Church witnesses to the Faith but it also blesses and challenges the world and its works. It must judge modern technology and encourage what is in accord with God's law and disapprove that which is opposed, all the while taking care not to make premature judgments or act hastily.

In light of the ever-increasing concern about nuclear energy, both as used in weaponry and in the generation of electric power, there is a recognized need to distinguish carefully between the use of nuclear energy for peaceful purposes and its employment in the production of terribly destructive weapons. But having made such a distinction does not *ipso facto* establish the moral legitimacy of nuclear energy even for purely peaceful purposes. This must be examined carefully. The workshop strove to keep the question of nuclear *warfare* out of the discussions, since this matter had already been discussed extensively by the bishops and their collected views expressed in the pastoral letter *"The Challenge of Peace: God's Promise and Our Response"*, issued by the National Council of Catholic Bishops.

The magnitude of the problem of nuclear energy is suggested by the single fact that in North America for example there are currently (1983) some ninety-four nuclear plants in operation with about sixty-two under construction. Western Europe has one-hundred twenty-two operating nuclear plants and fourteen more are being constructed. (See Zebroski, Chapter 2.) Each of these is in some archdiocese or diocese. The media has publicized the mounting opposition to these nuclear plants and a number have been closed down, temporarily or permanently. The economic and social impact, short and long range, have not been adequately assessed.

As moral leaders of the Christian community, bishops have been approached to take a stand on issues surrounding nuclear energy. Pressed both by opponents and supporters of nuclear power, the bishops need a balanced treatment of the topic. With this objective in mind, the workshop sought to present the most secure data regarding nuclear energy.

Accordingly, the advantages and disadvantages of nuclear energy were presented respectively by two speakers who were asked to discuss their material in a non-polemical manner. (A similar request was made of the other speakers as well). The organizers of the workshop relied on the expert knowledge and the personal integrity of the selected speakers to discharge their respective tasks in a responsible manner. The published papers stand as a witness to their success.

As with the issue of nuclear energy for peaceful purposes, the speakers for the other two subject-areas were selected in order to provide a broad spectrum of views.

Because the issue of personhood had been discussed in the preceding workshop (see, *Human Sexuality and Personhood*, St. Louis: The Pope John Center, 1981) but from a somewhat limited aspect, attempt was made in this workshop to discuss the issue on a broader, interdisciplinary manner. Accordingly personhood was addressed respectively from the perspectives of the empirical sciences (specifically psychology), philosophy (especially phenomenology), Sacred Scripture, contemporary theologies. Not wanting to leave the various pieces disassembled, the Pope John Center invited one speaker (Father Benedict Ashley, O.P.) to present an integrated Christian view that attempted to bring the facts and insights from the various disciplines into a coherent whole (see Chapter 11).

For the topics related to reproductive technologies, practicing clinicians were brought in to present the problems faced by involuntary childless couples, the various diagnostic procedures and the different modes of treatment, both traditional and the latest technological procedures such as in vitro fertilization and surrogate parenting. Because the latter has special legal problems, a federal judge with interests on the subject was brought in to address some of those issues. The questions raised for Catholics considering the use of some of these new reproductive technologies by the Church's teaching and canon law regarding the Sacrament of Matrimony, was treated by a leading canon lawyer.

To close the workshop, an educator with broad Christian and humanistic background as well as health care experience was given the task of bringing the lectures and discussions of the workshop into some focus.

The Reprise and Coda is the result of that undertaking: the Reprise highlights certain recurrent themes while the Coda brings a new note by making some suggestions for action.

It should be noted that rather than have one or more papers which would deal explicitly with the pastoral problems of these several topics, the plenary discussions (which also reflected the results of the small group discussions) were designed to allow these problems to surface naturally. What better source to identify the pastoral concerns of the bishops but the bishops themselves? While some came to the workshop already burdened with specific problems dealing with nuclear energy and/or reproductive technologies, for all the lectures and the discussions would call attention to the real issues as the bishops themselves experienced them. Consequently, the discussions (see Chapters 6, 12, 18) are important for a fuller appreciation of the topics covered in this workshop.

The Editors

The following letter was sent to the Workshop for Bishops for 1983 in Dallas, Texas (January 31 through February 4), from the Vatican, bringing greetings and blessings from Pope John Paul II to the Workshop and its participants. It was read to the assembly by the Most Reverend Pio Laghi, Apostolic Delegate in the United States.

Dear Brothers in our Lord Jesus Christ,

As you assemble for the Workshop on Pastoral Problems of Nuclear and Reproductive Technologies, I assure you of my pastoral interest and closeness in prayer. Again this year, you have judged it beneficial for your people and important for your own understanding of specific pastoral problems to gather for this time of prayer, study and reflection.

You come from the Antilles, Canada, the Dominican Republic, Mexico and the United States. Although you are from different countries, you are united as brothers in Christ who share a common mission on behalf of the universal Church, and as Pastors who are convinced of the importance of continuing study and reflection for the effective proclamation of the Gospel in the modern world.

You have chosen to focus your attention on pastoral problems associated with nuclear and reproductive technologies. Who is not aware of the tremendous advances which have been made in the various technologies in recent years, and in these two technologies in particular? Such advances bear witness to the creative genius of the human person, while they also remind us of God's command to man to subdue the earth and become its master (cf. Gen 1:28).

At the same time, we must acknowledge that the advances in technology have not been matched by parallel advances in meeting the demands of justice and social love, and in the development of moral and spiritual values. In fact, these technological advances have even been used for highly destructive purposes and for ends directly contrary to the dignity of human life. It was precisely of this tragic reality that I was thinking when I wrote in my first Encyclical: "The man of today seems ever to be under threat from what he produces . . . This seems to make up the main chapter of the drama of present-day human existence" (*Redemptor Hominis*, 15).

Modern technologies, then, present us with the promise of great good on the one hand, and with the threat of disaster and manipulation on the other. In the face of these opposing possibilities, man must learn how to direct technological progress toward the service of the human person in all aspects of life. Man needs, in other words, to learn how to exercise dominion over the visible world. In this regard, I said in that Encyclical: "The essential meaning of this . . . 'dominion' of man over the visible world, which the Creator himself gave man for his task, consists in the priority of ethics over technology, in the primacy of the person over things, and in the superiority of spirit over matter" (no. 16).

As Pastors in the last part of the twentieth century, we must help our people to exercise this dominion over creation. In particular we need to encourage the Christian laity in this task, for it is their special vocation to engage in temporal affairs, such as modern technologies, and direct them in accordance with God's plan. As the Second Vatican Council taught concerning the laity, "it pertains to them in a special way so to illumine and order all temporal things with which they are so clearly associated that these may be done according to Christ, and increase and exist for the glory of the Creator and Redeemer" (*Lumen Gentium*, 31).

In addition to these few considerations, I wish to remind you of the words of Saint Paul: "All creation groans and is in agony even until now. Not only that, but we ourselves, although we have the Spirit as first fruits, groan inwardly while we await the redemption of our bodies. In hope we were saved" (Rom 8:22–4). As we and our people engage, at times with anguish, in the struggle of all creation to be caught up fully in God's redemptive activity, let us be filled with hope and utter confidence in the Spirit of love and of life. And let us be heralds of this hope in the midst of a world drawn toward sadness and despair. For God has said: "See, I make all things new!" (Rev 21:5).

I would like to acknowledge those who have made this Workshop possible, namely the Knights of Columbus and the Pope John XXIII Medical Moral Research and Education Center. May the Lord reward them for their continued generous and loyal assistance to the Magisterium.

Upon all of you, my Brother Bishops, and upon all those who are assisting you during these days, I invoke the light and peace of the Holy Spirit. I entrust you to the loving intercession of Mary, Seat of Wisdom, and cordially impart my Apostolic Blessing.

From the Vatican, January 26, 1983

JOANNES PAULUS P.P.II

PART I

Prelude

Pastoral Problems of Nuclear and Reproductive Technologies

Introduction

One objective of the 1983 Bishops' Workshop was to present clearly, concisely and competently current data regarding 1), the use of nuclear energy for peaceful purposes and 2), the utilization of various technologies to assist human reproduction. As a basis for a consideration of the ethical and pastoral dimensions, several papers collectively presented a multidisciplinary study of the concept of personhood, since these awesome technological powers eventually must be evaluated in terms of whether they are of authentic benefit to human persons and human society.

A religious minded person will approach creation with a sense of awe and respect. Whether dealing with the tremendous power of nuclear energy or the intimate powers of reproduction, the human person is challenged to employ them in a non-manipulative fashion and with a reverence suggested by the expression of Bertrand Russell, "cosmic piety."

Nuclear Energy

The use of nuclear energy in North America must be viewed in light of global energy needs and resources. Not only have the supplies of oil and gas dwindled, but their global distribution is non-uniform. This combination has been a source of political and military instability, as well as placing a tremendous economic burden on the less developed oil-importing nations. Other energy sources are not sufficient of themselves to provide the energy required by the world to support the increasingly larger population at the current level of technological and cultural development.

For developed countries such as the United States, nuclear energy provides certain advantages. Among others, it can supply energy at levels which the exploitation of all other resources would fail to do. By doing so, it lessens the pressure for the importation of oil and thus provides greater availability of oil to the less developed nations. At the same time, proper use of nuclear energy reduces air pollution, toxic rain, and provides a more stable economic base by having an assured major source of energy.

As with most or all technology, the golden promise of nuclear energy can also be a deadly bane — even apart from its use in weaponry. Perhaps because nuclear energy was explosively introduced to the world, public fear and confusion concerning atomic energy is high.

Although a nuclear plant cannot blow up as if it were an atomic bomb, the worst scenario involves a complete melt-down of the reactor core because of cooling failure. This accident can result in a boiler-like explosion and the spewing forth into the atmosphere high concentrations of extremely radioactive chemicals. Lesser accidents can be visualized in which one or more humans may be exposed to lethal or near-lethal levels of radioactivity. The lack of an adequate plan for the proper disposal of radioactive wastes, with the potential danger of air and water pollution, further fuels public fears. Not far from the imagination of many are the dangers of sabotage and nuclear proliferation. All these dangers combined with the escalating costs — multibillions of dollars per nuclear plant — has made nuclear energy much less attractive as an energy source for many in America. On the international scene, it

2

remains for a number of nations the only viable source to meet the energy needs and demands of their peoples.

In thinking ethically about nuclear energy, one must consider and balance the values of safety and a healthy economy. Unquestionably, the safety and health of human persons is of paramount importance. At the same time, we do not and have never lived in a totally risk free society. With expanding populations on a finite surface with limited resources, the use and conservation of energy production becomes critical for the proper development of a truly human civilization. Neither an individual nor a nation may consider itself so isolated from others that it can ignore their legitimate needs and rightful share of this world's goods. Ultimately, nations and peoples will need to assess their needs and resources with greater integrity and trust, so that the relative affluence of one will be used to meet the corresponding poverty of another.

Personhood

The mid-century consensus among psychologists that the human person was basically the result of social learning and that the person was good, autonomous, and self-actualizing, has gradually crumbled as the importance of the biological component in human behavior has become more evident. The role of genetics and complex biochemical interactions in the formation of human personality has challenged the psychological hegemony. Christian psychologists have been quick to appreciate the role of theological realities in human behavior and personality formation. Considerable progress in understanding has been made in this area, but much more study will be required before an adequate "psychotheological" description of the human person can be formulated.

Contemporary philosophers working with a phenomenological approach identify the "moral sense" as the critical component of the human person. It is the moral sense an individual gradually develops which enables the establishment of interpersonal relationships and the existence of human communities. The individual consciousness of self and of other humans as other selves creates a social world, one which does not exclude nonhumans, for the person has to deal with the whole world responsibly and morally. Without this moral sense (or at least the capacity thereto), there can be no human person, according to this phenomenological approach.

For those of the Judeo-Christian tradition, a primary source for a theological understanding of the human person will be the Sacred Scriptures. In searching that source for guidance regarding the human person, one should not forget that there is a development within the Bible; the various books represent historical and cultural diversities. However, one can find certain constants. The human is a created, finite, corporeal being but yet containing, as it were, the breath of God by virtue of which he is empowered to "subdue" the earth. Notwithstanding this unique but delegated authority, the human person is rooted in, and completely dependent upon, God; he is totally answerable to Him. Human persons are social creatures, living and interacting in community with reciprocal responsibilities. Human beings and the world in which they live are beset by evil, sin, corruption, and death. Consequently, humans and through them the world, have need of redemption. All in all, the Bible portrays humans as wounded kings who can only be healed ultimately by God.

Contemporary Christian theologies see the human person historically, in the sense both of having been shaped by history and being the shapers of the future by the actions of the present. That history is both biological and social. There is an unfolding of potentialities in the individual, which is in part determined by his genetic history and in part by the psychosocial environment. God's action is seen as working through these natural forces. Even this unfolding is subject to another force. Jesus Christ, the Incarnate Son of God, is not only the model of what it means to be human, but He is also the model in whose likeness the rest of the human race was created. He and the Father have sent the Spirit to guide the world, through the Church, to its proper destiny.

Pope John Paul II represents a conscious and conscientious effort to incorporate the traditional Thomistic view of the human with the insights provided by a phenomenological approach. Rather than taking what some have thought to be a too static view of what it means to be human and then deducing ethical norms, John Paul as Karol Wojtyla, the philosopher, sought to find the guiding principles of human behavior from the subjectivity of his actions. It is the core of his self-determination by which man discovers his real being and his ability to transcend himself to interact with other humans as persons. This recognition and interaction of persons sets up in the human community the network of reciprocal responsibilities which provides the principles for evaluating these modern technologies.

4

Reproductive Technologies

Although there are secondary reasons for the development of the various reproductive technologies, the primary reason is in response to the pressing need of involuntary infertile couples. Studies have shown that about 10–15% of all married couples in the United States are infertile; that is, couples who have engaged in uncontraceptive intercourse for a year without a pregnancy. Because there are a variety of causes for infertility to be found in the husband or wife or both, it is necessary for such a couple to undergo thorough diagnostic testing.

Since the middle of the last century, artificial insemination has been available for humans. If the husband's semen is inadequate, semen from an anonymous donor has been employed. In the past 25 years about 250,000 children have been conceived by means of artificial insemination. However, this technique is of no help when the cause of the infertility has been an obstruction of the fallopian tubes. Until recently, surgical correction has not been very successful, but with the newer microsurgical techniques involving the use of the operating microscope, the results have been encouraging.

A concomitant development has been the techniques of in vitro fertilization and embryo transplantation. In simplest outline, the former technology involves the removal of one or more mature eggs from the ovary by means of laproscopy, the transfer of the egg to a Petri dish where it is mixed with a suspension of the husband's (or donor's) sperm. If fertilization has taken place and normal cell division takes place as determined by microscopic examination, the embryo is ready for the next step, which is embyro transfer. In this procedure, the embryo, which may be from one to three days old, is transferred from the Petri dish to the woman's uterus by means of a plastic tube and syringe, inserted through the cervix. If all goes well, the embryo will implant in the uterine wall and develop normally. As of March, 1983, some two hundred babies (world wide) had been born live after being conceived by in vitro fertilization. But the success rate is only about 10–15%; that is, for every 100 embryos transferred, only 10 to 15 children were actually born.

A recent development, which raises some special legal problems, is that of surrogate parenting. The most common form is where a third party, a woman, agrees to be artificially inseminated and after birth to give the child back to the couple, the natural father and his wife. In effect, the woman has contracted to bear a child on behalf of another couple. A number of legal problems arise. What if the woman refuses to relinquish the child to the couple? What if the woman for health or other reasons decides to abort the child? If the child turns out to be abnormal in some way, and the couple refuses to accept the child, is the surrogate forced to accept the infant? Or, if both the couple and the surrogate mother refuse to keep the child, who has responsibility of caring for the unwanted child? These and similar problems have already arisen, but the courts and legislation have yet to find satisfactory solutions.

These reproductive technologies present not only legal problems, but ethical and pastoral ones. Central to these issues is that of marriage. The sacrament of marriage is protected by the Church in part by Canonical legislation. The new Code views the ends of marriage in a non-hierarchial manner, but as two dimensions of the same fundamental reality. Consequently, in assessing the import of these new reproductive technologies on marriage, one needs to consider the good of the spouses as well as the good of the children. This good is not only the material and psychological good, but also the spiritual well being of the individuals concerned.

Reprise and Coda

A musical symphony is traditionally a complex but unified interaction of many sounds emanating from a variety of instruments. Human life is analogous in that a multitude of elements need to be integrated into the experience of the human person. The ultimate guiding principle by which humans achieve true integrity is God as realized in Jesus Christ and reflected in the teachings of the Catholic Church. With a rapidly accelerating rate, human beings as co-creators have developed new technologies and have acquired varying degrees of mastery over matter and the forces of nature. Two of these are extremely important because they are powers to subjugate things (and people) to the will of those controlling that power: nuclear energy for the generation of electric power, and reproductive technologies which confer some control over the generation of new human beings. A suitable theology and ethics must be employed to make sure that these two powers are used for the authentic well being of the human person. To determine what is the authentic good of persons, it is necessary to understand well the nature of the human person. This requires a consultation of both the empirical and theological sciences. For the Church to discharge her responsibility in the world to aid in its transformation to the Kingdom of God, she must encourage the development of intellectual leaders who can meet creatively the challenges of the technological advances. In turn, the Pastoral leaders, the Bishops, can provide the faithful the guidance they need to live as vital Christians who can affirm the goodness of creation and help shape the wonders of human creativity in a morally acceptable manner.

ASM

Keynote Address

The Bishop's Workshop for 1983

Christopher Derrick

Pastoral Problems of Nuclear and Reproductive Technologies

As a Catholic who talks far too much, I have from time to time found myself addressing an audience of priests, of *clerecia cautiva*. My heart always leaps up on such an occasion. "How lovely!", I say to myself; "Now I can pay the clergy back for all the long *boring* sermons I've had to listen through!"

But this present company is altogether too august to deserve any such punishment; and I assure you that if these introductory remarks of mine prove boring, this will be by reason of my failure and not by reason of any revengeful intention. I am in fact somewhat haunted by the risk of failure. I find this a distinctly intimidating occasion — one to which my personal revelance is far from obvious. You are here concerned with the moral and religious implications of two highly specialised subjects, nuclear energy and technologized *progenitura*; and about these (it might be said) only experts can speak. In the course of these few days you will be hearing from many experts, people of the highest standing in their respective fields: I cannot be included among these. Then, on your side, you are mostly Bishops, the chosen Apostles of Jesus Christ — even Archbishops in certain cases, even Cardinals. As such, you possess a sacramental grace and a divine *charisma*; and being thus strengthened, you most nobly discharge your specific duty of preaching the revealed Word in all its fullness and integrity, of defending the teaching and tradition of Christ's Church, its mysterious Faith and its exacting morality, in the teeth of all those clever and noisy people who suppose themselves to know better. What is there, of the moral or religious sort, that I can conceivably teach you? I am not a Bishop or even a priest: I am not a moral theologian, I am not even an immoral theologian. What place have I got on such an occasion as this?

If I can speak here at all, I can only do so as a representative or specimen of the common man — the man in the street, the Catholic in the pew. It is right and proper that somebody should speak here on behalf of that large constituency. We face these two alarmingly complicated things, nuclear energy and technologised parenting, and the experts will have much to say about them. But when all is said and done, it's the common man who will be their beneficiary — or, perhaps, their victim.

So, while I have conducted no kind of opinion-poll and can speak for myself alone, let me offer one common man's preliminary view of those two questions.

As I have said, I am somewhat intimidated by the occasion and the company; and I therefore find it my instinct to fall back upon a manner of thinking that prevailed widely in my younger days, before the Flood. According to that manner of thinking, it is the Church's principal job — in all matters of morals or behavior or action — to tell you *how far you can go,* and not only with your girl-friend. The moral theologians were very good at this. They went in for some remarkably precise mathematics, they almost went in for diagrams. We might be disposed to imitate their methods and the style of their conclusions. Take this question of nuclear energy, for example. As we all know, bad things have been said about it: it has been claimed that the dangers are appalling and totally disproportionate to the benefits. Others disagree; and no doubt we shall be hearing both sides of the argument in the course of this Workshop. But what *sort* of conclusion will we then reach as Catholics? Shall we perhaps express it in the language of the old moral-theology manuals?

"Whoever gives formal or material co-operation to the building of three nuclear power-stations sins venially: whoever gives formal or material co-operation to the building of six nuclear power-stations sins mortally". If we reach an adverse conclusion, shall we express it in some such form as that? My suspicion is that any such mathematics would yield only a deceptive appearance of precision and certainty, no matter how favourable or adverse our conclusion might be; and that's quite apart from the well-known fact (as some seem to think) that mortal sin was abolished by the Second Vatican Council.

It might seem, therefore, that this question of nuclear energy is a matter of prudential judgment alone, about which we — as Christians and Catholics — can have nothing particular or precise to say. There is talk of great benefits: there is also talk of great dangers. But these are incommensurables. We cannot possibly do sums with them: there is no conceivable calculus, no conceivable cost-benefit analysis by which we can evaluate a specified amount of available energy against a specified danger to human life and health.

We can of course invoke the Cardinal though pre-Christian Virtue of Prudence. "Be careful! Consider the consequences of what you propose to do! Are you sure that of balance, this operation will show a profit?" Something of that sort always needs to be said. But isn't it rather a tame and obvious thing for us to say? — we, who are supposed to be governed by the bloodstained Cross and the flames of Pentecost, and who therefore carry a unique and revolutionary message for mankind?

Things are perhaps a little easier when we turn to your second question — the question of technologized parenting. This also is a complex question and in some respects an indelicate one, at least by the standards of us sexagenarians. But here, we do not need to think in terms of prudential judgment alone. Those old-moral-theology manuals, backed up by the Church's ordinary *magisterium* at least, offer us several clear-cut and relevant negatives. We shall doubtlessly have these sexual and gynecological techniques explained to us, in possibly embarrassing detail, before very long; and as Christians and Catholics, we shall need to be vigilant. Do any of them possibly involve contraception, or abortion, or masturbation, frankly or in euphemistically camouflaged versions? Perhaps they do not. But if they do, we shall know what to think of them. We must never do evil that good may come.

10

For my part, I have no sympathy whatever with those who question or qualify the moral absolutes that are there at stake. But do they add up to the whole of the story? If so, the whole of this Workshop might be considered an unprofitable thing. You have come here at considerable expense, and so — though not personally — have I: what shall we take away with us when we leave on Friday? Shall we have anything new or special to think and say? About nuclear energy, shall we only be able to say "Be careful — weigh the benefits against the dangers"? And about technologized parenting, shall we only be able to say "Certain old familiar moral negatives are still in force"?

If so, this occasion will have been of great benefit to the airlines and to this hotel, but hardly to you or me or to Catholics in general, whatever may be said by the various experts whom we shall shortly hear.

I want to suggest one or two perspectives in which something more positive might be said, in which this Workshop might prove far from profitless; and initially, I want to say two rather negative things about Catholic moral theology as it used to exist. Some people reject this because it led to conclusions which they dislike. My objections to it are rather different; and I hope I won't be understood as suggesting that the new moral theologies of these post-Conciliar years — situational, consequential, and so forth — add up to an unqualified improvement on what went before.

In the first place and perhaps trivially, the older sort of moral theology seems to me to have been a rather scrappy science. If a legal analogy may be permitted, I see it as a vast mass of case-law, with very little in the way of codification or statute. Much has been written about *Humanae Vitae* since 1968, but few of us appear to have noticed how exceptional a document it was. During the previous centuries, there were —as far as I know — remarkably few occasions when the Church's supreme *magisterium* saw fit to pronounce as forcibly as that about *any* question of the moral sort.

Then and more seriously, moral theology seems to me to have been a rather insufficient science. It hardly existed outside the seminaries; and even there, it was seldom about the question of how to lead a good life, of how to love God and your neighbour, of how to put on Christ and walk in the Spirit. Questions of that more positive sort were largely handled in another department, one which terrified us sinful laymen by being called 'ascetic theology'. Moral theology was about something else: essentially, it was about how to hear confessions.

And it dealt with that practical subject on distinctive lines. Nobody (I hope) will want to question the desirability of not breaking the bruised reed, of not quenching the smoking flax: there is a very strong case for gentleness in the confessional, for not repelling the half-repentant sinner, and so for a certain probabilism. But all this did tend to make moral theology into a somewhat minimising thing, as though the Christian's key question were indeed "How far can I go?" — how far, that is, without definitely incurring the guilt of mortal sin and so needing to hold back from the altar next morning.

I don't think I'll be saying anything new if I suggest that we need something more positive than that, in connection with our two subjects as elsewhere. There is certainly a pastoral place for the question "How far can you safely go in a bad direction?" But it needs to be complemented — to say no more — by two different though no less pastoral questions: "In what good direction should you be heading?", and also "In what good direction should society be heading?". And these are universal questions. The first is not for monks and nuns alone, and it would be disastrous if we left the second in the childish hands of politicians.

The horrible fact is that we are called, individually and socially, to perfection; and while few if any of us will attain that in this life, we shall act ungratefully and ruinously if we aim at anything less. So our care must not only be for the hair's-breadth avoidance of certified mortal sin: it must also and primarily be for the ideal to which we are individually and socially called — for the Lord himself, that is, and for our own "imitation of Christ".

So I want to raise one or two questions of the more positive sort, questions which I hope will be remembered throughout the four days of this Workshop — and remembered, moreover, in their relationship to the tortured and bleeding body of Jesus, to the tears of the Sorrowing Mother, to the agony of the martyrs.

Here comes my first question. As we all know, the Commandment tells each one of us to love his neighbour as he loves himself, to seek his neighbour's good as he seeks his own. There are certain well-known complexities here. Some things can be good for one man but bad for another; and beyond that, one can renounce certain good things while still wishing one's neighbour to enjoy them. The Commandment does not oblige us to make all things exactly the same for everybody. But generally speaking, what kind of 'good' should we have in mind, for self and for neighbour too?

If we are materialists, we shall naturally think in terms of temporal good alone. We shall then lay heavy emphasis upon economic and political good, and also upon the rather mysterious psychological good that we call 'happiness'. That gives us something to do: we can certainly do our best for the economic and even the political good of self and neighbour, and according to a primary article of the American faith (though not of mine), "happiness" also is capable of being pursued. At the very least, we can aspire to a maximising of satisfactions and a minimising of sufferings, in oneself and in others.

But if we are to be Christians instead of materialists, how passionately should we set our hearts upon temporal good of any sort? How important should we consider it for ourselves and others to have all things exactly as preferred? The Christian ideal to which we aspire: should we see it as a world in which everybody finds all his desires satisfied at every point?

If that's how we see it, we are certainly doomed to failure. The real needs of a human being are simple; and apart from medical treatment in some costly versions, they can be easily and inexpensively met — that is, so long as there exists a general eagerness that they *should* be met. But the possible desires of a human being are infinite: in no conceivable world can all of them be satisfied. In practice, most of them are certain to be frustrated.

It's more to the point, I think, to say that no such view of the Christian ideal finds any support in the Gospel, or in the developed teaching of the Church, or in the writings of the great theologians and mystics and saints. What we find there amounts to a painful paradox. The Corporal Works of Mercy are of course obligatory: beyond that rockbottom level, we may certainly seek temporal good — in moderation — for self and therefore for neighbour. But even so, our badge is the Cross, not the supermarket or the credit-card. For oneself and for others, satisfactions can be lawful but are always dangerous, while suffering is not an absolute and unqualified evil.

So if I may drop back into the old language of morality, my question will take this form: could there be such a sin as "inordinate attachment to temporal good"?

I suggest that there is such a sin, widely committed and even taken for granted in these affluent societies of ours and even — in another version — in the poorer countries. I also suggest that our very proper concern for others, and for the duty of rich people towards poor people, can easily blind us to its dangers.

It is not always a matter of straightforward selfishness and avarice and gluttony. Let me cite one different and rather extreme case by way of illustration — a sadly familiar case, involving the other and more clearly satanic use of nuclear energy. At the moment, I do not live under a Communist government: I live much more comfortably than my fellow-Catholics in (say) Poland. Now it isn't in mere *egoismo*-selfishness that I cherish that as a temporal good and a very considerable one: I thank God for it, and I would like others to share it as widely as possible. (Note that I called it a *temporal* good, not a spiritual good. The blood of the martyrs is the seed of the Church, which comfort tends to make impotent and sterile. The Church thrives robustly there in Poland, and is all shot to hell in comfortable tolerant Holland.)

Not living under a Communist or similar government: that's a great temporal good, and I value it. But could I possibly value it inordinately? I would certainly do so if, in the hope of retaining it, I gave formal or material co-operation to any wholesale Massacre of the Innocents, such as is currently planned by the British government and some others.

I hope you all admire my mastery of the language in which those older moral theologians habitually spoke. It needn't be seen as a dead language: it still works. (Note, by the way, that abortion is another and closely-related instance of the same thing. It is a good thing for a young lady to feel unburdened and carefree. But her desire to retain or recover that pleasant condition will clearly be inordinate if it leads her to another Massacre of the Innocent, less spectacular but no less dreadful in its smaller way.)

A fully Christian attitude towards temporal good is easy to define but hard to live by. One can properly seek it for oneself and one's neighbour, within the moral law and moderately, but always with a certain light-hearted humorous detachment, since there are more important things: one should respond with gratitude when it comes and with cheerful resignation when it goes. It isn't the point of our existence or anybody else's, we shouldn't *care* about it too much.

In my belief and initially, that's the perspective in which we — in our specific capacity as Christians and Catholics, not simply as citizens and possibly as experts — can most usefully see the two subjects of this

Workshop, nuclear energy and technologized parenting, and (if it comes to that) technology in general. Everything of that kind is ordered towards some temporal good, some satisfaction; and we shall clearly need to be negative where the means proposed are inherently sinful, as in the two cases just mentioned. But don't we also need to be careful about the kind and degree of our attachment to the proposed ends? If we seek Christian perfection, if we identify with the dying Lord and his Mother and the martyrs, how passionately should we desire the temporally and temporarily good things that are thereby offered to us and to others?

Having your desires satisfied, getting your own way at every point — that isn't the greatest of causes, it isn't the name of our Christian game. It's very unlike what the Lord sought for himself and promised to his followers.

That goes for your two present subjects, along with everything else. Take nuclear energy, for example; and let us suppose that the alleged dangers have — for all practical purposes — been overcome. We can go ahead with no excessive rashness. But what's the point of going ahead? What's the point of nuclear energy?

That question needs to be answered with brutal frankness. Nuclear energy is about being rich.

Let me develop that obvious point a little. Some, though not all of us, live in affluent consumer-societies; and what makes them affluent is (among other things) their phenomenally rapid consumption of energy. This used to come in the form of coal, but coal is dirty and dangerous: then it came in the form of oil, but oil is only available on a precarious and temporary basis. There is much bravely ecological talk of wave power and wind power and solar power, but at the best, such things can only add up to a drop in the ocean. So we *must* have nuclear energy. Why? Because we in the affluent countries *must* continue to live in an extremely wealthy and extravagant fashion, and in fact *must* become wealthier and more extravagant as time goes on, *per omnia saecula saeculorum*. That's our great imperative; and then we remember — with a guilty start — that some people and some countries are not rich at all. About that fact, we talk a great deal and do very little. But at our best, we talk as though a universal enjoyment of our present affluence — or something like it — constituted our absolute, our ideal, possibly attainable or possibly not. That's our great imperative — for ourselves if we are selfish, and for all men if we are not.

It seems an arbitrary and un-Christian imperative to me. Look back at our grandparents' time. Their *per capita* use of energy was minute, by comparison with ours; and it would be hard to argue that they were worse men in the sight of God than we are, or even that they were less happy. Wealth, whether expressed in terms of energy-consumption or otherwise, has very little to do with happiness and still less to do with the natural or Christian virtues, with the love of neighbour or of God.

That being so, how seriously should we take these questions of energy-supply? The Lord told us not to bother very much about economics and our standard of living: we should leave all such anxiety to the heathens, the people who don't know about God.

There are some economists — notably my old friend E. F. Schumacher, the author of *Small is Beautiful* — who say that the dream of endless economic expansion is a dream indeed, an illusion; that our recent affluence is certain to prove a temporary thing, a freak of history; and that with or without nuclear power, we face a future of relative and perhaps extreme poverty. They may prove mistaken. But how grievously would we *mind* if they turned out to be right? if in our economic life, we reverted to something like the historical norm of the human condition? There's a moral and religious and pastoral problem there all right: let it be remembered throughout this Workshop and afterwards.

I am fully conscious of my own hypocrisy in raising such questions as these. I am no saint or Trappist, and I adore the fruits of energy-intensive afflluence when they come my way: the big steak, the jumbo jet, the Grand Babylon Hotel. I emphatically prefer the freeway, in some nice big comfortable car, to the 'Royal Road of the Holy Cross'. But would I do so if I really followed the Lord? if I really made Christian perfection into my daily working ideal? I fear that I may be among those who worship their own bellies, as St. Paul put it; or Mammon, or the Golden Calf.

"Inordinate attachment to temporal good": I suggest that there is a most serious moral danger of that sort, arising most notably in connection with affluence, and therefore in connection with energy, and therefore in connection with nuclear energy. And that danger would still be with us, I suggest, even if there were no poorer people to rebuke our gluttony with their hunger. I will even suggest that it can be no less dangerous for those poorer people themselves, if they come to resent their poverty and hate the silly rich.

16

When we turn to technologized parenting, things become a little more complex, and for two reasons. I take it that we are there dealing with technologies that enable people to have babies — and healthy babies — when Nature refuses to oblige in the conventional manner.

That isn't like the question of nuclear energy. For one thing, a desire to have babies is very unlike a desire to be rich. In effect, it frequently works out as a willingness to be relatively poor. In some simpler societies, children are an economic asset, but not in our kind of society: we find them an economic burden and a heavy one, as I know full well. Obviously selfish motives will seldom be at work here.

And then, our hearts naturally warm towards technologized parenting — as though by contrast — because of the enormous efforts now devoted to technologized *non*-parenting, to technologized sterility. As we all know, this has become a tremendous industry: so many couples are anxious *not* to have babies, when Nature is all too keen to oblige in the conventional manner. A converse development is surely to be encouraged?

Now in this matter, I do not propose to dwell on the simply moralistic question of 'How far can you go?'. I do consider it obvious that technologized *non*-parenting reeks of mortal sin from beginning to end: I also consider it probable that in some versions, technologized parenting may include elements of that same and simply wicked kind. About that latter question, we shall doubtlessly be hearing from the doctors and the moralists. But I want to put the emphasis elsewhere.

First of all, at the risk of shocking you, I want to say that here also, there could be a danger of inordinate attachment to temporal good. For their parents, children are among the very greatest of temporal blessings and are perhaps the greatest of all, while they can also be an occasion of spiritual good. It is entirely natural and right for a young married couple to desire parenthood. But while they probably cannot desire it too passionately, they can easily desire it in quite the wrong way.

To show what I mean, let me approach that desire by way of its converse. I have mentioned the consumer-societies in which some of us live; and a consumer-society is governed by the principle of "I want: therefore I am entitled to have, on my own terms and *now*". Where the thing wanted is abundant energy, that principle leads to the nuclear power-station: where one desires sexual satisfaction with no burdensome consequences, it leads to the contraceptive: elsewhere, it leads to such things as the credit-card. But that principle has its mirror-image or

17

converse: "I no longer want: therefore I am entitled to discard". If we live in a consumer-society, we also live in a throw-away society.

And it isn't only spent ball-points that we discard. There have been terrible news-items lately — stories of parents who, finding themselves less affluent than they were, have simply pushed their children out into the streets to fend for themselves. The children naturally drift into the big city and then into prostitution, male or female, and often into early death. Their parents no longer wanted those particular possessions: so, as by a kind of delayed abortion, they discarded them — rather as one might junk a car that one could no longer afford to run.

The key word there is 'possessions'. A parent naturally speaks of 'my' children, a couple naturally speak of 'our' children. But we should see there a partitive genitive, not a possessive genitive: if the parent has a spark of religion in him, he will know that the children are not his property but God's. They came into existence to serve his purposes, and that those purposes may be more commonly present and influential.

I retain an open mind about such probabilities. But I do want to say one thing dogmatically. As a general rule, the only decent and Christian attitude towards one's actual or potential children is one that we can express by adapting some well-known words of Job: "The Lord may or may not give: the Lord may or may not take away: blessed be the name of the Lord!". I offer that as a basic or normal philosophy of parenthood, a touchstone by which we should evaluate whatever may be said about technologized parenting in this situation or that: we must never get too far from it. And I offer it in full first-hand knowledge of what it feels like when the Lord does give, and also when he does take away.

But I would lay much greater emphasis upon a different *kind* of question, less moralistic and more strictly religious in scope, and relevant in its way to nuclear energy as well.

At this time, as we all know, it has become customary to talk about sexual matters with a frankness and freedom that would have surprised and probably shocked our grandfathers. One consequence is that our culture is suffused with verbal and visual pornography. But it would be a mistake, I believe, to see this entire development in altogether adverse terms. At this very Workshop, for example, we shall doubtlessly hear much frank mention of parts and functions which — until recently — would have been deemed unmentionable in polite and public and mixed and clerical company. An embarrassed whisper into the doctor's ear or the confessor's — that's the treatment they got in the good old days. If they get a different treatment here, that won't necessarily be a mark of our greater depravity.

But when we look at the wider scene, we do see a recent and most profound change in people's habitual manner of thinking and talking about sexual or reproductive matters, and of behaving as well. I have my own interpretation of this change, and I want to offer it as a background against which technological parenting can usefully be considered and evaluated by ourselves as Christians and Catholics and — more generally — as simply religious people. It is indeed a matter of religion rather than of morals. Please don't think that I regard the moral question as unimportant, or look with favour upon what they call the 'permissive society'. But what I want to talk about is something different — something about which a perfectly splendid book has recently been written, by me. (But perhaps commercials aren't allowed on this programme.)

What I refer to is a huge and widespread tendency which I call 'the desacralisation of Venus'. She used to be a goddess: now — for many people, and in Eliade's sense — she and her realm have ceased to be 'sacred' and have become 'profane'. Do not be shocked if I use this pagan language: in such matters, the Church always spoke practically everywhere in terms of the 'natural' or pre-Christian law.

The fact is that natural or pre-Christian or pagan or primitive man always attributed sacredness to the reproductive and especially the female functions of the body: he saw Venus as a goddess, and a delightful one — "laughter-loving" in Homer — but, as always with the sacred, a frightening goddess as well, as what Rudolf Otto called a *mysterium tremendum et fascinans*. It followed that everything connected with sex needed very careful handling. It wasn't always very moral handling: it was often very much the opposite, as with temple prostitution and the ritual orgy. But it was always very careful, very respectful, very religious, in theory and aspiration at least.

Then along came the Church, and took that natural perception a stage further. From being a goddess and of course fictitious, Venus was now to become an actual *sacrament*, a presence and action of the Dying God, the Mortal-Immortal whose necessity ran through all pagan myth. For us, *matrimonium* or sexual reproduction was to become one of the seven holiest things in all life, all human experience.

But we, in this age, have seen a progressive secularisation or desacralisation of all life and all human experience. Among our post-Christian fellow-citizens, this has gone very far indeed: as Eliade points out, they are the first and only people known to history or anthropology who have ever lived mentally in a totally profane cosmos. But it has gone pretty far among us Catholics too. If we wanted to sum up the liturgical and other changes that we have seen since the Second Vatican Council, we could cover most of them by the single word 'desacralisation'. Some of us consider that a good thing.

What has this tendency done to our bodily sexuality, to Venus? So far from promoting her into a sacrament, it has reduced her to a triviality — a consumer-good, an amusement or sport, something between personal hygiene and a box of candy. The Church still reiterates the ancient rules and rubrics that naturally govern the handling of something as perennially sacred as this — or the Pope does at least. But to the characteristically modern mind, these seem like nothing more than a set of arbitrary hang-ups or taboos. We are all familiar with the consequent arguments.

Those arguments are mostly concerned with particular questions of morality, and these are of undoubted importance. But I want to stress the religious angle instead. In any version of technologized parenting, somebody will be doing something with sexual parts and sexual functions. I am not a moral theologian, I have no *magisterium*, and I am certainly not going to tell him how far he may lawfully go. But I do want to remind him, very forcibly, that he will then be handling sacred things and must do so in a spirit of religious awe. It's rather like the question of how we should behave in church. We sometimes do profane things in the sacred building: the electrician goes in there to attend to the lights and the wiring, some devout woman goes in to vacuum the floor, and they do rightly. But they should never forget that they are in the house of God, in the presence of the crucified and risen Body.

Such considerations apply to medicine in general, of course, not only to technologized parenting. Primitive and pagan man usually saw the whole human body as a sacred thing, not only its reproductive functions, though the sacredness of those was exceptional: we call it the temple of the Holy Spirit, made one with that crucified and risen Body and sharing an eternal destiny with the soul. The doctors have too often seen it as a mechanism with which they can usefully tinker, very much as a mechanic tinkers with your profane car. But I hear rumours of a new medicine, more spiritual and holistic, more attentive to the totality of what a human being is, to all that 'personhood' implies in all its sacredness; and that's good news if true.

I would even extend the same principle to technology in general. Jacques Ellul has argued convincingly that technological development proceeds causally, not teleologically: it is not simply good or simply bad for us, it is mostly and simply irrelevant to real human needs. But it can also involve a manipulatory and Manichaean contempt for created Nature. How easily and unthinkingly we talk about 'Man's Conquest of Nature', as though this lovely planet — God's handiwork — were a kind of enemy, to be beaten down and then pillaged!

Bertrand Russell once said that if humanity destroys itself, this will fundamentally be because of our 'cosmic impiety', our lack of religious veneration for this world and everything in it. A kind of cosmic piety came naturally to most primitive people; and I suggest that we ought to do better than they, not (so dangerously) worse than they — we, who know that "The earth is the Lord's, and the fullness thereof". It isn't our property for profane exploitation: it belongs to God and should be treated accordingly. That goes for uranium among other things — even for plutonium. There's an important sense in which we are *always* 'in church'.

Now to anyone infected (as most of us are) by the dominant mind-set of this desacralizing age, I might seem to be offering a simply negative judgment upon both nuclear energy and technological parenting, as though we'd be better off without either of them. But in fact, I lack the competence and the desire to make any such sweeping judgment either way. I only want to express a kind of hope for this Workshop, and for Catholic thought in general. Where the frontiers of mortal sin need to be charted, in new and complex fields especially, let them be charted; and let us all respect those frontiers. But beyond that, let us always think and speak and act in a spirit of cosmic piety, as befits religious people whose Faith is an incarnational one, and who therefore cannot (like some) treat this visible world as evil or illusory or unimportant — and least of all, the human body and person. God loves his creation: he wanted us to live in it as in a garden, not as in a strip-mine.

Self-will and the gratification of all experienced desires, or as many of them as possible — that isn't the name of our Christian game. It isn't what we ought to desire for ourselves, and it therefore isn't what we ought to desire for our neighbours, even where the gratifications in question are more or less innocent.

So, from the position of a rather ignorant layman, I offer one or two perspectives which might usefully be remembered in the course of your discussion and afterwards. We must of course do good and refrain from evil. But there are certain courses of action which, although not technically and mortally sinful, would simply not occur — as possible options — to anyone whose mind was deeply and respectfully religious; who saw this life as a journey rather than a destination; and who habitually kept his attention fixed upon the Cross and eternity.

PART II

Nuclear Energy

An Overview

The problems which nuclear energy for peaceful purposes presents to the Central and North American continents have to be viewed against the background of energy needs and resources world-wide. Because of the increasing interdependency of nations, our energy problems need to take into consideration the energy situation of other nations and the impact which our action will have on them. Professor Deutch points out that the current choice for energy production is really between coal and nuclear. While our nations may have the capability to rely on coal exclusively, many other nations do not have such resources and therefore must rely on nuclear energy if they are to develop and avoid economic disaster.

The public media has made highly visible some of the dangers of nuclear energy by presenting the nuclear accidents in repeated and dramatic fashion. In his paper Dr. Ahearne seeks to present calmly and objectively the real disadvantages of nuclear energy while eschewing what he calls "debaters points." At the same time he provides sufficient details and descriptions of the potential hazards to give the reader a better grasp both of the hazards themselves and the impact they have had on the public. Ahearne emphasizes inflation, the borrowing of money at large interest rates, and the delay in construction brought about deliberately by the utilities who realize that they had overestimated future demand for electricity as significant factors in the great expense of nuclear plants. Although both proponents and opponents of nuclear energy in the scientific community agree that there are no unsolvable technical problems for the disposal of nuclear wastes, no country has yet been successful in actually selecting a site for such disposal. In this chapter, the author admits that he is concerned about nuclear power because he is skeptical of the willingness of those who utilize it "to put in place sufficient competence to handle this dangerous technology."

Dr. Zebroski points out in his chapter that in most regions of the United States where nuclear energy supplies about 30 to 50 percent of electricity generation (compared to 13 percent nationwide), a number of tangible and indirect benefits accrue such as 1) significant decreases in air pollution, 2) provision of a regiment of assured domestic supply with relatively stable fuel costs, and 3) limitation of the pressures of oil demand on world oil prices and the consequent increased availability of oil for developing countries. Fuller realization of benefits from nuclear energy have been notably limited, he asserts, by legislation, regulation and litigation which, in turn, are the result of public apprehension (and misapprehension) about nuclear power. He sees that these "excessive protectionists activities" may very well bear a responsibility for subsequent augmentation of human suffering resulting from the delay in the use of nuclear energy at a sufficient scale.

In the United States, private industry has done much to develop nuclear power plants for the production of electricity. An industry leader, Gordon Hurlburt, outlines the history of that development and notes that the rapidly accelerating costs of constructing such plants have slowed down the ordering of new plants. Agreeing with Zebroski and Ahearne, Hurlburt places much blame on those who through a variety of delaying tactics drive up the costs of construction. Whereas, in early days the United States was the leader in the use of nuclear power for the generating of electricity, now the momentum of growth has moved to Europe, Russia and Japan. In these countries, governments are much more supportive of the nuclear industry. The government regulations in the United States are such, Hurlburt notes, that the construction of a nuclear power unit now takes twelve to fourteen years, whereas, for example, in Japan, France or Taiwan, these same units take only five or six years. The costs have increased from about $135 per kilowatt of nuclear capacity in 1969 to $2,000 today, and are projected to be some $4,000 in the 1990's.

Professor Frederick Carney provides in his chapter an ethical reflection on nuclear energy values, obligations and virtues. He concludes with a qualified support of nuclear energy. While insisting on safety as a high value he realizes that nuclear energy, directly or indirectly, is an important factor in the economy of all nations. In this he is in agreement with those who presented the scientific papers. In trying to balance the two values, he echoes the position declared in 1981 by Monsignor Mario Perissin, the Permanent Vatican Representative to the International Energy Commission:

> Therefore, Mr. President, my delegation believes that all possible efforts should be made to extend to all countries, especially to the developing ones, the benefits contained in the peaceful use of nuclear energy . . . . . . The application of nuclear energy constitutes, however, also a risk for mankind because of the detrimental consequences which accidents in nuclear power plants and nuclear waste storage may entail . . . . . Those who hold that nuclear power can be utilized only in a "zero risk" or "no risk" situation are perhaps applying an unrealistic standard to endeavors which, like all human efforts, necessarily involve some risk.

In Carney's view, the well-being of the *community* of nations is important for the good of each. A basic integrity and mutual trust combined with technological and managerial competence are requisites for the proper development and use of nuclear power.

The Editors

Chapter 1

World Energy Assessment
to the Year 2000

John Deutch, Ph.D.

Editorial Preface

For the past 50 years nations have been employing finite fossil fuel resources, primarily oil and gas, to fuel their economies. The result is that oil and gas are becoming progressively scarcer and more expensive; the end of this source of supply is in sight. In addition, the distribution of oil and gas reserves on the globe is far from uniform and this has become a source of political/military instability as well as a major economic burden for less developed energy importing nations.

Electricity production can be accomplished by (1) oil and gas (2) coal, and (3) nuclear; the appropriate choice is between the coal and nuclear. For industrialized societies it appears that the high capital/low operating cost combination of nuclear is more economical then — providing everything goes as advertised. Beyond economics there are serious burdens from both energy sources as indeed there are for many economic activities. In the case of coal these burdens include miner safety, air and water quality, transportation and waste disposal;

fairly calculable risks. In addition, there is the long term issue of carbon dioxide emissions and its influence on global climate. In the case of nuclear energy the problems for (1) reactor safety, (2) radioactive waste disposal and (3) nuclear proliferation.

A modern industrial society such as the United States, France, Germany, Japan, and the United Kingdom should be able to manage the problems that accompany the utilization of nuclear energy if the proper technical and institutional mechanisms are in place. The record, however, of responsible utilization is not entirely reassuring.

Nuclear energy is important to this nation — it is potentially cheaper and less environmentally harmful than coal or oil and gas. Nuclear energy is even more important for our allies who do not possess the coal or oil and gas resources of this nation. Even if the United States were to decide to rely on coal electricity generation exclusively, it is highly doubtful that other industrialized nations should or would follow our example.

Introduction

The task here is to provide a context for consideration of the problems associated with the use of nuclear energy for commercial electrical power. The hope is that the energy context discussed will assist in evaluating the social costs and benefits of nuclear energy as compared to the alternative technologies which are available throughout the world.

World Wide Energy Outlook

As we think about the energy context and outlook, we should take a historical perspective and recall that over the past 50 years the use of oil and gas has increased dramatically, primarily to fuel the economies of industrialized nations. The recent consequence of this expanded use is that oil and gas are becoming progressively scarcer, progressively less available throughout the globe. This is not to say that oil and gas will run out tomorrow but that the end is, in fact, in sight on a time scale of several decades.

This dependence on oil and gas has led to two kinds of problems: a short-term problem and a long-term problem. The short-term problem arises because oil deposits are not distributed uniformly over the earth. They are generally located in highly unstable political regions, notably in the Middle East. Accordingly, there is a great concern about future supply interruptions and price increases similar to those experienced by all nations in 1973 and in 1979. Less than 10 years ago the price of a barrel of oil was $3.00; less than 5 years ago the price of a barrel of oil was $11.00; and today the price of a barrel of oil is approximately, in this state of Texas, about $32.00 a barrel. The expectation, if we forget about potential declines for a couple of years, is that by the end of the century in today's terms, the price of oil would reach as high as $50.00–$75.00 a barrel. This estimate is not based on the assumption that any conflict or political instability disturbs the pattern of oil trade which could push prices higher. The short-term problem posed by the possibility of real price increase and political instability places a substantial burden on the industrialized nations of the world, but it also places a greater burden upon the oil-importing underdeveloped nations which have to pay proportionately much greater amounts for their oil and gas. All this is the short-term aspect of the oil problem.

The long-term character of the problem is quite different. Basically, the nations of the world are going to have to make a transition, a transition from a primary reliance on oil and gas to alternative energy technologies. This transition must begin today. Such a transition need not fully take place for another 50 or 100 years. Yet, it must be recognized that the required amount of oil and gas will become increasingly difficult to obtain. We must plan now for transition to other types of energy technology.

What are they? Utilization of coal, utilization of nuclear energy, and utilization of renewable energy sources, by which I mean such technology as solar, wind, geothermal and hydropower. For both the short-term and long-term reasons here mentioned, it is important that we work towards a substitution by these other energy technologies for oil and gas as sources of energy.

Oil and gas are used for a variety of purposes throughout the world, namely, for transportation, for home heating, for petrochemicals, for fertilizers, and for electricity production. It is particularly in the last named area of electricity production that there is an opportunity today to substitute other kinds of energy technologies. In particular, in this end-use area of electricity production is where nuclear energy plays a role. Nuclear energy here competes not only with oil and gas, but also with coal and, indeed, with the various renewable energy of resources that are mentioned above.

28

Consequently, our efforts should be to evaluate the use of nuclear energy for electricity production relative, primarily, to coal and the aforementioned renewable energy sources. Such evaluation should take place in light of two different basic considerations: (1) in terms of economic factors, and (2) in terms of what I will term, environmental factors.

Let me address first the issue of economic factors in the evaluation of nuclear energy. For industrialized countries with large electricity demand it appears that the high capital/low operating cost combination of nuclear energy is somewhat better than coal. Indeed, either coal or nuclear will cost a great deal less, in this author's judgment, than oil or gas over the 30-year life of the power plant.

For industrialized nations, nuclear energy is likely to be less costly for the consumer than coal. What then is the problem? The problem is that there is a deep public concern about the risks and possible negative consequences associated with the use of nuclear energy. In fact, the whole controversy over nuclear energy concerns these issues which we will call the environmental factors in the use of nuclear energy. First, note that as in the case of all energy technology, what ever it may be, there are always associated environmental burdens. There are always environmental costs and burdens for mankind in its use of energy technology and other industrial activities as well. In the case of coal utilization, for example, there are substantial burdens. These include the relatively predictable risks of normal activity in coal mining (miners' safety, transportation accidents), effect on air and water quality, and acid rain (now a matter of great debate in this hemisphere). There are also *long-term* effects from the utilization of coal; for example, the carbon dioxide problem, namely, the increase of CO_2 concentration in the upper atmosphere and its effect on global climate.

In the case of nuclear energy, public concern in this writer's judgment focuses on three items, and we would do well to keep our attention on these three items for reflection and deliberation. Public concern focuses first on the issue of reactor safety, not so much the risk of a minor accident but the risk of a *catastrophic* accident. Secondly, it focuses on radioactive waste disposal — the toxic wastes that are produced in a nuclear reactor which will be a burden on future generations unless we establish an effective, practical and safe manner of eliminating them from the sphere of mankind's activities. The third area of public concern is nuclear proliferation or the prospect of the spread of nuclear weapons or of nuclear explosive technology as a result of commercial nuclear power operation. These are indeed very serious problems and they do influence public attitudes dramatically. We will return to deal with them in a moment.

Let us now ask the question which is in the minds of many, if there are these problems — problems with coal and with nuclear energy — why don't we now begin to rely for electricity production throughout the world on renewable energy sources? Certainly, the advantages of so doing are very evident. First of all, the energy sources of the wind, the sun and the tides are renewable. Secondly, environmentally they are said not to be a burden. Thirdly they create jobs. And fourthly, they are claimed to be less expensive for energy production than the conventional technologies of coal and nuclear. Indeed, it is this writer's view that over the next several decades we will need to rely more and more on renewable energy technologies to supply our energy needs. These technologies deserve both public and governmental support as well as that of the private sector. Yet, there are some real problems in saying that we can today rely on renewable energy technology for a major fraction of our electricity needs. Good intentions are not enough in this area. There are many problems that stand in the way of the utilization of renewable energy technologies in substantial quantities in the near term.

First, many of the most interesting and promising technologies are not yet technologically mature. We do not as yet know whether they can operate reliably at a reasonable cost for the long period of time required to make them economical. One example of that is photovoltaics (i.e., direct conversion of light to electrical energy), a technology in which some have great confidence, and as a matter of fact, on which a great deal of work is being done here in Dallas. Photovoltaic technology is not mature and is not ready to be introduced into the marketplace.

Second, many of the renewable technologies will end up costing more money — as compared to coal or nuclear. Such an increased cost does not mean that we do not have to use them but that they will remain an economically more costly way of meeting our energy needs. Third, the capital costs associated with renewable energy technology are likely to be substantially in excess of even the very considerable capital costs of nuclear energy. The consequences of these capital costs being so high is that it will prove more difficult than we would like to introduce these renewable energy technologies into the lesser developed nations, that it will also take a longer time to introduce them into the industrialized nations of the west.

In summary, with respect to renewable energy technologies, it is extremely important to nurture these possibilities and to spend money on the required research and development. These technologies will make an accelerating contribution to our energy mix but perhaps not until the end of the century. And we should recall that it is likely that it will cost more to utilize these renewable energy technologies. At the same time, we should be supportive of efforts to encourage research and development in conservation technologies, that is, in those technologies which permit us to perform the same activities with lower utilization of energy.

Let us now return to some of the problems of nuclear energy which we will be hearing more about. First of all, safety; there is a grave concern, especially after the Three Mile Island accident, of the risks of catastrophic accidents. Second, the public, in this nation, as in other nations of the world, lacks confidence in the ability of industry and the governmental regulatory bodies to pay adequate attention to safety. Third, at the same time, there is a concern with the sharply rising costs of nuclear energy and the availability of nuclear plants. In this author's judgement, it should be possible for industrialized nations such as the United States, Canada, United Kingdom, France, Germany and Japan to introduce the technology and institutional mechanisms required to run plants safely and efficiently. We should carefully note what others will be saying about the United States system in this regard because it is extremely influential in other parts of the world. Important, too, is how we are going to regain public confidence in the ability of our nuclear industry to run plants safely and efficiently.

The next area of public concern regarding nuclear energy needing discussion concerns radioactive waste disposal. It is a subject that has interested this writer for some time, and can be outlined briefly as follows: The reactor in nuclear power plants produces spent fuel rods which contain highly toxic radioactive materials due to the process of fission that occurred while the rods are in the reactor vessel. These fuel rods which are very hot and highly radioactive, remain a very serious concern for ten years and some concern for approximately 600 years. Their radioactivity does not fall to inconsequential levels for some 25,000 years. What disposition, then, is made of these dangerous materials? Presently, these fuel assemblies are held on-site at the 57 operating reactors around this nation and at operating reactors in most of the other countries which have nuclear power plants. Some have suggested that we devise a way for their disposal deep underground, or possibly in the sea beds of the ocean, in geological circumstances which are scientifically and technically believed to be safe. Others argue that there are technical solutions which involve reprocessing out a fraction of that radioactive material called plutonium that could be placed back into the reactors. This latter technological solution (chemical reprocessing), in my view, just trades a problem of the distant future for one of the present. The fact is that we do not have in operation a reliable way of disposing of radioactive nuclear waste. The public, naturally, is very concerned.

It is not that the public questions whether there is a theoretical or technical solution to this problem, but rather, whether there exists a *responsible*, credible implementing mechanism for taking care of these radioactive wastes. What is lacking is the combination of industrial and governmental measures which can give the public confidence that the implementation of a certain program will be carried out in an honest way and in an efficient manner. The issue, hence, is not technical feasibility, but rather responsible implementation. This lack of public confidence is a very serious problem, particularly in this nation, and it is becoming a much more serious problem in other nations, as for example, Germany.

The third area of public concern is nuclear nonproliferation. This is perhaps the most serious and potentially most divisive question among the different nations of the world. The concern is that nuclear materials and the technology of commercial power will be diverted to make nuclear explosives.

When this problem first became prominent in the mid-70s, it was discovered that western nations were selling nuclear plants and their associated technologies, such as reprocessing and enrichment plants to nations without regard to the potential spread of nuclear weapons capability. Deals were made between various western nations and such countries as Korea, Taiwan, Iran, Pakistan, Argentina, Brazil, and the Union of South Africa. These very elaborate deals transferred large amounts of nuclear technology to countries which many believe no sober individual would judge as being politically stable or located in stable regions of the world. The United States led an effort among nuclear exporting nations to control the export of nuclear technology. This program ran counter to a long international tradition, in nuclear energy — Atoms for Peace — which was introduced by President Eisenhower. Atoms for Peace was an implied promise between the U.S. and other developed countries and the underdeveloped countries that the industrialized nations would provide nuclear technology to the underdeveloped world. This promise was motivated in part by the assumption that in exchange for receiving western technology these underdeveloped countries would then be more reluctant to develop nuclear technologies in an independent manner. But there is a grave concern that some misuse of nuclear power has taken place. Evidence exists of some misuse having taken place in India and Pakistan, to mention two prominent examples.

In the judgement of some, an important issue for consideration is the following: Should industrialized nuclear exporting countries continue to restrict these exports and place controls on nuclear technology which go to Third World countries or to politically unstable nations where the possibility of misuse of this technology is greater? There are measures that can be put into place to restrict the prospects for misuse of the technology. These include, for example, prior agreements between exporting technology nations and recipient nations, and inspection mechanisms perhaps under international auspices. Surely the industrialized nations of the world have the responsibility to control the spread of nuclear technology, especially in those instances where misuse leading towards nuclear explosives is possible. The problem of nonproliferation of nuclear weapons will remain a major source of political friction between the developed and underdeveloped nations of the world, and a very serious threat to political stability.

Having surveyed the three problems of nuclear energy, namely, safety, radioactive waste disposal and nuclear nonproliferation, let us now spend a moment on some thoughts about the future. What is the future outlook for nuclear energy? First of all, the demand for nuclear power plants is declining, and indeed has been declining for some time, both in the United States and the world. In the United States we have approximately 57 plants in operation. In 1977 we estimated that at the turn of the century in the United States there would be 400 nuclear plants in operation. But today we estimate that at the turn of the century there will only be 165 major nuclear plants in operation. The decline is, in part, due to problems surrounding nuclear energy here discussed. But it is also due to very poor performance of the western economy and to the sharply higher energy prices mentioned earlier. Both these factors have had the effect of restricting demand. In this view, few if any new plants will be ordered in this nation before, let's say, 1995. Accordingly, opportunities exist to focus both our institutions and political processes on the problems of nuclear energy. We have had a welcome respite where we can work on some of these problems in a way that will permit us to use nuclear energy more fully. The progress will require the cooperation of both industry and government. Attention should be given to safety, lower costs and improved reliability of nuclear plants and to secure radioactive waste management. Our present emphasis should be on making today's technology better, and not worry about advanced technologies like chemical reprocessing or breeder reactors, which will not be justified for many decades.

At present the United States may perhaps have the luxury of not making use of nuclear energy because we have readily accessible coal and some remaining oil and gas, but our closest allies do not have that luxury. We must be aware that France, the United Kingdom, Japan, Germany and many other countries will indeed be making use of nuclear energy even should we make, in this author's view, a mistake and give it up. So, in fact, nuclear energy is going to be utilized by many of the western nations who are not graced as we are with deposits of coal, oil and gas. It is a part of the problem of the western alliance.

Let us conclude with this writer's own view of nuclear energy. It is important for the *world* to be able to make responsible use of nuclear energy. It is cheaper than oil, gas and coal. Nuclear energy is certainly, in this view, if handled responsibly, less environmentally harmful than the use of coal. It is an extremely important non-fossil fuel energy source. That the United States and the western democracies, and other nations of the world, learn how to use nuclear energy responsibly is of paramount importance. It is a highly critical feature in our future energy outlook.

Chapter 2

Nuclear Energy In North America — Advantages and Issues

Edwin L. Zebroski, Ph.D.*

Editorial Preface

Foreseeable rates of exploitation of all available energy sources do not supply foreseeable U.S. energy needs, given the evident constraints of declining resources and the high costs of expanding both conventional and novel sources. Nuclear energy for electricity production is currently only about 13 per cent of total U.S. electricity generation, but is 30 to 50 per cent of supply in three heavily populated regions of the U.S. In most such regions it provides both tangible and indirect benefits, including:

- *significant reductions in air pollution*
- *significant reductions in costs relative to coal, oil, or gas*
- *limits the loss of purchasing power and the consequent reduced economic activity due to the high costs of imported oil*

---

* This paper represents the author's personal views, and not necessarily those of any organization with which he has been associated in the past or present.

- *provides a segment of assured domestic supply with stable fuel costs*
- *restrains the rate of escalation of costs of alternate energy sources*
- *limits the pressure of oil demand on world oil prices — and on reduced availability of oil for developing countries*
- *use by U.S. helps to restrain the international tensions from competition for control of oil-producing regions and risks of disruptions of supply (probably significant factors contributing to the risks of wars).*

Public apprehensions on nuclear power — reflected in legislation, regulation, and litigation — are the principal limitations to fuller realization of benefits in the U.S. Unlike virtually any other human activity, intensive scholarly and technical efforts to prevent or contain accidents which might pose public hazards (as well as to reduce occupational exposures) have been the sine qua non of the industry. The risks of individual harm are lower than at least 50 other inadvertent sources of risk to society — including those from alternate energy sources.

The explosive growth of protectionist litigation as a major activity in the U.S. has made it possible to increase the costs of almost any long term project by procedural delays. This has been the largest single mechanism causing the decline in potential nuclear commitments and completions. To some degree the same effect is present in coal, chemical, steel, housing, transportation, mining, and many other industrial activities as well. The large waste of natural resources and human effort resulting from such litigation also helps to drive inflation, lower human productivity, cause decline or loss of industries and jobs, and contributes to the current recession — some aspects of which may be permanent.

A possible ethical/moral question is the extent to which excessive protectionist activities — no matter how well meaning — may bear a responsibility for eventual large increases in human suffering. There may also be a neglect of the grave or unforeseen consequences of the widespread use of such delaying tactics which may contribute to:

- *massive inflation and consequently reduced purchasing power of individuals and government*
- *reduced individual and national resources for improving health care and education*
- *reduced individual freedom of choice in occupation, housing, travel*
- *Increased social turbulence and crime or terrorism from declining standards of living and declining expectations*
- *increased likelihood of local and world wars over resources*
- *excessive steps for avoidance of both real or hypothetical hazards can*

have concomitant increase in human misery which may be much larger and more lasting than any which might have been possible from the hazards averted

Abstract

Forseeable rates of exploitation of all available energy sources do not supply forseeable U.S. energy needs, given the evident constraints of declining resources and the high costs of expanding both conventional and novel sources. Nuclear energy for electricity production is currently only about 13% of total U.S. electricity generation, but is 30 to 50% of supply in three heavily populated regions of the U.S., and in similar regions in more than a dozen countries which have larger proportions of nuclear energy than the U.S. has. In most such regions it provides both tangible and indirect benefits, including:

- significant reductions in air pollution;
- significant reductions in costs relative to coal, oil, or gas-generated electricity;
- limiting the loss of purchasing power and the consequent reduced economic activity due to the high costs of imported oil;
- providing a segment of secure, uninterruptible domestic supply with stable fuel costs;
- restraining the rate of escalation of costs of alternate energy sources;
- limiting the pressure of oil demand on world oil prices — and on reduced availability of oil for developing countries;
- use by U.S. helps to restrain the international tensions from competition for control of oil-producing regions and risks of disruptions of supply (probably significant factors contributing to the risks of wars);
- U.S. actual and planned use through 1990 is about one half of the potential capacity which was once considered desirable and new commitments are unlikely in the 1980's; however overseas commitments continue apace;
- worldwide use, driven by the economic, resource, and strategic advantages over available alternatives, is now over 50% larger than U.S. The capacity under construction and planned is over 200% larger than that in the U.S. The world total in the 1990's is equivalent in energy to about 10 million barrels/day of oil.

This can be a primary cushion in helping to restrain world tensions over access to resources, and in limiting deprivation in countries which do not have abundant indigenous energy sources.

Limits To Nuclear Power In The U.S.

Public apprehensions of nuclear power — reflected in legislation, regulation, and litigation — are principal sources of limitations to fuller realization of benefits in the U.S.[1] Civilian nuclear energy was developed almost from its inception with a painstaking concern for possible hazards to the environment, with unique emphasis on hypothetical worst-case accidents. There was also, generally, great caution on the assumed possible effects of low levels of radiation exposure, even relative to those inherent in the natural world. The preoccupation with safety issues was an early example of the idea of social responsibility for potential long-term risks, but this also has contributed to exaggerated public perception of the hazards.

Unlike many other industrial activities, intensive scholarly and technical efforts to prevent or contain accidents which might pose public hazards (as well as to reduce occupational exposures) have been the *sine qua non* of the industry. These efforts have been redoubled since the accident to the reactor at Three Mile Island, even though public radiation exposures were small relative to variations in natural radiation backgrounds.

The concerns on civilian nuclear energy are not insignificant but the confusions of real issues versus unfounded perceptions is widespread. The risks of individual harm are lower than many other inadvertent sources of risk to society — including those from most alternate energy sources.

The literary and entertainment genre of exaggerating fears and hazards is well developed. It tends to work especially on the gullible segments of the public which have difficulty in discriminating fact from mythology. (We note more than two decades of declines — sometimes to near-zero — of education in the natural sciences.)

There have been no new reactor commitments in the U.S. and several dozen projects have been cancelled since 1978. These also reflect the complex of economic conditions resulting from the "oil price shocks" of 1974 and 1978. Worldwide inflation, high interest rates, increased expenditures for oil and the widespread economic recession have reduced discretionary purchasing power and availability of capital. Reduced availability and increased cost of borrowing contributes to delays or cancellations of many long-term projects which require capital. Reduced industrial demand for energy has also helped to rationalize some cancellations in some regions, but the completion of projects in such cases would still have been prudent if capital were available.

Nevertheless, a rapid increase in the number of civilian reactors in operation in the U.S. is occurring from the completion of projects which have been under construction since the 1970's. This results in up to 29% increase in U.S. nuclear capacity in 1983–84 and about 70% increase in capacity to 1990 (versus 1982).

A major part of the increase in costs of large construction projects arises from the increased cost of interest during construction, plus the delays experienced during and after construction. The explosive growth of protectionist litigation as a major activity in the U.S. has made it possible to increase the costs of almost any long term project by procedural delays. This has been the largest single mechanism causing increased costs and the decline in potential nuclear commitments and completions. To some degree the same effect is present in coal, chemical, steel, housing, transportation, mining, and many other industrial activities as well. While some litigation is necessary, perhaps some concern for litigation which is mounted only for the sake of delay is appropriate. It amounts to an almost unlimited power to impose denial-by-delay on most productive activities. The large waste of natural resources and human effort resulting from such litigation — and the corresponding effects in regulation — also helps to drive inflation, lower human productivity, cause decline or loss of industries and jobs, and contributes to the current recession — some aspects of which may be permanent. The need for limits-to-growth of excessive due process may be as urgent to human welfare as limits to growth of other aspects of society.

Comparative Risks of Energy Production From Various Sources

There is extensive historical data on the occupational and public health impacts of conventional energy sources, including fossil fuels, hydro, and nuclear. Inhaber (2) (3) (4) has extended such risk estimates to include a variety of less conventional energy sources. For each, he evaluates six components that are required to produce energy from any given source:

1. material acquisition and construction
2. emissions associated with the production of the required materials
3. operation and maintenance
4. back-up energy system requirements
5. energy storage requirements, and
6. transportation and distribution

The health effects associated with the production of a ton of steel, concrete, aluminum, glass, etc. are based on historical data of the actual numbers of injuries, deaths, and health effects. The contribution to a given energy technology from material sources covered by the first two elements is in proportion to the amount of materials required. Similarly, the contribution of the other four elements have considerable areas of commonality in requirements, and in data available. Inhaber further estimates health effects and risks of these to the general public as well as occupational health effects.

Inhaber's work leads to the conclusion that various energy sources all exact considerable tolls in both occupational and public health effects. This conclusion is less surprising when one considers that essentially all energy sources are now costly, and (with one or two useful but limited exceptions), newer sources are more costly than older ones. High costs reflect the requirement for high content of materials, energy, and labor. These in turn have their associated human and environmental costs.

Many less broad-ranging risk assessments have been carried out by other analysts and agencies — with generally similar results. (Reference 3 has an extensive bibliography — over 600 references — and review of many of these studies.) Analysis in several other countries also have given generally similar results. (5) For example, the British Health and Safety Commission (6) estimates 1.8 deaths per 1000 megawatt years of electricity production from coal, versus 0.3 for oil and gas, and 0.25 for nuclear. (The nuclear figure includes fuel reprocessing and waste disposal.)

Inhaber gives a variety of tabulations of his results. Perhaps the most general condensation of his results is Figure I-A, which compares the total man-days lost associated with a unit of electrical energy

40

produced from each source considered. Man-days lost include losses due
to injuries, disease, and premature deaths. The analyses for each source
results in a range of values. Fig I-A shows this range. For example, the
range for coal is 610 to 1900 man-days, for wind it is 50 to 91 days, etc.
One should not attribute any precision to the numbers given that
uncertainties of 50 to 100% are unavoidable. The basic relationships
can be summarized in a short table as follows:

Health Effects of Principal Sources of
Energy Used To Generate Electricity

MAN DAYS LOST PER MEGAWATT YEAR (FOR THIRTY YEAR LIFETIME OF PLANT)	ENERGY SUPPLY SOURCE
200 to 2000	coal, oil
20 to 200	methanol, solar (for space heating, photovoltaic, or thermal-electric) wind, hydroelectric, ocean thermal
2 to 20	nuclear & natural gas

Many aspects of these results have been challenged or refined in
quantative terms by advocates of both conventional and unconventional
energy sources, and have been further refined after several extensive
reviews. Several changes in the numerical values have resulted from
extensive critiques (4), but they have not changed the rankings shown. *

The supporters of conventional fossil energy sources grant that
there are substantial social and health costs involved in energy production. For new or unconventional sources, such measurements may seem
insignificant or irrelevant at the stage when a new source provides a
miniscule fraction of total energy needs, but these small effects can

---

*For example, a substantial range of values is found for the amounts of steel and labor involved
in drilling a successful oil well, on land or in the ocean, and in the average expected yield of the
well over its lifetime. For the newer sources, there is reasonable hope that advancing
technology may in time reduce the amounts of material, construction, and associated transportation and storage which will eventually be required. However, large changes in requirements would have to be achieved to affect the relative ranking of any given source.

become significant social impacts when uses grow more widespread. In special circumstances, some benefits can (and should) be exploited at very small marginal risk. For example, simple measures in proper orientation of a new house can reduce heating energy required by up to 30%. This energy contribution would fall into the lowest category of added risk.

A decision to develop one of the more hazardous sources — say deep-mined coal or ocean bed oil wells — is not necessarily unreasonable or immoral. It represents a social value judgement that the risks and consequences of insufficient supply may outweigh the commitment of human risks and lives involved in such enterprises. Figure I-B illustrates the relative contribution to total risk of energy production from 11 different conventional and unconventional sources.

The nuclear contribution to public health impacts is comparable to that of natural gas — when the latter is used to generate electricity.** This result is subject to caveats on the validity of such comparisons. For example, it is argued that the mere possibility that a large scale "worst case" catastrophe might occur implies that an added weighting factor "social risk aversion" should be applied. That reflects a judgement that the social impacts of accidents involving several or many people at one time are inherently more damaging to society than the same number of health effects or deaths spread over a longer period of time. The implication is that greater regulation effort and greater costs for risk reduction are warranted socially or politically when multiple deaths or injuries are potentially involved. This may be valid to some extent, but it begs the question of the need to look even-handedly at all technologies or human activities for very low probability accidents with large consequences. At the level of one-in-a-million chance per year, few if any activities are free from "worst cases" with very large consequences to the public.

The current "worst case" for a nuclear accident, used in standard safety calculations for licensing purposes, was developed at the Massachusetts Institute of Technology for the Reactor Safety Study — the Rassmussen Report (7). This study is now believed to overestimate the environmental and health impacts of worst case accidents considerably, (see later discussion).

**Gas use for space heating is not included. It would show considerably larger numbers for man-days lost from injuries or deaths due to fires and explosions.

The details of any estimates and the methodology of risk comparisons of different energy sources inherently have considerable ranges of uncertainty. A large and increasing body of scholarly literature indicates the level of continued analysis and review. The second law of thermodynamics can be paraphrased as "there is no free lunch." All human activities involve the acceptance and experience of some degrees of both known rates of health effects, injuries, and deaths, and estimated or hypothetical risks of such effects where there is little or no actual experience.

Risk Perception

There is a widespread folk mythology that civilian nuclear energy has been one of the more damaging enterprises of mankind — despite the excellent actual experience. The hope of the Atoms for Peace Program initiated by the U.S. Congress and successive Administrations in the 1950's and 1960's was that civilian nuclear energy, despite its arising as a byproduct of a war-time effort, would become the equivalent of Isaiah's injunction — "beating swords into plowshares" — and that it would be so perceived by the public. It was part of the basis for the non-proliferation treaty — now subscribed to by over 100 countries. The industrial countries which had nuclear technology would assist other countries in developing civilian aspects of nuclear technology. In return, the signatory non-weapons states would agree to refrain from clandestine development of nuclear weapons, and to this end to agree to permit inspection of nuclear-related facilities. This approach rested on the observations that:

1. Civilian nuclear energy could help offset the disparity in world distribution of energy resources and population.
2. The basic science and technology of nuclear weapons was already available to almost all countries.
3. Civilian nuclear technology did not facilitate weapons technology.
4. Open and inspectable civilian facilities would produce less international tensions and risks of war than closed or covert military facilities.

However, the juxtaposition of the word "nuclear" with a mental picture of a mushroom cloud was firmly fixed in people's minds before there were any civilian values to nuclear matters. This image and perception cannot be erased merely by good performance or by stating

43

the physical impossibility of making a nuclear reactor function as a nuclear bomb.

For historical perspective, Tables II-A, B, and C summarize recent U.S. mortality experience and sources of deaths from accidents and diseases.

Possible Large Accidents Versus Many Small Accidents

Another school of thought on risk assessment argues that probabilities, however small, are of little significance to public perception and acceptance of risks. Only the "worst conceivable" accident should dominate public decisions. If this principle were generally applied, it would prevent or inhibit a great many human activities. One wonders, for example what would be the effect on the safety of air travel if a principal concern in the regulation and operation of aircraft was the consideration of the possibility that a fully loaded jumbo aircraft might someday crash in flames into a sports stadium containing 50,000 people. This risk in fact exists. It has been estimated to have about one chance in 80,000 per year of such a crash near a major airport in California. (8) There is more than one in one hundred per year chance of such an event nationally, and still higher chances on a world basis. For perspective, Table II-D shows recent experience on actual accidents with multiple victims.

The range of fatalities for such a crash is estimated in the referenced report to be from 6,000 to 32,000 with the lower value considered average. The same study considers the average chance of a crash in any given square mile within five miles of a major airport to be about 24 expected fatalities in a 30 year period (not counting passenger fatalities).

For the large accident, the expected value of fatalities in the same period is four chances in 10,000 that such an accident might happen in 30 years, near any single airport.

A conceptual difficulty in treating small chances of large hazards is well illustrated here. The "expected value" of the payout risk — in an actuarial or insurance sense — would be calculated as .0004 × 6000 or 2.4 likely fatalities in 30 years. The less dramatic accidents, involving only a few people at a time, are ten times more "risky" than the large accidents. For 100 airports which have sports arenas nearby the "expected value" would be 24 fatalities in 30 years. Or finally — an insurance actuary would estimate that for one hundred airports, the risk of such a large accident is a 50% chance in 500 years.

Inhaber's results total up the man-days lost including the actual production of electricity, plus the production of the materials and the construction involved before electricity can be generated plus the public risks from possible accidents. (He excludes the injuries or fatalities connected with the use of electricity in the home and in the industry, since these are independent of the means by which electricity is generated.) One basic caution on this kind of risk assessment is that it represents an estimate of public health consequences over the 30 year lifetime of a typical generating source. As in the case of aircraft risks, this begs the question of the possible distinctions in public perception, public policy, and morality between an occasional injury or death — say at the rate of one or two per year, versus the same or even a smaller total number of injuries or deaths which occur in a shorter period of time. For example, oil burning generating stations typically have an accident rate of considerably less than one fatality per year. Some have operated 30 years without a fatality. However, occasionally a severe event has occurred. For example, a few weeks ago a power station in Venezuela had an accident in which about 30 people were killed and a larger number injured.

Historically, society and regulation have tended to discount low probabilities of large events, even when evident, as with aircraft, gasoline, butane and chemical trucks, high speed ground travel, etc. Hypothetical or unprecedented events have been ignored almost completely. The practical and political focus is commonly on situations in which visible numbers of fatalities or injuries are evident each year. The exception to this — until recent years and to some extent continuing — has been the curious tolerance of accidents, injuries, and health effects which are removed from everyday public experience. Occupational health effects now get intensive attention by regulatory agencies, but there is rarely a public outcry that coal or oil use should be banned because of the large numbers of occupational deaths and injuries which occur each year.

Starting with the increasing attention and litigation for environmental issues, the concern over hypothetical events now sometimes overrides the concern for actual current fatalities and injuries and their highly predictable continued occurrences.

There is perception that at some level of probability, accidents involving hundreds or even thousands of people are possible from several sources, notably including nuclear energy. The most difficult risk to treat in a rational and moral way are the risks of episodic occurrences such as wars, civil disturbances, epidemics of particular crimes, and natural disasters including hurricanes and tornadoes, earthquakes, tidal waves, and volcanoes. Recent general experience on sources of deaths from natural events is shown in Table II-E.

Inhaber's thesis explicitly involves the idea that evaluation of risks should include consideration for losses to the human condition of all kinds, whether they be actual shortening of life-span from disease or injury, or loss of effective days of lifetime through illness or injury. He also assumes that all lives are equally valuable, whether miners, construction workers, producers or consumers (Presumably these losses must be evaluated by the extent to which they exceed some typical levels of death or injury of disease compared with the "normal" levels prevalent in a given society). This work raises the question whether it is socially or morally responsible for regulators to be equally sensitive to situations which systematically result in several actual deaths per year (on the average) relative to situations in which a similar number of people might be killed — hypothetically — in the course of 30 years.

Low-Level Radiation

The concerns in respect to civilian nuclear energy have included those over possible effects of very low levels of radiation from normal operation and from waste disposal. They have been even more intense in respect to hypothetical large-scale accidents which might conceivably affect many people. The objective information on low level radiation effects is increasingly solid and encouraging that the possible exposures to the general public are not significant.

The moral dilemma in this area is the following: exposure to many materials or natural forces — at some levels — are known to have harmful effects. The "conservative" assumption is that if one gram of a material can kill one person, then one thousand people exposed to one thousandth of even one millionth of a gram each must be prevented by legislation and regulation. Fortunately, there are many exceptions which have been deemed politically unenforceable. (For example caffeine, tobacco, pepper, and constituents of many common foods can be toxic at high levels, but are not banned.)[20]

The evidence of nature is that organisms often need small amounts of some materials or exposures to thrive — while larger amounts of the same can be injurious or fatal. For example, most medicines, minerals, or vitamins needed for health can be toxic in large amounts. Sunshine, fluorides, or radiowaves can be fatal in excess, but normal amounts are harmless or even beneficial.

Yet there has been enormous amounts of research and polemics on whether small amounts of radiation exposure should not be treated for regulatory and litigation purposes in a unique way. In its most extreme form, this amounts to the proposition that if a snowball can cause injury, an avalanche of snow can kill, so the falling of snowflakes on many people, might eventually injure or kill.

This gives the regulators and courts an insoluble conundrum since the natural lifetime background of radiation can be 3 to 10 units (REMs) and can be increased to double or more by where and what kind of house one lives in, what one eats, by travel and by many occupations remote from nuclear energy. The nuclear energy contribution to the nearest people is unlikely to reach 1/30th of a unit, or less than one percent of nature.

An even more difficult dilemma has been posed from hypothetical genetic effects. If 100 units of radiation to one organism cause a detectible mutation, does .001 of a unit applied to each of one hundred thousand people cause one mutation?. The total dose to tissue is the same but the question is unanswerable by any test since natural muta- tion rates are many thousands of times greater. Fortunately, it has been established that most mutations are recessive and do not aggregate over many generations. But the fear of genetic damage is pervasive.

Even if a large number of nuclear reactors operate for long periods of time, their contribution to the background of radiation already existing in nature is very small. The most basic *de minimis* reasoning arises from the observation that just the *changes* alone in any individual's annual exposure from nature from ordinary human activities, are far larger than from all nuclear power. For example, moving from one building to another or from one city block, or country farm, to another can give *changes* in exposure many times larger than the maximum public exposure to radiation from nuclear power stations. There are many locations in the world in which the local background from nature is more than ten times higher than the average values in the United States — and such regions have been inhabited for many centuries. (For example there are such places in Brazil, India, and at increased elevations in several places in the world). Finally there are common occupations — such as airline flight personnel — (and some "frequent flyer" passengers) who receive 100 percent to 500 percent more radiation than typical natural background. This is a result of natural radiation to which aircraft are exposed at high altitudes.

It is likely that low-level radiation exposures from television sets and from computers are many times greater to the population as a whole than that which would accrue from replacing all fossil fuel electricity with nuclear sources. Even staying in close proximity to another human results in a measurable increase in radiation exposure. It is even true that minor changes in eating habits can affect natural radiation exposure by substantial amounts since foods and liquids can differ by factors of more than 10 in the amount of natural radiation content. The practice of building homes out of brick or stone, or sod or adobe has contributed to larger changes in human exposure to radiation than are likely if all electricity were produced by nuclear power. Energy conservation by better sealing of homes and buildings in recognized as a major increase in public radiation exposure. This source of radiation exposure is *many times* greater than from nuclear power even if all electricity were nuclear-generated.[21]

Apprehension and Perception of Large Accidents

This leaves as a principal valid concern the possibility and probability of large accidents which might disperse major amounts of radioactivity to the environment. The possible consequent effects would be significant exposures, say 10 to 100 units — to people immediately downwind of an accident. The effects would be mostly latent cancers — which typically develop 20 or 30 years after the exposure. There is also possible localized interdiction of property use — for some time, if a region were to be heavily contaminated by the spread of radioactivity.

The actual experience to date is about 750 years of large scale power reactor operation in the U.S., over 1600 years of such operation worldwide; and wll over 5,000 reactor years of operation if reactors used for navy propulsion are also included. There have been more than four dozen occurrences of major damage to plant equipment, some of which involved some radioactive spills or emissions. The record in terms of actual impacts or public health is more than a satisfactory one, not in comparison with a zero-risk ideal, but in comparison with virtually any other productive human activity, and lower than most industrial activities. The question is whether such a good record will continue indefinitely.

The record is so good that most people do not perceive it or believe it. The reason for this is that "harmless" exaggeration in the media is so pervasive that it is an unarguable part of folklore — which is more powerful than reason. Two examples serve to illustrate this. When President Carter visited Three Mile Island soon after the accident, there were several cartoons in virtually all of the national media showing him glowing in the dark, presumably from exposure to radiation. This is monumentally silly, but has enduring public impact. There have been literally hundreds of cartoons which show a mushroom cloud or a skull and cross-bones, superimposed on the nuclear plant. The emotional, non-rational impact of such messages has been repeated over the years in thousands of ways. In songs, theater, movies, and television as well as cartoons, this has built a folklore which is largely immune to reality or reason. Here — as in other fundamental social issues — "history may be a race between education and disaster" (H. G. Wells).

Perception and Risk at Three Mile Island

The so-called "worst reactor accident in history" in the United States was at Three Mile Island in March 1979. Virtually all of the radioactive gas in the reactor escaped to the environment. However, the total worst individual or group radiation exposure was equivalent to no more than one or two months of natural background radiation and the average added exposure for people in the adjacent town was equivalent to one or two days of natural background.[9] The *natural* background measured before the TMI plant was built, varies by 50 to 100 percent in the few miles immediately adjacent to Three Mile Island, with the lowest values near the river at which the plant was situated. The irony of the situation is that the people who evacuated their homes within sight of the plant — moving to motels or to other homes a few miles away — would in a great many cases have experienced a larger increase in radiation exposure from the difference in natural background — than they would have experienced if they had stayed near the damaged reactor. (The radiation exposure history was extensively monitored at the time, and the data studied and documented by the presidential Kemeny commission and by three federal agencies).[9]

There actually was a more severe accident in the U.S., but not to a civilian reactor. An accident to a small military reactor in Idaho resulted in three fatalities and severe damage to the reactor core. The fatalities were primarily due to mechanical forces such as can result from a conventional steam boiler accident, rather than from radiation.[10]

Current Evaluation of Hazards of Actual Reactor Events

Each year, news and electronic media carry stories of occurrences at nuclear power stations with the evident implication that these are "near misses" to a possible catastrophe.

Intensive analysis of these events is now regularly done by two non-profit research institutes as well as the staff of the Nuclear Regulatory Commission, a National Laboratory, and several contractors. Approximately 30,000 incident reports which have been studied and analyzed for the period 1969 through 1982. About two dozen (including Three Mile Island) show some reduction in the normally very large margins of safety. A perspective on the nature of these hazards is that for most of these two dozen events, they would have to be repeated about 1,000 times before there would be significant likelihood of damage to the reactor core. Even if the reactor core is damaged, as at Three Mile Island and a number of other accidents, there still remain considerable margins and time for remedial actions to prevent public exposures. All such incidents are now subject to intensive effort to make changes in equipment, procedures, and training to reduce the likelihood of occurrence. Few of them will continue to occur repeatedly and any such will get even more intensive attention to preventative measures.

Even if core damage were to occur, it is now recognized that the effectiveness of the containment building and the effectiveness of water in retaining radioactivity give further levels of protection. Many studies show probabilities greater than 99 percent — that emission of amounts of radiation greater in effect than annual natural background will not occur even if the core were to melt. These studies confirm the theoretical analyses conducted for many years, notably by Massachusetts Institute of Technology, and by about a dozen subsequent studies of similar depth, that estimate the risks of reactor accidents. Those which might release appreciable amounts of radioactivity are in the range of 1 in 1000 to 1 in 50,000 years of reactor operation.[7] These estimates of risk are indeed small relative to most other industrial activities and relative to those from other sources of energy. These estimates do not take into account the now ongoing process for rigorous learning from experience.

In addition to Three Mile Island, several dozen less publicized accidents (involving some damage of fuel and some spread of radioactivity) have occurred. A severe accident of this type occurred in 1957 at Windscale in northern England.[11] A small air-cooled graphite-moderated reactor used for plutonium production became overheated. Its magnesium-clad uranium metal fuel actually caught on fire. Unlike civilian reactors, the production reactor had no containment building and was air-cooled. Some of its radioactivity escaped to the countryside. The main effect was the spread of about 20,000 curies* of radioiodine (an isotope of iodine with a half-life of about 7 days) to the nearby areas — which included a number of dairy farms. For several months farmers were required to dump the milk from cows which had grazed on the iodine-contaminated grass until the radioactive iodine decayed away. There was no general alarm or evacuation of people. Subsequent health studies, conducted over several decades, showed no discernible effects on humans or animals.

The reactor accident at Three Mile Island involved a much larger reactor, with roughly a 100 times larger content of radioactivity than the reactor at Windscale. Based on conventional calculations, such as those used by MIT or Inhaber to calculate public exposure risks, the expected release of radioactivity to the environment should have been many times larger than at Windscale. However the surprise was that no more than 20 curies of radioiodine where released to the environment[9] — about one one-thousandth of the release at Windscale. The small release was due to the effectiveness of water in the containment building in retaining most of the iodine.

The issue illustrated by the unexpectedly small release of radioactivity from the Three Mile Island accident is now called the "source term" issue. Nearly all of the radioactivity other than gases which escaped from the damaged fuel was found to have stayed in the water which remained in the reactor containment building. The effect of the water present in the reactor system, (or which drains into the basement

---

*A "curie" is a measure of an amount of radioactivity equivalent to one gram of radium.

of the containment building if the reactor system leaks) has the ability to hold up essentially all of the non-volatile radioactivity, even if the fuel and primary system are badly damaged. This prevents non-volatile radioactivity from being airborne, and also holds up virtually all of the slightly volatile radioactivity such as iodine. Basic chemical analyses and laboratory tests now confirm these observations. These observations make it likely that the proper "source term" for water-cooled reactors is ten to one hundred times smaller than assumed in past accident studies — (and it may be as much as a thousand times smaller for most realistic situations). This would mean that even "worst case" accidents in which all of the multiple and redundant safety systems fail simultaneously or consecutively, and the containment building also is grossly breached and no remedial actions are taken for many hours or days — that even for such highly unlikely cases, the plausible consequences of such accidents might range down as low as zero-to-one potential cancers, occurring some decades after the accident.** This is not to imply that all due diligence to prevent and contain possible accidents is unwarranted. Substantial efforts are essential for economic and social reasons even if the perspectives on extreme accidents become more tame.

The circumstantial evidence of a number of reactor accidents involving fuel damage, as well as laboratory experiments, now all point in the direction of the lower values of "source term." However, the Nuclear Regulatory Commission prudently discounts virtually all of this evidence, including the observations of the Three Mile Island accident, until a long series of systematic, well-controlled experiments can be conducted. Furthermore, still further scenarios can be envisioned in which all of the large inventory of water available in a reactor systems and in its auxiliary systems somehow is made to disappear, and the non-flammable ceramic oxide fuel somehow converts itself to fine airborne smoke — or else melts its way slowly through ten feet of concrete to reach bedrock or sub-soil. Even given that these hypothetical conditions are reached, these processes take many hours or days to

---

**The "worst case" dose estimate for a person who might have stood at a particular spot on the site boundary at Three Mile Island for a full two weeks during which the leakages occurred, would have received about 100 "millirems" of thyroid dose from radioiodine. (9) (The uncertainty in the calculation is such that it might equally well have been less than 10 millirems.) These doses are roughly a thousand times smaller than the thyroid doses which often occur in the common medical use of radioiodine, which themselves have been shown to produce negligible health affects. (A "millirem" is a measure of radiation exposure which is one thousandth of the unit mentioned earlier).

52

occur. It requires a further set of unlikely assumptions that none of the various backup means available are used to add or spray water into the containment building. (For example, a fire engine pumper can supply enough water to maintain fuel in a non-volatile condition indefinitely even if all of the protective systems and containment were damaged or breached and all installed sources of cooling water were lost.) To reach worst-case assumptions requires the further overlay of another set of highly unlikely circumstances over the one-in-a-million kind of estimates found in the Reactor Safety Study of 1975.[7]

Nuclear Reactors Created by Nature

There is evidence that nuclear chain reactions have occurred naturally on the earth.[12] Four confirmed instances of such reactors have been discovered in Gabon in Africa and others are suspected in Colorado.

The ratio of fissionable isotope of uranium (U-235) to ordinary uranium (U-238) is closely fixed in most of nature to slightly above 7/10 percent by weight. Samples from hundreds of different locations in the world and from meteorites usually agree to three decimal places. The French mining operation was astonished to discover a large body of uranium ore in which the uranium-235 content of the uranium was lower than the normal value, in some samples less than one-half of the normal amount. (Under 4/10 percent by weight.) Over a number of years, the story of the natural reactors has been worked out. In earlier times, the percentage of U-235 in U-238 in nature was several times higher than at present. (U-235 has a shorter half-life and has decayed more rapidly than U-238.) At higher concentrations of U-235, a natural uranium ore above a certain richness could become "critical" and sustain a nuclear chain reaction, with ordinary water from nature serving as the moderator. The results of this would be a natural boiling water reactor. The evidence from the analysis of the remaining elements is that such reactors continued to operate in nature for tens to hundreds of thousands of years, gradually depleting the U-235 content in these locations by nuclear fission, and producing fission products, possibly in ton quantities.

An important implication of these discoveries is that most of the radioactive products occurring from these long periods of reactor operation — including plutonium and the fission products — were localized in and around the natural reactors due to the nature-made safety systems and contained effects. All of the fission-produced radioactivity, including plutonium and fission products, has long since decayed away, but the stable daughter elements remain to provide clear testimony to the events and processes which occurred. This provides an important clue to the reasonableness of safe disposal of radio activity from modern reactors. It can be safely sequestered deep underground, in stable geological formations while it decays to inactive elements.

Improvements in Reactor Safety and Operations

The accident at Three Mile Island led to extensive reappraisals of reactor operations by both government and industry. Even when the findings were confirmed that no appreciable public damage had occurred (beyond that caused by apprehensions) the financial and social impacts were much greater than those from similar events in other kinds of activities. Except for the absence of deaths or injuries, the other consequences were much greater even than from accidents which actually have involved large numbers of casualties. One of the principal "lessons learned" was enunciated by a Presidential Commission.[9] This . Commission was headed by Dr. George Kemeny, President of Dartmouth College, himself a noted scientist and mathemetician. This "lesson" was noted as the lack of a systematic nationwide process for accumulating, analyzing, and sharing the detailed lessons from operating experience. They noted the need to disseminate and apply the results of such analysis for continued improvements in equipment and operation.

In the months following the accident at Three Mile Island, two new institutions were established by the U.S. utility industry with the encouragement of the Presidential Commission (The industry group includes federal and state-owned public utilities, municipal utilities and co-ops, and investor-owned utilities). The new institutions formed were the Nuclear Safety Analysis Center in Palo Alto (now a part of EPRI, the Electric Power Research Institute); and the Institute of Nuclear Power Operations (INPO) in Atlanta. These are independent non-profit institutes. EPRI does energy-related research covering broad areas of energy as well as nuclear safety research. INPO monitors all U.S. civilian reactors and advises utilities on how to improve their technical and management operations. Similar monitoring and advice has been routine for Navy reactors, several hundred of which have operated safely during the last 25 years.

Prior to the accident at TMI, studies of possible reactor accidents were done to some extent by the government, and at the design stage by reactor designers. Studies of operating experience were done largely by the reactor suppliers, and to some extent by the government. However, these activities were not rigorous, comprehensive, or timely. Several less damaging events had occurred, generally similar to first stages of the TMI accident, but were not recognized as needing corrective actions. A specific incident occurred at the Davis-Besse reactor which had many similar features to the initial stages of the TMI accident. It was terminated safely by the operators without significant damage to fuel or equipment. This event was actually reviewed by the reactor supplier and by the government, but the results were communicated to the utility people at TMI some 18 months after the event at the Davis-Besse unit — and only after the TMI accident.

There now exists at the Institute of Nuclear Power Operations in Atlanta, a rigorous and comprehensive system which analyzes all reactor operation incidents involving reactor power system malfunctions of almost any kind, including very minor ones. There were some 19,000 such incidents reported prior to TMI, but a comprehensive process of analysis and communication of recommendations was not in place. The present system is analyzing between four and five thousand such reports each year. The overwhelming majority of these incidents are minor. Only a few dozen of these events meet commonplace definition of industrial "accidents" in the sense that significant equipment damage, or some leakage of water or radiation occurs within the reactor containment. However, even the seemingly minor events are analyzed to see if they could lead to, or be parts of, a chain of events which might have more serious consequences if extended.

This evaluation process now includes rapid communication on all events which are considered significant, using a computer-assisted teleconferencing system. This system promptly reaches all utilities in the United States, and also reaches those in thirteen other participating countries which have major nuclear programs, in Europe, Asia, and South America. (See Fig. IV-D)

The occurrences which are found to be significant are subject to intense technical and operational analysis by highly qualified teams of engineers, operators and analysts. Detailed recommendations are developed for practical means to reduce the likelihood of occurrence and to limit the consequences if such events, nevertheless, do reoccur. The process is similar to that used by the Federal Aviation Administration and the National Transportation Safety Board for analyzing aircraft or other transportation accidents or malfunctions, and for developing remedial actions. A similar process has been used by NASA to raise the reliability and safety of spacecraft and satellites to a high degree.

The process of comprehensive evaluation of all operating experience started late in 1979, and reached its present developed state by mid-1981. Some of the recommendations made take several months or even several years to implement in practice. It is too early to measure a noticable change in the frequency of significant malfunctions. However, a majority of the malfunctions which have been analyzed in the last three years are "repeaters" — that is to say, a number of prior examples can be found for almost all of them. There is already a trend evident that as remedies are more widely implemented, the frequency of the "repeater events" decreases. Since "repeaters" form a large fraction of the total number, it is expected that the total frequency of troublesome events overall will decrease, even with more reactors in operation.

Possible large accidents involve a chain of several — or many — malfunctions or abnormal conditions. These individual steps or partial sequences are of the same kinds of those which are reported each year as individual events. Analysis shows that reduction in the frequency of the kinds of malfunctions which are involved in severe accident sequences will decrease the likelihood of such severe accidents in proportion to the reductions in the individual steps. For example, the remedial measures taken following the Three Mile Island accident have reduced the likelihood of some chains of events (in the same general family as the Three Mile Island accident) by a factor of ten to a hundred.

We can estimate the likelihood of a chain of events similar to that of a Three Mile Island historically as being one such event in seven hundred years of domestic power reactor operation to date. If all reactors implement and maintain the remedial actions now available and practical, the likelihood of that type of chain of events falls to less than one in about seven thousand reactor years of operation and possibly to about one in seventy thousand years. This implies that there is now a high degree of assurance that such an accident can be avoided even with as many as 150 reactors in the U.S. operating for their 30 to 40 year life-times. This takes us well into the first quarter of the next century before a possible accident of this type involving serious reactor core damage becomes likely. Even this small possibility should decline still further as the implementation of the process of learning from experience becomes universal.

The benefits of such a cumulative learning process can accrue fully only if all of the utilities which operate reactors make timely use of such information and implement it fully in practice. To this end, the Institute of Nuclear Power Operations also conducts a continuing cycle of evaluations of plant operation, training, quality of technical support, maintenance, and plant management. The evaluations have an assistance or tutorial function which provides constructive examples of good practices. (The Nuclear Regulatory Commission also reviews all plant operations, but is constrained to a policing and punitive role.) Together these reviews contribute to the effectiveness with which operating experience is understood, and its lessons applied. The specific implementation of the recommendations from operating experience are also tracked in the evaluations by INPO.

Despite the relative newness of these programs, most utilities have implemented most of the applicable recommendations which are given a priority rating, at the time of the INPO evaluation visits. These visits are now on a cycle of about 15 months, with a follow-up after six months.

Systems for the reporting and evaluation of operating experience are also in place in France, Sweden and Belgium — which have larger percentages of nuclear energy relative to total electric capacity than does the United States. Similar systems are also under development, or being considered, in most other countries which have major nuclear programs.

The Likelihood of Reactor Accidents in the Future

The lessons learned from Three Mile Island are generally understood in all organizations worldwide which operate civilian power reactors. Nevertheless, the approximate frequency of damaging events is roughly predictable. There have been fifty-nine occurrences (through 1982) of circumstances which required that reactors be shut down for considerably longer periods than the normal times required for refueling. Many of these prolonged outages were not the result of "events" or accidents as such, but which resulted from testing or inspection of

57

particular systems or equipment which demonstrated an inadequacy in function of condition in need of repair. However, some of these extended outages were a result of events which occurred during operation, and a few of them had consequences extensive enough to be regarded as accidents and to make some headlines.

For perspective, all of the events which occurred amounted to a "forced outage rate" of about 8 percent — which is favorable compared with heavy power generation equipment, for example coal-powered plants. The duration of some of these events was extended by the need for extensive review by the utility and the Nuclear Regulatory Commission to determine whether sufficient repairs or corrective actions had been taken. The amounts of regulatory outages have been substantial in the last several years because of the extensive requirements for "backfits" (which are changes in equipment and instrumentation), mandated since the accident at TMI. These were estimated to amount to over six billion dollars worth of mandated changes as of 1981 — in some cases greater than the initial costs of building the plant. Many additional changes continue to be required by regulation. The consequence of the observations above is that a significant amount of plant outage in excess of the times normally required for refueling and routine maintenance is likely to continue, even with substantial improvements in operations and equipment. Part of this is due to the time required for accomplishing of the improvements themselves, and part of it is due to continuing increases in regulations and in vigilance in inspection and repair.

A further important observation is that despite such requirements, the overall operating capacity factor of nuclear plants continues to be excellent, and slightly better than that for large coal plants. The difference in favor of nuclear plants is likely to increase with time as the backlog of improvements is completed — and as coal plants become increasingly complicated to accommodate processing equipment required to meet standards for air quality. Such equipment is called for to limit the increases in the enormous tonages of gaseous and particulate emissions and of gases and particles which can contribute acid rain, which would otherwise occur.

Cost Differences — Nuclear and Fossil Energy

Many studies, both domestic and foreign, show a substantial cost advantage for nuclear power over oil or gas-fired electricity sources. (13) (14) The cost of power is a combination of the capital costs, operating costs, and fuel cost.[13, 14] The cost of power is a combination of the capital cost, operating cost, and fuel cost. For nuclear units, it is now common to add accruals or sinking funds for the processing and disposal of spent fuel, and for the eventual decommissioning, disposal, and return to original site conditions for the plant itself. (Both of the later costs are a small part of the total annual costs since they are spread over a 30 to 40 year operating lifetime.) The cost comparisons also show a significant cost advantage for nuclear units over coal units. The advantage is small enough that it may be considered essentially a stand-off, or slightly in favor of coal in regions which have excellent access to supplies of high quality coal. Where coal is not available nearby, or when high sulfur coal is present, the cost of using coal for power generation is substantially higher than nuclear. This characterizes most of the United States. The extra cost is necessary to pay for the additional capital and operating costs of emission control equipment, or to pay for the shipping of high quality coal to replace or to blend with lower quality coal.

There was a policy determination during the Carter administration that the use of coal for power generation should be doubled by 1985. Nuclear plant commitments were discouraged by policy and by practices which started the flow of cancellations of partly completed units. Only a modest increase in coal use has actually occurred, and the market for coal is relatively weak. The cost of coal and of energy from coal has continued to rise due to the increasing costs of control of environmental and occupational hazards.

Basis for Cost Comparisons in Operating Units

The cost comparisons referred to so far are most relevant to decisions on which type of plant to build when additions to capacity, or replacement of capacity is needed to retire obsolete equipment. For plants which are already in existence, the decision of which ones to run or to reduce in power as load demand varies is controlled by the incremental costs of each additional kilowatt of generation. That is to say the fixed charges (paying off the bonds which supply the money for the capital cost) continue unchanged for all types of plants whether they are run at full power, half power, or not at all. The operating costs — which cover the labor costs and materials and services other than fuel — are only weakly related to the extent to which a plant runs, unless it is actually shut down for a prolonged period.

Fuel costs vary almost directly in proportion to the number of hours which a plant runs at full power. For plants already built, the effect on the consumer and on the economy is primarily from the fuel costs. Comparisons here are instructive. Not only is the cost of power generated by oil or gas considerably higher than the cost from Nuclear source, but the fuel costs *alone* are higher than the total cost — capital plus operation plus fuel — for existing nuclear plants. The incremental fuel cost *alone* is commonly as much as 10 times higher than the incremental fuel costs for a nuclear plant.

The Department of Energy maintains comprehensive study of fuels markets, and intense economic analyses of the factors which control prices. Tables III-A and III-B show the "middle of the road" forecasts for oil, coal, gas, and nuclear — either as total cost of generation — or fuel cost alone in the case of oil and gas. The low side projections of these costs are only modestly lower, and still show some increase in real terms. The "high side projections" range as much as 50 percent higher for fossil fuels.

The projections for uranium prices are much more stable, since the supply through the 1980's is almost entirely domestic, is already under contract, the mining and milling capacity is in place, and the demand is precisely forseeable from the amount of capacity in operation. The U.S. uranium reserves already known are sufficient to operate about 600 large reactors for their full lifetimes. (Fewer than 200 are likely to be in operation in this century.) Despire this highly favorable position in respect to domestic supply — including mining and milling capacity in place — some foreign procurement of uranium is contracted for; increasing in the 1990's — since even more favorable price terms are available from other countries.

The conclusion of these observations is that the continued full operation of all of the nuclear capacity operating and under construction in the U.S. is strongly to the advantage of the consumer and to the national economy.

The foregoing conclusion is not at variance with the observation that most U.S. utilities are not likely to be able or wish to commit added nuclear plant capacity for the next few years. This is due to the combination of lower rates of load growth, the high costs and low availability of capital. But the dominant factor — even if load growth resumes with economic recovery — is due to the uncertainty in the time required to license, to build, and to acquire permission to operate a new nuclear unit. Licensing and construction cycles of 50 to 70 months were at one time regularly attained in this country — and continue to be attained regularly in France, Taiwan, Japan, Spain, Belgium and in other countries. In the U.S., the combination of financial and regulatory limitations, together with reduced or zero load growth in economically depressed regions, has resulted in stretchouts of reactor completions. Some of these in recent years have run in the range of 10 to 12 years. Similar durations occur in the Soviet Union. A few units in the U.S. continue to find more favorable circumstances and are completed in 6 to 7 years. The effects of the long construction cycles mean that the overwhelming majority of the cost of the nuclear plant now is the cost of the money tied up during construction and licensing. The direct cost of the high technology equipment portions of the plant is now as little as 10 percent of the total costs seen by the utility and the consumer. For whatever reason these costs of delay occur, they add to the consumer's burden for the entire lifetime of the plant. The costs of delays diminish, but do not entirely remove, what otherwise would be very large cost advantages to consumers — and to the national economy — from civilian nuclear energy.

About one-third of the plants still under construction have experienced delays much greater than the average. This results in high capital costs, up to twice the median costs for units completed since 1980. Such units will have relatively high power costs, initially higher than fossil fuel alternatives. Some of these plants are likely to be cancelled. However, most of those which are already more than 50 percent complete will probably be finished. The already sunk costs in manpower, materials, and resources generally make it less costly to complete them than to cancel and eventually replace with costly future plants. Even some of the high-cost units can become satisfactory for the consumers after a few years' time due to the effect of inflation on both fuel and capital costs of alternate fossil energy sources. The nuclear plants' capital charges — largely bonds — are fixed, and nuclear fuel costs are relatively small and much more stable than fossil fuel costs.

Units which were completed before the middle 1970's, now represent remarkable bargain sources of energy. In that time period, capital costs were low, construction periods were stable and relatively short, and labor productivity was high. For the utilities fortunate enough to have these early plants, they can point to savings to the consumer of many hundreds of millions of dollars per year for each unit.

The saving in fuel costs may equal the total cost of some of these plants in as little as three years. These savings help to cushion the otherwise drastic increases in the costs of electricity which would occur where oil or gas are primary fuels (as in New England and California) and also where coal is used under less than the best conditions.

World View Of Prudent Planning and Decision-Making in Respect to Energy Sources

Decisions to augment or strengthen a nation's energy supply in the face of rising population or rising industrialization in third-world countries, require the exercise of a long-term sense of responsibility to human welfare and to the public in general. Even under the most favorable financial, environmental, and regulatory conditions, it takes 4 to 6 years to build a coal plant of appreciable size. It now takes five to eight years to build a nuclear plant overseas. For small countries, a single large coal or nuclear unit may amount to half of the capacity available. It may displace most of the oil consumed for generating electricity — if that is the principal source. The project can then be viewed and decided in the context of a single defined set of actions.

For large countries, the significance of another energy source must be viewed in terms of being able to forsee a consistent plan and pattern of commitments which can produce 10 to 20 percent or more of the total energy, if it is to have a significant overall impact on national energy costs and availability. For the United States, this process will take roughly 25 years from the initial relatively small commercial units, to the point of producing 15 to 20 percent of the total electric energy supply of the United States. Figure IV-A shows the percentages of total electricity production from nuclear units (projected for 1985) for nine regions of the U.S.

Eleven other countries will have reached or exceed the level of 15 to 20 percent nuclear energy for electricity by 1985. (See tables IV-B and IV-C) These include France, (43%), Germany (Federal Republic) (20%), Japan (16%), Spain (20%), Sweden (26%), and the United Kingdom (19%). Most of these countries (except France and the United Kingdom) were initially importers of reactor systems, components, and technology. They, as well as the U.S. and the Soviet Union, now have substantial capability to produce reactor systems themselves and to design and build systems for export as well. The other countries

62

reaching 15 to 20% generation do not have capabilities to build entire plants themselves. These include Belgium (38%), Bulgaria (26%), Czechoslovakia (12–18%), Finland (20%), Germany (Democractic Republic) (17%), Hungary (16–23%), Korea (20%), Switzerland (22%), and Taiwan (31%). Nearly all of these countries also have considerable capability to manufacture much of the equipment needed for nuclear power stations.

Many countries recognize the need for long-term planning horizons on issues as vital as energy supply. Twenty-two countries have some nuclear capacity operating as of 1982. This appears reasonably certain to rise to about 28 countries by the late 1980's or early 1990's. Eleven other countries have initial projects underway for the mid-1990s. Figure IV-D shows a world overview by world regions. Most countries which already have one or more reactors, have in place plans to produce more than 20% of the total capacity as nuclear by the late 1990's. A half-a-dozen countries plan to have more than half of all generation to be nuclear by the end of the century. As with any long-term projections, no particular level of certainty can be assigned to such projections since they are subject to vicissitudes of costs and economic conditions of the same kind as we have discussed for the United States. However, the existence of such projections, and often rather detailed planning at both the government level and the level of the operating agency (a nationalized utility in many countries) indicates the long-term time horizons which such enterprises always must involve.

The exigencies of high interest rates force a short-term planning horizon. The level of foresight which is practical to exercise is now shorter in the U.S. than that which has prevailed over most of the last two centuries. The time-horizon for planning of long-term, long-time-to-payoff projects, becomes smaller, falling more than inversely with the increase in the cost of money. In recent years the cost of money for many enterprises (including interest, taxes and insurance) has exceeded 20 percent per annum.

Where is the Responsibility for Energy Decisions and Energy Planning?

In considering the moral-ethical issues involved in any aspect of energy, some observations on limiting and controlling factors may be useful. These can help identify the *situs* of decision-making and the constraints or imperatives which may act in ways which are not obvious or evident in commonly available literature.

Most productive industry has been treated by ethical theorists as purely utilitarian, and generally act-utilitarian rather than rule-utilitarian. An important observation is that utilitarianism has significantly different dimensions in generally affluent and resource-rich circumstances than under conditions in which resources are becoming scarce or expensive, and in which appreciable levels of deprivation are present. For example, in a generally affluent situation one evident dilemma of a utilitarian ethic is the difficulty of choosing among a variety of potential goods or benefits. There is also the problem of the ranking of benefits which is affected by the time frame chosen for measuring the benefits.

In a situation of declining resources and affluence, the choices theoretically remain equally broad. Realistic constraints arise from the priority which is normally and humanely given to avoiding precipitous declines in benefits already available. These are almost always perceived as "deprivations" on a relative scale even though the deprived state may have seemed like affluence several decades earlier — or currently in other parts of the world. The effects of the social disruptions caused by rapid demise of some enterprise or industry are painful, even if basic essentials of life are maintained. The dimensions of the choices available under utilitarianism become even more constrained when there is already a history of significant deprivation in the sense that life is — or can become — "nasty, brutish, and short" for some portions of society. Under these conditions, the imperatives of supply of essential necessaries of life begin to demand priority in virtually all moral-ethical structures, especially where the absences of supply can cause a visible and direct increase in human misery and death.

In complex and highly interdependent societies, direct relationships between productive actions or inactions and the consequences to human welfare are subtle and often indirect, but nevertheless real. For example, the effects of a recession in a generally affluent society for many people can be equated to little more than a minor amount of belt-tightening or dispensing with some luxuries. However for most people a decline in disposable income, both individual and national, has direct effects on nutrition, health care, education, and social services. Even without gross signs of mass starvation, there will be subtle increases in malaise, incidence of diseases and injuries, and eventually in increases in infant, juvenile, and adult death rates. Even where these do not actually worsen, it may not be possible to implement the available opportunities to improve conditions.

It has been fashionable to discount teleological aspects of utilitarianism as begging the question of "whose values?" or "whose view of the appropriate timeframes?" A difficult problem is posed for all ethical viewpoints when the connections between a particular course of action (or inaction) are subtle. They may be indeterminate — causing first one result, then another. They may unexpectedly have long-term consequences which are different or opposite to those which were expected in good faith.

Some Observations on Participants in the Moral-Ethical Choices Which Involve Energy Production

In public policy matters, the application of moral-ethical judgements is more commonly used to rationalize (or criticize) existing decisions rather than to define the decision principles to be used in specific practical situations. To help discuss applicable decision principles, it is important to distinguish for the various agencies involved in energy the range of decisions available (or made unavailable) to a given participant by various constraints.

The range of choices available to utilities has been preempted by basic changes in social-political structures and in the technical and economic circumstances. The number of state and federal regulations has increased by over 1,000 percent in the last decade. New projects can involve as many as 40 different agencies — state, federal, and local, for permissions, for rules or constraints to be observed, fees to be paid, papers to be filed, and hearings to be prepared. Even after construction is done, the interest of multiple branches in several federal agencies and in several state and local commissions must be served. Every utility executive must nowadays become to some degree a lawyer-bureaucrat in order to survive and to deal with the array of requirements. The State Public Utility Commissions have nearly unlimited control of what costs are allowable, and what rates may be charged, and what changes can be planned or made. With full exercise of these powers, they can become in some sense virtually the general managers of utility enterprises since they can determine what changes can or cannot be made.

Another imperative constraint now is that of capital and its availability — or more commonly, the unavailability which results when the revenue from the allowed rates of return are frozen, while many costs to utilities inexorably rise. A certain amount of capital investment is required even in a zero-growth situation in order to replace aging equipment. Capital is also needed to take advantage of technical improvements in operation which can produce direct gains in safety, reliability, fuel utilization, efficiency, and in overall costs. However beneficial such improvements may seem, they are often precluded because the capital expenditures must precede the benefits — usually by several years — and the capital often cannot be made available from the limited amounts of current revenue which is reflected in lower bond ratings and higher cost of raising capital.

The cancellation of some nuclear units for which virtually all of the equipment had been procured and delivered, and a large part of the construction completed, reflects the workings of some of these imperatives. The lack of capital availability, in part due to restraints on utility rates, precludes the completion of the units. This happens even though the operation of the units would more than pay for the capital costs in a few years from fuel savings alone (and thereafter provide an increasing cost-savings and security of fuel supply and costs to all rate payers — and their children — for several more decades).

In addition to the roles of the controlling interests of regulatory agencies and utility commissions, moral-ethical values are often embedded in legislation and in court decisions. The effect of this is that under many circumstances, utilities simply strive to thread their way through a maze of partly contradictory regulations, legislation, and court rulings. They strive to find "the most good for the most people". Some of the decisions forced in this environment are non-utilitarian. In some cases the moral dilemma of the utility executive can approach that of the soldier on the battlefield of a war of dubious purpose. He is constrained to serve by personal and patriotic loyalties, but may well wonder if the political or field strategists have a coherent sense of purpose. He strives to provide security of supply, within environmental requirements, and at best attainable costs — yet all of these once-noble aims are now to some degree thwarted or deprecated.

Non-Available Futures and Decisions

Some implied ethical or strategic decisions for utilities have never really been in their purview or range of choices. For example the option of a zero-growth society is a favorite theme of some environmentalists (either in terms of economics or in terms of population growth). This would indeed simplify many aspects of energy supply, not to mention air pollution, urban crowding or the like. Another choice is the possibility of mandating the use of renewable energies, for example solar, wood burning, hydro, or fusion. None of these are within the range of choice for significant levels of implementation by utility decision-makers. To implement any of these against public disinclination — usually due to higher costs, implies either coercion, or the provision of artificial stimulus (subsidies, tax advantages, or threats of penalties). These means are those sometimes available to governments, but not to legal private organizations. A noteworthy exception is utilities' initiatives for small pilot projects. When these are technically feasible — even marginally, some utilities have mounted significant pilot projects, for example for biomass, wind machines, and for active and passive solar heating, and solar thermal electricity, to encourage the use of such alternate energy sources. Even though considerably more costly than conventional sources, they sometimes fill a particular niche.

Utilities have also subsidized energy efficiency improvements for homes and businesses — sometimes by State regulation — but also because the subsidy cost of reducing the growth of consumption is sometimes less than the marginal cost of maintaining (or increasing) the energy production which would otherwise be required.

Some Relationships of Environment, Economics, and Carrying Capacity of Land Areas

In the western world, the issues of energy resources, energy supply, and forms of energy supply have been commonly treated in terms of supply and demand, which is to say the economic descriptions of the situation. In the recent decade, questions of energy supply in the U.S. have increasingly been treated as an environmental and esthetic issue. Energy production involves the use of resources, land, and the capacity of the environment absorb various kinds of emissions. Energy supply and production also has esthetic dimensions especially in regions where there is aversion to large industrial structures. An explicit assumption of much environmental philosophy is the concept of "deindustrialization" with the implicit assumption that this is an unmitigated practical as well as esthetic gain in the human condition. A further implicit assumption is that economic decline or restraints on productive activities which lead to deindustrialization — at least those which involve large-scale operations — can be accomplished without serious negative impacts on the human condition. These assumptions need to be examined.

It seems likely that the relationship of energy supply to human survival and welfare is at least as basic a consideration as most environmental and esthetic aspects. The principal hazards to human survival today for much of the developed world are the threats of regional wars, and possibilities of still larger wars. For the less developed world there are the additional realities of many actual ongoing conflicts plus the uncertainties in supply of basic human necessities of food, clothing and shelter.

Energy supply, and the resources which are required to produce energy supply, are central to most aspects of survival. The "carrying capacity" of a given region for human welfare and survival is related to the sum of directly useful resources, plus available energy supply.

With appropriate human ingenuity and with sufficient energy supply — even relatively barren regions can be made to sustain life at better than subsistence levels. More productive regions can be made to sustain more people — at better levels — if secure energy supply is available. If the energy supply in such regions is reduced (either through interruptions of supply or substantial increases in cost) the conditions of life can fall to — or below — subsistence levels. The "carrying capacity" of the regions may decline and some people can become, in effect, surplus to that society. The correlation between energy, resources and "carrying capacity" is easy to overlook when these are abundant. When they are not, the advocacy of actions which reduce the supply of energy (and the related resources) is tantamount to advocating retroactive birth control.

The condition of developed countries like Japan and France — with most of their energy supply imported — is clearly perilous if external sources should be reduced or interrupted. This is also true of many developing countries that have raised themselves above the subsistence level and increased the ability to carry more people using imported energy supply.

For both the developed and less developed worlds, tensions over access to the materials essential for energy supply and production are one of the most pervasive historical forces which have produced many conflicts and wars — and which continue to be a driving force for the principal threat to human welfare and survival which is posed by the risks of wars.

In the developed world — and especially the United States and Canada — convenient, reliable, and relatively cheap energy supply has been taken for granted for most of this century. The cost of energy for transportation (the largest single sector of consumption) and for electricity has been decreasing for most of the last half-century. Electricity has had continually decreasing cost (in real terms) for 50 years prior to 1975. Reliability of supply, low cost, and freedom from significant interruptions has been so secure that until recently, energy in most forms has been regarded as a common good — almost in the same category as air and water — by most people in the United States.

Under these conditions, the "oil shock" of 1973–1974 and shortages of supply of gasoline created near-panic conditions in this country. This led to discussions of forceful intervention and considerable degree of actual deployment of military forces in regions near the mid-East. There were even discussions of potential conditions of use of such forces. Economically this initial shock was absorbed with limited impacts by the U.S. since the real cost of oil in constant dollars was not much greater than it had been ten years earlier.

The second "oil shock" in 1978-79 — when oil prices tripled for the second time has not yet been absorbed. It has contributed directly to a large unfavorable balance of trade for the United States and for many other countries. The resulting massive export of capital is regarded by most economists as one of the principal sources of U.S. and world inflation and recession. For both the developed and less developed world, the increase in their costs of oil have been much greater than the declines in consumption. There has been a corresponding loss of purchasing power for other human needs in both the developed and less developed worlds. The decline in purchasing power has resulted in reduced ability to pay for other human desiderata — including food, housing, education, medical services, transportation, and the like. This in turn has driven a worldwide decline in most basic industries, in work available, and probably contributes to continuing widespread unemployment and recession.

The disruption in the normal financial relationships has led to a potential threat to the stability of the world financial system. Some even speak of the possibility of collapse in some areas of world financial relationships driven by defaults on large blocks of credit by developing countries. This situation adds to threats of wars and to increasing social turbulence, chaos, terrorism and the consequent human misery.

The present decline in oil prices, the oil and "gasoline glut" of 1982–1983, may tend to make some people hope or believe that there is no crisis or threat arising from the questions of energy supply and resources. The future options and trends of energy supply are far from reassuring. The continuing vulnerability of many countries to possible interuptions in oil supply, or further shocks of price increases if portions of world supply become unavailable, is still the most visible source of world tension and threats of war for the remainder of this century. The recent declines in oil prices are encouraging, but the economic drain from oil imports continues to be a massive drag on world economies and especially on those of the developing countries.

What About Alternate Sources of Supply?

In principle, the United States has coal reserves roughly 50 times larger than the oil reserves. Uranium-fueled power plants — more than two times as many as are now projected for this century — can be fuelled for their full lifetimes with low-cost domestic uranium already discovered. In principle, renewable energy sources such as solar thermal, solar electric, biomass, ocean thermal and the like, eventually should be able to supply many times more energy than fossil fuel sources — and supply such energy indefinitely. None of these options appear to be growing at a sufficient rate to reduce the vulnerability to oil-related shocks for the next two decades. One reason why the alternate means are not growing enough to become significant is that each of them requires the commitment in advance of a great deal of human resources and wealth — which is to say capital investment. Such effort and investment are available only at a limited rate in any society even under healthy economic conditions. Under the present conditions of worldwide recession, high rates of capital investment are essentially precluded for most countries. The available resources must give priority to the basics of food, clothing and shelter. Over 15% of the U.S. population now fits the official designation of "poverty level."

High interest rates worldwide force a short time horizon for planning on both an individual level, and at the levels of societies and governments. Because of the large size of the existing energy system for electricity supply, even a hypothetical new source which was competitive in cost, reliable, environmentally acceptable and immune to regulatory delays would take 25 years, and more likely more than 35 years, to reach the point at which it would supply 20% of present electricity consumption.

Some Possible Paths to A Viable Future — The Role of Conservation

Nearly all serious studies of energy supply and demand on both a national and world level lead to the conclusion that substantial reductions in per capata energy consumption are essential for the developed world.[15] If this is a mandated or forced reduction in use, over a short time period, it becomes equivalent to serious deprivation for considerable portions of society, and at the margin, results in increases in human misery. Conducted at a practical pace, conservation has a major constructive role. Intensive measures for conservation, which is to say more efficient utilization of limited energy supplies, is clearly more humane. Some degree of conservation is readily available with little or no investment — by avoidance of wasteful practices. However, many conservation options — no matter how cost-effective for the long term — also tend to be capital-intensive in the short term. For example, the per capita energy consumption for heating, cooling, and transportation might be cut in half by sufficient investment in measures which produce conservation and improved efficiency of use. However, in the near term, additional energy and costs must be expended to attain conservation. For example, double or triple glazing saves heating energy, but requires increased investment in construction and materials, and increased short-term energy inputs to manufacture, transport and install more glass. More efficient automobiles are appearing rapidly on the market, but it will have been more than ten years before the fleet average mileage per gallon of gasoline has increased from 13 to 20 mpg.

Growth of the U.S. Workforce

Population growth in the United States is relatively slow compared with the rest of the world outside of Europe. However, even in the United States at net increase of approximately 30 million adults will enter the work force in two decades ending in the year 2000. It is evident that even in the absence of a recession, the level of amenities which were taken for granted in the last quarter century in the U.S. will be much more difficult to come by and are practically attainable much more slowly, if at all, for most of the newcomers. This situation implies a period of generally declining expectations — and realization. In principle one can view this with equanimity — considering that even the declining expectations are generally more ample than most of recorded history starting 25 years back — and are higher than all but six other countries at present. However, history teaches that in a society with a prolonged period of declining expectation and realization, increasing sectors of the society can become disadvantaged and disaffected. Historically, the seeds of social chaos, crime, political extremism or dictatorship, and war, are found under these conditions. Accordingly, some of the decline in amenities should ideally be offset by improved efficiency of use, plus conservation, plus exploitation of all economically available domestic energy sources. The key observation is that despite a considerable decline in per capita use and intensive conservation measures, there still is a net upward pressure of demand of several forms of energy supply including electricity.

Quality of Energy

In a practical sense, as well as in well defined scientific and economic senses, available energy has a range of quality levels. Heat at low temperatures is the lowest grade and cheapest form of energy, and becomes somewhat more expensive as higher temperatures are required.*

Another form of energy is work, which is the ability to produce mechanical motion such as is done with a steam engine, jet aircraft engine, or gasoline or electric motor. Work energy is the most expen-

---

*(More accurately this should be stated at higher temperature *differences* which takes account of the increase cost of cooling and refrigeration as temperature differences are increased.)

sive form of energy, and also has the highest value. It displaces human muscular effort, and extends the possibilities of transportation, manufacture, earth-moving, and construction far beyond the possibilities of muscular efforts alone. Electricity is unique in its transportability and its "readiness to serve." The ease of control provides high efficiency of use in many application. Electricity is also unique in that the production keeps in step with consumption almost instantaneously. (Small but valuable exceptions are being developed such as the use of pumped storage, batteries, fuel cells, and other means to provide a cushion between instantaneous supply and demand.)

A characteristic of electricity is that — up to some point — the cost of producing electricity by conventional means declines with increasing size of the supply facility, whether it is a coal plant, a nuclear reactor, a hydroelectric dam, or a solar or wind facility. An important hope for the future, although apparently some decades away, is the refinement of technologies and social-economic conditions which will permit smaller scale units of production which are still economic. At present, small units are marginally economic in parts of the country for low grade energy. For example passive solar homes which are specially designed to catch and hold heat from solar radiation are now economic in some locations. Despite the economic advantage, there is still a capital-intensive price to be paid in advance if more than marginal low-value heat is to be captured. Wind energy is making a useful incremental contribution in some locations, as long as it is a small part of the total local capacity.

An occasional lesson on the value of secure supply is generally appreciated. For example, the New York City blackout for half a day in 1981 had a social cost estimated to be in excess of $300 million.

Values of Security of Supply

Because of the high stability and security of supply of energy in general, and of electricity in particular, the value of security of supply is easy to overlook in the United States. For other countries, security of supply is a compelling national goal and necessity. For example, both France and Japan have virtually no indigenous resources for energy production. For either or both of these countries, an interruption in supply from the Mid-East for even a few weeks would result in massive dislocation of society, and if persisting for a few months or more could lead to severe deprivation, possible starvation, and likely calls for military actions. Because of the evident risks of such a path, both countries have chosen to develop a substantial nuclear energy source of supply near-term, and with capability for further rapid expansion. Neither country has significant uranium reserves. Nuclear units commonly carry sufficient fuel to operate for three to five years, and stockpiles of 10 years supply or more are technically and economically practical because of the relatively small volume and low raw material costs compared with other fuels. In a ten year period, some breeder reactors which produce more fuel than they consume, could be brought into operation. Both France and Japan have built small breeder reactors and are building larger ones.*

Nuclear energy supplied 12.5 percent of U.S. electricity in 1982. The units still under construction, if all are completed, will raise nuclear generation to about 20 percent of the U.S. total. In terms of fossil fuels, this is the fuel equivalent of over 4 million barrels of oil per day or over 40 billion dollars per year if replaced by oil. The capital investment represented by this capacity is now in excess of 150 billion dollars (expressed as original cost). It would take several times this amount of investment if it were to be replaced by future construction of coal, hydro, or solar capacity, if these were available. (Replacement by oil or gas for electric generation is now prohibited by federal regulation.)

Replacement by oil or gas capacity is possible in principle, but would bring an additional net negative effect on foreign exchange of over 20 billion dollars per year. Some economists have noted that a dollar spent for imported oil has at least three times as large an impact on the national economy as an equivalent expenditure for something which is supplied domestically and which circulates as added economic activity within the U.S.[16]

Available Versus Non-Available Futures

The story of energy in the last decade is another chapter of the "tragedy of the commons". In affluent societies energy has come to be regarded as an entitlement, a generally available commodity like air and

---

*The U.S. operates two small breeder reactors. Five other countries have built or are building breeder reactors. Largescale units have been in operation in France, Britain, and the Soviet Union for several years.

water. It has been easy to assume that someone else or other parts of the country will bear the responsibility and the burden for the continuity and cost of supply. Hardly anyone feels the responsibility to pay for the cost of an additional coal mine, an additional railroad to transport coal, or an additional generating plant, whether it be coal, nuclear, hydro, or whatever. There is general enthusiasm for alternate sources such as solar and biomass, but little or no enthusiasm for paying the advance capital costs which these entail. Subsidies to accelerate the introduction of solar energy have often soured. In California — state tax subsidies for solar heaters have enabled people who can't afford swimming pools to help pay for solar heaters for those who can afford swimming pools.

The enthusiasm for alternate sources is both technically and economically sound, when viewed as an evolutionary development over the next half century. There is no question that the world cannot support an adequate standard for the world increase of four billion souls expected during the next 50 years — unless the renewables are brought into widespread use. These can supplement — and by the 22nd century — *must* largely supplant, fossil fuels. [15] For the next several decades, and certainly for the immediate needs of the next decade, society has no prudent choice but to exploit all economically available sources. The replacement of a reasonable fraction — perhaps as much as one fourth — of the *growth* of U.S. energy supply is desirable by using a combination of more efficient use, reduced per capita use, and alternate sources. Three quarters of near-term replacement for oil and gas is mostly coal and nuclear. There is no conceivable way of *replacing* a large fraction of the enormous bulk electricity supply now provided by coal, nor the substantial fraction of the bulk supply provided by nuclear capacity, by any alternative source in the next one to two decades. Much of the argument on alternate energy sources and conservation disappears, for reasonably well-informed people, when the near-term and long-term alternatives are distinguished and when the basic logistics of feasible growth rates, and of the resources required for the different options are more fully understood.

The Quintain's Revenge

In medieval times, knights in armor practicing jousting against a dummy supported on a cross-beam mounted on a pivot. A dynamic stroke at the dummy could cause it to swing around in a full circle so swiftly that the knight was knocked from his mount by being hit from behind by the dummy.

The "quintain's revenge effect" must be considered in any social, political, and even ethical-moral decisions. All too often the intended good result brings with it other consequences which cause more damage than the good attained. Lack of foresight of possible unprecedented consequences or neglect of potential and evident consequences is often evident in social-political decision-making.

There is a corollary source of neglect of consequences — the syndrome: "that's not my department." This syndrome manifests itself as a too-narrow range of consideration from over-specialized experts, or from bureaucracies with narrowly defined scoupes. The solution of a narrowly perceived problem can fall heir to the quintain effect. The undesired results cancel the hoped-for benefit. Worse yet, the actual net result obtained is sometimes the oppositie of the one which was promoted and promised.

For the last half century, the narrow view of energy supply took it for granted that ever-growing supply and ever-lower costs were an unmitigated good. Changing circumstances, increased environmental impacts — increased vulnerability of supply and costs were not taken into account — the quintain's revenge on this kind of narrow view arrived in the 1970's.

More recently it has been a popular notion — especially in the most affluent parts of our society that it would be pleasing to "de-industrialize America" and to live carefree in a park-like Utopian world without heavy industry and with a purified environment. This view, while perhaps once noble in essence, has contributed to the political, legislative, and procedural constraints which have led to stasis or decline of many industries. Constraints of many productive activities — by legislation, regulation, political action, and by activist protests have been remarkably effective. The environment has improved (or further deterioration arrested in many respects). The construction or renovation of many industrial facilities has been halted. Nuclear energy has been an especial lightning-rod for this enthusiasm — providing the symbol of highly visible but dimly understood high technology.

Over one third of the nuclear units under construction in 1979 have been cancelled and more may yet fall under the weight of delay and high interest costs. But the quintain's revenge has come full circle. The loss of jobs and the decline or disappearance — perhaps forever — of some domestic industries will increasingly be measured by many and varied increases in human misery. Some of the overenthusiastic demobilization of industry — through not necessarily intended or perceived as such — may exact a much higher social price than envisioned.

When such aftereffects are long-term or unprecedented there is loss of responsibility for untoward consequences of decisions which affect the public welfare. Even when some voices call attention to the possible and likely dimensions of the quintain's revenge, others can press forward with risky policies with the knowledge that they can't and won't be held responsible.

Perhaps an obvious but often overlooked aspect of morality in the energy arena is the need to recognize such responsibility more fully. Responsibility for decision-makers (and moralists) must include great and thorough concern for the unexpected and undesired damaging byproducts of social policies, decisions and actions, even when the primary or near-term objectives, when viewed narrowly and politically, seem virtuous and noble.

The concern for by-product effects should temper the enthusiasm for the hoped-for benefits. In the realities of politics and most other human and organizational relations, enthusiasm is essential for decision and for resolution of choices. But the need for enthusiasm should not blind the enthusiast to the danger signals from unwanted but likely consequences. Concerns over the hypothetical effects of reactor accidents should be tempered by equally thoughtful concerns over chronic or intermittent insufficiency of supplies of energy, and the resulting deprivation and impacts on increased regional and world tensions.

Epilogue

A central ethical/moral question is the extent to which excessive protectionist activities — no matter how well meaning — must bear a responsibility for the possibility of eventual large increases in human suffering. Many productive activities have been delayed or stopped on the grounds of lack of full knowledge of all of the future consequences. There may also be a neglect of the unforseen consequences of the widespread failure or chronic delay in the fulfillment of human needs. There is also the responsibility for actions — or calculated inactions — which has the effect of increasing the vulnerability of existing means to painful dislocations.

List of Figures

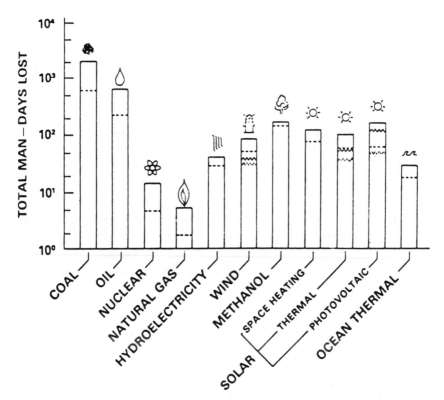

Fig. I-A   Comparative risks of alternate Energy sources (Inhaber, 1982, ref. 4)

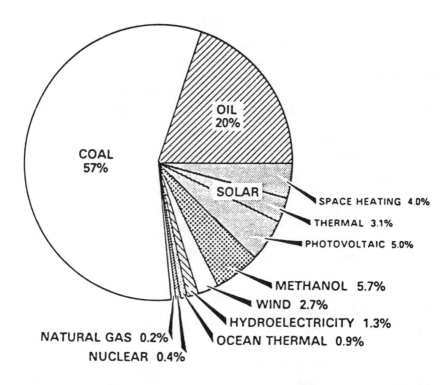

Fig. I-B   Relative proportion of total risk for equal amounts of energy from II conventional and unconventional energy sources, (Inhaber, 1982, ref. 4)

Fig. II-A

Deaths From Disease and Accidents — 1978*
(Total — 1,927,800)

Rank	Type	Number Per 100,000 People	Percent
1	Cardiovascular	443	50.2
2	Heart	334	37.8
3	Cancer	182	20.6
4	Cerebrovascular	81	9.2
5	Other Causes	70	7.9
6	Other Diseases	63	7.1
7	Accidents	48	5.4
8	Pneumonia, Flu	27	3.1
9	Arterial	25	2.8
10	Diabetes	16	1.8
11	Unknown	14	1.6
12	Cirrhosis, Liver	14	1.6
13	Suicide	12.5	1.4
14	Infancy Diseases	10	1.1
15	Bronchial	10	1.1
16	Homicide	9.4	1.1
17	Genetic Anomalies	6	0.7

*Statistical Abstracts of U.S. (1980), p. 78

Fig. II-B

Accidental Deaths (1978)

Cause	Rates/100,000
1. Motor Vehicles	24
2. Falls	6.3
3. Fires	2.8
4. Drowning	2.7
5. Industrial Accidents	2.4
Traumas 1.6	
Electrocution 0.5	
Explosion 0.2	
Burns — 0.1	
(Including Radiation)	
6. Poisoning	2.2
7. Swallowing Objects	1.4
8. Medical Procedures, Complications	1.4
9. Air Transport	0.9
10. Firearms	0.8
11. Water Transport	0.7
12. Other Vehicles	0.6
13. Railway	0.3
14. All Other	2.5

Fig. II-C

Accident Injuries and Deaths — 1979
(In 1,000's)

	Total	Motor Vehicle	Home	Work	Public
Deaths	103.5	51.9	22	13.2	21
Permanent Impairments	360	150	90	80	60
Temporary Disabilities	9600	1850	3200	2200	2500

Fig. II-D

Accidents with Five or More Victims*
(1971–1978)

Rank	Type	Deaths	No. of Accidents	% of Deaths
1	Air Transport	1986	151	
2	Tornadoes	1976	77	
3	Motor Vehicles	1418	212	
4	Fires, Home	1181	199	
5	Fires, Non-Home	1111	99	
6	Misc. Causes	438	36	
7	Water Transport	307	22	
8	Mining	151	7	
9	Rail Transport	85	6	
I	Travel	3796	391	44.6
II	Fires	2292	198	27.0
III	Weather	1976	77	23.2
IV	All Other	438	36	5.1

*Statistical Abstracts of U.S. (1980)

Fig. II-E

Annual Losses from Natural Events (No. 22)

Hazard	Deaths per 10 Million	Injuries per 10 Million	Property Damage [1] [6] $ per Capita
Avalanche	.35	.48	
Coastal Erosion	—	—	
Drought	—	—	
Earthquake	.38	?	
Flood	3.90	?	
Frost	—	—	
Hail	—	—	
Hurricane	2.52	119.52	
Landslide	—	—	
Lightning	5.43	10.95	
Tornado	5.24	90.48	
Tsunami	1.57	?	
Urban Snow	5.19	3.19	
Volcano	NA	NA	NA
Windstorm	4.65	29.42	

NA — Not Applicable

Fig. III-A

Prices of Energy Sources[1]

	1965	1973	1979	1985	1990	1995
World Oil $/Bbl	6.5	7.1	24	33	49	67
Nat. Gas — at						
Wellhead ($/M cu. ft.)	.39	.38	1.3	4.6	6.4	7.2
Delivered	2.5	2.1	3.0	5.4	7.4	8.7
Gasoline $/Gal.	.75	.66	.92	1.4	1.8	2.2
Electricity ¢/KWH	5.5	4.1	4.5	5.9	6.0	6.3

[1]Doe Report to Congress February 1981, Table 19 (All in 1980 Dollars)

Fig. III-B

U.S. Prices for Energy Supply Sources

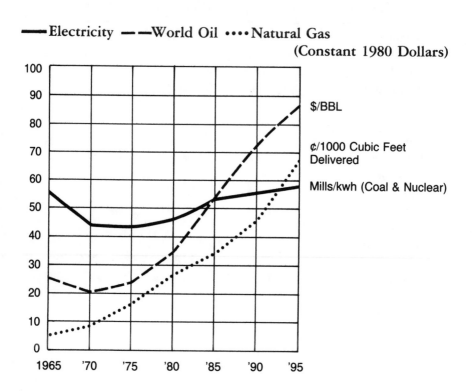

Source: DOE Report to Congress, Feb., 1982

Fig. III-C

Free World Oil Consumption & Production[1]

	1980	1985	1990	1995
Consumption (M Bbls/day)				
US	17	17	16	16
OPEC	2	3	4	6
Other	30	29	30	32
Total	49	49	50	54
Production (m Bbls/day)				
US	11	10	10	11
OPEC	28	26	26	28
Other	10	13	14	15
Total	49	49	50	54

[1]DOE Report to Congress February 1981, Table 30, Midprice Projections

Fig. IV-A

U.S. Projected Electric Power Generation
from Nuclear Power, 1985

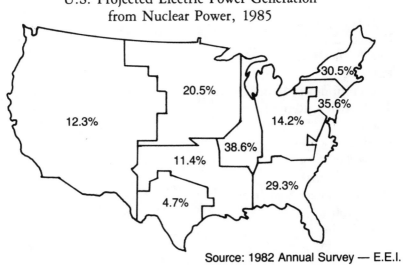

Source: 1982 Annual Survey — E.E.I.

Fig. IV-B

World Nuclear Power Plants in Operation and Under Construction
1983

	Operating Units	Units Under Construction (>0%)
Argentina	1	2
Austria		1
Belgium	5	2
Brazil		3
Bulgaria	3	1
Canada	11	10
Czechoslovakia	3	8
Finland	4	
France	32	25
Germany		
(Democratic Republic)	5	2
(Federal Republic)	12	8
Hungary		4
India	4	4
Italy	4	4
Japan	25	9
Korea, Republic of	1	8
Mexico		2
The Netherlands	2	
Pakistan	1	
The Philippines, Republic of		1
South Africa, Republic of		2
Spain	4	10
Sweden	10	2
Switzerland	4	1
Taiwan (China)	4	2
Union of Soviet Socialist Republics	37	13*
United Kingdom	33	10

Fig. IV-B (Continued)

World Nuclear Power Plants in Operation
and Under Construction
1983

	Operating Units	Units Under Construction (>0%)
United States	83**	50***
Yugoslavia	1	
Total	289	184

*To be completed by 1988
**Includes licensed units
***Terminated, deferred, and under-review units not included

Data Source: Atomic Industrial Forum, *International Survey*, 1981
Atomic Industrial Forum, *Nuclear Power Plants in the United States*, January 1, 1983
Nuclear News, February 1982
Nuclear Power '83 (Southern Science)
Nucleonics Week, December 23, 1982

Fig. IV-C

Projected Nuclear Generating Capacity
Outside the United States*
1985

	Percent of Capacity
Argentina	8.5
Austria	N/A
Belgium	38.0
Brazil	1.0
Bulgaria	26.0
Canada	10.5
China, People's Republic of	0
Cuba	0
Czechoslovakia	12.5–18.5
Denmark	0
Egypt, Arab Republic of	0

Fig. IV-C (Continued)

Projected Nuclear Generating Capacity
Outside the United States*
1985

	Percent of Capacity
Finland	20.0
France	43.0
Germany, Democratic Republic of	17.4
Germany, Federal Republic of	18.7–20.7
Greece	0
Hungary	15.9–23.1
India	2.6
Israel	0
Italy	3.1
Japan	15.6–16.8
Korea, Republic of (South)	20.0
Libya	0
Mexico	5.0
The Netherlands	3.0
Pakistan	2.2
The Philippines, Republic of	10.5
Poland	3.2
Portugal	0
Romania	0
South Africa, Republic of	7.0
Spain	20.3
Sweden	26.3
Switzerland	21.9
Taiwan (China)	31.0
Thailand	0
Turkey	0
Union of Soviet Socialist Republics	10.0
United Kingdom	18.9
Yugoslavia	4.3

*Includes units in operation and those with construction over 75% done.

Source: AIF International Survey, 1982 Energy Information

Fig. IV-D

**World Distribution of Nuclear Power Plants
Operating and Under Construction (1983)**

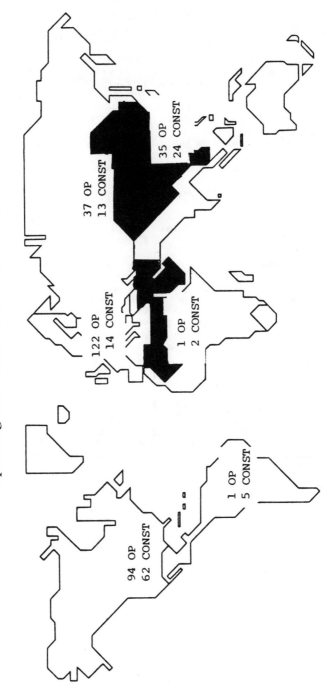

Reference: See Fig. IV-B

91

References

1. Ahearne, J. Nuclear Power: A Greek Tragedy? *Progress in Nuclear Energy* 7, No. 2 (1981) 77.
2. Inhaber, H. *Science*, Vol. 203, 23 February (1979), 718.
3. Inhaber, H. I.A.E.A. Bulletin, Vol. 23, #1 (Feb. 1979), 16.
4. Inhaber, H. "Energy Risk Assessment," Gordon & Breach, N.Y. (1982).
5. "Health Implications of Nuclear Power Production," World Health Organization, Proceedings of Conference, Brussels. December 1–5, 1975.
6. "The Hazards of Conventional Sources of Energy," by the Health and Safety Commission, HMSO, Great Britain (1978).
7. Reactor Savety Study, WASH-1400, N. Rassmussen, Project Director, MIT, (1975).
8. K. A. Solomon *et al*, "Airplane Crash Risk to Ground Population," UCLA-Eng. 7424, (March 1974).
9. J. G. Kemeny, (Chairman) Report of the President's Commission on the Accident at TMI, Pergamon Press, NY (1979).
10. The SL-1 Accident, *Nucleonics*, V. *19*, 2 Feb. (1961) p. 17–23.
11. The Windscale Accident, *Nucleonics*, V.*15*, 11 Nov. (1957) 130.
12. Proceedings of Colloquium on Oklo Phenomenon, I.A.E.A., Vienna, Leiberville, Gabon, 23–27 June (1975).
13. G. A. Vendryes, "Discovery of a Prehistoric Nuclear Reactor In Republique Gabonaise" November 1972.
14. H. Crowley, J. D. Griffith, *Nuc. Eng. International* (UK) June (1982), 25.
15. Lewis J. Perl, "The Economics of Nuclear Power," National Economic Research Associates, New York, June 3, 1982 and Coal-Nuclear Costs for 1981, Department of Energy Report DOE/EIA-0173 (81) Volume 3.
16. Häfele, W., "Energy in a Finite World," — "A global Systems Analysis," Ballinger (Harper & Row), Cambridge, Mass. (1981), (Sponsored by the International Institute of Systems Analysis, Laxenburg, Austria; with Academy of Sciences or equivalent from 17 countries participating.)
17. R. Stobaugh and D. Yergin, *Foreign Affairs*, 58, 3 (1980), 563. *Harvard Business Review*, Jan.–Feb. (1980), 57.
18. World Almanac and Book of Facts, 1981.
19. Statistical Abstract of the United States, 1980.
20. Ames, B. N., Dietary Carcinogens and Anticarcinogens, *Science, 221,* 4617 (1983).
21. Hurwitz, H., Residential Radiological Standards, *Science, 219,* 1377 (1983).
22. White, G. F. and Haas, J. E., Assessment of Research on Natural Hazards, M.I.T. Press, Cambridge (1973) p. 68.

Chapter 3

Nuclear Energy for North America: Disadvantages*

John F. Ahearne, Ph.D.

Editorial Preface

The United States and Canada have large nuclear power programs. Mexico has indicated strong interest in developing nuclear power. However, public opposition has strengthened following the Three-Mile Island Accident. To consider objectively the issues concerning nuclear power is beyond the ability of most people involved in these debates. This paper sketches the following major arguments against the use of nuclear power:

(1) The general public has grown skeptical of commercial power. Reactors are not understood and radiation is a mystery.

(2) The multi-billion dollar cost of a new nuclear plant strains the financial system of any country.

---

*"Reprinted by permission of the U.S. Nuclear Regulatory Commission."

(3) A nuclear plant can blight the local landscape with nonradioactive emissions.

(4) Major questions have been raised about the health hazards from normal operations and from accidents.

(5) Many opponents link the international growth in nuclear weapons to nuclear power.

(6) No site has been chosen to permanently store nuclear waste.

Nuclear power is a dangerous technology. The problems associated with its use demand high competence form operators and managers — competence that may neither be present nor even seem to be necessary. North America will need more energy sources. That is clear. Nuclear power probably will not fill a significant part of that need. Whether it should is a difficult question to address objectively.

My topic for this morning is Nuclear Energy for North America: Disadvantages. I have been a member of the Nuclear Regulatory Commission (NRC) for the last four and one-half years. The Commission is neither an advocate nor a devel's advocate. I am not used to speaking on advantages or disadvantages of this subject but rather try to reach objective judgments on what conditions are necessary for the safe use of nuclear power in the United States. In order to balance the program, I will speak on disadvantages. However, I will not offer you debaters points that a dedicated opponent of nuclear power would be likely to make. Rather, I will attempt to outline for you what I believe to be the real disadvantages of nuclear power.

Nuclear power is an appropriate subject for this gathering in that it has often been described as a religion, and the fierce arguments between its supporters and its foes are tinged with religious fervor. Many of the subjects I will touch on and many of the issues and controversies in this field are quite technical, revolving around detailed mathematical analyses, and in some cases substantial mechanical or electrical engineering work. Nevertheless, the basic issues are policy questions and questions of practicality, and these we all can address. In addition, even in the addressing of a very technical question there will be a strain of ethical consideration, if only in the way the process of analysis is done.

I. Current Status for North America

To begin, I believe we all should have an understanding of the current and future status of nuclear power in North America. Figure 1 gives approximate numbers, appropriate at the end of 1982, for operating reactors, reactors under construction, and planned reactors for the United States, for Canada and for Mexico. The figure gives generation capacity in megawatts and (in parentheses) the number of plants. A megawatt is a million watts, or a thousand kilowatts. For example, the figure shows that in the United States there currently are 77 nuclear power plants that can generate 60,300 megawatts of electricity. To give you a feeling for what this represents: most U.S. nuclear power plants generate about 1,000 megawatts, enough electricity to supply a U.S. city of 500,000 people.

The table does not include research reactors or U. S. Government reactors used in the nuclear weapons program. As you can see, most of the reactors in North America are in the United States. Canada has a different type of reactor from the United States reactors. The United States reactors are so-called light-water reactors. Canada uses a heavy-water reactor. The Mexican reactors under construction are light-water reactors.

The U.S. utility industry first generated electricity using nuclear power in 1960. In 1977 nuclear power passed hydropower as a source of electricity in the United States, in 1980 it passed petroleum, and nuclear now ranks third behind coal and natural gas. In 1981 nuclear power generated 12 percent of the electricity in the United States and 11 percent in Canada. The leading nuclear country, not in numbers of plants but in the percentage of their electricity generated by nuclear power, is France, where 38 percent of the electricity in 1981 was generated by nuclear power. North America has 40 percent of all the commercial nuclear power in the world. The U.S. accounts for roughly one-third of world nuclear power.

For many years the U.S. Federal Government estimated nuclear power would grow to be 20 percent of electrical capacity by the end of the century. The latest Energy Department forecast is about 16 percent. However, as you can see by the figure, only two additional reactors are planned in the United States and one in Canada. For Mexico I show a question mark. Until the economic problems of the past year, the Mexican official plan had at least 20,000 megawatts of nuclear electrical power by the end of this century. The plan was then scaled down to take smaller steps, with recent discussions focused on 2,000 megawatts. At present there are no official plans for more nuclear plants in Mexico.

In the United States, as of November of last year, 22 plants had been cancelled after they had received a construction permit and 48 were cancelled while the NRC or the Atomic Energy Commission (AEC) were reviewing requests for construction permits. Even nuclear industry representatives, who have always been the most optimistic, in their latest estimates have told the NRC they have no knowledge of any near-term construction plans. A recent industry study concluded there will be no new nuclear plants ordered prior to the mid-1980's. That leaves open whether there will be any new plants after the mid 1980's.

Consequently, the discussion of nuclear power in North America is primarily a discussion of nuclear power in Canada and the United States, essentially of that in the United States, and it is a discussion of existing, not future, power plants.

II. Disadvantages of Nuclear Power

A. Public Fear

Nuclear power is a mystery to most people. It is a mystery which they fear. Few people have ever seen a nuclear plant other than in pictures. Editorial cartoons show the large cooling towers, leading some people to believe these towers are the reactors. The wasp-waisted tower has become an ominous symbol. Very few understand what the core of a nuclear reactor is or how nuclear fission works. Most people are comfortable with the idea of using oil or gas or coal to heat water to generate electricity, which they believe is basically what a nonnuclear power plant does. Radiation is known to be the hazard of a nuclear power plant, but very few people know what radiation is. Explaining radiation as alpha, gamma, or beta rays leads to greater puzzlement and growing apprehension. It is known that radiation is invisible, tasteless, odorless, and obviously can cause great damage to the body. This air of hazardous mystery is a major problem for nuclear power.

The public has some concern about nuclear plants being objects of terrorist attack or war. This is not an unfounded concern. There is growing debate about the effects of nuclear weapons and the catastrophic damage that would occur were a nuclear war to break out. The weapons that are usually discussed are 100 kilotons, 500 kilotons, and larger. In a nuclear reactor fission products are produced as the nuclear core generates heat. A typical 1,000 megawatt reactor that has been operating for one year at full power will generate in its fuel in a day the same amount of fission products as would be produced by the explosion of a 50 kiloton nuclear weapon. The reactor continues to accumulate fission products while operating. It is this large collection of fission products whose distribution around the countryside could cause significant health hazards. There have been concerns that nuclear reactors therefore would be major targets in war. However, in a large scale nuclear attack hundreds or thousands of weapons would be used. The resulting destruction would be so great there would be little need to target nuclear power plants, whose destruction would lead to only marginal increases in radiation levels. Targeting power plants would be primarily to eliminate the electrical system, which would be eliminated anyway in a large scale nuclear attack because transmission lines and distribution points would be destroyed.

William Lowrance has described the hazards associated with nuclear power:

> "Nuclear power plants are thought to be essential by those who believe that the alternative ways of generating power will not meet energy demands. For the general public, the risks are inescapable once these expensive plants are in operation. What the risks really are is quite controversial. The risks will be both to those who work in the plants and to the general public. Effects will be both immediate, in the event of a catastrophic accident, and delayed, with any radiation exposures. There is a possibility, even if slight, of misuse such as sabotage. Both the radiation hazards and the unlikely-but-horrible explosion hazards carry overtones of dread."[1]

The Three Mile Island (TMI) accident substantially changed the attitudes of the American public, and of many people around the world. The fear that is represented in those who oppose nuclear power is hard to describe. Let me attempt to do so by reading two extracts for you. The first is from a contention, an issue that was raised before the NRC Licensing Board that was considering whether or not the undamaged reactor at Three Mile Island, TMI-1, should be allowed to operate. This is a contention by one of the groups opposing the restart of the plant:

> "Many residents of Central Pennsylvania were thoroughly and completely terrorized by the March 28, 1979, accident at TMI-2. This terror has turned the lives of many otherwise happy people into a living nightmare, because they know the

accident at TMI-2 is not over, and that unannounced releases of radioactive materials continue. . . . Metropolitan Edison has created a climate where people know that they are no longer safe in their own homes, they are afraid to grow food in their own gardens, and many will soon have reason to distrust the very water they drink. . . . One certain result of the reopening of TMI-1 will be a substanial increase in the tension. . . . The outward manifestation of this tension may well appear as increased suicide rates, divorce rates, incidences of child beating, a general lowering of the general mental health of the populace, quite probably, acts of civil disobedience . . . and possible acts of violence. . . ."[2]

A less articulate but more emotional message is from one of the people who appeared in front of the Commission in a November meeting that we held in Harrisburg, Pennsylvania. At this meeting members of the local public presented their views on whether or not the undamaged plant should be allowed to restart. The woman whom I now quote lives in a small town immediately adjacent to the reactor and works in a day-care center:

"I am scared to death to be here, but what scares me more is, I'm the one who has to take my children out of town if we have to evacuate. I have 14 children I'm responsible for. I see them every day. I know when they are happy and when they are sad, and I know when they are scared.

"My children told me today when I came up here, to tell them one thing: That Daddy won't be able to come home. Why won't their daddy come home? Because he'll be dead from TMI. He is left behind. The last time when we evacuated he stayed behind to help. His job was to drive a bus out of town if anybody in Middletown didn't evacuate with us.

"My kids were scared. I was scared. I'm still scared.

"I don't understand. I teach my children right and wrong, and no means no, no matter how many times you say it. But we keep saying it and saying it. Nobody hears us. I don't understand. . . .

"I don't know what else to say to you people. What do we have to do? Do we have to get down on our hands and knees and beg you to close that place down? Because if that's what need be, I'll help. I'll get on my knees, I'll beg, I'll crawl. I want it closed. . . .

"You worry about the big people and taking care of all the big brains and everybody that has money, but you don't care about the little kids that are left behind.

"I would just like to ask you, please, for God's sake, close it, for the children if not for anybody else."[3]

Fears like this have led to intense bitter opposition to nuclear power.

Public opposition to energy projects is not limited to nuclear power. Citizens have been opposed to liquid natural gas terminals, to pipe lines, to transmission lines, to many projects. Much opposition to energy projects has come from local citizens who are concerned about the impacts of technology, perhaps removal of or damage to local scenery, perhaps the influx of large numbers of temporary workers. Nuclear power projects are able to draw opponents hundreds or even thousands of miles because they are seen as much more than merely local issues. A political science professor has argued that "hostility to nuclear power is strong and deep seated . . . America has many people in its midst . . . who now oppose the basic principles of the technological society. . . . [These people see themselves] as standing with nature, against the insensitive engineer. . . . Nuclear power is seen as an ultimate transmutation of matter. . . . It is man's manipulation of nature, expressive of an arrogance unknown in earlier technology. . . ."[4]

Public opposition to nuclear power has grown throughout the world. In the United States the majority of the public still may favor nuclear power plants, but even that is now questionable. The Three Mile Island accident significantly changed public opinion. Figure 2 shows responses to the question "in general do you favor or oppose the building of more nuclear power plants in the United States?" The numbers are approximate but they show that the opposition jumped and leveled off at a higher percentage following Three Mile Island. I believe this new plateau, which brings the opponents of nuclear power to over 40 percent, may be the fatal flaw for nuclear power in the United States.

Margaret Maxey, who was then a Professor of Bioethics at the University of Detroit, in a talk on radiation effects to the National

Academy of Sciences spoke about "the frustrating dilemma of a policy maker who wishes to set safety standards on the basis of informed consent. . . ." She came to the conclusion "that at the heart of the matter lies a misconception about safety, especially as it relates to risk estimates and risk acceptability."[5] The difficulties that nuclear power has with respect to these misconceptions were clearly illustrated in a series of studies down in Oregon. The authors asked various groups to judge the risk of dying across all U.S. society as a whole as a consequence of 30 activities, one being nuclear power. The questions were asked of members of the Eugene, Oregon, League of Women Voters, of students who responded to advertisements in the University of Oregon student newspaper calling for participants in psychological studies of judgment, and of a group of experts in risk assessment. The next series of figures will show their judgments of the seven most risky activities. The groups were asked to assign numerical risk values by giving a rating of 10 to the least risky and then rank the others relative to that least risky activity. The first slide shows the League of Women Voters estimated nuclear power to be 25 times more hazardous than the least risky activity, which they voted to be vaccinations. The next overlay shows that college students also consider nuclear power as the most risky, but almost twice as risky as did the League members, and approximately two and one-quarter times as risky as the next activity, which they estimated to be handguns. The third overlay shows that experts concluded smoking is the most risky activity, followed closely by motor vehicles, dropping significantly to alcoholic beverages and handguns and then surgery. The experts put nuclear power far down on their list. The same authors also asked: "How many people are likely to die in the U. S. next year, if next year is an average year, as a consequence of these activities and technologies?" All sources of death were to be included. For example, fatalities from nonnuclear electricity should consider the mining of coal and other energy production activities as well as accidental electrocution of workers. As a guideline, the respondents were told the total number of deaths in the U. S. averages about 2 million per year. Figure 4 lists the major categories of the 30 that were either listed in Figure 3 or showed up in answer to this question. The first column shows League of Women Voters' estimates of deaths. The next overlay shows their previous rankings. Their rankings are relatively the same as they were for risk for motor vehicles, motocycles, handguns, and smoking. The significant differences occur for alcoholic beverages, which moves up to number 2, for surgery, which comes from 10 to 5, and for nuclear power, which drops from first to last place. The next overlay shows the deaths estimated by college students. Motor vehicles are now first, alcoholic beverages, second, and smoking, third. The rankings of the first four are now equivalent for college students and League members. The final overlay shows the college students' risk ranking. Nuclear power, which had been first, is now last.

In this series of studies the participants were also asked to provide a multiplying factor to indicate how many times more deaths than the average would occur if next year were particularly disastrous for the activity being considered. This estimate would bring in concerns about catastrophies. Whereas the average multiplier for the other 29 activities never exceeded 3, that for nuclear power was greater than 85. More than 40 percent of the people had multipliers for nuclear power of greater than 1,000. Using the multiplier times each respondent's estimate of expected fatalities, almost 40 percent of the respondents estimated greater than 10,000 fatalities for nuclear power and more than 25 percent had estimates exceeding 100,000. The authors also had a group of 28 students write scenarios describing their image of the maximum credible disaster that might be produced during their lifetime. The authors of the study commented that "neither the disaster scenarios for nuclear power nor the fatality estimates associated with them would be considered reasonable by most technical experts."[7] One-third of the scenarios had an explosion within the reactor, which is consistent with several public opinion surveys which have found that 40 percent or more of the people questioned believe that nuclear power plants can explode like an atomic bomb. However, a nuclear reactor cannot explode like an atomic bomb and no honest technical person will tell you that it can.

B. Financial

On August 25th of last year, the Tennessee Valley Authority Board of Directors cancelled four nuclear power plants. These were not the first cancellations in the U. S. However, one of the plants was almost 30 percent complete. The four together when cancelled meant the utility was writing off an investment of $1.85 billion. Other recently cancelled plants also represented sizable investments: the Bailly plant in Indiana was a $127 million investment; the Pilgrim plant in Massachusetts, $291 million; the Hope Creek plant in Delaware, $172 million; the Harris plant in North Carolina, $187 million; and perhaps the most talked about plants, those in the State of Washington, whose current estimated cost of cancellation is two billion dollars. There are many others, including North Anna 3 in my own State of Virginia, which represented a $550 million investment. The cancellations are many and the costs are large.

The two principle arguments for nuclear power in North America have been that the United States and Canada have large deposits of uranium that can be used for us and for other countries, and the low cost of nuclear power. In many other countries the argument for nuclear power has been based on the advantage seen in a method of generating electricity that requires import of a small amount of material, uranium, from Australia, Canada, and the United States, countries believed less likely to apply economic blackmail than are the oil exporting countries. The oil embargoes of the 1970's and the continued instability of Middle East oil producing regions have increased the interest in both developing and developed countries in the potential of nuclear power. In the 1950's nuclear power had been described as a very low cost means of producing electricity. An AEC Commissioner said electricity from nuclear power would be too cheap to meter. As late as 1976, an estimate of new electrical generating capacity for the Northeast showed that a coal plant would cost 28.1 mill sper kilowatt hour and a nuclear plant, 25.7 mills per kilowatt hour.[8]

Investment cost is a strong argument against nuclear power plants. Figure 5 shows the capital costs of nuclear power plants currently under construction.[9] Thus a 1,000 megawatt plant in New England will cost $1,470,000,000. The Washington Public Power System plants drive the Northwestern United States costs. Except for the Southern United States, the capital investment for nuclear power is substantially greater than for coal plants, even with scrubbers. Fuel and operating savings had been expected to overcome this large capital difference. However, inflation has driven up wages and other costs associated with building a large facility and has made it more difficult to raise the money that is required to make the capital investment to gain that advantage. In addition, public utility commissions use a depreciation system which in general keeps the nuclear power plant out of the rate base of the utility until the plant is ready to operate. The ratepayer is then hit with a very large increase. Over the lifetime of the nuclear power plant there may be significant cost savings over an equivalent coal plant or replacement oil plant. But these cost savings are typically seven or eight years out from the beginning of operation and few ratepayers have that long range perspective or can afford the economic perspective to realize they are going to save money over twenty years even though they are going to have to pay a lot more this year.

A recent Department of Energy study indicates that nuclear power plants may have lost their cost advantage over coal even on a long term basis.[10] This is shown in Figure 6 which lists lifetime costs for new plants in each Federal Region. (Region 1 is in the Northeast and Region 10 is in the Northwest). Nuclear is favored in only four regions, whereas coal is favored in five. These estimates were done by the Department of Energy, which one can imagine would try to be objective but is not going to be as critical of nuclear power as some opponents would be.

One of the more expensive regions for oil or coal in the United States is New England, because coal must be brought in over long, old rail lines and there are no New England oil refineries. However two recent power plants under construction in New England hint that even this apparent advantage has been lost. The Millstone plant in Connecticut would appear to have cost advantages. It is a large plant, the third plant at an existing site, and is being constructed by a company that has built many other power plants. Nevertheless, the utility has recently estimated the breakeven point with respect to oil will not be reached until somewhere between 1989 and 1994, depending upon the estimated cost increases in the price of oil. *The New York Times* commented "if oil prices triple, Millstone III might look cheap."[11] The New Hampshire Public Utilities Commission now estimates the Seabrook plant with cost between $6 billion and $7 billion. In objecting to this cost, the utility said it estimates the plant will only cost $5 billion.

Why are nuclear power plants so expensive? The principle reasons reflect a single fact — it takes a long time to build a nuclear power plant. Inflation eats at cost estimates. Something that was estimated to cost a certain amount of money will end up costing much more if the dollars have to be spent in years when inflation is much higher than originally expected. A large part of the cost growth in nuclear power plants is due to inflation driving up construction costs. In addition, the utility has to borrow large amounts of money to build a nuclear plant. When prime rates are high, interest charges for a nuclear plant exceed $100 million per year. Finally, completion schedules have been extended for many plants. When schedules are extended, additional interest is added on to the total cost. One reason for the extension is that the NRC has required changes to be made to plants to meet our requirements, many of the changes resulting from reviews of the Three Mile Island accident. Another reason is that utilities overestimated future demand for electricity. While plants were under construction, the owning utilities have realized the plants would not be needed when they would be finished. Therefore some utilities have slowed down construction to better fit completion dates when the plants will be needed.

C. Local Impact

Although most of the debate around nuclear power centers on effects due to radiation, there are arguments about other local impacts. The method of cooling a nuclear plant has been argued in many hearings. Once-through cooling, in which the cooling water is dumped back into either a river or ocean, is cheaper than building a large cooling tower and also avoids the eyestore of the enormous cooling tower. (A typical cooling tower is 460 feet tall and 400 feet in diameter at the base.) But there are problems with dumping this hot water. For example, in 1973 the Atomic Energy Commission licensed one of the Indian Point reactors to operate. A major issue in that hearing was what effect the hot water discharged by the plant would have on the striped bass population in the Hudson River. The Licensing Board concluded that between 20 and 80 percent of the fish in the entire middle Atlantic fishery region came from the Hudson River. The NRC staff estimated that operation of the Indian Point plant with a once-through system could cut this population of striped bass by as much as a third. The staff suggested that 15 million fingerlings, that is, baby fish, would have to be supplied per year. At that time 3.3 million fingerlings were produced in all the fish hatcheries in the southern United States. Thus, to avoid disastrous effects upon a very large portion of commercial fishing in the eastern United States would require the use of six times the output of these hatcheries. The cooling system question was not resolved until last year.

In the case of Seabrook plant in New Hampshire, the concern about the hot water impacting the clam beds offshore led to the requirement that a three mile tunnel be constructed under water so the hot water would exit far away from the beds.

The cooling towers themselves, however, have additional problems. Since they work on the basis of evaporation, a spray mist goes over the local regions. Particulate matter, mainly salt, condenses out and this salt spray can be an environmental hazard. Recently a group of farmers filed a petition regarding the Palo Verde plants under construction outside Phoenix, Arizona. The farmers argued that salt drift from the cooling towers and from plant ponds will cause major environmental damage in the surrounding crop land and "potentially devastating economic injury to the members." Experts hired by the farmers have concluded . . . "that salt deposition from [the nuclear power plants] could measurably reduce the productivity of farms in the [region] . . ." and . . . "even conservative estimates of losses . . . could conceivably drive some area farmers out of business."[12]

D. Health Risks

The nuclear power debate is a debate about health risks. Underlying arguments about probabilities, proliferation, and deceit are concerns about the health hazards of radiation. Before discussing some of the specific features of radiation hazards from nuclear power plants, for this nontechnical audience it is probably necessary to briefly describe what radiation is and some of the effects about which I will be talking. You have been exposed to radiation all your life; you are being exposed right now. I have attached an appendix to this paper to briefly describe radiation, some of its effects, and how they are measured. Here let me briefly mention radiation exposure comes from gamma rays, alpha particles, and neutrons. Gamma rays are high energy photons, as are x-rays. Radio waves and sunlight are made up of low energy photons. An alpha particle is essentially the nucleus of a helium atom. A neutron is a heavy building block of atomic nuclei. Neutrons are given up in the decay and fissioning of uranium. They trigger and propagate the chain reaction in a nuclear reactor. Alpha particles and gamma rays are also given off in the decay of fission products.

In the nuclear reaction uranium splits to produce energy and the energy is used to heat water, which is then used to run turbines to generate electricity. After the splitting of the uranium atom, what is left over includes unstable elements which then decay, giving off radiation. These radioactive leftovers, called fission products, produce the health hazard from nuclear power accidents. All of these types of radiation are called ionizing radiation, which means that when they pass through material they knock off electrons and leave ions, which are electrically charged atoms or molecules. This forming of charged particles in material is a predominant source of biological damage from radiation. Gamma rays transfer small amounts of energy per unit length of passage through material, whereas alpha particules and neutrons stop in a short distance and give up large amounts of radiation per unit length. The result of this difference is that alpha particles are primarily hazardous if their sources are absorbed inside the body, either by breathing in or digesting food or drink, whereas gamma rays from external sources can be quite hazardous.

The main unit of measurement for radiation exposure is the rem. It is difficult to describe what a rem is without talking about such things as roentgens and quality factors. The appendix attempts to do that. Let me here merely say the rem attempts to measure the effect of a unit of radiation interacting in a person. The rem unit includes the biological effects of radiation. One other commonly used term which you may have heard is the curie. I won't be talking about curies because a curie is not a measure of damage, but a measure of disintegration, of how rapidly is a radioactive atom decaying. The number of curies of a material tells how many atoms decay per second. It does not tell how hazardous the decay is, unless you also know what kind of material is decaying. Some materials have decay products which are relatively harmless, because they have little penetrating ability or low energy, whereas others are extremely hazardous. Knowing both the curie value and the material, a technical person can determine the hazard.

As described by the National Academy of Sciences, the possible harmful effects from radiation that are of concern are the following:

- "early deaths and injuries (occupational and public);
- "delayed deaths and illnesses (occupational and public) in the present generation or its immediate descendents;
- "deaths and illnesses produced in more distant future generations;
- "damage to property or means of production;
- "damage to [the] environment (e.g., ecosystems, climate);
- "damage to social or political institutions."[13]

The National Academy states that "several kinds of immediate causes might be responsible for such effects:

- routine releases of radioactivity, or exposure of workers, associated with normal operation of the various facilities making up the nuclear fuel cycle;

- occasional accidental releases of radioactivity from such facilities;
- gradual, though perhaps unanticipated, escape of radioactivity to the environment over long periods of time (e.g., from waste disposal sites);
- intentional employment of materials or facilities of a nuclear power program for dispersal of radioactivity or construction of nuclear weapons."[13]

How much radiation is harmful? Much debate has focused on whether there is a threshold, i.e., is there some dosage or dose rate below which there is no harmful effect. I do not believe it is possible to give a *precise* answer based on any scientific data. The dose rates that are involved are so low that the effects end up being impossible to determine in a statistical sample. Consquently let me instead talk about the recommended limits. The International Commission on Radiological Protection (ICRP) has published recommended annual limits. These limits for workers are 50 rems to particular tissues and 5 rems for uniform irradiation of the whole body. For the public, the limits are 5 rems to any one organ or 500 millirems, that is one-half of a rem for whole body irradiation. (One millirem is 0.001 rem.) For pregnant women, the ICRP recommends a reduction to 60 percent of the worker exposure.

How much is lethal? The National Academy of Sciences estimates that "[if] all parts of the body are equally exposed, a dose equivalent of 300 to 350 rem over a short time will result in 50 percent [of the people dying] in the absence of medical treatment; with [medical treatment], 50 percent mortality might be reached at 500 rem. At such doses death usually occurs in weeks; very much larger doses are required to cause death within hours."[14] For low doses the estimates usually accepted are from 3,000 to 10,000 person-rems for cancer death, if a body is uniformly irradiated and if one averages over all ages and other vital factors in the population. There is some continuing debate on this number although much of it is only on questions of factors of two. The Government Accounting Office concluded "[t]here is as yet no way to determine precisely the cancer risks of low-level ionizing radiation exposure, and it is unlikely that this question will be resolved soon."[15]

The dose in person-rem is found by multiplying the total number of people receiving a dose times the dose received. Using person-rem one can calculate deaths due to very low doses if those doses are given to large numbers of people. For example, a dose of 100 millirem is far short of the mortality level. However, if one million people were to receive this 100 millirem dose, the total dose would be one hundred thousand person-rem (1,000,000 × 0.1), which would then be equivalent to 20 deaths (100,000 divided by 5,000 person-rem per cancer death). To put these numbers in perspective, Figure 7 shows recent National Research Council estimates of the annual doses to the general public.

Figure 7[16] shows that the typical person who gets medical x-rays will receive around 200 millirems of radiation a year. The natural background from cosmic rays is very sensitive to altitude. For example, 28 millirems is typical for sea level, but at an altitude of 3 kilometers, for example on some of the plateaus of Mexico, a person would get about 100 millirems per year.

Radioactive emissions during normal operation of a nuclear power plant are restricted so that the maximum exposed individual, who is taken to be someone standing at the plant boundary, will get no more than 25 millirems of radiation per year. Concerns about the normal operation of power plants do not focus on radiation acting directly on people but rather on radioactivity entering the food chain. The National Academy has pointed out that the most important food chain pathways for ingestion of radioactivity by humans are:

- "Deposition from the air onto vegetation, which is then eaten by cows whose milk is drunk by humans. . . .
- "Deposition directly on food products, particularly leafy ones. . . .
- "Consumption of seafood and freshwater fish . . . In many situations, 90 Sr [strontium 90] and 134, 137 Cs [cesium] turn out to be the most important nuclides; Cs is biologically concentrated in fish by factors of tens to hundreds. . . ."[17]

This radiation is produced not only by operating plants but also in other parts of the fuel cycle: mining uranium ore; milling the ore to extract uranium; converting uranium into a gas so the uranium can be enriched, or concentrated; enriching the uranium; making fuel; reprocessing the used fuel, if there are any such plants; and finally transporting the fuel or waste to storage and disposal sites. The National Academy has estimated that these other parts of the fuel cycle contribute less than 25 percent of the radiation exposure for workers but dominate that for the general population. The primary general population radiation dose comes from the mining operation, with reprocessing next, if that is done. The lifetime dose commitment, with reprocessing, is approximately 1,000 person-rem per year per thousand megawatts of nuclear power.

This relatively benign conclusion on normal operation is not universally accepted. For example, in 1979 the Department of Environmental Protection of the University of Heidelberg used an ecological model to assess the operation of a planned nuclear power plant in Wyhl, Germany. The authors concluded radiation doses from the plant would greatly exceed those allowed by Geman law. For example, whereas German law would allow a maximum value of 30 millirems per year whole body dose, the authors calculated the plant would lead to a dose of 940 millirems per year. Whereas the law would have restricted the radiation dose to the kidney for adults using Rhine River water to 90 millirem per year, the authors calculated the plant would lead to a dose of 1,338 millirems per year.[18]

The NRC reviewed the Wyhl study in detail because of its implications for any operating nuclear power plant, including those in the United States. The NRC staff selected 18 operating nuclear power plants at random and compared the measured values of a large number of isotopes on which the Wyhl report was based with those calculated in the Wyhl report. The typical differences were several orders of magnitude. The NRC concluded the Whyl report was based upon erroneous parameters, such as the intake of cesium 137 by grass, cabbage, turnips and other leafy vegetables. I believe the NRC report discredits the Heidelberg effort. Nevertheless, this study represents one group of people who do not believe that normal operation is safe, although calculations as well as measurements indicate it is.

Another example of individuals who do not believe that normal operation is safe was a group in Maine. They charged that since the Maine Yankee nuclear power plant began operating in 1972, there had been a noticeable increase in leukemia around the plant. This led to a study by the National Center for Disease Control (CDC) of leukemia rates from 1969 to 1980 in the areas around Maine Yankee. The CDC study concluded: "No association was found between leukemia incidents and residence near the power plant, and no statistically significant excess cases occurred in [the affected counties].))[19] This has not quieted

109

the opponents. A biostatician at the Roswell Park Memorial Institute in Buffalo has argued that the CDC study was inappropriate and used the wrong estimates for the number of leukemia cases to be expected in a population of the size and age distribution in the Maine counties.

A second hazard of normal operation is worker radiation exposure. In 1980 there were significant increases in worker exposure compared to previous years. For example, boiling water reactors averaged over 1100 person-rems per reactor and the total occupational dose in 1980 was approximately 53,800 person-rems, a 35 percent increase over the 1979 total. The 1981 figures show an increase to 54,100, primarily due to the larger number of reactors operating. These 54,100 person-rems were distributed over 82,000 workers with measurable doses.[20] The average dose per worker still remains under the protective guides and the maximum levels of exposure in cases of overexposure still are small. However, the total person-rem is rising. In addition, the use of so-called "jumpers" may be a serious problem. These people are hired for a short period of time to work in very high radiation areas. Concern about this practice has been increasing as plants have had to make repairs to steam generators, in areas with extremely high radiation levels. Currently the Federal Government has poor data on transient worker dosages.

Finally, there are concerns about transportation, principally of spent fuel from nuclear reactors. The spent fuel, highly radioactive because it contains a large amount of fission products, must be transported from the reactor to another reactor for storage, to another storage facility, or to a disposal site. Even though spent fuel is transported in large, heavy casks, some critics have argued a terrorist could stop the vehicle and use plastic explosives to widely disperse the fission products. In 1982 a New York organization, the Council on Economic Priorities (CEP), raised a number of issues regarding potential hazards from such an accident. They claimed "under calm meteorological conditions, with a 10 percent release of cesium, hundreds to thousands of early deaths could occur within ¼ mile of the accident. Outside the ¼ mile area, delayed cancer fatalities would result if anyone remained in the area. Assuming 100,000 people per square mile did stay, 50,000 latent cancers would develop. An area of ½ square mile would be off limits to people for several hundred years."[21]

The NRC response to this claim has been that the 10 percent release is "excessively high" and that the bases for the CEP estimate cannot be understood without more detail. The NRC staff believes CEP used an outdated 1974 model. Our response was provided to the authors of the original study early in 1982. In May the CEP indicated they would provide their analysis. So far they have not done so.

E. Accidents

Accidents can happen. If the public were convinced accidents could not occur at nuclear power plants, there would be no public fear. If technical analysts were convinced accidents could not happen there would be far less criticism of nuclear power. The Three Mile Island accident has convinced much of the public and many technologists that nuclear power may be unacceptable. The Three Mile Island accident is the most disastrous that has occurred to a nuclear power reactor in the noncommunist world. (Our information about accidents in the communist world is extremely limited.) The TMI accident so severely damaged the reactor that four years later the reactor vessel has not even been opened, much less cleaned up, because of technical, political, and financial problems. The accident has put a large utility on the verge of bankruptcy. It frightened many people. It apparently did not cause any physical harm. Secretary of Health, Education, and Welfare Joseph Califano reported to Congress that his health staff predicted approximately one additional case of fatal cancer, one case of nonfatal cancer, and one additional genetic defect as a result of the accident. He noted that this one cancer would be added to the 350,000 deaths from cancer expected among the 2.1 million people living within 50 miles of Three Mile Island and consequently would not be detected.[22]

Much larger numbers of deaths have been estimated for accidents. The NRC currently is involved in a very controversial hearing addressing the two operating nuclear power reactors at Indian Point, approximately 30 miles up the Hudson River from New York City. In testimony before the NRC hearing board the senior energy scientist of the National Audubon Society estimated that an accident at Indian Point with the wind blowing towards New York City could lead to 6,000 to 50,000 delayed cancer deaths and a total of as much as 64,000 deaths. He also estimated that if the wind were to blow in the opposite direction, into the agricultural area, that between 240 and 3,300 square miles would be contaminated for longer than 40 years.[23]

More recently, the day before the November elections, newspapers published articles concerning a study done for the NRC of the consequences of nuclear plant accidents. The *Washington Post* reported the "death-toll could exceed 100,000 and damage could top $300 billion. . . ."[24]

These very high death figures result from fairly straightforward calculations. They use estimates for causing death of between 2,000 and 20,000 person-rem, quite reasonable, based on scientific studies. The amount of fission products within the reactor is not disputed. The argument always turns on how probable is the radiation dosage. The NRC has had studies done on the probability of major accidents. Within the technical community the most famous is the study published in large 1975, called WASH-1400, the Rasmussen Report, and also known as the Reactor Safety Study. More recently the Oak Ridge National Laboratory reviewed ten years of reports on things that had gone wrong in nuclear power plants to try to identify events which could have led to a severely damager nuclear core.[25]

The Oak Ridge study indicated that the probability of severe core damage during that eleven year period was higher than had been expected from the Reactor Safety Study. The Reactor Safety Study estimated the likelihood of a severe core damage or core melt accident as about one chance in 20,000 years of reactor operation. The Oak Ridge Study indicated about one change in 1,000 years of reactor operation. The Oak Ridge authors estimated their assessment could be optimistic by a factor of two-to-three or pessimistic by a factor of ten-to-one-hundred. To put one-in-one-thousand in perspective, there are about fifty reactor years accumulated every year in the United States so that it would take twenty years to accumulate a thousand years of reactor operation. Therefore, if there were no changes made to reduce the probability of an accident, the Oak Ridge study would indicate there will be another severe core damage accident between now and the turn of the century. The NRC argues that changes made as a result of the Three Mile Island accident will significantly lower that probability. The opponents of nuclear power argue these changes will not.

As I mentioned, the estimates of 100,000 deaths came from a study done for the NRC. The *Washington Post* led many readers to believe there was a 2 percent chance that this size accident would happen in the United States before the year 2000. These stories received considerable attention because this number of deaths is the nuclear power catastrophe people fear. The NRC's comments on the errors in the story did not receive much attention. This Sandia study[26] calculated the worst cases. The authors assumed large scale melting of the core, assumed failure of the safety systems, assumed failure of the containment to hold the fission products, and then assumed the radioactive material is formed into a plume, the plume blows at a close-by large population center, and assumed that when the plume gets over the population center a rain storm comes to deposit the radiation on the ground. Finally, after the rain, the people stay in the area for 24 hours rather than evacuating. These events are calculated by the NRC staff to have a probability of approximately one chance in one billion. Sandia Laboratory disagreed with the *Post* and commented that "the likelihood of experiencing the Post peak consequences for a given plant is about once in a billion years (about ⅕ the age of the earth)."[27]

These calculations, discussions, estimates illuminate the central point of the nuclear power argument — the Omega point — catastrophic consequences and vanishingly slim probabilities. They are both calculations. The proponents argue if one set of calculations is believed, then so should the other. They argue that if you believe the consequences can be very high you should also believe the probabilities are very low. Risk is a product of multiplying the consequences times the probability. Something that is high risk needs to have both high consequences and a high probability, although if the consequences are sufficiently large the probability need not be too large to still have a high risk. The proponents of nuclear power argue that the probabilities being discussed are such that there is one chance of the catastrophe in a period of time comparable to the time on which man has been on the earth or perhaps even as long as the earth itself has existed. Consequently, they argue, these high consequences are not relevant. The opponents argue as did the Audubon scientist at the Indian Point hearing:

> "The true probability of [radiation] release could be orders of magnitude higher or lower than the limited estimate given [by the NRC]. As a result there is no way to *guarantee* the public safety at Indian Point. Nor is it even possible to state that there is reasonable assurance that the public safety can be protected."[28]

The proponents of nuclear power ask you to consider what they would argue would be a more probable event: the collision of two large aircraft fully loaded with fuel over Shea Stadium in New York City on an afternoon when it is sold out for some major sport event, or the crash of one aircraft into the stadium. This they note could easily lead to tens of thousands, even fifty thousand deaths. Yet, they argue, aircraft are allowed to take off while nearby sports stadiums are packed.

F. Sabotage

Nuclear power plants are vulnerable to sabotage, as are all complex equipment. Plants have been sabotaged. In 1980 a tank which adds chemicals to the reactor supply system of a nuclear plant in New Jersey was found to have unacceptable sodium and chloride added. At this same plant valves were incorrectly positioned on one of the diesel generators used to provide emergency power, which would have prevented that generator from starting. In 1981 a chain and padlock twice were removed from valves at a plant in Pennsylvania, and in one case a valve that was supposed to be open was closed. A diesel generator could not start at a plant in New York State because a fuel oil drain had been tampered with. Instrumentation and control cables were cut at a Midwest plant under construction. A metal clip was used to short a circuit in the shutdown system in a plant in New Jersey. Detector guide tubes were bent at a plant in the Southeast, which significantly degraded equipment used to signal the reactor protection system to shut down the reactor. At a plant in New England a cup-full of metal clips, some bolts, and nuts were discovered inside the oil reservoir that provides lubrication oil for the reactor cooling pumps. Other events have been reported which could make sabotage easier[29]: the former Security Director of the AEC gambled away over $170,000 of money borrowed from fellow AEC employees and failed to repay it; a security guard at a plutonium fuel fabrication plant, arrested in connection with an armed robbery, was found to be a convicted and paroled armed robber who had been hired under a false name; in 1974 an analytic laboratory used by the Japanese nuclear industry to monitor waste products from power plants was shut down by the government for falsifying and fabricating test results.

Nuclear power plants are large, technically complicated systems. There obviously will be opportunities for sabotage of these systems. Plant security is maintained by guard forces, but many questions can be raised about the quality of these contract guards. Nevertheless, the issues involved with sabotage are really no greater than the issues involved with other health hazards for the plant. The major questions are whether an accident can be triggered and what are the results of those accidents. The principal criticism of nuclear power with regard to

114

sabotage has been that not enough effort has been spent trying to calculate in what ways a plant can be sabotaged. Guards and the security system around nuclear power plants are aimed at preventing takeover or sabotage by a small number of people. A large force of armed invaders would have a much greater chance of being able to occupy a plant. They could then destroy the plant and themselves in a terrorist action.

G. Proliferation

Pope John Paul II has spoken frequently on the unacceptable moral risk of nuclear war: " . . . the only choice that is morally and humanly valid is represented by the reduction of nuclear armaments. . . "[30] Nuclear power has been connected with nuclear weapons. The highly discussed and respected report by the Ford Foundation Nuclear Energy Policy Study Group said:

"By far the most serious danger associated with nuclear power is that it provides additional countries a path for access to equipment, materials, and technology necessary for the manufacture of nuclear weapons. We believe the consequences of the proliferation of nuclear weapons are so serious compared to the limited economic benefits of nuclear energy that we would be prepared to recommend stopping nuclear power in the United States if we thought this would prevent further proliferation."[31]

The Flowers Report, a United Kingdom Report on nuclear power, had similar remarks:

"The spread of nuclear power will inevitably facilitate the spread of the ability to make nuclear weapons and, we fear, the construction of these weapons."[32]

There are many discussions and arguments about why new countries develop nuclear weapons and, once committed, how difficult is it for such a country to do so. A recent article[33] included these points:

" . . . The main technical barriers to acquisition of fission weapons . . . are a weapon program's requirements for a sizable cadre of highly trained specialists and for a source of fissionable raw material plus the facilities for converting it to weapons-useable form.

"A commercial nuclear power program lowers these barriers in three ways:
- it assembles people having the same skills needed for a weapons program. . .
- a nuclear power program cannot avoid solving the problem of fissionable material. . .
- such programs often provide directly the means for converting the raw fuel into weapons-useable material. . ."

Countries develop nuclear weapons for three fundamental reasons: (1) because of a clearly perceived danger to national survival which the leaders believe might not be averted unless the country has nuclear weapons; (2) because of national prestige, to increase the country's standing among other nations, particularly in their area of the world; and (3) to achieve national goals. The countries of concern currently come under two categories: (a) non-nuclear weapons states that are not parties to the Non-Proliferation Treaty and in which certain nuclear activities are not under International Atomic Energy Agency (IAEA) safeguards. These are India, Israel, Pakistan and South Africa. And second, with respect to the Tlatelolco Treaty: (1) Argentina has signed the treaty but has not ratified it; (2) Cuba has neither signed nor ratified it; and (3) Brazil has signed and ratified it but not waived it into force.

There is no direct link between nuclear power and atomic weapons. A nuclear reactor will not explode like a bomb. And it is also true that no country that has developed nuclear weapons is known to have developed them through a nuclear power program. But developing a nuclear power program does bring with it the knowledge and skills needed to develop nuclear weapons. The attempt to reduce proliferation is primarily through the Non-Proliferation Treaty and the IAEA safeguards system. However, events in Pakistan and India show the difficulty of trying to use IAEA safeguards in a country which does not want to allow them. The case of India is particularly illuminating. The 1974 Indian nuclear explosion led to the United States' Nuclear Non-Proliferation Act, which restricts our nuclear exports, and gave impetus to strengthening IAEA safeguards. Neveretheless, the United States and India over the last five years have been arguing about selling more fuel to India for its existing reactors in return for India accepting IAEA safeguards on all its nuclear facilities. India refused to do so and the United States finally refused to send fuel. Recently an arrangement was struck between the United States, France, and India by which France would send the fuel. For several months France and India debated what would happen to the safeguards when the United States-Indian Agreement ends in 1993. The United States' position had been that safeguards would continue. India's had been that they would not. A trade journal reported:

> "As they had hoped, French Government Officials managed to blur the issue with semantics. . . . 'It's due to the diplomatic skills of (French Ambassador to India) Andre Ross,' said a French source close to the talks. 'He scored a notable triumph in persuading the Indians that the French had capitulated (on the perpetuity question) when in fact they haven't.'"[34]

This continues the tradition of ambiguity which permits countries that do not want to apply safeguards not to apply them and increases the belief in the world that safeguards are only applied by countries that have no intention of developing nuclear weapons.

F. Nuclear Waste

In 1979, Burns Roper reported on a recent study in which the Roper testing service asked people how concerned they were about various sources of radiation, not just nuclear energy. He was surprised that the first thing that people were "very concerned" about was storage and disposal of nuclear waste. "Some 55 percent expressed themselves as very concerned about storage and disposal, another 21 percent moderately concerned, for a total of over three-quarters."[35] The Nuclear Regulatory Commission has spent the last two years studying whether we can have confidence nuclear waste can be safely disposed of. We conducted extensive hearings and received testimony from opponents and proponents of nuclear power: from state, public interest, and industry representatives, and from scientists.

The general consensus of both opponents and proponents was that there are no unsolvable technical problems for the disposal of nuclear waste. Although recognizing the great difficulty in making predictions for thousands of years, it is not a substantial technical concern. The general technical community believes that nuclear waste with long-term radioactivity can be successfully contained and deposited in locations where the likelihood of the radioactivity reaching people, animals, or water is sufficiently slim as to not be of great concern. This does not mean nuclear waste problems are solved. The Congress of the United States, as a last gasp of its lame duck session, just barely passed a Nuclear Waste Bill. After over 20 years of struggling with this issue, the United States' Federal Government finally has a law which lays out how a waste repository is to be developed. It is still at least 10 years from when we could possibly have a waste repository built, and more likely at least 20. The little booklet, "Nuclear Energy Facts", published by the American Nuclear Society, in its discussion of "Why Hasn't the Waste Disposal Problem Been Resolved?", points out that "the problem, then, is a political one, centering around Federal licensing of facilities, states rights in siting, and the need of fuel reprocessing to concentrate the waste."

The political question of siting is killing the programs for developing nuclear waste sites. I believe another handout was a colored brochure entitled "The Management of Radioactive Waste". At the end of that booklet is an interesting table showing who is doing what with high-level waste and where. If you carefully read down ths table you find the following: Belgium is "investigating" clay formations for a repository; in Canada methods of disposal in underground rock formations "are being developed"; Finland is "investigating" rocks for a repository; France is "investigating" rocks for a repository; in the Federal Republic of Germany salt formations "are being studied" and they are "investigating" rock formations; in Italy disposal in clay formations is being "investigated"; Japan is "investigating" rock formations; the Netherlands is "investigating" salt formations; Switzerland is "investigating" evaporite formations; the United Kingdom is "investigating" certain rock formations; in the United States deep geological disposal concepts are being "considered"; and in the Soviet Union geological disposal concepts are being "studied".

Throughout the world governments are still considering and investigating, but have not *chosen* locations. Everytime the United States Government attempts to choose a site the local population gets very upset and rises up against it. This is true in other countries also. Local attitudes in the United States can be seen in the following statement by Utah Governor Matheson, who was then Chairman of the National Governors' Association. In opposing the Department of Energy even examining Utah for possible high-level waste repository, he said:

> "I am holding judgment in reserve until we have all the facts. I recognize that there is a national problem, and if this is the best site, then I might not oppose it. But I have not reached that conclusion, and there is a legion of factors that have not been resolved."[36]

The unarguable facts are that nuclear waste is generated by the operation of nuclear power plants and there is as of yet no site chosen for permanent disposal of that nuclear waste.

III. Future Problems

A. Accidents

There was a long period in which the nuclear industry—designers, builders, operators, and regulators—believed that an accident could not happen. This led to neglecting data from experience and led to concluding that worrying about the qualifications of and procedures to be followed by the operators was not necessary. It led people to conclude that if the reactor were designed so well that an accident could not happen, then it was unimportant to think about: whether labels are easily read or instruments clearly marked; whether on/off switches or signal indicating lights and other indicators were the same across the control panel; if red means "on" in one place, does it mean "on" in another place; are controls and the related instruments to tell what is being controlled close together; do operators understand what is going on in the reactor; are there instruments that could tell the operator what is going on? The answers to all these questions were "no." But no one paid much attention to the human side of designing nuclear reactors. The results were poorly designed control rooms, badly instrumented reactors, inadequately trained operators—a result also was the Three Mile Island accident.

The Three Mile accident did happen and near misses have occurred here and abroad. How likely is another major accident? First, I have to define what is meant by a major accident. In answering that question I use three categories:

(1) An accident in which a large amount of radioactivity is released off site. There have been no accidents like this in the non-

119

Communist world, with the possible exception of a 1957 release at Windscale in England.

(2) An accident which leads to a substantial damage to the reactor and, therefore, a very large expense to the utility. There are the Three Mile Island and Browns Ferry accidents. This category and (1) are major accidents.

(3) An accident in which some damage occurs and there are costs primarily due to the reactor being down and replacement power being purchased. However, if some additional event should happen or if operators do something differently, then the accident could shift into one of the first two categories. In this country this type event happened at Rancho Seco in California, Davis Besse in Ohio, and Crystal River in Florida.

Using these accidents and other accidents in which less dangerous things happened, a simple probability analysis leads to estimating the chance of another major accident occurring in the United States before the year 2000 to be between 8 percent and 20 percent, *if* the changes introduced by the NRC and the industry have reduced the probability by a factor of 10. If they haven't, the chance of a major accident before the year 2000 is about 80 percent.

I believe there will be an accident. The only question is whether offsite damage can be prevented.

B. Industry Attitudes

The President's commission that reviewed the accident at Three Mile Island examined the utility that ran the plant had said:

> ". . . the analysis of this particular accident raises the serious
> question of whether all electric utilities automatically have
> the necessary technical expertise and managerial capabilities
> for administering such a dangerous high-technology plant.
> We, therefore, recommend the development of higher stan-
> dards of organization and management that a company must
> meet before it is granted a license to operate a nuclear power
> plant."[37]

The NRC's independent review of the Three Mile Island accident concluded:

> "This account suggests two conclusions. First, the operators

on duty had not received training adequate to ensure that they would be able to recognize and respond to a serious accident within the first hour or two after it occurred. Second, neither the operating crew nor their supervisors in the site management group possessed the necessary combination of technical competence and familiarity with the plant to diagnose a totally unanticipated situation and take the appropriate corrective action.

". . . [E]verything we have learned in this investigation suggests that the problems in this area revealed by Three Mile Island—inadequate training, unreasonably scanty manning levels, lack of any requirements for minimum onsite technical supervisory competence—are common to many, probably most nuclear plants."[38]

Last year the executive in charge of reviewing requirements for the NRC spoke on nuclear power plant construction. He said:

"The problems in construction are real. . .

"At one site, . . . because of improper welding, the wall would probably not withstand accident-generated shear forces. . . .

"At another site, safety-significant voids, surface defects and honeycombs occurred in concrete. First attempts to patch them were unacceptable. . . .

"At still another site, safety-related structures have settled excessively because of inadequate specifications and poor compaction of foundation backfill. . . .

"In a final example, another utility has experienced costly delays due to defects in the quality of cadwelds, concrete, cable separation, and piping welds in safety systems.

"The point of these examples is that real defects were built into these plants. . . . I am gravely concerned about shoddy construction because of its potential impact on public health and safety."[39]

The nuclear industry's Institute for Nuclear Power Operations (INPO) has evaluated U. S. power plants. Last Fall, thirty-four of the forty-five completed evaluations had been made public. Utilities were having difficulty releasing the others. Utilities complain this kind of information is harmful. For example, it gives ammunition to intervenors, or, as a Chief Executive Officer mentioned, reports on being made public reach audiences that are not always friendly. In his view, these audiences pressure public service commissioners to look for excuses to deny utilities badly needed rate increases.

Quite frequently, it appears that INPO only is able to take action when the NRC is about to. Apparently one of the most powerful arguments that the President of INPO can bring to his Board of Directors is that the NRC is about to do a study or look into an area. That will energize INPO's Board of Directors to authorize INPO to look into it.

As an example of the difficulties with industry, last year the NRC staff approached the Institute of Electrical and Electronics Engineers (IEEE), the largest international professional engineering society, and asked whether they would be willing to develop a program to accredit laboratories to test equipment for nuclear power plants to see whether the equipment is qualified to operate in accident environments. Most electrical equipment is not made to operate in the radiation levels, high temperatures, perhaps high pressures, and with the steam that equipment in nuclear power plants may have to endure during an accident. The NRC requires utilities to show their equipment is qualified. The showing is usually done by a testing laboratory. We asked the IEEE whether they would be willing to develop a program to accredit the testing laboratories.

After substantial negotiation and discussion, IEEE agreed it would be a very difficult task but they would do it. They put a lot of time and effort in during the past year to develop a program. However, the NRC is not going to use the IEEE program. We are not going to because industry objected vehemently, with many specious arguments. As best as I can tell, the real concern is that perhaps the IEEE would only accredit laboratories who would be very rigorous in testing the equipment.

Another problem with industry attitudes is seen in the area of operator qualifications. The Three Mile Island accident led many of us to conclude operating personnel in nuclear power plants ought to be very skilled people. It is true that what they do most of the time is very boring, but occasionally to prevent or to mitigate an accident they are challenged to perform extremely difficult integration of a large amount of information and to react promptly under great pressure. I believe this requires an individual who is very knowledgeable and is very competent. This translates into high qualifications and it also translates into high pay. The airline industry understands this; the utility industry is not interested. They are really interested in keeping operators at the lower end of the utility pay scale. They believe in taking a high school graduate and giving him a few years of training, and have bitterly fought, successfully so far, any attempt by those of us who are interested in placing higher requirements on operating personnel.

IV. Summary

The views on both sides of this debate are harsh. The views of the proponents of nuclear power toward the opponents can be summarized in the following quote:

> "The real battle is, instead, between those who believe in a rationalist world and those who reject it.
>
> "This is not a minor disagreement. Rather, it is the most fundamental of all.
>
> "For the movement which believes the secret of running the world lies mainly in having the right values is bound in the end to ignore almost any practical problem which threatens to interfere with the attainment of their hopes.
>
> "It is a movement not much interested in technical arguments, expert opinions or rationalist excuses which delay the mission. For it postulates that the very reason its goals have been so long postponed lies precisely in the opposition of just these forces. So it now seeks simply to overturn them."[40]

The opponents of nuclear power would say, as does Amory Lovins:

> "We are more endangered by too much energy too soon, than by too little, too late. . .
>
> "We know next to nothing about the carefully designed natural systems and cycles on which we depend; we must therefore take care to preserve resilience and flexibility, and to design for large safety margins . . . recognizing the existence of human fallibility, malice and, irrationality. . . .
>
> "People are more important than goods; hence energy, tech-

nology, and economic activity are means, not ends, and their quantity is not a measure of welfare. . . .

"The energy problem should be not how to expand supplies to meet the postulated extrapolative needs of a dynamic economy, but rather how to accomplish social goals elegantly with a minimum of energy and effort. . . .

"The technical, economic, and social problems of fission technology are so intractable, and technical efforts to palliate those problems are politically so dangerous, that we should abandon the technology with due deliberate speed. . . .

"Ordinary people are qualified and responsible to make these and other energy choices through the democratic political process. . . ."[41]

Opponents of nuclear power raise hard questions:

"Proponents of endless energy growth are fond of saying that we need the energy to accomplish our goals. What goals? Goals imply that they are bounded, are finite, can be attained; but a goal of 'more' has no end. Whose goals? How much is enough? Enough for whom? If we cannot say how much is enough, do we need more? Who has enough already? Do the Germans think they have enough? Do they think the Americans have enough?

"Do the Indians think the Germans have enough? Who thinks the New Zealanders have enough? Which New Zealanders? How far does tomorrow's growth steal from our children? What would they say about that?"[42]

There are many who oppose nuclear energy because they don't understand it. They fear the mysterious and the unknown. There are many who fear nuclear power because they hear others who they think are responsible describe the horrors of nuclear radiation and imply that accidents are very likely to happen. There are others, like myself, who are concerned about nuclear power because we are skeptical about the willingness of those who use it to put in place sufficient competence to handle this dangerous technology. And finally there are those whose primary concern about nuclear power relates to nuclear war and they see an indissoluble link such as Jacques-Yves Cousteau, who said at the United Nations in May of 1976:

> "Despite the best efforts and intentions of the people of the United Nations, human society is too diverse, national passion too strong, human aggressiveness too deep-seated for the peaceful and the war-like atom to stay divorced for long. We cannot embrace one while abhorring the other; we must learn, if we want to live at all, to live without both."[43]

In preparing for this paper, I found it difficult to describe the intensity and bias which characterize much of the nuclear power debate, both pro and con. An excellent summary of the debates has been given by a Columbia law professor who conducted a conference on the issues you are addressing:

> "The picture which emerges is, we believe, somewhat different from that which one is apt to glean from the daily press. The contest is seen not as one between certainties—of certain disaster on the one hand or happiness ever after on the other. . . . [R]isks and benefits are hard to quantify. Safety emerges as a primary objective, but absolute safety does not exist, and the trade offs between power costs and the 'last ounce of prevention' are very hard to measure. . . .

> "Perhaps the strongest message is that our present structures are inadequate. Even if we decide, as an abstract matter, that we should proceed more or less vigorously to pursue the nuclear option, there are many troublesome questions, political, institutional, and psychological, which must be faced. It is not at all clear that we can mobilize the necessary resources to do what is necessary even if we can agree on the ultimate objective. . . .

> "It seems useful to point out that the nuclear question may be only part of a larger problem of long-term resource management and the management of technology. It is hard to know how we got to this point at this time. Looking back to twenty years ago it seems almost inconceivable that we should have reached the point where the giving up of the nuclear option is a distinct possibility. In part, the opposition to nuclear power appears to be a product of long resentment of arrogance

and high-handedness on the part of some members of the nuclear establishment; in part it may be more broadly antiscientific in nature, with nuclear power as the symbol of science in general. Certainly it seems to reflect a disenchantment with the highly touted benefits of technology which many took for granted for so long.

"Finally, it seems to reflect a belief in simple answers to complex problems and an unwillingness on the part of many people to face up to the difficult problems of choice with which we must deal. It may turn out that as a society we are simply not able to live with the idea of risk. It may, in the last analysis, be that both the pro- and the anti-nukes will turn out to be wrong and that the society when confronted with the question will make no choice at all. In that event it seems highly likely that we will simply drift along from crisis to crisis—that we will neither live with nuclear power nor reconcile ourselves to living without it."[44]

FIGURE 1
NUCLEAR ELECTRIC GENERATION CAPACITY
Megawatts (Number of Plants)

	US	CANADA	MEXICO
Operating	60,300 (77)	6,260 (11)	0
Under Construction	66,300 (60)	8,000 (14)	1,300 (2)
Planned	2,500 (2)	600 (1)	?

FIGURE 2
PERCENTAGES RESPONDING TO HARRIS POLLS

	Taken Over the Three Years Prior to TMI	Taken Over the Two Years After TMI
Favor	47–69	46–60
Oppose	20–39	39–51
Not Sure	10–20	6–16

FIGURE 3
ESTIMATES OF RISK

	League of Women Voters	College Students	Risk Experts
Alcoholic Beverages	161	150	4,614
Private Aviation	114		
Handguns	220	193	2,189
Motorcycles	176	155	651
Motor Vehicles	247	169	15,220
Nuclear Power	250	449	(90)
Pesticides		188	
Smoking	189	192	15,571
Surgery			1,422
X-rays			608

	League of Women Voters		Previous Rank	College Students		Previous Rank
FIGURE 4 **ESTIMATES OF ANNUAL DEATHS**						
Alcoholic Beverages	12,000	2	6	2,600	2	7
Handguns	3,000	4	3	1,900	4	2
Motorcycles	1,600	6	5	1,600	5	6
Motor Vehicles	28,000	1	2	10,500	1	5
Nuclear Power	20	30	1	27	30	1
Pesticides				84	20	4
Smoking	6,900	3	4	2,400	3	3
Surgery	2,500	5	10			

FIGURE 5
CAPITAL COSTS FOR POWER PLANTS
CURRENTLY UNDER CONSTRUCTION
(1980 Dollars per kilowatt)

Nuclear
    New England   1470
    Southern United States   955
    Northwestern United States   2295

Coal
    Bituminous, high-sulfur, with scrubber   1057
    Bituminous, low-sulfur, without scrubber   877

Oil   654

FIGURE 6 COMPARATIVE BUS-BAR COST FOR NUCLEAR AND COAL-FIRED POWER PLANTS (Mills/KWh[a])										
REGION	I	II	III	IV	V	VI	VII	VIII	IX	X
Nuclear	43.0	45.0	41.9	40.6	43.5	40.6	42.5	42.3	44.8	44.8
Coal	46.8	44.1	41.1	44.1	42.4	29.5	42.9	31.0	44.8	46.5
Margin	3.8	0.9	0.8	3.5	1.1	11.1	0.4	11.3	—	1.7
Favored	N	C	C	N	C	C	N	C	—	N

[a]1980 Constant dollars levelized over 30 years of plant operation beginning in 1995.

FIGURE 7 ANNUAL DOSE RATES FROM SIGNIFICANT SOURCES IN THE UNITED STATES	Millirems/ Year
Natural Background	
Cosmic	28
Terrestrial	26
Internal	28
Total Background	82
Medical X-rays (if have)	
Medical Diagnosis of Adults	103
Dental Diagnosis of Adults	3
Atmospheric Weapons Tests	4–5
Commercial Nuclear Power Plants (Normal Operation) (Population within 10 miles)	<< 10
Building Materials (Population in Brick and Masonry Buildings)	7
TV Viewing	0.2–1.5
Airline Passengers	3

Notes

1. Lowrance, William W., *Of Acceptable Risk: Science and the Determination of Safety*, William Kaufman, Inc., Los Altos, CA, 1976, pp. 93–94. Quoted in "A Nuclear Power Primer: Issues for Citizens," League of Women Voters Education Fund, Washington, D. C., 21 (1982).
2. "Certification to the Commission on Psychological Distress Issues," TMI-1 Restart Hearing Atomic Safety and Licensing Board, A-3, (February 22, 1980).
3. "Public Meeting on the Restart of Three Mile Island Unit 1," Harrisburg, PA, USNRC Transcript, pp. 38–40, November 9, 1982.
4. Hacker, Andrew, "Nuclear Power and the Hamilton-Jefferson Debate," *Electric Perspectives*, Edison Electric Institute, New York, pp. 1–13 (Summer 1980).
5. Maxey, Margaret N., "Radiation Health Protection and Risk Assessment: Bioethical Considerations," Proc. Fifteenth Annual Meeting of the National Council on Radiation Protection and Measurements, NCRPM, Washington, D.C., 23 (March 1980).
6. Fischhoff, Baruch, *et al.*, "How Safe Is Safe Enough? A Psychometric Study of Attitudes Towards Technological Risks and Benefits," *Policy Science 9*, 127–152 (1978).
   Slovic, Paul, *et al.*, "Images of Disaster: Perception and Acceptance of Risks from Nuclear Power," in *Energy Risk Management*, Goodman & Rowe (eds.), Academic Press, London (1979).
   Slovic, Paul, "Miages of Disaster: Perception and Acceptance of Risks from Nuclear Power," Proc. of the Fifteenth Annual Meeting of National Council on Radiation Protection and Measurements, NCRPM, Washington, D.C., pp. 34–55 (March 1980).
   Slovic, Paul, *et al.*, "Perceived risk: psychological factors and social implications," Proc. R. Soc. Lond. A *376*, 17–34 (1981).
7. Slovic, 1980, op cit., 45. See also Reference 13, 52.
8. "The Economic and Social Costs of Coal and Nuclear Electric Generation," National Science Foundation, 28, 49 (March 1976).
9. Department of Energy Annual Report to Congress, Vol. 3, Supplement 2, Tables 27 and 30 (February 1982).
10. "Projected Costs of Electricity from Nuclear and Coal-Fired Power Plants," DOE/EIA-0356/1, Table 7 (August 1982).
11. Wald, Matthew, "How Atomic Power Costs Just Grew," *The New York Times*, E-7 (October 17, 1982).
12. "Memorandum of Law in Support of the Petition of West Valley Agricultural Protection Council, Inc.," Palo Verde Atomic Safety and Licensing Board, 1, 15 (October 14, 1982).
13. "Risks Associated with Nuclear Power: A Critical Review of the Literature," National Academy of Sciences, Washington, D.C., 3 (April 1979).
14. Ibid., 9.
15. "Problems in Assessing the Cancer Risks of Low-Level Ionizing Radiation Exposure," EMD-81-1, U.S. General Accounting Office, Washington, D.C., iv (1981).
16. *The Effects on Population of Exposure to Low Levels of Ionizing Radiation: 1980* (BEIR III), National Academy Press, Washington, D.C., Table III-23 (1980).
17. "Risks Associated with Nuclear Power," op. cit., 29–30.
18. "Radiological Assessment of the Wyhl Nuclear Power Plant," Department of Environmental Protection of the University of Heidelberg, Germany, NRC Translation 520, 113–114 (July 1979).
19. "Feds Reject Leukemia Claim About Maine Yankee," Waterville, Maine *Sentinel* (October 9, 1982).
20. "Occupational Radiation Exposure at Commercial Nuclear Power Reactors 1981," NUREG-0713, Vol. 3, U.S. Nuclear Regulatory Commission, Washington, D.C. (1982).
21. Resnikoff, Marvin, Project Director, Council on Economic Priorities, letter of May 14, 1982 to William J. Dircks, Executive Director for Operations, U.S. Nuclear Regulatory Commission.
22. Califano, Joseph, quoted in Fredrickson, Donald S., Testimony on Low-Level Ionizing

Radiation, Committee on Science and Technology, U.S. House of Representatives, 12–13 (June 13, 1979).

23. Beyea, Jan and Palenik, Brian, "Some Consequences of Catastrophic Accidents at Indian Point and Their Implications for Emergency Planning," Testimony before NRC Indian Point Licensing Board, 7, 30, 40 (June 7, 1982).

24. "Nuclear Study Raises Estimates of Accident Tolls." *The Washington Post* (November 1, 1982).

25. Minarick, T. W., and Kukielka, C. A., "Precursors to Potential Severe Core Damage Accidents: 1969–1979, A Status Report," NUREG/CR-2497, U.S. Nuclear Regulatory Commission, Washington, D.C. (June 1982).

26. Aldrich, D. C., *et al.,* "Technical Guidance for Siting Criteria Development," NUREG/CR-2239, U.S. Nuclear Regulatory Commission, Washington, D.C. (January 1983).

27. McCloskey, David T., Manager, Nuclear Fuel Cycle Safety Research, Sandia National Laboratories, letter to White House Office of Science and Technology Policy (November 3, 1982).

28. Beyea, *op cit.* 10.

29. Lovins, Amory B., *Soft Energy Paths: Toward A Durable Peace,* Ballinger Publishing Co., Cambridge, Mass., 191–192 (1977).

30. Pope John Paul II, Angelus Message (December 13, 1981), quoted in Origins *12:*315 (1982).

31. Nuclear Power Issues and Choices, Ballinger Publishing Co., Cambridge, Mass., 4 (1977).

32. Flowers, B., *Nuclear Power and the Environment* Sixth Report of the Royal Commission of Environmental Pollution, Her Majesty's Stationery Office, London, 76 (September 1976), quoted in Holdren (see ref. 33).

33. Holdren, T. P., "Nuclear Power and Nuclear Weapons: The Connection is Dangerous," Bulletin of the Atomic Scientists, 41 (January 1983).

34. Nucleonics Week, 1 (December 2, 1982).

35. "Nuclear Radiation: How Dangerous Is It," National Academy of Science Forum, National Academy of Sciences, Washington, D.C., 52 (September 27, 1979).

36. "Utah is Ready to Fight U.S. on Atomic Waste," *Baltimore Sun* (September 22, 1982).

37. "Report of the President's Commission on the Accident at Three Mile Island," Washington, D.C., 23 (October 1979).

38. Rogovin, M. (Director), "Three Mile Island: A Report to the Commissioners and to the Public," U. S. Nuclear Regulatory Commission, Washington, D. C., 103 (January 1980).

39. Stello, V., "A Regulatory Perspective of the Role of Construction in Revitalizing the U.S. Nuclear Industry," IAEA-CN-42/253, presented to the IAEA International Conference on Nuclear Power Experience, 2 (September 13, 1982).

40. Bremner, J. E., "The Crisis of Expertise," Financier VI: 51–52 (September 1982).

41. Lovins, *op cit.,* 12–14.

42. Ibid, 166–167.

43. Ibid, 171.

44. Murphy, Arthur W. (ed) *The Nuclear Power Controversy,* Prentice-Hall, Inc., Englewood Cliff, New Jersey, 6–7 (1976).

Appendix

Taken from the statement by Donald S. Fredrickson, M.D., Director, National Institutes of Health given to the Subcommittee on Energy Research and Production and the Subcommittee on Natural Resources and Environment, Committee on Science and Technology of the House of Representatives, June 13, 1979.

Types of Ionizing Radiation.

The most important form of human radiation exposure is from gamma rays, high energy electromagnetic rays which can be produced either by nuclear reactions or by the bombardment of metallic targets with electrons, the common source of production of x-rays in medical applications. Beta rays or, more accurately, beta particles are electrons emitted from an atomic nucleus which, like gamma rays, may cover a wide range of energies. In general, because most beta particles are less penetrating than gamma rays, they produce less biological damage.

Alpha particles, emitted from the decay of certain heavy atomic nuclei, are charged particles containing two protons and two neutrons. Alpha particles are thousands of times heavier than beta particles and, therefore, do not have the penetrating power of gamma rays or beta particles. Nevertheless, they can be an important source of biological damage if alpha-emitters are deposited within a living organism. A fourth type important in producing human health effects is neutron radiation. The neutron, emitted in certain types of nuclear reactions, especially in nuclear fission, is moderately heavy but uncharged and thus is quite capable of penetration into biological tissues.

All of these types of radiation or particles are called ionizing radiation. While each is different physically and may come in a variety of energies, they all undergo numerous collisions with matter. The predominant result of these collisions are ions; that is, charged atoms, molecules, and subatomic particles which in turn can interact with the surrounding matter to alter it. This is the predominant source of biological damage from radiation.

However, while ion production results from all such radiation, it is important to make the distinction between different types of ionizing radiation, since the nature of the biological effects produced by each may differ considerably. Gamma rays, and to a lesser extent, beta rays, are considered to be low linear energy transfer (LET) forms of radiation; that is, as each passes through matter, it gives up its energy over relatively long distances. So-called high LET radiation is represented by alpha particles and neutrons, which give up the same amount of energy over much shorter distances. Therefore, the type of damage that each of these kinds of radiation may elicit upon passing through the same type of matter, including biological tissue, would be expected to differ.

Radiation Measurement.

Radiation is measured in one of two ways. The curie is a measure of quantity of radioactive material and is equal to 2.2×10^{12} disintegrations per minute. Clearly, the amount of energy or amount of ionization produced by the same number of curies will differ, depending on the particular radioactive isotope that is decaying. Therefore, this is not a particularly useful measure upon which to assess human health effects.

The classic unit of radiation exposure is called the roentgen. One roentgen is equal to 2.58×10^{-4} coulombs of electrical charge produced per kilogram of air. It is used only for electromagnetic radiation such as gamma rays or x-rays. However, a more useful quantity which has been used over the past two decades is a measure of absorbed dose called the rad, which may be used for all types of radiation, and is equal to 100 ergs of radiation energy absorbed per gram. A more meaningful unit is assessing biological effects is the quality does equivalent, which is the product of the absorbed dose in rads times the quality factor. This is an empirically derived adjusting factor accounting for the differences in the effectiveness of certain radiation in producing biological damage.

There is clearly some uncertainty in determining what this quality factor is. However, this unit, called the rem, which stands for *r*oentgen *e*quivalent to *m*an, includes for fast neutrons a quality factor of ten, or for alpha particles, a quality factor of one to twenty. This is the high LET radiation. For gamma rays and electrons, the quality factor is approximately one. Therefore, for the latter types of radiation, dose in rads and dose in rems is generally the same, whereas the dose in rads for neutrons and alpha particles will result in a substantially higher equivalent dose if measured in rems.

Practically, in order to determine radiation absorbed, it is necessary to measure these different types of radiation. This is clearly one of the current sources of uncertainty in assessing the radiation exposure and, therefore, the radiation risk to man. Certain types of radiation, such as gamma rays, are relatively easy to measure accurately. However, many of the gamma ray detectors do not measure beta rays. Alpha particles and neutrons are generally more difficult to measure and are, therefore, not usually detected by the normal film badges or ionization chambers.

Alpha particles, however, because they are not penetrating, are difficult to measure but also are usually important biologically only when the emitters of such particles are deposited within the body. And only a select population—those working with fissionable materials or working around particle accelerators—would be exposed to neutrons, which, because they are uncharged, special means must be taken for their measurement.

Population Exposure to Radiation.

The natural background radiation to which every human being is exposed throughout his or her lifetime is in the vicinity of from about 60 to 140 millirem per year. Approximately half of that comes from cosmic rays and the other half due to rocks, soil, and radioactive decay in the environment and in the human body. There are wide variations, however. The exposure to cosmic rays differs substantially, depending on the altitude at which one lives. When one flies in an airplane at high altitudes, the radiation due to cosmic rays increases considerably. Similarly, the amount of radiation received from rocks and minerals differs substantially, depending on where one lives, whether or not one lives in a building made of granite or bricks, and whether or not radioactive mineral deposits in the earth have been disturbed and brought to the surface in a particular area. The last century of man's development of technology has contributed, in some cases, significantly to the radiation exposure of individuals. For example, coal, for many years the chief energy source in the civilized world, contains on the average two parts per million of uranium. Coal ash, therefore, contains a substantial quantity of radioactivity. Even natural gas contains polonium, which also increases the radiation level where it is used.

The chief man-made source of radiation is, however, medical and dental x-rays. On the average, this accounts for an annual exposure of about 85 millirem per year per person in the United States. However, unlike background radiation, this varies considerably between individuals. Many receive no exposure from medical x-rays. Yet there is a small percentage of the population—particularly those undergoing extensive diagnoses or radiation treatments—which may receive many rem per year for medical purposes.

It is noteworthy that fallout from past and present nuclear weapons tests conducted in the atmosphere still contribute approximately seven millirem per year to each man, woman, and child living in the United States. The estimates of average exposure to the general population from nuclear power plants currently in operation in the United States and assuming normal operation—that is, without accidents of significance—is about 0.1 millirem per year per person, although estimates vary. Consumer products, such as television sets, smoke detectors and radium dial wrist watches, contribute overall less than .1 millirem per year per person. All of these figures represent exposure values averaged over the entire U.S. population. The contribution of each of these sources to a given individual may vary considerably.

Adverse Human Health Effects from Ionizing Radiation

On the basis of the information that has been gained from the study of certain special populations exposed to low-level radiation, the predominant adverse effect of radiation is an increase in the incidence of cancer and of cancer deaths. Each year approximately 400,000 people in the United States die of cancer. There have been a number of epidemiological studies on different populations exposed to various doses of radiation and exposed to different types of radiation. Not only do the conclusions differ from study to study, but analyses by different scientists of the same body of data often result in different conclusions.

At several times in the past few years the existing body of data and studies have been analyzed in an attempt to come up with an assessment of human risk from radiation. The National Academy of Sciences Committee on the Biological Effects of Ionizing Radiation, the so-called BEIR Committee, published a report in 1972 and just recently [1979] have released a draft report updating their 1972 findings. These questions were also addressed by the UNSCEAR Report (United Nations Scientific Committee on the Effects of Atomic Radiation) in 1977 and by the DHEW [Department of Health, Education, and Welfare]-sponsored Interagency Task Force on Ionizing Radiation, which will release its final report in 1979. None of the epidemiological studies,

135

such as that done on the Hanford nuclear workers, the Portsmouth Naval Shipyard submarine reactor workers, leukemia deaths in Utah, and even the atomic bomb survivors in Japan, is without some measure of uncertainty. Difficulties in accurate dose measurements of each type of radiation, including body burdens, problems in identifying control populations, the identification of confounding variables, and small sample size complicate most of these studies.

Animal data have been collected for a variety of controlled experiments to assess the biological effects of radiation. However, no certain model for the extrapolation of animal risk data to human beings for the various types of ionizing radiation exists. The best data seem to indicate, however, that radiation effects are cumulative, that there is no threshold dose below which there are no biological effects, and that the shape of the extrapolation curve differs between high LET and low LET radiation. While that statement may require some qualification and clarification as we learn more about the repair of radiation damage in human beings, there is not now any compelling evidence for a threshold nor that the dose rate over which radiation is absorbed makes much difference over a wide range of values. However, occupational and population exposure limits and risk estimates are still based on the dose received per year.

Most reports which attempt to assess human risk treat all radiation the same; that is, that a rem is a rem, no matter how it is produced or how or where it is received. Risk is generally estimated over a range of values. The data simply do not allow one to be any more precise than this.

The BEIR report of 1972 predicts a lifetime risk of cancer from a single radiation exposure to be from one to six cancer deaths per 10,000 person-rem of low LET exposure; that is, exposure primarily to gamma rays or x-rays. The 1979 BEIR report gave an estimate in approximately the same range, from about 1 to 3.5 cancer deaths per lifetime per 10,000 person-rem from exposure to low LET ionizing radiation.

Risk estimates for high LET radiation or for specific isotopes deposited in the body, while discussed in the BEIR report, were not estimated due to the lack of exposure data, epidemiological data and reliable risk estimate models. It is generally conceded, however, and there is some evidence to support the contention, that specific isotopes which find their way into specific body organs may, per rem of exposure, produce more serious health effects than the same amount of radiation received from gamma rays or x-rays coming from outside the body. These would include iodine 131, which is deposited in the thyroid gland, particularly in children whose thyroids are much more sensitive to radiation damage, and strontium 90, which replaces calcium in the bone and, therefore, results in the substantial concentration of radiation to the bone marrow cells, producing a higher risk of leukemia than if the same dose were received externally. A concern for those working around reactors or in the processing of fissionable materials is the toxicity of plutonium, a heavy metal alpha emitter, which, once it becomes ingested or lodged in the body, is retained for long periods of time. It is believed that, like most heavy metals, plutonium is concentrated in the liver. It is these types of exposure which are of considerable concern, both from fallout due to nuclear weapons tests, from possible nuclear reactor accidents, and for workers involved in milling operations of fissionable materials, both in the weapons industry and for nuclear reactors.

However, the bulk of radiation exposure to the U.S. population is of the low LET type and from external sources; that is, from background radiation or from medical x-rays. While we must continually cite the degree of uncertainty in our knowledge of radiation risk, we may, with the appropriate caveats, apply the range of risk estimates from the BEIR report for low LET radiation to assess the risk of cancer to the population. Taking an average value from the 1979 BEIR report of two fatal cancers per 10,000 person-rem of exposure, one would predict about 4,000 fatal cancers per year from natural background radiation in the United States population. This would account for approximately one percent of all cancer deaths in the United States. Given the range of values in the BEIR report, this number may be somewhat smaller than 4,000 or it may be somewhat larger. The limits of uncertainty of risk in the 1972 BEIR report result in a range of 2,000 fatal cancers per year to 12,000 fatal cancers per year, or a range of .5 to 3% of all cancers being due to background radiation. It should be mentioned here that some scientists would put the figure considerably above or below this range.

Again, assuming the mean value in the 1979 BEIR report, of two fatal cancers per 10,000 person/rems, the healing arts would result in approximately 3400 fatal cancers per year in the United States population, or approximately an additional 1% of the cancer deaths in the United States. Thus, taken together, the total contribution from both natural background and medical radiation, accounting for better than

137

90% of the total radiation exposure in the United States, we would predict between one and six percent of all cancer deaths due to these sources. By way of comparison, we can estimate that approximately 100,000 cases of fatal cancer per year, or about 25%, are due to cigarette smoking—the only other area in which we have both a large body of data and a very strong adverse effect.

The Editors

Chapter 4

Nuclear Energy
in the Private Sector

Gordon C. Hurlburt, M.E., M.B.A.

Editorial Preface

The use of heat from controlled nuclear fission as a source of steam to produce electricity emerged from the military program which developed the propulsion units for naval vessels such as the submarine, NAUTILUS. Westinghouse, General Electric and others launched the business of providing what are technically known as "nuclear steam supply systems." Utilities, urged on by the promise of a low-cost, environmentally clean central station system of power generation, provided a strong market and stimulus.

Construction delays due to many causes both internal and external to the utility industry caused the cost of each new nuclear kilowatt to climb rapidly. A new nuclear kilowatt cost $135 in 1969. One ordered today for the 1990's would cost a projected $3,200 — with $2,000 being the cost of finance. Under the impact of such rising costs, and of anti-nuclear activities, the market has declined. No new nuclear plants have been ordered in the United States since 1978.

Regulation has played a role both in the growth and decline of nuclear electricity in the United States. Changes are needed to speed up licensing, and cut construction costs.

Internationally, nuclear electricity continues to expand rapidly, threatening the United States with a loss of its technological leadership. Domestically, the public debate on technical subjects such as radiation and waste storage has created a negative political climate, and will probably continue through the present period of electricity surplus.

For American manufacturers, nuclear electricity is still a good business. The new unit market is now international. The domestic market centers on the fueling, service, and maintenance of plants on line or in production.

This offering is a personal viewpoint on nuclear electricity — the view of a businessman trained as an engineer who has a heavy obligation toward productivity, profit and society.

First, let me offer a brief sketch of the history of nuclear electricity from a manufacturer's experience, with some references to our customers, the world's electric utilities.

Westinghouse took its initial steps into the age of nuclear energy in the late '30s — some years before the first sustained fission reaction at Staff Field in 1942. We built what was then called an "atom smasher" near Pittsburgh, and a small but brilliant group of scientists did a great deal of theoretical work on the fission process. Other companies, notably General Electric, had similar early programs.

We were part of World War II's nuclear weapons programs in an indirect support role, but we have never engaged in the design or manufacture of the weapons themselves. Our first substantial experience with the process of creating heat and then steam in a nuclear system was, however, for a military application. Westinghouse engineers helped design and manufacture the first nuclear propulsion system for the U.S. Navy — the one which powered the famous NAUTILUS when it sailed under the North Polar Ice Cap in 1958. We have remained active in naval propulsion. In fact, we have the contract for the propulsion system of the Navy's new nuclear-powered aircraft carrier.

Using on our Navy propulsion experience, we designed and built the first commercial nuclear steam supply system used to generate electricity. When President Eisenhower threw a remote switch in the

White House in 1957, he initiated a sustained reaction in a Westinghouse reactor at Shippingport, Pennsylvania. The Shippingport plant generated electricity for 25 years. We remain proud that we were part of that project.

There followed a period of high activity in the design and manufacturing of nuclear power plant systems for electrical generation. The accomplishments of the 25 years following Shippingport support our belief that we and General Electric were the world's most successful manufacturers of such systems. The French program today, for instance, is based almost totally on technology which Westinghouse transferred to that Country. Our reactor designs pepper the globe — especially in countries such as Spain, South Korea, Taiwan, Japan, Italy and Sweden.

The rapid expansion of nuclear electricity in the United States and worldwide was fueled by its economic promise; for plants now operating, that promise has been fulfilled many times over. The first wave of nuclear expansion in the United States has now been halted, however, because the economic promise of nuclear electricity here is, at least temporarily, no longer bright. The degree to which the economics of nuclear electricity has changed in the past quarter century is all but astounding. Let me offer you a few figures.

In 1969, a new kilowatt of nuclear capacity was projected to cost $135. Some nuclear plants were brought on line in the early 1970s for costs in this neighborhood. The Westinghouse-designed Robinson plant in South Carolina, for example, was completed at a utility cost of $105 per kilowatt. Today, plants are coming on line which cost $2,000 per kilowatt. And projections are that a plant ordered today for the 1990s, assuming that we do not become more efficient in licensing and building them, would cost nearly $4,000 per kilowatt when it went into service.

These high costs of nuclear power plant construction have been well publicized, as illustrated by recent press coverage of the Shoreham plant in Long Island, New York. Westinghouse had no involvement in Shoreham, so I have no inside knowledge to share. But I can give you a businessman's perspective on what appears to have happened.

In 1968, two applications for construction permits for nuclear electric plants in New York were filed with the Atomic Energy Commission: the Shoreham plant and the Fitzpatrick station on Lake Ontario. Both were for boiling water reactors of basically the same design, and from the same supplier. Both used the same architect-engineering firm for detailed plant design and construction services. Both settled on 820,000 kilowatts as the size. But there, the similarities ended. Seventeen months after the application, a construction permit was issued for Fitzpatrick. For Shoreham, on the other hand, five years were required to obtain the construction permit, much of that time spent in public hearings. Shoreham then slipped ever deeper into a regulatory-judicial quagmire, dealing with continuing escalation of federal regulatory requirements and legal challenges. In that environment, the physical costs of design and construction mounted rapidly, the soaring interest rates of the mid-seventies delivered the second half of a one-two punch.

The Firzpatrick station — spared most of this relentless intervention — went into operation in 1975, and has generated over 30 billion kilowatt-hours since then. The reported capital cost of $419 million, I understand, has already been recovered several times over from savings on the fuel oil the utility would otherwise have had to burn. In stark contrast, Shoreham is only now nearing completion. Its reported costs of $3.2 billion are nearly 8 times those of its sister unit. To pay for its construction costs, the ratepayers will be faced with substantially higher electric bills. Both the public and the utility will pay dearly for the delays which were imposed on Shoreham by those who opposed it. They made the plant not one whit safer than Fitzpatrick; they succeeded only in making it far more costly.

Today, a utility executive who contemplates the role that nuclear energy might play in his system's future power generation must be concerned with this situation, and he must consider the financial risks that come with the political and regulatory uncertainties that attend the construction of nuclear power plants. When faced with such factors, he cannot readily choose the nuclear alternative.

Domestically, regulatory and political uncertainties have helped to bring the market for new nuclear electricity plants to a standstill. A drop in the growth of the demand for electricity is also an important factor. Prior to the Arab oil embargo of 1973 and the subsequent dramatic increase in the price of oil, the demand for electricity was growing at about 7 percent a year. Conservation and economic conditions since then have caused the growth rate to fall to about 2 percent annually, and in 1982, because of the depressed condition of the economy, there was no growth at all. In that climate, many nuclear plants have been either canceled or deferred in recent years. The same is also true for coal plants. Last year, seven nuclear plants were canceled and two were deferred. Two coal plants were canceled and eight were deferred. No new plants of either kind were ordered.

The absence of new orders for nuclear plants, and even the cancellations and deferrals, do not suggest that electricity from nuclear plants is unimportant to the United States, or that it is going away. Far from it. Nuclear electricity has, in the past 25 yuears, become a significant segment of the Nation's energy mix, and it is still growing. As of the end of last year, there were 143 nuclear power plants in some stage of planning, construction, or operation in the United States, with an aggregate power generation capacity of more than 132 million kilowatts — more U.S. nuclear capacity than the total installed electrical generating capacity in all but a handful of nations. Seventy-nine of those plants are licensed to operate.

At the beginning of this year 74 of them were in commercial operation, actually producing electricity for the American consumer, and five were in start-up testing. These 79 plants represent more than sixty million kilowatts of generating capacity. In 1982, nuclear plants were the source of 12.5 percent of America's electric power. In the U.S., nuclear plants are now producing more electricity than our entire country produced 35 years ago. Billions of dollars have been invested in nuclear electricity, and hundreds of thousands of engineers and workers are employed in designing, building, operating and servicing nuclear plants. In 2.3 trillion kilowatt-hours of electricity that have been generated to date from nuclear fission in the United States represent the energy equivalent of one billion tons of coal or 3.5 billion barrels of oil. According to Atomic Industrial Forum surveys, the differential savings in 1981 to the nation's ratepayers from nuclear-generated electricity compared to other major sources amounted to $1.4 billion over coal or $12 billion over oil plants. Nuclear electricity in the United States may not have reached the overwhelming dominance initially predicted for it, but it is a strong and viable segment of our energy infrastructure. Its benefits are measurable. In Chicago, for example, Commonwealth Edison has reported that in 1981, its six largest nuclear plants generated electricity at two cents per kilowatt-hour, while its six largest coal plants cost 4.7 cents per kilowatt-hour.

As new construction has tapered off in the United States, Westinghouse and other manufacturers have redirected our capacities toward service work — the task of keeping the operating plants efficient and modern. In addition, the fueling of nuclear plants is a major undertaking, and an important part of our activities. The fuel business is growing at about 15 percent a year. Today, nuclear activities represent about 10 percent of Westinghouse sales. Nuclear manufacturing, fueling, and service are, for us, an attractive business, and we expect them to remain that way for the foreseeable future.

I sketch this pattern of business activity because it is a view of the nuclear experience in the United States that is not normally emphasized or understood. While all the debating and fence climbing have been going on, nuclear electricity has arrived in substantial force in America. It is here, and I believe it is here to stay. What is open to question, however, is the likelihood of new units being ordered in the United States for the future. There have been no domestic orders since 1978, and frankly we don't expect any for at least five more years. There is a pause. Contrary to public belief, this pause was not caused by Three Mile Island — only exacerbated by it. The nuclear and coal plants ordered prior to the Arab Oil Embargo of 1973 were based on the assumption that the seven percent growth rate of the past would continue. Of course, it has not. Consequently, for the moment, most regions of America have more than adequate electrical capacity on line or coming on line. It is also interesting to note that Japan and other countries are building nuclear plants to displace oil-fired plants on an economic basis. U.S. regulatory practices and indecisiveness have priced nuclear electricity out of the oil substitution market.

Will nuclear electricity stage a comeback in America? Not unless we make drastic changes in the way we regulate and build them. Nuclear electric power plants can be built in America for half, perhaps even one-third, of what they cost today. We need to reduce the time it takes to build them from the 12 to 14 years required in the United States to the 5 to 6 years required to build the same Westinghouse design in Japan, France or Taiwan. Cutting construction time to that degree does not compromise safety. The Japanese have strong feelings about nuclear safety, and the French take risks only in romance.

I mentioned a moment ago that if we signed a contract today to build a nuclear power station in the United States for the 1990s, the project cost of each kilowatt of capacity would be $4,000. Of that amount, $3,000 would be spent on interest and inflation. Only $1,000 would end up working for the consumer. That's what time delay does to the cost of nuclear plants. The same effect has been felt to a lesser extent with coal-fired plants. It almost brings a tear to the eye to recall that in

1969, when each nuclear kilowatt was projected to cost $135, only $20 of that amount was attributed to interest and inflation. I wonder if there isn't a small ethical consideration right there. Some interveners have fought nuclear power by deliberately delaying it in order to make it more costly. But the added cost is paid from the pockets of the consumer, in charges that dig deep into the poor man's pocket. Does the end justify the means?

We know how to cut the time it takes to build nuclear power plants. All we need is common sense regulation, as opposed to the politically timorous regulation which has been the fate of the peaceful atom so far. We might begin by agreeing to build our nuclear plants to a realistic safety standard — one that is carefully formulated and is equivalent to other risks to which the public is exposed. That safety standard should be published and left unchanged unless new evidence suggests that the original risk assumptions were substantially in error. We also ought to agree that once the construction of a plant has been started, we will let the architects, engineers and contractors do their jobs in peace. Today, nuclear plants are often built in an environment of demoralizing chaos, as change follows change, and what was built last month is torn down and replaced today. The morale and productivity of construction workers at nuclear plants has been falling substantially. It's not difficult to understand why.

Nuclear manufacturers and electric utilities do not spend much time praising the Nuclear Regulatory Commission. We think that substantial changes are needed in regulation. But when the NRC takes a step in the right direction, we are happy to offer them all the praise they deserve. On January 10 this year, the NRC took such a step. The Commission voted to accept a series of safety goals for nuclear plants. It would take too long to describe them, and to attempt a brief explanation would not do them justice. But in general, the NRC took the view that the public's exposure to the risk of accident or cancer from nuclear power plants should be no more than one one-thousandth of the risks which are part of everyday living.

The attempt made by the NRC to draw a line on safety is realistic and courageous. They are trying to call "halt" to an otherwise endless and vacuous debate. How safe is safe? Someone has to decide. Then engineers, architects and utilities can do their job, and the public can be served. The availability of established safety standards can also do much to speed up the construction of nuclear plants. The MRC's January 10 decision is a major step in the right direction. We'd like to see many more changes of that kind.

So far, we have kept the focus of remarks on industry's nuclear experience within the United States. Until recently, we thought largely in those terms. Now, the momentum of growth in nuclear electricity has shifted from America to the world around us. The contrast between what is happening here and what is happening all across the world is sharp.

When we look at the international pattern of nuclear development, the first factor to note is the cooperative working relationship between other governments and their nuclear industries. The French and Japanese can build safe nuclear plants in five to six years because they are supported in doing so by governments which understand the value of lower cost homegrown electricity to the quality and stability of a nation's life. It's that simple. Some of those government-industry relationships are a little too close for American tastes. The electrical industry is nationalized in many countries. We don't want that, but we could do a better job if we had a far less adversarial relationship with our own government.

In the Soviet Union, the endless American debate about nuclear energy is taken to be yet another capitalist aberration. Nuclear energy is viewed, according to a report that has come out of the Los Alamos National Laboratory, "not as an energy form which must be used reluctantly, but as well proven boon." There is genuine irony in the fact that totalitarian governments are quicker to realize the potential of a technology such as nuclear energy than are democracies. They can dispense with debate. Frankly, I'd rather have the debate any time, but the price of technological process for a democracy can be high.

The Soviet Union has a vigorous nuclear program. It plans to obtain almost all of its additional electric generating capacity in European Russia for the balance of this century from nuclear plants. The USSR now has 15 million kilowatts of nuclear capacity on line (compared to 60 million in this country). They intend a five-fold increase, to 80 million kilowatts, by 1990, to supply about one-fourth of their electricity. The Soviets have abundant oil and gas reserves in the eastern part of their country, and pipeline projects to pump them westward. They hope to gain an economic advantage by selling the oil and gas to Western Europe rather than burning them in their own power plants. The same pattern holds true for the Soviet satellite nations. Czechoslovakia, for example, put its last fossil-fired plant on line in 1982, and will build no more of them. From now on, all new electric power plants in Czechoslovakia will be nuclear.

Today, France already generates about 40 percent of her electricity from the heat of nuclear fission and is aiming at 60 to 70 percent in the next decade. Finland, Switzerland and Belgium all produce from one-fourth to one-third of their electricity from reactors. Japan plans to produce 30 percent of her electricity from nuclear sources by 1990. Nuclear electricity is an inherent part of the energy mix and plans of Brazil, Spain, China, Taiwan, South Korea, West Germany, the United Kingdom, Sweden and Italy. The 27 countries which today have nuclear electricity programs are operating 281 plants, have 227 under construction and are planning 165 more. The world's total nuclear power program now includes 673 units, capable of producing more than half a billion kilowatts of electricity.

There is no implication intended that the world has embraced nuclear electricity without debate or doubt. The "greens" of West Germany oppose nuclear energy. Sweden, which now gets about 40 percent of its electricity from nuclear reactors, has recently passed a referendum which, although the most pro-nuclear choice on the ballot, would phase out all nuclear power by the year 2010 if no further action is taken. Nonetheless, in general, the acceptance of the nuclear alternative is widespread and growing. Nuclear energy is a dynamic technology around the world. For a manufacturer of nuclear equipment, the lesson is obvious: The immediate future of our business for new units is international. Only 10 days ago, I returned from a trip that literally took me around the world visiting Westinghouse projects and prospective customers.

The worldwide benefits promised by nuclear electricity seem to me enormous, especially for those nations whose people are just stepping firmly into the industrial age, with all that it promises for the common man. When such nations must buy oil to fuel their growing industries, they become dependent on the politics and greed of other nations. Down that road lies towering debt, political instability and strangling limitations on growth . . . all inevitable even if the cost of oil is reduced from its present level. For the emerging industrial nations, the nuclear electrical option is literally a godsend. I know because I have been with them and talked with them . . . and felt the power of their hopes for the future.

An American nuclear manufacturer, then, can be assured of a strong service and fuel business in the United States, and growing market potential for both new units and service around the world. But the business does not come easy. We face 11 nuclear plant suppliers from 7 overseas countries. Perhaps our most difficult competitive factor is the uncertainty felt by nations who regard the United States as an erratic and unpredictable trading partner.

There are many benefits to be gained by keeping American industry strong in the international nuclear electricity markets. The export of a turnkey nuclear plant from the U.S. supplies 60,000 man-years of work for American engineers and production workers. It also provides a continuing business base for manufacturers so that they can finance research and development for simpler, more reliable nuclear plants. Such sales also help the U.S. balance of payments problem. They can also create continuing export business over the lifetime of the plant.

It might seem possible that what has been said so far will be misleading in one important aspect of what it has meant to be a producer of nuclear designs and equipment for the electric utility industry. I refer to the church's specialty — the ethical context. I don't want anyone to conclude from my business-oriented discussion of markets that we have operated outside of the realm of ethics all these years. For quite awhile now, we and many other manufacturers have engaged in nuclear advocacy. We have employed and still employ staffs of intelligent, well educated men and women who examine the assertions of those who attack nuclear electricity, and then try to answer those objections — including ethical objections — in a rational voice. These employes use no bullhorns. They try to fight quietly with facts. They are, of course, biased — as I am. But their bias fllows in great degree from a profound understanding of nuclear technology, and from an equally profound respect for the industry's remarkable safety record.

They understand that a manufacturer of nuclear systems and equipment faces some very difficult ethical questions. It would not do to pretent that we have been able to answer them all — even to our own satisfaction. One begins after awhile to have great sympathy for Pontius Pilate. What is truth? How safe is safe? How clean is clean? One American manufacturer, for example, was recently involved in negotiations to sell nuclear fuel to India, a nation which is widely suspected of having detonated a nuclear weapon. India denies this, but the suspicion is enough to raise an ethical question. At first, the answer might seem easy, especially if you believe that the nuclear fuel used in electric power reactors is just what the weapons maker wants. That does not happen to be the case.

The uranium we insert into nuclear reactors has been enriched to contain some three or four percent of the U-235 isotope — the one that fissions. Just three or four percent. To make a uranium bomb, you must have an enrichment of more than 80 percent. Weapons can, of course, be made from plutonium, which is produced along with many other isotopes and elements in the fuel as the reactor continues to produce power. A commercial nuclear reactor, however, is the most expensive way to produce plutonium, does not provide a good isotope of plutonium for weapon production and, in any event, requires a high level of technical sophistication to safely separate the plutonium from the other residue of spent fuel. Such separation can be accomplished only in a complex, expensive reprocessing facility. A far more direct route to nuclear weapons-grade fuel is the research reactor, which can produce plutonium for the making of bombs much more efficiently. If India did, in fact, build a nuclear bomb and test it, this route — the research reactor — was the one taken. It costs less. It's faster. And It's easier to cover up — except in Iraq. In plain fact, every nation which today possesses nuclear bombs, with the possible exception of India, had those bombs before it began building peaceful reactors to make electricity. China today has nuclear bombs, but has not even one nuclear electric generating station.

Keep this seldom understood but essential distinction in mind as the very serious subject of proliferation is debated. Let me repeat: Nuclear electric reactors are not the road to nuclear bombs. No one has ever taken that road, and no one is likely to try it. But the question lingers. Right now, we at Westinghouse are attempting to persuade our government to allow us to sell the People's Republic of China its first nuclear power stations, which would, of course, have to be fueled. We think it's a good idea — good for the U.S., good for the world, good for China, and good business for us. Our government is hesitating.

Claiming the high moral ground has not proved to be especially effective in such matters. President Carter tried to prevent American plutonium from moving around the globe in an effort to prevent proliferation, and succeeded only in losing any chance to control proliferation. You can't stop the ball game from being played unless you are the only one with a ball.

149

The question of nuclear proliferation would not seem to have any relationship to the business of designing and manufacturing peaceful reactors worldwide — not as long as the great distance between the two technologies is appreciated. But there can be a constructed relationship, one that might limit or even stop expansion in the number of nations developing bombs, and which might, in the process, do much to alleviate the poverty and instability of great sections of the world.

I think that the peaceful reactor should be the reward which the weapons-possessing nations use to bribe — yes, bribe — the non-weapons nations into staying that way. The principles which can underlie such international relationships are well established. They were formulated in President Eisenhower's "Atoms for Peace" program in 1954, and enhanced in the Nuclear Proliferation Treaty which went into effect in 1970. In such agreements, the weapons states would provide technology, enrichment services and reprocessing on spent fuel. They would act as international "bankers," if you will, of nuclear energy credits. The "banking" function, coupled with strict international inspection, will allow the supervising agency to keep track of every fuel rod in the world's inventory. Such a stabled international mechanism, based in reverence for the benefits which nuclear electricity can provide, and in a genuine fear of what proliferation might bring, may in fact be our only hope for significant control of weapons capability. Certainly, any further attempts by the United States to exercise such control unilaterally must inevitably prove counterproductive.

The second most thorny nuclear issue in the minds of most serious people is the question of storing the waste products of nuclear fuel processing and use. Most of the nuclear high level waste which exists today has been produced by weapons programs. But there is a growing amount of similar material accumulating in temporary storage at the nation's nuclear reactor sites. These materials pose a moral question. Is it moral for us to leave behind something that can be dangerous to succeeding generations for 500 years? A good part of the answer will clearly lie in the ability of our technology, which has created the problem, to develop a solution. My company has entered the business of nuclear waste disposal. We are working with the Department of Energy to develop safe methods of handling such wastes, and we are confident that a rational solution will be defined in the near future. There are some people, perhaps a bit overconfident, who feel that it is here already. We know with certainty that nuclear wastes can be converted either to a glass-like substance or to a ceramic, which can then be stored in geologically stable places deep in the Earth's crust. If we take this approach, we will know that we are applying a solution which is completely natural, since the Earth's crust is pocketed with areas of higher than average radioactivity. We also know that the technology of moving such materials cross country is well proven.

Does the disposal of nuclear wastes present us with a question which has no ethically affirmative answer? I don't think so, but once again, I would not claim that the question is an easy one. Radioactivity, in general, is one of the most perplexing of the questions which will add interest to your discussions. I can only suggest that in the end, you may choose to draw a safety line somewhere this side of zero radioactivity. But where is that line? We think we have reasonable answers to that question, and in practice we have been extremely conservative in our designs, just as utilities have been extremely conservative in their operations. But the question is difficult because it cannot be answered with a simple "yes" or "no," not in a universe characterized by radioactivity of all kinds and dimensions. The sharply pointed questions are: How much? What kind? How often?

I think it's fair to note, in summation, that the nuclear industry — encompassing the manufacturers, architects, consulting engineers and utilities of America — has a right to suggest that it has never done its job in an ethical vacuum. The technical people who serve at the heart of the industry have always understood its dangers. If at first they overestimated its benefits, they have never, to my knowledge, neglected its risks. If you have the interest, or find the time, to plunge into the engineering details of a typical American reactor, you will find safety system stacked upon safety system. Where safety is involved, redundancy and even double redundancy is the rule, and has been the rule since Shippingport. It was the cumulative effect of hundreds of such highly conservative safety decisions which made the Three Mile Island reactor stand up to events which might have overwhelmed it. Three Mile Island is seen by most people as testimony to the dangers of the nuclear age. Inside the industry, there is another view. It is seen as a monument to the responsibility of the thousands of engineers and regulators who have contributed to modern reactor design. The reactor was tougher than anyone would have predicted. I submit that ethical people made it that way.

To this day, after a quarter of a century of the nuclear age, not one person has died as the result of a nuclear-related accident at a commercial nuclear power plant. Not one. In terms of ethical behavior, this is a unique attainment. I am proud to be part of the industry which has accomplished it.

Chapter 5

Issues of Equity
and Ethics in
Energy Production

Frederick S. Carney

Editorial Preface

The aim of this Chapter is to set forth the major moral notions that are relevant to thinking ethically about nuclear power and its alternatives, as well as to employing these moral notions, together with pertinent factual information, in arriving at reasonable conclusions about the role of nuclear power in meeting energy needs both at home and abroad. Three types of moral notions are identified and applied to energy matters: values, obligations, and virtues.

The discussion of values centers initially around human safety, and then the maintenance *of a healthy economy (or, in most of the Third World, the* development *of a healthy economy). Both values are very important, but neither is absolute.*

The prime obligation notion under consideration is that of beneficence. In energy matters this points to the duty to help those in need (both in our society and

153

in the Third World) and the duty to restrain, by morally justifiable means, the proliferation of nuclear weapons and to work toward their overall reduction.

The notion of virtue is applied both to persons and to communities and nations. The chief virtues to be discussed are integrity and faith. Integrity is relevant in energy matters in assessing facts, setting forth arguments, and deciding among nuclear and other energy alternatives. Faith pertains to how we shall live in a world that, with the best of human efforts, still contains risks of many sorts.

A position of contingent support for nuclear power is reached in the presentation. At the same time, it is hoped that the moral analysis provided will be of use both to supporters and to opponents of nuclear power in thinking ethically about energy matters.

Though I am not a Catholic, I have long appreciated the rich theological and ethical tradition of the Catholic Church and I give thanks to God for the moral leadership her bishops provide our society at a very difficult time in its history. A few years ago, H. L. Mencken wrote, "for every human problem there is a neat, plain solution, and it is always wrong." So it is with the moral problem of nuclear energy, all neat, plain solutions to it, whether pro-nuclear or anti-nuclear, turn out, when carefully examined, to be wrong, for they all involve a naive simplicity that fails to address the complex, factual and ethical dimensions of energy production and distribution.

Now this kind of situation, however, is certainly not new to Catholic Bishops. They have had to resist, over the years, other oversimplified solutions to complex moral problems such as that abortion is a neat and plain solution to the problem of inconvenient pregnancies, or that a hedonistic and self-centered life-style is a neat and plain solution to the search for human fulfillment. Solutions that bishops, in the exercise of their pastoral responsibilities, have rightly declared to be wrong. So, instead of offering at this time yet another neat and plain solution, I want to set forth some major moral notions that are relevant, I believe, to thinking ethically about nuclear energy, and I intend to employ these moral notions together with pertinent factual information, in proposing some conclusions about the role and limits of nuclear power in meeting energy needs both at home and abroad.

These moral notions are not temporary facts or of dubious standing, rather they are drawn deeply from within the moral tradition of the

154

west, both religious and secular, and to which tradition the Catholic community throughout time has made especially important contributions. These moral notions are all a part of what Matthew Arnold once called the best that has been thought and said in the world. Now, what are these moral notions? There are three types of them. First, there are values which respond to the question — what things or states of affairs are important and which ones are more important than others? Second, there are duties or obligations which respond to the question — what ought to be done or what ought not to be done? And third, there are virtues which respond to the question — what qualities of a human person or of a human society are truly worthy of praise and cultivation?

I shall employ two moral notions from each of these three types, six moral notions in all, and discuss with you their relevance to the moral assessment of nuclear energy. In so doing, I shall also set forth a position of qualified support for nuclear energy. I am well aware that some of you may disagree with this position, nevertheless, it is my hope that what I have to say to you may still be useful to you in thinking ethically about nuclear energy and what it means to take a moral position, whether for or against, the deployment of nuclear power in the production of electricity. One of the two values I now want to examine is human safety, for human safety is and ought to be a major concern in the moral assessment of nuclear energy. More precisely, we want to know how safe nuclear reactors and their fuel cycles are, because we attribute considerable importance or value to human safety. But what kind of value is human safety? Surely, it is not an intrinsic value or what St. Thomas Aquinas called a final end, that is, some state of affairs like love of God, or human happiness or human excellence, that is good in itself and not merely good as a means to some other value, for we are quite prepared to relinquish safety, or risk losing it, under some circumstances, for the sake of freedom, or in mountain climbing for the sake of achievement. Thus, safety is not intrinsically worthwhile in itself, rather we value it because of other values that safety serves. Therefore, it is an instrumental value.

But to what is safety instrumental? What values does human safety serve for the sake of which we rightly esteem it? I think you will agree that the most important value safety serves is the intrinsic value of human life. The safety of nuclear reactors is of concern to us because we attach great value to human lives that might be lost or harmed by them if they are not properly designed and operated. If you have any doubt about the commitment of our society to human life as intrinsically valuable, consider what happens when coal miners are trapped underneath the ground in a mine disaster. Rescuers undergo considerable risk to their own safety and very expensive procedures are often employed in the effort to save them. Or reflect for a moment on the deep concern of people throughout the western world a few years ago for the lives of American citizens being held hostage in Iran. Nevertheless, we still need to inquire whether either the instrumental value of safety, or the intrinsic value of human life is an absolute value. Is either of them a value to which we give preference over every other value? Is either a value for the sake of which we consider it proper to sacrifice any other value that comes into conflict with it? The answer is clearly no. And the evidence that supports the denial of any absolute character to the value of safety or even human life is very strong.

Let me suggest some examples. Consider airplane travel. We can reasonably project, on the basis of recent experience, that at least a thousand lives will be lost this year from airplane accidents on scheduled airlines throughout the world, and considerably more if accidents in general aviations are also included in our projections. Do we, therefore, close down airplane travel in order to absolutize the saving of human lives? The answer is obviously no. And the reason is that we also value other goods that airplane travel makes possible, including a more productive economy, the nourishment of family ties and friendship, and opportunities to expand our first-hand experience of the world by personally visiting places of our choice. Moreover, consider cigarette smoking. We know that we could save thousands of lives every year if we prohibited the production and sale of cigarettes in our society, but we do not do so, because we also believe the value of human autonomy, the opportunity of persons to make their own decisions and figure out their own destinies. We know that thousands of lives are now lost in highway accidents that could be prevented if we spent considerably more money on the design and construction of highways than we now do. Why do we not do so? Because we are also concerned with other values that make competing claims upon our finite resources, including education, both public and private, and we are unwilling to make absolute the saving of lives on our highways at the cost of the impoverishment of human minds in our schools.

Let us now apply this ethical analysis to the nuclear generation of electricity. Obviously, our strong commitment to the instrumental value for human society and the intrinsic value of human life should lead us to do all that we reasonably can to make our production of electricity, whether by nuclear or other means, as safe as reasonably possible. But we should also ask what other values are present in the production and distribution of energy. There is at least one other value that impresses me as being of very considerable importance, and that is the health of our economy. It, too, like safety, is an instrumental value, not finally important in itself, but important as a means to serve other values, especially intrinsic ones. There are, I think, two intrinsic values for which a healthy economy can be understood to be essential. One of these is human freedom. Without the good-functioning of industrial and technological base, and other components of a healthy economy, who would doubt that our chances of our defending and nourishing human freedom, not only for ourselves but for other nations as well, would be small indeed? To the extent that we value human freedom, and I think that we value it very highly, it is instrumentally important to take all necessary steps to see that nothing necessary to the good functioning of our society is missing. Here, of course, we have especially in mind adequate sources of electricity at reasonable prices.

The second intrinsic value of major relevance to our analysis is the activity of helping those in need, whether at home or abroad. And that, too, is an intrinsic value. Whatever measures we may want to take in behalf of improving the welfare of the disadvantaged in our community and in the world at large, depends to a very considerable extent upon the maintenance and nourishment of a healthy economy. So here again we are necessarily concerned with adequate electricity supply at reasonable prices in order to support our industrial and technological base.

So now we have two instrumental values, the one of human safety, and the other of a healthy economy. Both of them serve important intrinsic values, the one serves human life, the other serves human freedom and service to others. Surely, neither should be absolute ties at the expense of the other. Some trade-offs need to be worked out between them when they conflict, as we already do when values conflict in airplane travel, in cigarette smoking and in highway construction. Furthermore, whenever an improvement can be brought about in one of these areas without loss to the other value, this is a happy choice that we should be quite ready to accept. Thus, when improvements in safety can be effected in energy production without impairing the economy, or when improvements in the economy can be realized without increasing the safety risk of energy production, it is obviously in keeping with our deepest value commitments to make them.

Now, let me apply this value analysis to the question of nuclear energy directly. There would seem to be five energy sources for the production of electricity in the next twenty years, oil, natural gas, coal, nuclear and hydro. I rule out solar electricity from this group on the basis that presently known technologies and projected cost make it highly unlikely that it can produce more than one or two percent of the electricity used in any nation in the world by the year 2000, although some increased use of direct solar heating for space and water may displace another one or two percent of electricity usage, in some places. But of these five *major* sources for electricity production, the prospects of significant increase of hydroelectricity at competitive costs seem very limited in the United States, although the prospects are considerably brighter in some countries such as Egypt and Pakistan.

Furthermore, we are already phasing out natural gas for electricity production because of the limited availability and greater usefulness for other purposes — that is, of natural gas for other purposes. And it will not be too long before the same situation will prevail for oil. This leaves coal and nuclear as the major sources of energy for any growth that is to occur in electricity consumption and for needed replacement, over time, of existing generating facilities. So far as safety is concerned, nuclear energy has a far better record than coal. Every year thousands of persons lose their lives in America alone as a result of the burning of coal for electricity production. Yet, not a single person has yet lost his life from the operation of a nuclear reactor devoted to electricity production in America. It is true that some persons have lost their lives in the mining of uranium, but even here the number is far less per unit of electricity produced than in coal mining.

Most of the concern today about the safety of nuclear energy centers around the question, "What if some bad thing 'X' were to happen?", rather than the determination of what, in fact, has been our experience with nuclear power. About this I shall have more to say later. The other issue, the one that bears especially upon the value of a healthy economy, is cost. Nuclear has considerably heavier front end construction cost than does coal, but a much lower operating cost over the years. As a result, the very high interest rates of recent years have had a more devastating effect upon the economics of new nuclear construction than upon new coal-using construction. Yet, with interest rates beginning to come down, this situation may well be changing quite considerably. There are at the same time very lengthy periods of construction, because of management problems and regulatory delays, which seriously effect the front end cost, and thus effect the economic competitiveness of nuclear energy by comparison with coal. There are reasons to believe that this situation is now undergoing some improvement for nuclear energy.

Now, if we are genuinely concerned for the maintenance of a healthy economy, in order to serve the intrinsic values of human freedom and service to others, we shall want to secure our electricity at the most reasonable rates that we can. On the question of cost, there should be no bias, either in favor of nuclear energy or against it. We should let the marketplace work, subject only to reasonable safety standards for both nuclear and coal. If cost factors in the next twenty years favor coal, then on this score coal should have the advantage. If, however, cost factors turn somewhat in favor of nuclear, then nuclear should have the advantage. Nevertheless, there may be benefits of maintaining a viable program in both areas, provided their cost is not too far apart, in order to diversify our electricity production, and thereby reduce our vulnerability if unforseen negative effects become apparent in either of them.

Thus, from a viewpoint of a value analysis there seems no reason to count nuclear power out of our energy plans for electricity production, provided, of course, that my factual analysis is substantially correct. Indeed, there would seem to be strong reasons from the standpoint of safety for counting it in, and possible developments in the area of cost as they effect the national economy in general, to consider nuclear energy is a quite viable moral option. Nevertheless, such a value analysis is not the entire territory to be addressed under the rubric of issues of equity and ethics. There is also the realm of obligation or duties to which I now turn. You will recall that this realm pertains to actions that morally are to be done or morally ought not to be done, as distinguished from what things or states of affairs are important and which are more important than others in the value realm that we have thus far been discussing.

The two duties I should like to focus attention upon are those of beneficence and non maleficence; that is, the obligations to do good to others and not to do evil to them. And although I could employ these two notions in energy matters domestically, it is to the international realm that I would like to turn now in discussing them. Ever since the

Atoms for Peace Program was launched by President Eisenhower in the 1950's, we in the United States have understood ourselves to have a moral duty to help other nations, especially Third World ones, to receive some of the benefits of nuclear energy for peaceful purposes. Some of these benefits are, of course, medical, but others were envisaged as pertaining to electricity production, a vitally needed commodity in much of the Third World, if standards of living there are to be raised.

Thus we assumed, quite rightly I think, a national duty of beneficence. At the same time we assumed another commitment, which became more fully and specifically developed in the non-proliferation treaty of 1970. This commitment pertains to the prevention of the spread of nuclear weapons and to negotiations concerning the reduction where they already existed. It can be understood, I believe, as a duty of non-maleficence. That is, a duty not to do evil, and it is a duty we attempted to get other nations to share with us. Thus, for example, we agreed to provide Third World nations low-enriched uranium for electricity producing and research reactors, provided the recipient nations agreed to forego the reprocessing of this uranium to produce weapons-grade fuel.

Thus, we were rightfully attempting to prevent or at least restrain *horizontal* proliferation of nuclear weapons; that is, a proliferation of increasin the number of nations possessing nuclear weapons. But what we did not take with sufficient seriousness was the other part of this duty of non-maleficence. That is, the implied commitment to reduce *vertical* proliferation; the increase of nuclear weapons and of their destructiveness on the part of nations who already possess them. Now some Third World nations viewed this situation as decidedly unfair and inherently discriminatory against them, and refused to sign the non-proliferation treaty, for on the one hand they are required by it to forego nuclear weapons altogether, while certain other nations, including the United States, are required by it only to negotiate about the reduction of their own stockpiles. On the other hand, the period of such negotiations has actually witnessed a substantial increase in vertical proliferation, which has further upset the world-wide power balance between "have" and "have-not" nations in nuclear weapons.

Now this problem led to an unfortunate series of events centering around India's Tarapor reactor, which supplies a very large part of the electricity for Bombay, the second largest city in India. The United States agreed in 1963 to provide India's Tarapor reactor with low-enriched uranium fuel for its operation for thirty years, that is, until 1993, provided India agreed to forego any proliferation potentialities from this nuclear installation, and to put the entire installation at Tarapor under international inspection. India agreed to do so, and until the United States broke its commitment, faithfully carried out its side of the agreement. But in the later 1970's the United States insisted that India place not only the Tarapor reactor, but all of its nuclear facilities, under international inspection. Failing to do so, the United States would deny the low enriched fuel necessary to the operation of this important source of electricity for the city of Bombay.

The bearing in any relationship now of these two moral principles of beneficence and non-maleficence in this situation are interesting indeed. Acting from the principle of beneficence the United States set out to help India obtain a higher level of electricity production for the benefit of a nation that badly needs to improve its standard of living, but we became more obsessed over time with the relatively minor risk of a Third World nation having one or two small nuclear weapons than we were with the immensely more important issues involved in our own continuing vertical proliferation, together with that of Russia. We sought to remove the mote from our neighbor's eye without considering the beam in our own, and we thus broke our commitment to India, which is a kind of maleficence in itself. One of the results has been that we have not really done much thereby to restrain horizontal proliferation. Indeed, we may have advanced it, for we have thus served notice that we are an unreliable source of nuclear fuel for electricity production, and have thus given occasion to India and other Third World nations that they had better provide for their own fuel cycle facilities if they can manage to do so, rather than rely on us. And to this extent we have increased the potentiality at least of horizontal proliferation in the Third World. There is much more to be said about that, I am sure.

Now I turn finally to the realm of virtues in the ethical analysis of nuclear energy. By virtues I mean the qualities of both persons and societies that are worthy of praise and cultivation, for instance, integrity. By integrity I have in mind the intellectual honesty in energy matters, particularly in assessing facts, setting forth arguments, and choosing among nuclear and other energy alternatives. One of the curious things that has developed in energy debates in the last ten years in North America and Western Europe is what I call value-determined

161

facts, that is, the determination of the facts of the matter under discussion by one's prior commitment to values.

Now this is a very different situation from the intellectual milieu in which I was raised, for there and then one believed the facts could be commonly agreed upon independently of a person's values, and were epistemologically "hard." On the other hand, values were understood to vary somewhat from person to person, and were considered to be epistemologically "soft"; indeed, as varying, in terms of the values held by their analyzer, yet such is now all too often the situation.

Two areas in which this especially occurs in energy matters is in estimates about the possible risk of low level radiation and in predictions about future electricity consumption, or the relative contributions of various energy sources, nuclear, coal, solar, etc. in meeting future electricity needs. It is important about both of these kinds of statistical exercises to notice that the facts that one brings forth, and claims to be objectively valid, often depend to a very considerable degree upon the assumptions one begins with; and these assumptions are usually selective in keeping with what side of the fence one is on in the energy debate. The same is often true of arguments made on the basis of facts. Arguments are chosen to support one's predetermined position and are too often not applied objectively across the board. Now this represents, I think, some lack of integrity wherever it is found. I simply want to call this to your attention at this time and observe that public discourse among those who disagree about nuclear and other matters would be considerably enhanced by some agreement about the facts, which in itself requires a reasonable degree of integrity.

Now the final notion that I wish to discuss, a notion of virtue (and its application to nuclear energy) — is the notion of faith as trust. We obviously live in a world of considerable risk, not merely in the question of energy production or electricity production, but also in other arenas as well, such as some others I've mentioned (such as airplane travel, etc.). It is possible to respond to those risks in two ways. Either we can look realistically at the nature of the risks and attempt to reduce or remove them where possible, and to live with those that we cannot, and to maintain a certain sense of inner freedom in the face of a world that does contain risk; that is, to live in faith; or we can do what Robert DuPont once referred to in a study he made for the Media Institute, that is, we can engage in phobic thinking, or phobias. DuPont was asked by the Media Institute in Washington (which is supported by the major

162

media in America) to make a study of the combined news broadcasting and commentary on the major networks for the 13 weeks immediately following the incident at Three Mile Island; all of the commentary and news broadcasting that pertained to it.

Robert DuPont is a psychiatrist, and a very good one, and after studying the combined records of what was said to the American people during this time, he came to the conclusion that the media were basically propagating phobia. He defined phobia as always asking the question — "What if something happens," rather than what is the case, and he used this in an analogous situation of a person who, every time he or she gets into an airplane, is constantly preoccupied with the question: "What if there should be an accident?". Of course, there is always the possibility of an accident, but ordinarily we do not allow this to paralyze us, because we look rather realistically at the facts — and the percentage of risk is very small. But in phobic thinking one loses one's freedom; phobic thinking is the opposite, basically, of true faith as trust, which contains, when properly exercised, a very considerable amount of inner freedom.

I had the pleasure a couple weeks ago of engaging in a debate at the LaFarge Institute in New York City with Dr. Jim Harding, who is a representative of Friends of the Earth in America. The subject was Nuclear Power. One of the men in the seminar was Monsignor George Lentoka, the Catholic pastor of the Church of Seven Sorrows in Middletown, PA, the community closest to the Three Mile Island reactors. I was amazed to hear some of the things he had to say about the experience of his own community during that accident. He observed that one of the things that kept him (and as a consequence, to a large degree, many of his people), calm during the events that occurred, was that a member of his Church was a superintendent at the facility. He was able to consult from time to time with this man, and also to observe that this man decided, without any particular pressure or feeling of short-changing his family, simply to leave his family in place, near the reactor. As a result, he contended that the response of the Catholic community, which constituted about half of the population of Middletown, was rather calm during this. He also observed that the common judgement in his own Church at this time was that it was not the nuclear energy that lost credibility during that accident; it was the Media. And the basic reason is the same one Dr. Robert DuPont gives, that the Media engaged in high-level phobic thinking, yet people on the scene, who had lived there a considerable part of their lives, were able to make adjustments to the whole nuclear incident in ways that others a further distance away (such as ourselves), did not have available to us.

I want to close with a modification of a prayer that you have heard many times, here applied to nuclear power or any kind of situation in which we find ourselves at some risk, nuclear power, coal generation of electricity, or airplane travel. "God, give us the courage and determination to remove those risks that can be removed, the faith and the trust to live with those risks that cannot be removed, and the wisdom to know the one from the other."

Chapter 6

Pastoral Concerns Regarding Nuclear Energy

This chapter presents the morning and afternoon plenary discussions between the bishops attending the workshop and the speakers of the day on nuclear technology, and Fr. Benedict Ashley, O.P., as theological resource. The dialogue has been edited slightly for brevity's sake from tape recordings of the proceedings.

Morning Discussion,
February 1, 1983

Question 1: Surely we can agree that a barrage of statistics from one side or another can be very confusing. I get a bit apprehensive, like people quoting scripture at me. You can prove anything with selective quotes. My question really could be addressed to both of you, Dr. Ahearne or Zebroski. For instance, Dr. Ahearne, you emphasized at some length the evaluation of various groups — college students, housewives, and so on. Are the fears warranted or are they unwarranted? If they are unwarranted then the approach would be one of education. So, it is not just because people, maybe in their ignorance, are fearful of all these major risks that are or might be, but the question should be, what really are the risks? And then, Dr. Zebroski, along those lines, the statistics you were citing pertain more to the various incidents of risk associated with the various technologies. So many people may be hurt in this industry, and so many peoples' health and lives are endangered in another as compared to those working in nuclear plants. But what is the quality or the enormity of the risk? One accident in a nuclear situation could add up to all the rest. So the question: what is the worst thing that can happen? The man on the street would say, "well, even if you say that's only going to happen once in a hundred years or a thousand years, that is still too much to risk. Is the question clear enough?

(Ahearne) One of the biggest disadvantages of nuclear power is that people are very much afraid. But should they be afraid? That is a question of one's judgment of risk. Risk in quantitative terms is a combination; it is the *probability* of the event happening times the *consequences* of it happening. There is a considerable amount of radioactivity inside a nuclear reactor, and if all of it were to get out, then the consequences could be very severe, many deaths possible. The fundamental question is, how probable is that event? It is very, very unlikely. People like Zebroski, myself and others in the industry are working diligently to reduce that probability. One of the critical issues of nuclear power is whether people are willing to live with such a risk. Can people agree that although a full scale nuclear accident could be a catastrophe, the probability of it occurring is so low they are willing to accept that risk? Much of the nuclear power debate is really a debate about that issue even though it may not be always clearly defined.

(Zebroski) The real issue is not whether you need to select between a risk and zero risk, but rather which risks do you tolerate. We have killed, for example, several hundred people at a time in a hotel fire, but we don't ban hotels. We can kill 400 people at a time in an aircraft accident but we don't ban aircraft. We have killed 2600 people at one time in a dam accident in Italy, but we don't ban dams. The problem is that we have not been even-handed in our view of risk, and I believe this attitude is a disease of affluence. We have lived for 20 years with those who promised us the unattainable: a risk-free, park-like society.

Question 2: But, pardon me, it is the risk of what?
(Zebroski) This is one issue on which Commissioner Ahearne and I disagree scientifically. I have worked in the nuclear energy field for 30

years, and I am now firmly convinced that the so-called worst-case accident has been over estimated by a factor of between 10 and 1,000. Some of the Nuclear Regulatory Commission staff as well as those in Germany and Britain are beginning to have the conviction, namely, that the worst-case accident, the one-in-a-billion event, may even be physically impossible as long as you have water in the system. One can overlay, in addition, another one-in-a-million chance that there is no water and nobody ever brings it. But now one is arriving at probability levels which are considerably smaller than the likelihood of a meteorite falling on one's head.

Question 3: Are we sufficiently knowledgeable to measure realistically the risk involved in nuclear production? For example, are we able to measure the anticipated radioactive fallout when we have an accident like the Three Mile Island? I understand that if they had not shut down the nuclear reactors, In one more hour the reactor itself would have been melted down and only the Lord knows what would have happened subsequently. Secondly, are we that well educated in the use of nuclear power that we are able to contain a serious accident, box it in, as you suggested that we are able to do? We heard this morning, for example, that it takes 25,000 years for a uranium rod to be completely rendered innocuous. Can you respond to some of those concerns?

(Zebroski) There are two questions, the first one is the perception of risk and Three Mile Island. I happen to be co-director of the team that was called to the plant immediately after the accident to help address just that kind of question. We had about 100 of the country's leading technical people, including the present Chairman of the Nuclear Regulatory Commission, working on this team for that month. In order to get to the condition many people fear, it would be necessary to overlay what actually happened with the further assumption that no one did anything correctly for another 100 hours before you would have radioactivity in anyway threatening the *containment*. Then, you would have to assume further that no one would bring water in by any means — and there were many means for bringing water into the system *if* the installed systems did not work. But they did work when the installed systems were turned on. But even *if* the installed systems failed (which they had not) and further that you could not bring water in (which you could, even with a fire engine), and that no one did anything correctly for hundreds of hours, even then the result is only to make the mess

167

inside the reactor worse. The environment is still not threatened. Only after a good many hundreds of hours would there be the potential for melting through the concrete and hitting bedrock with the possibility of eventually contaminating the ground water.

To your second question, I will get anecdotal. God, if you will ran a number of nuclear reactors in the early geological history of this planet. There are at least four such reactors known in Africa. These reactors ran for some 100,000 years and we now know that there were probably about 5 tons of fission products and perhaps a ton of plutonium. The residues — long since decayed — are still largely unmoved from where they were and those which did move did not move every far. Here is an example, without safeguards, without special engineering, of the natural geological structures and forces taking care of nuclear waste for millions of years. To encapsulate fission products (and plutonium if necessary) into suitable canisters, to bury them 2,000 feet under ground, and to pick a site which is geologically stable without any water moving, I think is a relatively straightforward procedure that can be done. The difficulty is that we have not developed the institutional process to make it happen at a reasonable rate, as Professor Deutch has said.

(*Ahearne*) There is one additional comment I would like to make relative to the continuing hazards of radioactivity. When we talk about 25,000 years for uranium to still be hazardous, one ought to put that fact into perspective. There are many chemical wastes which are "forever" hazardous; yet, it eventually decays away. However, there are many chemical wastes which never change their form, they always remain hazardous.

Question 4: When Professor Deutch spoke, he said that the Soviet Union seemed to be more responsible regarding nuclear proliferation and careful in its regulations of nuclear materials especially to those sold to unstable governments. It seemed that Dr. Zebroski disagreed very clearly on that point. We would like him to explain the nature of his disagreement.

(*Zebroski*) The reason I was shaking my head at Professor Deutch's comments was that I was involved in discussions in India and Brazil and as well as in several other countries during the late 50s and early 60s. The Russians were always there pushing their approach, and generally they were not commercially successful; they did not offer suitable financial terms and they wanted some political domination as a result of any deal. For example, they really wanted to staff the nuclear plant with their advisors as a condition of the sale. The Soviets offered India a Breeder reactor in 1961 or 62, after having built one in the Soviet Union. I think they have refrained from aggressive selling largely because they are not really commercially adept. Most nuclear projects that have been sold by either the United States, France, Germany, England have been multi-national cooperative projects: parts from here, parts from there. In most cases the country receiving the reactor wants parts to be made domestically as much as possible. I think the Soviet Union, at least until recently, has had much more difficulty because they have not had enough productive capacity for their own industry.

(Ahearne) I cannot speak of the years that Dr. Zebroski is talking about, but certainly in the late 1960s and the 1970s the Soviet Union has been a very strong supporter of linking safeguards to any of its sales. I would agree with John Deutch that — to the extent that I'm familiar with and that is during this last 10 years primarily — the Soviet Union has been a consistent supporter of tight safeguards for what it sells. It may well be that it does not see much of an opportunity for economic sales outside the Soviet Union, but for whatever reason (I think its safe to say) it is the only area in international negotiations of which I know where the Soviet Union is not only on the same side as we are but in many cases slightly ahead of us.

Question 5: Given the information that you gave us this morning regarding the escalating cost of energy not only the present sources of energy, but even the future ones, what would be recommended for the Third World where the resources, financial research and otherwise, are so limited? What is being done at the international level to assure a more equitable distribution of energy around the world?

(Zebroski) That is really an extremely difficult question because as seen by many Third World people, there is a slowness of the Western world in formulating an adequate energy policy. The U.S. has a *de facto* energy policy, namely, to burn more oil. In principle, we had the opportunities in the mid-60s to make policies which would have largely eliminated oil imports. One administration actually had something called Project Independence which was laughed out of court. To advocate the idea that one pays up front for an improvement to be gained

only 5, or 10, or 15 years later takes a rare kind of moral and political leadership.

(Ahearne) The energy technology into which the United States puts most of its effort, tends to be one that can be successfully developed in the U.S.; these are usually high technology, high cost. Such technologies are readily transferable to the underdeveloped areas. To whatever extent we are developing technologies that are transferable, it is, I think because industry may see there the development of a market. As far as the federal government is concerned, it has not been doing much in that area and, in fact, in the last two years it has done much less than it had over the previous years.

(Zebroski) There is one technical point to be noted, namely that there is a great effort in the Western world and especially in this country to make the reasonable cost options work on a smaller scale. Right now, all the good cost options are very large scale, namely, these thousand megawatt [million] plants we talk about. I think there is a reasonable hope that plants which are considerably smaller can be made which benefit from the lessons learned from nearly 5,000 unit years of reactor building and operation. Smaller, less expensive coal plants have been built; there is hope with new power fuel cells. Hence the idea of smaller units, which is really what most of the developing world needs, is a very important and useful approach to the needs of most nations of the world.

Question 6: Our group would like to raise two questions: 1) How much of the decision-making involved in nuclear policy and nuclear development is controlled by financial institutions and is related to the international and political scene? 2) While we certainly appreciated the effort to present the disadvantages and the advantages of nuclear energy, in the light of some of the pre-workshop material sent to us, was the position of the Union of Concerned Scientists [UCS] adequately represented this morning?

(Ahearne) As far as the first question is concerned, I speak as a member of the organization of our Federal Government which has the responsibility of developing suitable regulations. I have been on the Commission for 4½ years and was Chairman of the Commission for about 16 months. Hence I can assert without any doubt that I never received, much less felt, any pressure from any financial institution as to which way I ought to decide on any issue. As a matter of fact, the only significant pressures I ever experienced were from the Congress and from

the public interest groups. I have received essentially no pressure from industry either.

The second question is very difficult to answer because you would really need to ask the UCS people as to what is their position. I quoted from and my paper give larger quotes, from the UCS position. For example, the representative from the National Audubon Society, who testified at Indian Point, was really testifying on behalf of the Union of Concerned Scientists. But I did try, I believe, to present the UCS's principle arguments. However, as I pointed out earlier, I did not attempt to give the kind of debater's points which a dedicated opponent would make.

Question 7: Two questions surfaced in our group: 1) Why is it that the peaceful use of nuclear energy receives such distortions in the media with regards to its dangers, risks and fears, and what can be done to present nuclear energy more positively to people? 2) The second question is really connected with last night's point that the need for the use of nuclear energy is based upon the style of our consumer society; is, then, nuclear energy really needed?

(Zebroski) With regards to the question of whether nuclear energy is really needed, one can look at the studies of how do we get from here to the next century with an additional four billion people to feed and clothe. The items necessary for life are made from raw materials and energy. If you have more energy you can use lower grade raw materials. Many people believe that it is necessary. If ongoing projects are completed in the 90s, this will supply energy equivalent to 10 million barrels of oil per day. That is a substantial reduction in the international pressure and competition for oil. We have not mentioned the biggest risk and one which we often ignore because we do not know how to calculate it: the risk of war and specifically a war resulting from competition over resources, including oil. To reduce that pressure — if I were to do a statistical calculation on that, I would get a fair size probability of a very large saving in lives by reducing the likelihood of war. So, I believe that is really the dominant question of this meeting.

Regarding the media question, I can only speculate, but I can observe, as other people already have, that nearly 90% of the print media writers are of the generation which is generally against technology of any kind. They are the Shumacher generation, you might say, which Mr. Derrick reflected: small is beautiful, so let us deindustrialize the country. We have not weighed the risks of de-industrializing the country. For speakers in the electronic media, that same poll showed that higher than 95% were of that generation, so if you see something in that media which is just terribly unfactual, and some of the most famous commentators on television have made such statements, it is impossible to get equal time to set the record straight. In a large part of the media there is really a monopoly on one side of this debate, and I do not know how to correct it.

Question 8: I must raise a general question in our continued discussion, and one I think to be very important. Are we being asked to accept some rather broad assumptions as the preface of our discussion? I feel that we are somewhat boxed in by assumptions which leave me uncomfortable. Let me illustrate by an example (and this is no reflection on the Deutch lecture which I found interesting): the title of that lecture states, "World Nuclear Energy Assessment," but in the whole presentation I found the world equated generally with the industrialized nations. We are then presented not with what I consider a world assessment but the classic argument in favor of the mega energy project. When the question of biomass and its use was raised it was then summarily dismissed as not economically feasible. But in fact, there are other countries in the world presently using biomass very adequately to provide for the needs of millions of people, and China is only one illustration. While I have not read that broadly in the field, I find it hard to accept when we are told this is not economically feasible while we know it is already being done.

This causes me to raise a serious question as to whether these decisions, the so-called *economic* decisions, are not really *political* decisions. Is it that the decision makers are saying, we don't want to do it that way, so we are going to tell you that our interpretation (the mega energy project which we have selected for political reasons) is the only model within which we can discuss this matter? For me that is a serious question which confronts our whole seminar. I am raising it for possible future consideration. Are we really opening up the debate and clarifying the assumptions or are we being asked to discuss within pre-determined models?

(Zebroski) In my written paper I address the issue of biomass at some length with somewhat the same viewpoint that you expressed. It has an important resource niche and an important economic niche. One

of the tragedies of the polarization which marks the "nuclear debate" is the failure to recognize that no one solution has to solve all problems in order to be good. One does not have to prove that biomass can displace all coal, oil and nuclear in order to make it worthwhile; where one needs it, one should use it. Yet, if one were seeking to generate a thousand kilowatts of electricity by burning biomass you would find it an extremely expensive and dirty, high-waste and polluting operation. So it does not fill that resource niche.

We have really missed one other dimension in all these discussions in which, I think, is to be found the essence of the answer to your question: the temporal in the time sense, not in the secular sense: the time it takes for change to take place in a community. Because Society is accustomed to doing things in a certain way, although one might find an alternative which is good, feasible and even economic, even with good will and the best of financing, and a healthy economy it would take a long time to replace an institution which is already very big. For example, if somebody came up tomorrow and said I can give you an automobile engine which is twice as efficient, it would take some time for a fleet of a hundred thousand or a hundred million vehicles in this country to be replaced, even with good will and sound economics. So, I think the opposition (or the delay) to biomass is that it is like many of the other alternative energy options, it gives you the privilege of prepaying your energy bill a few years; it is capital intensive upfront, except on a small scale.

(Ahearne) I would like to add a point to that regarding the energy use per person (or per nation). When there is a greater energy use per person, on the average, there is associated with them the large scale production of energy. That is the picture of the world as it is right now. One of the challenges to any technology is to try to modify that relationship. From a technologist's point of view, what is to be done is to design more efficient energy production utilization. Much more effort needs to be expended in the proper use of various supplementary energy resources: biomass, solar, tidal, geothermal, wind, river power, etc.

The non-technological issue pertains to the question of the energy use per person, which is, in some ways, equivalent to the standard of living. There is a question of whether that should be somewhat reduced. If one can *bring down* the energy use per person and *bring up* how much energy can be obtained from these supplementary source technologies, you can begin to get to this more equal distribution. It is a very tough problem, for there is not enough effort, I think, placed on either side, either reducing the energy consumption per person, or bringing up the contribution from supplementary sources.

(End of morning discussion)

Afternoon Panel and Plenary Discussion
February 1, 1982

(Ashley) I want to raise two issues that remain on my mind after hearing these several excellent papers that we have had. The keynote speaker last night raised the first one, a very fundamental question which was subsequently touched on in some of the questions but to my mind remains unsettled. That issue is whether or not this whole problem arises from our insistence and our assumption that human economy needs to be a growth economy and one which attempts to more and more satisfy every human need, not merely the basic human needs, but "needs" (or, desires?) that have been artificially created. In striving to make a growth economy that assumption may lead us into accepting types of technology which are of dubious value or safety. Our speakers have given us a number of arguments to show that, in fact, nuclear energy is relatively safe. While I have not been phobic on this issue (though I'm very phobic on the question of nuclear weapons), those people who are very concerned about it are in that state basically because they feel that in spite of these good arguments there are still many factors about which we are not very clear or sure. Nuclear energy is a type of technology which is not very well understood and perhaps has great perils. That is the first question — whether or not we have to rule nuclear energy out on the grounds that it is a dangerous technology — or dubious technology — the requirement for which is based on the assumption of greater and greater economic growth.

The second difficulty is that I strongly maintain the idea that some things are intrinsically wrong. Dr. Carney has considered this from the viewpoint that it would not be intrinsically wrong to establish a nuclear plant near a large city. That seems to be a question which is on many people's minds. If there were a *real* danger of an uncontrollable and incalculable catastrophe, then it seems we have done something which is intrinsically wrong just as the argument opposing nuclear weapons is

174

based on the fact one is using a weapon which is uncontrollable. This is what makes it intrinsically wrong. It has been said here, and I suppose that it is true, that there is no danger of a nuclear explosion which would resemble the explosion of a nuclear bomb. Bujt nevertheless, if it is true that there is a real risk of an uncontrollable disaster, does not that render the building or the planning of such a facility in a population center an intrinsically wrong act and therefore not justified by any and all the other arguments that have been brought forward?

A few more points — the human element is a most important consideration for nuclear power since, to me at least, the weak parts in the entire enterprise are those associated with the building, the operating, and the managing of a nuclear power plant. To me, at least, these are not questions of complex technology, but questions of responsibility. To some extent, there is no perfect safety system. Nuclear energy is a dangerous technology for there are very serious potential risks associated with it. But there also are very serious potential risks associated with flying in airplanes. Let me give you an analogy which is not that far-fetched. The Shea Stadium in New York City is quite frequently filled to capacity, some 60– 70,000 people during a sports event. Kennedy International Airport is only a few miles from Shea Stadium and jet aircraft including Jumbo jets such as 747s, for example, take off from Kennedy for overseas flights filled with people, cargo and huge quantities of fuel. One of these jets could veer off course and crash into Shea Stadium, which could very easily result in the deaths of thousands of people. The probability of this occurring is very, very small and, consequently, aircraft are allowed to take off while the Stadium is full and the Stadium is allowed to be used while the aircraft are taking off. But no technology is absolutely safe.

Nuclear proliferation is another tough issue, and the question of whether or not the United States is acting responsibly or irresponsibly has been debated for years. Proliferation of nuclear armament is far broader than a North American question. At this point in time it is very difficult to understand how one can best limit proliferation.

Finally, I would like to address three points. The first is — is more energy necessary, regardless of whether it is nuclear or not? Unless we have some unforeseen breakthrough in technology or God provides food in a totally unexpected manner, unless we can provide the fertilizers and the irrigation, unless we can provide the energy to do all this, at least a fourth of the world's population will go to sleep hungry every night and many will not awake. I believe that it would be immoral for us to foreclose the option of providing the energy that is necessary for one-quarter of the world to survive and have longer life and a more human life. It seems to me that nuclear energy has to be a portion of that option.

The second point I would like to make is that historically, truth has come in the technical arena when the peers who are knowledgeable have had the opportunity to debate the situation and to come up with a consensus of what is true in the specific technical domain. I would urge that the non-technical segment of society for scientific and technological assessment depend on insitutitions such as the National Academy of Sciences or the National Academy of Engineering which have a membership representing a broad spectrum of scientists and engineers. We ought to pay particular attention to what they say as differentiated from the comments of any individual proponent or opponent because, in my judgment, we have the best chance of *technical truth* from such a group. Obviously, value judgments are another matter.

The third point I want to make is that the United States certainly must show the leadership in the non-proliferation arena. As I understand it, the Soviets will not send another load of fuel until the old one has been sent back. But we cannot, I want to emphasize, we cannot operate unilaterally. We are not the only one with the technology: the British, the French, the Japanese, for example, have that technology. When we try to be arbitrary we lose the leverage that comes with being in negotiation. I think unilateral action in this matter is doomed to failure. The only solution to nuclear proliferation, in my judgment, is dialogue and consensus. That means all parties must have trust. The United States cannot operate unilaterally and arbitrarily as it has in the past.

(Zebroski) I would like to respond first to the question of the growth assumption of Father Ashley. Growth assumption is intrinsic, I think, to what most people here have talked about, but it is not growth in amenities or in hedonism. Rather it is growth resulting from the expectation of seeing on this planet Earth another four billion souls in about the next 50 or 75 years. No one who has looked seriously and competently at the energy situation expects anything other than a substantial decrease in per capita consumption in the Western world, achievable by a combination of restraints and greater efficiency in usage and, at best, a very slight increase in per capita consumption in the

developed world. It is this net effect which, combined with reduced availability of easy resources, makes the nuclear option so appealing and necessary to fill the gap. So it is certainly not growth in the sense that Mr. Derrick spoke, the falling in love with temporal amenities to a too great extent. No responsible planner sees the hedonistic pursuit as either desirable or likely or even possible.

Regarding the second point of the intrinsic wrong of placing a highly dangerous entity near a city, I think the Europeans have struggled with this issue much more strenuously than we have in this country — and we have struggled with it here. Nearly every nuclear plant site in Germany or France or England is an urban site by our standards. They have struggled very hard with the question of making sure that even if the worst were to happen and everything broke the containment is very secure and the public is protected. They have satisfied themselves that the idea of a massive threat to the much higher population densities with which they must cope still leaves the probabilities in the range of one-in-a-billion and makes it acceptable, at least, to informed people.

On the final point and Mr. Hurlbert's comment on the Soviet Union and non-proliferation, I heartily agree. They have been reliable suppliers but they have also taken back the fuel from the satellite countries where they have supplied reactors. In that sense they have been superior to the United States because for a period we were advocating suppression and repression instead of cooperation. These tactics have been counter-productive and so we have never taken back fuel from the reactors that we send overseas. So in that sense I agree.

(Carney) In responding to Father Ashley, I myself have no particular interest in a consumer society so far as it pertains to middle class and upper class people. I do not think there is anything important about increasing our level of consumption. I do worry, however, about that part of our society which is in a situation of under-consumption, and I deeply worry about peoples in other parts of the world who are desperately in need of food, clothing and housing, as well as occupational opportunities. The two values which I thought were important with reference to the maintenance of a good economy had to do not with increasing our own consumption but rather with human freedom and service to those in need. I would like to see some expansion of the economy so far as it is directed to those purposes. I realize that the middle class is always also going to benefit concurrently. I can anticipate that will occur, while at the same time not cherishing that as a goal or an

end. But a growth economy is important in a world that contains so much poverty, *provided* we can learn ways to direct some of the growth into the hands of those who need it so desperately.

As Father Ashley, I also believe in intrinsically wrong acts, but I didn't discuss obligations under the rubric of intrinsic acts. I only discussed intrinsic values.

I do believe in intrinsically wrong acts, but I am not at all convinced that building a nuclear reactor near a big city is intrinsically wrong. I think it might be proportionately wrong but I see nothing evil in itself about it. I would call your attention to the fact that it just depends on what are one's assessment of the risks. There are other people who assess the risk in a significantly different way from us. Consider, for example, the placement of the Soviet reactors — the electricity-producing reactors. They observe, of course, that heat is a by-product of the reactor and they can use this by-product which we call oftentimes waste, and which the environmentalists refer to as heat pollution. The Soviets vote that they can use that by-product to heat homes. The building of some of the reactors near the cities in the USSR has been a deliberate strategy in order to be able to make use of the various resources available. They have a low view of the degree of risk that is involved in the reactors.

Regarding the India question, which is what I think Dr. Ahearne had primarily in mind, I too am very much interested in trying to restrain horizontal proliferation. I've had no problem with that goal — not to do evil and to restrain it. The point which I wanted to make is that in carrying out an intelligent and moral non-proliferation program, we had better make sure that we proceed in ways that make us reliable as human persons and human societies. It seems to me that our big fault in India has not been in our attempt to discourage India from proliferation, but rather that we did not keep our commitments to India, and we tried *ex post facto* to revise and change them. At the same time we were guilty of our own proliferation. So, I want to control proliferation, but I also want to do it in ways that express integrity.

(Zebroski) We had a question submitted taken from a pamphlet from the Union of Concerned Scientists which holds the position that a moratorium on the construction of new plants would allow an orderly assessment of the problem and the time to carry out research and development to decrease the risk. At first hearing it sounds like a very responsible and thoughtful suggestion. But, I submit that if it was

made with full knowledge then it is mischievous because a delay in the construction of a plant which is nearly ready to operate will cost the utility, and ultimately the consumer, about an extra half-million dollars a day. The reason is simple; the extra costs result from the paying for bonds and not producing anything. Many utilities would go under financially. There is one utility which currently is in default on its bonds. That raises the question whether it can get the further bonding money to bring to operational level one plant which is 95% complete and a second one which is about 65% complete. This is an enormous waste of resources. How can it be said that experience is needed when there is to date nearly the 5000 years of reactor operation, which is quite a large body of experience?

I think what has been missing is a comprehensive and rigorous harvesting of this experience for its lessons, as well as the implementation of effective remedies. I believe the industry and the NRC are really stepping up to this issue now in a much more systematic way than they have in the past. As a consequence, what is being asked for here is actually being achieved, but without the great economic dislocation that a construction moratorium would bring.

There is another statement in this pamphlet which makes moratorium seem like a nice thing to do: Nation-wide our 1980 capacity is 33% greater than peak demand. However, that statement is not correct in two dimensions. The 1980 reserve over the peak demand nationwide average actually is about 8% because part of the capacity always must be taken down for routine maintenance, for required inspection, repair, refueling, and so on. I am referring not just to nuclear but coal and oil capacity, so the 33% is a fictitious number. It would be like saying you could run your automobile for 4000 hours without stopping. In principle you could, but in fact if you do not maintain it every 100 hours or so of operation it will break down. The assertion of a 33% over capacity has another misleading aspect. A large part of that margin capacity, even the more accurate 8%, is obtained from oil and gas energy sources. This is the most expensive peaking capacity and therefore it is used as little as possible by responsible dispatchers and utilities because it costs so much more to run. To the extent that there is a margin one would still prefer to generate that electricity with something which does not burn so much gas and oil.

Question: A small group of us have agreed that despite the location of our homes, none of us is going to fly home, or will any of us ever again see a game in Shea Stadium. Having said that, however, and desiring to be really complimentary about the individual presentations, we felt that coming as a group not committed to one side or another of an extraordinarily complex and difficult question, that the speakers, not as individuals but as a body, failed to present another side which is not being heard here today. Clearly we are not experts in that field, but the only presentation from the Union of Concerned Scientists was their small brochure which had been sent to us as pre-workshop reading. I appreciate the fact that they got in at least for that one moment. While we do want to reflect appreciation for the marvelous presentations, at the same time we do feel a certain amount of disappointment in the absence of the other position.

(Ahearne) Can I say something here? You actually did not see either of the two sides. Perhaps you are most familiar with the UCS phamphlets but there are just as vociferous people on the pro side, for example, the American Labor Party and the Fusion Party; you have not heard from them either. There are people on the affirmative side who will tell you there is absolutely no hazard in nuclear power. There never could be an accident. They would assert that there is never any danger, and in fact one could locate plants in close proximity to cities, and that by not going ahead with nuclear power we are destroying the fabric of the United States, that it is an abomination to allow any regulation, and that there are cowardly people who are raising issues against nuclear power. That is the pro side. You did not hear that. It is true there is a strongly opposed side which you did not hear in their words. Having spent 5 years being bombarded from both sides, it is very difficult for me to describe the other side accurately. Their argument includes a mixture of statements, some of which are not very responsible. Zebroski just pointed out how the percentage of capacity over peak demand, 33%, is a misleading number. It is very difficult to find, I think, objective people on the two extremes. Perhaps that is typical of extremes, and it is extremely difficult in a short period of time to listen to someone hold an extreme position and carry away some correct factual information. Yes, you are correct, you did not hear the pitch from one side of the extreme, nor, however, did you hear from the other side.

Panelist) I think Commissioner Ahearne is far too modest. I read his 79-page paper last night and I think it is the most devastating and comprehensive summary of the opposing arguments that I have read anywhere. It is only temperate in that it avoids what we hear in a

180

passionate debate, which are the cheap shots, the statements which are made for emotional effect. Obviously he did not use them. Because of the time restrictions, he could only give a limited number of factual concerns, but he outlined the ones which he could only touch.

Question: Dr. Carney, our group wondered whether in the debate which you described in your presentation, you could cite the valid argument given on the other side of the issue. That would be one question. the second question would be, is it inevitable that the expansion of nuclear energy contributes to the expansion of nuclear arms?

(Carney) I was merely reporting the pastor's judgment that his constituency, which comprises about half the community and which is not organized on the basis of pro- or anti-nuclear positions around the Catholic faith, seems to be overwhelmingly in support of the pro-nuclear position and is also very desirous that the Three Mile Island Reactor #1 which was not involved in the accident be restarted. I did not meet anybody from Middletown at this particular meeting two weeks ago who has anti-nuclear, so I really cannot report the arguments there. The other question is concerned about the availability of nuclear materials used for electricity production for diversion to nuclear weaponry, or possibly to terrorist activity. I myself spent a year working for the Congressional Office of Technology Assessment on exactly that topic. It was the panel on nuclear proliferation and safeguards that reported in 1977 to the Congress. I think the risk that might develop would come with reprocessing. As long as we are using low enriched uranium and as long as most other nations — Third World Nations — do not have enrichment equipment which is enormously expensive and technologically very involved, that is, as long as reprocessing, which is a chemical process at the end of the fuel line, does not occur, then the risk of proliferation from nuclear energy into nuclear weaponry is very, very small. If one moves into reprocessing, then a greater possibility exists.

(Ahearne) Let me address at least the first half of the question . . . are there people in that area [the Three Mile Island region] against nuclear power? In November the Nuclear Regulatory Commission held a public meeting in Harrisburg, Pa. Approximately 1200–1400 people came out to the High School Auditorium. The majority were strongly against nuclear power, and were extremely emotional, crying, screaming, and weeping; terrified, I would say, is the accurate description,

completely frightened about nuclear power, adamantly opposed to allowing the undamaged reactor to restart. A referendum was taken in the three counties around Three Mile Island. As is typical in American voting, the majority of the people did not vote, so the results represented a minority of the people who could vote, but to those who did vote, the majority in three counties favored not allowing the reactor to restart.

I would like to add something to the probability of weapon development if we have increased consumption of nuclear electricity. That outcome depends on the wisdom of all governments, but particularly of our government. If we fail to keep our part of the bargain to supply nuclear technology and support peaceful use of the atom, because people have the same desire that we have for an abundance of goods and an economical source of energy, they will go ahead on their own. Enough technology is available for them to go ahead on their own. When they go ahead on their own, they will put in the facilities for enrichment and reprocessing. That will increase the risk of proliferation. However, if we live up to our commitment, to our part of the agreement, and nuclear energy goes under international inspection, in my judgment, increased consumption of nuclear energy in the Third World will actively reduce the risk of proliferation. The counterargument runs that then nations will be more trained and therefore will have more technical capabilities. But I think there is plenty of capability in the world now for some one to build the enrichment facilities if they have a strong enough incentive to do it without commercial nuclear power.

How can we make sure — what could we do to make sure that the development of nuclear energy, in fact, does go to and help the Third World countries? The obvious course of action is for us to develop adequate and just international policies. But what do we do to *assure* that the Third World countries will, in fact, benefit from the development of nuclear energy? When Korea first purchased their nuclear plants they paid for it in the differential between the oil price that they would have had to pay for the energy and the cost of the plant in 30 months. They got a 30-month payback which allowed them to have a standard of living substantially better than they would have had. If one believes that electrical power from nuclear energy is generated at a substantially lower cost than from burning oil — which is what most of the developing countries now have — then developing nations should be able to service their debt on that nuclear plant better than they could service the debt from the procurement of the oil.

(Question: Let me make a comment. It is not obvious to me that nuclear power is really appropriate for a Third World country if you are really talking about the very poor countries who are struggling to make a life of some dignity for their people. Not because nuclear power is evil or bad, but because it is a high technology. It is not obvious that the limited amount of technical competence that tends to be in those countries should be focused on nuclear power plants. If the real problem in the world is poverty, is this the type of technology we really need?

(Panelist) The difficulty, Bishop, with the way you just phrased the question, is that the issue has shifted from the underdeveloped countries to a world issue, and what I was focusing on was what is appropriate for a very poor country trying to struggle its way up. On a world basis there are some highly industrialized countries which need very large and efficient supplies of electricity. Hence, when you ask do *we* need this type of technology, in a narrow parochial sense that now narrows down to the United States. That is an entirely different question than it is for some country, say, in Africa or some of the South American countries.

(Panelist) I'd like to speak about one country where I lived last year, namely Egypt. At the present time Egypt only has about 4800 megawatts of electricity production. In order to overcome its problem of poverty, its leaders believe that by the year 2000 it has to increase its electrical production to about 19000–20000 megawatts of electricity production. It plans that a major part of that should be nuclear power. It will also develop to some degree its hydroelectric potential. It plans to build eight nuclear reactors before the year 2000 and is already currently involved in negotiations with France for the first two reactors. One thing which gives hope is that in their operation of the Suez Canal, the Egyptians involved a good part of their top technological and administrative people. As a consequence, the Canal has been excellently run. Their plans are basically to do the same thing with the nuclear energy.

The other observation I would like to make is that if solar electricity were a real possibility, Egypt would be a primary candidate. One reason being the fact that 96% of the population of Egypt is gathered either within a few miles of the Nile River or in the Nile Delta. On either side of the Nile River there are enormous expanses of what most of us would consider wasteland, namely, areas where you could easily place solar collectors. But at present they see no future in solar electricity, and while they have no coal, they do have plenty of oil, which they are exporting today. They are producing about 750,000 barrels a day, a third of which is going into exports. To finance these nuclear reactors, they plan to put a good chunk of their oil revenues, about 250,000 barrels a day, into the financing of the nuclear reactors.

Question: Will the introduction of nuclear energy into the developing countries result in their being more impoverished, more dependent on the industrialized countries?

(Panelist) The question is — Does the adoption of a nuclear option by a less developed country make it more dependent? This also relates to a question that Father Ashley asked a little earlier which needs to be addressed, that is, do we need the nuclear option at all? I think the answer must be considered on a case by case basis, and let me give an example. The high technology components involved in a nuclear power plant can be a relatively small part of the total cost. A very large fraction of the construction material — the concrete and the steel and so on — can be largely domestically supplied. So, for countries at a sufficient stage of development, dependency on foreign supply is very limited. The experience has been that most of the countries which have passed through that stage, very quickly get the capability to be suppliers of substantial pieces of the plant equipment. For countries not at that stage, I think it is true that it would not be appropriate. Under those conditions assistance from the developed world, I think, depends on two elements: one, to get our own economy healthy so we can have the means to give aid at the level that was once common, and secondly, to emphasize the principle that it is better to teach a man how to fish than to give him a fish. Certainly we have not done all we can in that regard.

Ashley Question: Could I ask, what about nuclear fuel? Would not these countries be dependent on us for fuel and would not their agreements put them under some kind of control by us?

(Panelist) That is true. However, the whole attraction of the process is that the fuel costs are relatively low and there are at least four international suppliers now, providing these countries with diversity in supply sources. The controls have to do with the agreement that if the country accepts help with its power program, it will accept a restraint on clandestine activities which might lead to nuclear weapons. I think everybody believes that is a fair trade.

Question: I wish that we also had had advocates of the soft energy path, so that it would be from the basis of a comparison of alternatives that we could have judged the nuclear option.

(Hurlburt) Our corporation is actively involved in the soft energy program. We are building windmills, doing a great deal of work in solar voltaics, and we have a contract on the use of ocean thermal currents. We are planning to begin selling fuel cells but we are off by a factor of about 10 in cost per kilowatt hours. In many circumstances we ought to be able to use the soft technologies instead of conventional gas, or coal fired, or oil or nuclear plants, to generate electricity. If there is available a good source of gaseous fuels, fuel cells may be a very good answer because one can put them in small units. It is not necessary to build a 1000 megawatt plant, one can perhaps build a ten-megawatt plant to be competitive.

(discussion's end)

Part III

The Human Person

An Overview

Speakers on the middle day of the Workshop focus on the reality which stands in the middle of contemporary technological issues of energy and of reproduction: the human person.

Doctor Paul Vitz chronicles the rise of an approach to the human person which dominated the field of psychology in the 1970's. This approach has now been profoundly challenged by a new generation of psychologists.

Doctor Anna T. Tymieniecka presents a phenomenological approach which sees the "Moral Sense" as a capacity which distinguishes the human person from the infra-human world in which he or she is immersed.

Donald Senior summarizes the three-fold emphasis of Sacred Scripture on the human person as meaningless being unless he or she has a relationship to his or or her God, a place within a human community, and a sense of his or her full existence as a body-soul entity.

Since the 18th century Enlightenment, massive abandonment of ideas previously accepted as "common sense" has produced at times a subtle, but almost universal scepticism about the human person's ability to know truth with an abiding univocal meaning. Philosophical movements during the same period focused increasingly on the "inner space" of man's "subjectivity", that is, his uniquely human mental process. Michael Hines sees these developments as freeing our vision of the human person from any changeless concept of "human nature" and, therefore, from claims which pose illegitimately as natural law.

Benedict Ashley expands upon the classical thomistic concept of *person* in light of the psychological, philosophical, scriptural and systematic theological developments of the first four papers.

The Editors

Chapter 7

Empirical Sciences and Personhood: From an Old Consensus to a New Realism

Paul C. Vitz

Editorial Preface

In the United States around 1970, a general consensus regarding the human person quite definitely dominated the field of personality theory, its application in clinical psychology and ethical formation, and most importantly, popularized versions of psychology. This 1970 consensus peaked around 1975, but continued to have a definite though declining following thereafter. Today it is in disarray, subjected to scientific as well as philosophical challenges from all sides. No new consensus has yet arisen to replace it, though there are signs of the data and philosophic considerations that will have to be integrated into any new consensus.

The old and now much discredited consensus tended:
1) *to ignore any biological basis of the human person;*
2) *to presume that each individual, if not hindered by bad societal influences (including parents), would by innate tendency develop correctly;*
3) *to believe that increased individual independence or autonomy was automatically to be equated with healthy mental growth;*
4) *to encourage awareness and expression of one's various emotions, simply for the sake of expressing them cathartically;*
5) *and for some, to concentrate, not on the content of the mind, but on the structure of the mental operations by which the mind moves to cognition.*

Most of these five elements were found, at least implicitly and usually explicitly, in the work of the best-known names in psychology in the 1970's: Rogers, Fromm, Maslow, May, Perls, et al. *Moreover, out of this same consensus came many of the techniques adopted in social and educational psychology: Transactional Analysis, Values Clarification, Ethical Formation Stages (Kohlberg), etc.*

Researchers prior to 1970 (Piaget, Skinner, et al*) had prepared the way for all this, though the original Freudian and Jungian tradition generally had not. While philosophical roots could be traced back for centuries, the existentialism of the 1940's as well as the thought of Dewey, Whitehead, Russell* et al, *were a more immediate matrix of the 1970 consensus.*

Around 1975, however, the 1970 consensus began to totter under the onslaught of psychological research by a new generation. The new researchers criticized the older consensus for ignoring the biological basis for both normal and abnormal mental states and activity. The use of highly sophisticated drugs in therapy, the function of the two hemispheres of the brain in determining one's analytic vs. synthetic propensities, the biological basis of sexual differences, the effect of inherited genetic components on behavior, and the almost immediate presence of post-natal cognitive activity in infants were all factors which the older 1970 consensus had practically ignored. The newer psychologists emphatically re-affirmed them.

They also maintained that the older consensus had played to the worst weaknesses of an affluent but centrifugal American society. The plush, pleasure-seeking, unscrupulous, self-fulfilled James Bond type displaced the ideals of life-long commitment and cohesiveness, self-control and self-sacrifice, which were the foundation of family life. Family life crumbled in the 1970's as never before in a tidal wave of divorce. The new researchers are convinced they have clearly identified the massive suffering which resulted.

190

Critiqued also by the new researchers was the old consensus' ignoring of uniquely feminine moral sensitivity, as well as this same consensus' enslavement to a consumer society, content, it seems, only in consuming more and more. In the economic hard times, however, "millions of Americans are beginning to learn that it is very hard to actualize one's self at today's prices."

The new psychological researchers are also rejecting the myth that social science as practiced recently has been science in the pure, empirical sense of the term. Often psychologists and psychiatrists labeled as "mental illness" patients' attitudes which the practitioners happened not to share for (unacknowledged) philosophical, political, or (anti-) religious reasons. Some of these were uncritically rationalistic, individualistic, politically liberal, capitalistic and even Americanistic. Many of the new researchers now deny the possibility of a truly objective "empirical" study of the human person, at least at the theoretical level.

Finally, the older 1970 consensus is being critiqued from a moral and religious point of view. Morally, psychological counseling must give clients a direction; but this is impossible without the practitioner having moral convictions. Religiously, the very concept of "person" is the fruit of Jewish and Christian theological consideration, especially of experience with the Person Who is the Lord. Sundered from this experience, "the person" becomes only "an autonomous, self-actualizing individual who is devoted to the growth of the secular self." The past few years have seen the emergence of a number of theorists and practitioners with a "Christian psychology", consciously articulated as such.

I have been asked to answer the question: "What do the empirical sciences, primarily psychology, tell us about the nature of the person? That is, what is today's consensus in the relevant sciences about the origin and development of personality and the person?"

This is a pretty tall order under any circumstance, but to present an answer in only a few pages is a truly Herculean task. Thus, in order to give a reasonable response, I shall have to restrict my answer to a broad summary of the present situation. The advantages of such a procedure are that it concentrates on the most important features of the subject, that it can be grasped without much specialized knowledge, and that it avoids getting bogged down in the details of the countless particular experiments and particular theories. The danger, of course, is that of over-generalization. With these caveats aside, let us begin.

The Old Consensus, Circa 1970

We can best understand the situation today by comparing it with the situation roughly ten years ago, about 1970. *For there was then a general consensus about the nature of the person* — at least there was in psychology and related disciplines, a consensus which could easily be found in the textbooks of psychology, counseling, and education. Much of the same consensus was also clearly present in the popular psychology of the time as represented in the many paperback best-sellers that featured psychology. It was a consensus which had been building for at least 60 years, and which became dominant in the period of the 1950's and '60s. It clearly appears to have peaked in the early 1970s. The major assumptions, concepts and emphases of this consensus were as follows.

1. Learning, Social Roles and Experience

A central assumption was that *personality was overwhelmingly the product of learning,* primarily of social learning. To a large degree, a person consisted of learned social roles derived from his or her family, social and cultural experiences. These social roles were interpreted as culturally relative, and hence as essentially arbitrary in content. Any possible innate or biologically determined bases of the person were almost entirely ignored.

2. Human Goodness, Natural Morality and Moral Relativism

It was widely assumed that human nature was intrinsically good and that people had no natural tendency toward what theologians call evil — no tendency to aggress, to hurt, to exploit others; no tendency toward narcissistic self-indulgence at the expense of others. Although a few psychologists and psychiatrists were holdouts, the dominant theoretical interpretations all assumed that "bad things" came from outside man. Evil, which was usually called "sickness" or "a bad self-image", came from the family, or from social institutions (especially the Church — seldom the University), from the culture at large, or from "ignorance." Therefore, if the social sources of evil could be removed or counteracted, a person would naturally become happy and fulfilled, and a just society would result. These assumptions meant that among other things morality was viewed as relative, as something to be determined by the individual who had been freed from the crippling effects of the past, especially the traditional family, religion, and much of the rest of society. A consequence of this position was that a person could pick his own values and do his own thing (In this sense it was subjective. Indeed, all of the characteristics of the old consensus were part of a very general emphasis on subjectivity — a subjectivity that can be well described as narcissism). The possibility of an objective morality, much less of traditional morality, was ignored or derided.

3. Autonomy, the Self and its Actualization

The 1970 consensus assumed that a person developed by moving to autonomy or independence from others, and from the past and present culture. Great emphasis was placed on the self. In fact, the ego or the self was conceptualized as the center of the person, as the master category. It was the perpetual growth of this ever-changing self that was described and prescribed as the goal of the person's life. This was usually summarized under the term "self-actualization" or "self-realization."

4. Feelings and Emotion

The consensus in question placed a great emphasis on the expression of a person's emotions as central to the process of becoming a person. This required that one become aware of or "got in touch" with one's feelings. The content or quality of particular feelings — for example, anger, rage, anxiety, desire, depression, didn't matter, since catharsis was the goal. It was the expression that mattered, not what was expressed. Besides, the self, as mentioned, was assumed to be trustworthy in whatever it expressed. This expression of feelings was considered an important step in freeing the self from the negative, neurotic effects of parents — and of husband, wife, children, and of society. It was part of the move toward self-actualization. This emphasis on emotional expression was widely found in theories of psychotherapy, counseling, and popular psychology.

5. Structuralism and Cognitive Development

A final characteristic of the 1970 position was its preoccupation with mental *structure* or the dynamics of cognition, in contrast to the *content* of the mind. The dominant theories of this period were then cognitivist, that is, they focused on the organization of the mind: what mattered was *how* you thought, not *what* you thought. Changes in structure were called processes. Mental or personal growth was described as the natural development of changes in structure, or just as a continual movement from one content to another, that is, being into something new. The essential point is that the content of your thought or emotions received little attention as long as their expression and change, i.e. "growth," were taking place.

Examples of the 1970 Consensus

Some examples of the theories which formed this consensus will help to make it clearer and more specific. They are represented in two groups: the *self-psychologists* and the *cognitivists*. The self-psychologists are probably the most representative of the foregoing descriptions. The writings of Carl Rogers (1951, 1961), Erich Fromm (1947, 1955, 1966), Abraham Maslow (1954, 1968), Rollo May (1963, 1958), and Fritz Perls (1969), are all examples of Points 1–4 (above). The fifth point is not found in the approach of these psychologists to any great degree. They did, however, consider the self to be created largely through conscious choice, so their emphasis on consciousness and choice puts them in general agreement with the second group, the cognitivists. Most of the cognitive theorists were academic and research-oriented, while, in contrast, the self-psychologists were clinically oriented and much more interested in application. The self-psychologists' lack of attention to cognitive structures, however, did not imply any great theoretical opposition.

The popular psychology of the time, as found in Transactional Analysis (e.g., Berne, 1964; Harris, 1969), and many others, was in substantial agreement with the first four points. Again, these writers largely ignored any detailed treatment of cognition, but they had no serious opposition to it. The popular psychologists also emphasized choice, but left the specifics of cognitive structure and decision making to the academic psychologists.

The psychology of moral education and development in the 1970s is also a part of the old consensus. The Values Clarification theorists (Raths, Merrill, & Simon, 1966; Simon, Howe, & Kirschenbaum, 1978), fit all the first four points well; they also left the details of cognitive structure to others. Into their model of morality, they incorporated decision-making and a kind of unspecified discussion which directly advocated moral relativism (Unfortunately, their advocacy of moral relativism was done under the guise of moral neutrality. See Baer 1977, 1980; Bennett & Delattre, 1978; Eger, 1981; Gow, 1980; Lockwood, 1977, 1978; Vitz, 1981, 1982).

The social psychologist Kohlberg (1971, 1981), whose theory of moral development is very much a part of the 1970 consensus, did not concern himself with emotional expression (Point 3), but otherwise his approach is a good example of this consensus (For recent criticisms of Kohlberg see Kurtines & Grief, 1974; Adelson, 1975; Gilligan, 1977, 1982; Hogan & Emler, 1978; Vitz, 1981b, 1982; and Levin, 1982).

The social psychology and personality theory of the time was also in general agreement with the consensus — although these approaches were much narrower and usually focused on concrete concepts capable of being investigated in a reasonably precise manner. Leon Festinger's theory of cognitive dissonance (1957), had little to say about emotional expression in the typical sense. However, Festinger's approach explicitly assumed a cognitive approach to the mind, focused on the autonomous individual, and assumed that cognition came from social learning. Walter Michel's (1968, 1971) theory of personality was explicitly cognitive and individualistic, as well as based on social learning as the source of the cognitions. Albert Bandura (1969), who developed probably the first social learning approach to child psychology and personality development, also fits much of the consensus picture, although Bandura did sometimes emphasize the content of what was learned, including moral learning, which takes place during childhood.

Entirely outside the 1970 consensus were traditional Freudians with their emphasis on the unconscious. Those Jungians who emphasized self-realization were part of the consensus, but those who focused on the unconscious, dreams, and symbols were not. Most of the work of such psychologists as Erik Erikson, Karl Menninger, and Victor Frankl, also remained outside the consensus.

The somewhat earlier contributions of Piaget and Skinner are in most instances examples of the 1970 consensus, although once again, their concerns were much more specific and oriented toward academic research. Skinner heavily emphasized social learning via reinforcement, assumed human goodness or at least human moral neutrality, and assumed that the self was important but not autonomous, since his philosophy was one of strict determinism. He had little to say about emotion, but was quite willing to grant thought an important place as long as it was admitted that thought structures were learned, not innate (On this he opposed Piaget and Chomsky).

Piaget was primarily a cognitive psychologist who interpreted the environment as the crucial factor in developing the intrinsic structural capacities of the mind. Piaget had relatively little to say about the other aspects of the consensus, although there is no reason to think that his concept of the self was much different from the other psychologists noted here.

In retrospect, the big theoretical disagreements between people like Skinner and Rogers don't appear so large (Rogers, 1956). Skinner argued for a very hard nosed, deterministic kind of psychology, based on behaviorism. Rogers argued for a soft-minded approach which allowed human free will and choice. But these were rather abstract theoretical arguments, and in practice the applied approaches of both were often taught in the same graduate programs of clinical psychology and counseling. Both were secular humanists who optimistically believed that individuals could control their social and personal environment in such a way as to greatly increase happiness and justice. Both rejected biological factors, both strongly rejected traditional religion and traditional morality, both assumed a self at the center of their systems, and both believed in the power of the conscious rational mind to understand and control reality. One sign of this basic compatibility is that the social learning theorist Michel considers his sophisticated behaviorist approach consistent with existentialist psychology (see Maddi, 1976). Bandura (Ibid., p. 589) would seem to belong to this same camp.

The Origin of the 1970 Consensus

The roots of this consensus go back at least to the Enlightenment. But as a consensus existing within the explicit and presumably empirical study of personality, it had its origins in the major psychologists of the first part of the century, for example, Behaviorism, Piaget, Freud, Adler, and Jung. Philosophical influences were also important, especially Dewey, Existentialism, Whitehead, Russell, etc. Thus, most of the major theoretical contributions on which the 1970 consensus was based were published before 1940. The founding ideas were laid down a generation or so before they became the popular psychology of academia and much of upper middle class America.[1]

The Collapse of the Old 1970 Consensus

The interpretation of the person embodied in what I have called the "old consensus of 1970" is today in the process of disintegration. As a result, the present is a period of intellectual transition as to the nature of the person and personality. There is no new consensus; perhaps for reasons given below there never will be, but in any case, the old framework is falling apart.

In some respects the situation in psychology is analogous to that in economics, where the old Keynesian consensus holds no longer, but no new agreement has been reached. If anything, the awareness of crisis in economics is more advanced than it is in psychology. In the world of economics, failure is fairly quick and objective; economic bankruptcy must be dealt with. In the world of psychology, failure is slower, harder to observe and easier to rationalize — but in the long run it is every bit as destructive as inflation and unemployment.

The demise of the old consensus in psychology is partly the consequence of the exhaustion of the basic ideas of the older viewpoint. As mentioned, these ideas were first published decades ago, and in the intervening time most of the implications of these ideas for research and theory have been drawn out. In short, the concepts of the old consensus appear to have little potential left in them for generating new insights. It is no wonder that the younger and better minds are being drawn to very different paradigms. [2]

However, the weakness of the old consensus is only partly due to its apparent intellectual exhaustion. The major causes for its disarray are new research findings, new conceptual frameworks for interpreting the person — and new highly effective criticisms as well. These new factors make very clear that the old consensus was substantially wrong. [4] Since this new evidence is very important and interesting in its own right, I will summarize it. And, of course, any possible new consensus must take this research into account.

The Biological Critique

A radical challenge to the older position presently comes from recent biologically oriented research. One substantial contribution has come from the now widespread use of biochemical and psychopharmacological (drug) treatments of mental illness. Very briefly, there was the discovery in the late 1950s of chlorpromazine, e.g., thorazine, as a major help in the treatment of schizophrenia, and the finding that reserpine could be used as a tranquilizer. More recently there has been the development of such antidepressants as imipramine for mood elevation. The use of lithium for people suffering from bi-polar mood swings, that is from chronic manic-depressive cycles, has provided a major new benefit. Valium and librium as anti-anxiety drugs have also proved helpful. Although the use of these drugs is not without serious side effects and social risks,[4] it is nevertheless true that today the dominant model of personality in the medical world of psychiatry is a biochemical one. That is, psychiatry has moved from frequent, long, talk sessions to short interviews followed by drug prescriptions. All people working in pastoral counseling need to be aware of these therapies, and to be able to recognize when a person probably needs referral to this new psychiatry (See Cooper & Bloom, 1982; Lipton, Damascio, & Killam, 1978; Snyder, 1975.).

A second major biological factor stems from the work of Nobel Laureate Roger Sperry, who pioneered the understanding of the differences between mental functioning of the two brain hemispheres (Sperry, 1968). The distinction, now well established, is between the verbal, rational and analytic left brain, and the spatial, intuitive, and synthetic right brain. In spite of some past excesses of interpretation, the distinction continues to generate important new findings in neuroanatomy and in physiological and experimental psychology (e.g., Davidson & Fox, 1982; Lacoste-Utamsing & Holloway, 1982). In particular, it seems that these differences help explain different types of people as a function of different hemisphere structure and specialization. For example, the differences between right- and left-handed people appear related to hemisphere differences (see Marx, 1982). Also, a number of important sex differences can be interpreted within a brain hemisphere framework (Blakeslee, 1980, has a good summary of the brain hemisphere literature).

In fact, the biology of sex differences is a third new challenge to the old consensus, which assumed that there were no important differences between men and women. Research in the last ten years or so has uncovered many reliable neurological differences, with important behavioral implications. The most basic finding has been that the male nervous system is biochemically masculinized before birth and shortly thereafter. This masculinization of the brain controls much of the later adult sex-linked behavior (see Goy & McEwen, 1980). Important evidence supporting sex roles has also come from the recent systematic work on the social aspects of human and primate behavior (Hamburg & McGown, 1979; Symons, 1979; Robert May, 1980). The older consensus assumed that sex specific behavior, so widely observed in all cul-

198

tures, was an arbitrary learned stereotype; the newer research based on far more objective evidence implies that many of these differences are rooted in basic biological structures.

Closely related to the sex difference research has been the research demonstrating the large number of other behaviors shown to have a strong genetic component. For example, alcoholism is now known to be very significantly influenced by a person's heredity (e.g., Goodwin, et al., 1973). Some recent work on identical twins raised apart also indicates the role of heredity in many personality characteristics (See Buss, Plomin, & Willerman, 1973; Gottesman & Shields, 1972; Shields, 1976; for a recent balanced, but conservative, summary, see Farber, 1981).

A final area of research with strong biological implications comes from child psychology. Here studies with human infants show that the baby has a rather sophisticated mental capacity before he or she is a year old, often very much sooner. For example, at 36 hours of age, infants can recognize such basic human emotions as happiness and fear expressed in the human face. They can demonstrate their recognition by mimicking the adult facial expression. Also, long before they can actually speak, infants can recognize many essential speech sounds in the same way that adults do. Infants can also recognize the appropriate lip movements for speech as shown by adults before the adults begin to speak (Kuhl & Meltzoff, 1982). One implication of this is that such distinctive human capacities as speech have a strong biological basis. In short, the older assumption derived from behaviorism, that the baby was a kind of *tabula rasa* on which the environment could write any kind of instruction, is now pretty thoroughly rejected (For good recent summaries see Osofsky, 1980; Lamb & Campos, 1982).

All of the preceding research points in the same direction: namely, to the dramatically increasing importance of biology for understanding human nature and human personality. This is not to suggest an acceptance of thorough-going biological determinism. Instead, the point is that biology does place serious constraints on the person — we are embodied persons and this embodiment has been grossly neglected by the old consensus. A thoughtful understanding of this long over-due position is now in the making. I should add that it also implies that psychology as a field will become less important in the future as its over-extended theories get carved back by the rising tide of biological findings.

Furthermore, the growth of biological models of man will, in time, have a profound effect on public policy and attitudes in general. Certainly, the older consensus affected much of American public life, most especially our theories of education. For example, the secular models of moral education, such as Values Clarification and Kohlberg's model, routinely assumed that humans were entirely intrinsically good. Already the new sociobiology is beginning to emerge with something of the opposite message: humans are biologically programmed to look out for their own interests or for the interests of their group. That is, what has normally been considered as a built-in altruism doesn't exist, only individual or group self interest. Thus, just as the earlier social science assumed that people were naturally all good and completely free to choose whatever kind of person they wanted to be, the new science is implying that people are overwhelmingly determined, "programmed" by biological factors to be selfish.[5] So far, this biological emphasis is a dose of welcome realism in the face of the older inflated and socially destructive consensus about human goodness and changeability. But this new morality is likely in time to become a harsh justification for the self-interest of those with power — of the governing class, whoever they might be. Since this position will be argued from an extensive biological base, it will be far harder to refute than the fading, over optimistic position which has had weak empirical support. Thus, it behooves all Christians to be forewarned and to sharpen their philosophical and ethical arguments in advance.

The Social and Economic Critique

Recall that a central tenet of the older consensus was that *the person developed to the extent that he or she became autonomous and self-actualizing.* The entire emphasis was on being separate and independent of others. Social bonds and interpersonal loyalty as positive factors were entirely absent from these theories. The unit for consideration was always the individual. (The one-to-one nature of most psychotherapy is a common expression of this bias.)

Thus, for example, there was no emphasis on marriage as involving commitment, or on the stable family as an important necessary determinant of human personality. Indeed, in not one of the theories of personality from Freud to Rogers is there any focus on abiding interpersonal commitment as intrinsic to the formation of what it is to be a person. The whole gist of the old consensus was toward breaking entangling commitments, toward autonomy, toward doing your own thing — and moving on (see Vitz, 1977). I suppose the secular ideal was rather like the James Bond of movie fame. Ironically, Bond was a man without any bonds. He lived in a world with no family, commitment, or even serious friends — the perfect autonomous unit.

But a family critique of the 1970 consensus is now being established. Research has dramatically shown the need of children for both a father and a mother — for what has been called a "whole home." Investigation has documented the many seriously destructive long-term effects of divorce on children. The best estimate is that 35 to 40 percent of children of divorce suffer serious long-term psychological depression, anxiety, apathy, delinquency, etc. as effects of divorce (Wallerstein & Kelly, 1980). In the United States alone this means that about 400,000 children are made into long-term psychological casualties every year. *Much of this suffering must, I suspect and fear, be laid at the door of the psychological theories of the immediately preceding period.* Their emphasis on the search for personal fulfillment, plus the total neglect of the needs of children for parental commitment, have been major factors in the sorry state of the modern family. Ironically, it has been this very pathology of the modern family which has allowed social scientists to observe that the stable traditional family is a major positive contributor to adequate personality formation. One should add that other social pathologies, e.g., abortion and euthanasia, still remain largely and sadly uninvestigated from a psychological perspective.

Along with the documentation of the pathology of divorce has come recent theoretical understanding of what is known as *separation anxiety.* This anxiety allows one to understand why divorce should have such disturbing effects. Separation anxiety is the child's fear of being abandoned by the parental figure, usually the mother or father. Divorce commonly results in the abandonment of the child by one parent, typically the father; and it often makes the child seriously anxious that the remaining parent will also leave. Since separation anxiety is now understood as the deepest fear of children, the trauma of divorce for children is now reasonably well understood (Bowlby, 1969, 1973, 1980). There are other hurtful conditions which divorce creates as well, such as lowered financial support, less time with the remaining parent who now commonly must be out of the house at a job, less parental supervision, etc.

201

Another example of a social critique of the old consensus understanding of moral development comes from Carol Gilligan (1977, 1982). Her research has shown that women respond very differently than men to moral dilemmas. In general, women are much more concrete, and concerned with people, and with avoiding suffering, than are men. Gilligan's work exemplifies a positive acknowledgement of sex differences, a special emphasis on the actual content of the moral life and a rejection of abstract, cognitive functioning. I should add that her findings (not her philosophical framework) have much to recommend them in terms of Christian concepts of morality.

Yet, another strong critique of the old consensus is an economic one — a criticism found in the psychological literature, but even more effectively experienced by millions in the current economic reality. The old psychology of true self was implicitly based on economic prosperity, especially the wealth of the large corporations and government bureaucracies and programs. People who accepted this psychology did become independent from their family and traditional values. But in the process, they became dependent upon the economic health of the corporate and government world. They became flush — but they certainly did not become autonomous or truly independent. Today, as harsh economic realities are driven home to those raised on self-psychology, they are more and more aware of their true helplessness. Autonomy has turned out to be an illusion held out by the economic interests of the corporate and consumer society — aided and abetted by much of the so-called "helping professions." Those who fell for it no longer have family or friends to fall back on. Their anxiety is feeding a new kind of desperate survival-at-any-cost mentality.

As we look back on the prosperity of the affluent society in the period 1945–1975, the connection of the self-psychology to the economy appears clearer and clearer. Indeed, the proposed ideal of self-growth looks more and more like an expression of a Chamber of Commerce psychology in which self-realization can be interpreted as nothing more than a rationalization of the ideal consumer so needed to keep the economy going. It was from the beginning a psychology for the well-off secular American suburbanite who had no worry about such things as a job, much less about food. Today, as the world-wide economic crisis calls into question the survival of many large corporations and even such programs as Social Security, the secular psychology of the self seems increasingly irrelevant. Millions of Americans are beginning to learn that it is very hard to actualize one's self at today's prices (Vitz, 1977).

A serious empirically based challenge has come from Myers (1981) who has shown the many ways in which the self is intrinsically prone to make large errors of judgment to its own advantage — for example, most people think they are above average on most positive traits.

A final social criticism — implicit in the preceding — is a cultural critique. Briefly, it is now apparent that *the old psychology was an especially "American" psychology* (for example, see Kilpatrick, 1983). The emphasis on the autonomous individual and the hostility to society and tradition is a mixture of modernist ideologies with many especially American ideas and values. In a nation started by a Declaration of Independence, with an old tradition of the "self-made man" who was always changing and becoming more up-to-date; in a nation with a long history of enthusiasm for growth and change, the 1970 psychology is not hard to see as typically American. For Americans to develop, to believe in and export such a psychology was perfectly natural, but to imply that its truth value derived from empirical and objective science was questionable, to put it politely. In any case, as the psychology of personality becomes less American and more international, the old consensus will erode still further.

The Ideological and Philosophical Critique

In many respects the most devastating and far reaching criticism of the old consensus, and indeed of all social science, has been the recent ideological analysis and criticism of social science as practiced today. The bottom line has been to show that ideology in the form of political and philosophic presuppositions has played a controlling role in theories of the person, put forward as supposedly objective models of man. I will touch briefly on only three of the relevant critics here.

One of the first to criticize effectively the ideology of psychology, and especially psychiatry, was Thomas Szasz (1964, 1978), whose arguments are still having repercussions. Szasz's basic point is that psychiatry as a branch of medicine, has turned into a kind of new "secular priesthood" which uses its diagnostic categories to enhance its own power and the power of the institutions it serves. Szasz effectively argues that any notion of "a distinctively human, normal, or well functioning personality is rooted in psychosocial and ethical criteria."

Thus, what is diagnosed as mental illness is often in reality an expression of a person's having social needs and lacking social power, which have little or nothing to do with some supposed underlying medical problem. To warn against such false supposition of medical illness is not, of course, to deny the obvious biological base of many psychiatric cases (unfortunately, in his extreme position Szasz has done a disservice, for many people do suffer greatly from biologically based mental illness). Szasz's important point is that psychiatric labeling has been over-extended, and that many abuses of psychiatry stem from the social and political ideology of psychiatrists (See Bobgan & Bobgan, 1979, for a good critical review of psychology and its tendency to label quite normal and ordinary unhappiness as mental illness, or at least as neurosis). As far as I can judge, most of the "neurotic" unhappiness I encounter in people ages 20–40 *today* would be seriously reduced by (a) a good job, or (b) a good marriage, (c) a community of good friends, or (d) medical help for their biologically based problems, including biologically based mental problems. These are, of course, reality problems. The irony is that "social science" has done much to make both a good mate and good friends harder to find in today's society, and to make biologically based mental illness harder to diagnose and understand.

More recently, Christopher Lasch, in a strong attack on modern social science or the so-called "helping professions," has cogently argued that the modern psychology of personality is an expression of the peculiar economic and social situation of the last few decades (1975, 1979). In particular, he interprets the growth of the psychological professions as an extension of the late stages of capitalism. In the first stage the father and work were taken out of the family and transferred to the factory; now in the late stage of consumer capitalism, the mother and child are taken out of the family, the mother to a job in the service economy, and the child to the school and to the psychological clinic. Lasch, in his analysis of the narcissistic consequences of modern psychology, thus interprets the popularization of psychological definitions of personality and the person as a procedure for extending the power of the psychological professions, and above all, of the government and corporate institutions which they largely represent. Once the person is safely in the hands of the "helping professions," then the family is no longer in control of child rearing, and the economy and the state can more effectively create people who serve their interests.

Among other things this means that the value of being a mother —

to say nothing of the value of being a father — must be downplayed (and it certainly has been). Other values, such as those of the supposedly autonomous individual and of having a self-actualizing career, must be promoted. And, of course, values that support a traditional strong family life must be actively attacked.

A third ideological critic is Robert T. Hogan (1975, 1978, 1980), who has identified the many philosophical and political assumptions built into much of recent social science. A detailed discussion of Hogan's analysis is not possible here. However, he identifies a number of major biases in social psychology, and by implication, most of social science as it was found in the established theories in the 1970s. He notes that social science has been overwhelmingly rationalistic, individualistic, and politically liberal in its basic assumptions, and that these biases are embedded in theory and experiment in a disguised manner. As a result, social scientists have falsely represented their theories and results as the unbiased findings of scientific research. Hogan (1978) is especially critical of Lawrence Kohlberg's theory of moral development for its incorporating liberal political philosophy in the guise of empirical science.

Other widely influential critics of psychology who focus on ideological moral, and philosophical bias are Phillip Rieff (*The Triumph of the Therapeutic,* 1964), and Ernest Becker (*The Denial of Death,* 1973; *Escape from Evil,* 1975). The result of these criticisms, and of many others in recent years, such as the Christian psychology of Myers (1978), has been to challenge radically — in fact to reject — the very idea of an unbiased, objective social science, at least at the level of theory and interpretation. This conclusion is of great significance. For it means, among other things, that what I was to do in this paper cannot really be done. I was, as you recall, asked to summarize the consensus about the empirical nature of the person. Well, this is no longer viewed as possible, since no notion as theoretically loaded as "person" can be separated from ideology, philosophy, etc. But perhaps this issue can be better addressed within the context of the next type of criticism.

The Moral and Religious Critique

Finally, another major type of critique has recently emerged from a moral and religious perspective. First, the moral critique: The basic point is that there are no facts without values. Instead, facts and values

205

go together like nouns and verbs, or like a particle's mass and its velocity. Even to attend to a particular fact is already to give it a value with respect to those facts ignored. In psychology, in all social science, this problem becomes so pervasive that the notion of scientific objectivity must be seen as impossible when it comes to theory. Once central problem is that within the traditional, objective scientific paradigm, there is no way to go from what is observed as a fact to a valuing of that fact. There is no way to go from what *is* to what *should be*. Now with the physical, and to a large degree the biological sciences, this is not so acute a problem; although the new biological interpretation of the person and even more, the realities of genetic engineering, raise immediate and profound moral issues.

But in psychology there cannot be a theory of the person without associated values. There cannot be a practical application of psychology in therapy or counseling which does not immediately bring in values. At present, much of clinical and counseling psychology recognizes this general difficulty — but, to my knowledge, not one textbook in abnormal or clinical psychology has any systematic treatment of the actual values implied in the different theories and in the different kinds of treatment recommended! Of course, if textbooks did treat this issue, it would become obvious that psychology is deeply involved in ethics, philosophy, and social ideology. This whole issue lies behind a number of recent criticisms of the status quo, and again, it is forcing a painful re-evaluation of psychological practice by many (Bergin, 1980).

A final critique of the once and former consensus is explicitly religious. The problem is that *the very concept of person is itself religious in origin and character* — and explicitly Christian.

But psychologists don't know this. They do usually know that the word *"person"* comes from the Latin *"persona"* which meant *"mask"*, and also of the theatrical role that went with the mask. But the origin of the word "person" is not the significant thing; what is important is that the *concept* of a person which is unique to the western world was first introduced as part of basic Christian theology. That is, the first use of the word for *person* in the modern sense arose out of the theology of the Trinity and of the Incarnation: God as three persons, and Christ as both the second person of the Trinity and as the perfect expression of a person in human form. It is in the image of this trinitarian God that we are all created. Now of course in certain significant respects, the origin of the idea of a person is found in Judaism, in which from the beginning God was understood as a person, as a personal God. In any case the concept of a person "remained unknown to ancient pagan philosophy and first appears as a technical term in early Christian theology" (Muller & Hadler, 1969, p. 404). The concept of a "person" then developed and remained within the context of Christian philosophy and theology for hundreds of years, and this concept of a person "still determines modern thinking to a great extent" (Muller & Hadler, p. 404).

The notion of personality in its contemporary psychological and utterly secular sense is quite recent, being no more than 50 or 60 years old. In view of the anti-theistic character of modern personality theory, it is not surprising that these secular theories should end up by reducing the concept of a person to something like the pre-Christian pagan idea which was essentially a purely naturalistic idea of an individual — without the dignity, the moral and spiritual importance of the Judeo-Christian understanding of a person (Indeed the widespread loss of respect for the person in recent decades can be attributed in part to the rise of prominence of the secular humanist or modern pagan understanding of personality. This reduced idea of a person is a common factor in such diverse positions as abortion, fascism, Stalinism, etc.). This means that when Carl Rogers (1961) titles his best known book "On Becoming a Person," he is simply wrong. Instead, what Rogers wrote was a book about becoming an individual — an autonomous, self-actualizing individual who is devoted to the growth of the secular self. But he is not talking about the *person*. The psychologist Adler apparently understood this, since he termed his theory "individual psychology"; likewise Jung put "individuation" at the center of psychological growth and development (The distinction between the person and the individual is a very old one in philosophy. See, for example, Maritain, 1947).

The Christian understanding of the person, then, has strong psychological implications. This brings me to my final critical point, which is to mention that *in the last few years a consciously articulated Christian psychology has begun to emerge* (Adams, 1970, 1973; Bergin, 1980; Bufford, 1981; Collins, 1977; Crabb, 1978; Fleck & Carter, 1981; McDonagh, 1982; McLemore, 1982; Solomon, 1982; Strong, 1977; Tournier, 1962, 1965; Van Leeuwen, 1982; Vitz, 1981, 1982). If this approach continues to develop, and it shows every sign of being young, lively, and growing, then the notion of the person will have a very good chance of being understood both psychologically and spiritually (see Groeschel, 1983). And, of course, it will be necessary for a

Christian psychology of the person to be deeply informed by Christian philosophy and theology.

Conclusion

Let me sum up the major new evidence and its significance for the newer, more realistic understanding of the person.

1. Increasingly, human nature is being interpreted as rooted in biology. This biological evidence makes clear that all individuals operate within a set of biological restraints and limits. While social learning will still have importance, especially in such areas as morality, character, and social beliefs, biology will be given more and more weight in understanding man.

2. Increasingly, healthy personality formation is being understood as needing the nurturance of a stable, committed family, ideally of both a father and mother. Further, the need for strong social bonds (committed relationships) with friends and a community, is becoming understood as essential in supporting a happy and productive personality.

3. The ideological criticisms have now made it clear that any theory of the person, any interpretation of an ideal individual, any proposal for what people should become, is rooted in philosophy, social ideology, and often religion. As this becomes more widely appreciated, it will force all interpretations of the person to distinguish carefully between the empirical evidence being cited and the interpretation being proposed.

More specifically: Since the very concept of a person is derived from Christian theology, future interpretations of the person will not only involve ideology and philosophy, they will have to explicitly deal with religious issues. As noted, most of the so-called theories proposed by secular psychology are, in fact, theories of the individual, since they are without any acknowledged spiritual, or moral, or theistic character. Certainly the new empirical findings are most important and must be understood, for if grace perfects nature, it is still necessary to know what our nature is. However, the way in which grace perfects nature so as to truly "actualize" a person, is a topic for the emerging Christian psychology — and ultimately, of course, for Christian philosophy and theology.

Footnotes

1. Important historical influences came from Freud, Jung, and Adler, the three founders of personality theory and of modern psychotherapy. Freud's early concern with dreams and the unconscious and his essential pessimism about human nature were, however, mostly rejected. Instead, his ideas were Americanized, if you will, by the rise of psychoanalytic "ego-psychology," with its positive conept of the ego as having its own autonomous sphere of mental activity (Hartmann, 1958). This new ego-psychology easily fit into the American self-psychology consensus with its optimistic emphasis on change and growth. Alfred Adler's psychology, with its concern with the social environment and with a person's "style of life," did much to create humanistic psychology. That part of Carl Jung's psychology that focused on the self and self-realization fed the popular self-actualization psychology. As noted, much of the rest of Jung, however, lay outside the 1970 consensus.

The early writings of the behaviorists such as Watson, Hull, and Skinner set up the rationale for social learning as central to the formation of personality while Piaget, Bartlett, and Lewin laid the foundations for many of the later cognitive models of the mind. In child psychology the writings of Baldwin and Piaget introduced the first extensive cognitive interpretation of the child.

The important recent philosophical influences behind this consensus came from three major sources. The first might be called the emphasis on experience and learning developed in the philosophy of John Dewey and which had such an impact in education. Whitehead and his process philosophy also had some influence in this regard. Another source was the tough-minded philosophic position of Bertrand Russell and the European positivists with their concern with reason, measurement, and observation. A third influence came from the European existentialist concern with the individual self which because it exists in a world without God, must create its own meaning. This meaning is created by making choices unconditioned by others or society. The growth of such a self requires a continual making of such choices — thus bringing the so-called "authentic self" into existence or actualization.

2. A very thoughtful, philosophically sophisticated discussion of the need for paradigm change in psychology, especially social psychology, has recently been published by the Christian psychologist Mary Stewart Van Leeuwen (1982).

3. A very recent example of the collapse of the 1970 consensus surfaced in social anthropology while I was writing this paper. Derek Freeman's book, *Margaret Mead and Samoa: The Making and Unmaking of an Anthropological Myth*, was discussed in advance of publication by Harvard University Press in the *New York Times* (January 31, 1983; see also the *New York Times* Science section the next day; also *Science*, 1983, *219*, 1042–1045). According to those who have already read it, Freeman shows quite convincingly that Mead's picture of Samoans as a peaceful, happy people who condoned adolescent free love is simply wrong — and in some respects "preposterously false." None of the anthropologists cited (January 31, February 1) denied Freeman's evidence, although several excused Mead on the grounds that when she did her study in the 1920s anthropological methodology was not very advanced. But, Mead's major weaknesses, according to Freeman and unchallenged by others, were: (1) She had very little knowledge of the Samoan language; (2) She did no preliminary study of Samoa prior to her visit; and (3) When she was there she lived with expatriate Americans, not in a Samoan household. (4) She only stayed nine months. Since these failings, even in the 1920s, violated the most elementary common sense of ethnological study, the critical judgment of Mead must, I believe, be severe. Freeman makes the case that Mead's professional shortcomings were primarily the result of her doctrinal baggage: "it was her deeply convinced belief in the doctrine of extreme cultural determinism, . . . that led her to construct an account of Samoa that appeared to substantiate this very doctrine" (January 31). Mead's message of cultural relativism and "free love" was spread around the world through the sales of millions of copies of her book; its message has widely influenced laws, social policy, and child rearing. As the *New York Times* article also notes, the social learning approach to anthropology has given much ground in the last decade to biological views of behavior. Mead's misleading social anthropology is no isolated example. Much of her other work has also been strongly criticized by other anthropologists. Also, Ralph Linton, a prominent anthropologist with anthropological views similar to Mead's, has been

raked over the coals by his colleagues for misrepresenting Marquesan culture. The critique of Linton is similar to that leveled against Mead (see Symons, 1979).

4. Some of the negative biological consequences from extensive, long-term use of psychopharmacological treatment will probably not get discovered for a good number of years.

5. See *The Selfish Gene* by R. Dawkins for a philosophically naive and troubling expression of the biological approach to morality.

6. A few of the many others whose writings seriously call into question the possibility of objective social science, especially an objective psychology, are: Andreski (1972); Hudson (1972); Koch (1969, 1973); Polyani (1964); Coan (1977); Vitz (1977), Gross (1978).

References

Adams, J. E. *Competent to Counsel.* Nutley, NJ: Presbyterian and Reformed Publishing Company, 1970.

Adams, J. E. *The Christian Counselor's Manual.* Nutley, NJ: Presbyterian and Reformed Publishing Company, 1973.

Adelson, J. Psychological Research on a Profound Issue. *Science,* 1975, *190,* 1288–1289.

Andreski, S. *Social Sciences as Sorcery.* New York: St. Martins, 1972.

Baer, R. A., Jr. Values Classification as Indoctrination. *The Educational Forum,* 1977, *41,* 155–165.

Baer, R. A., Jr. A Critique of the Use of Values Clarification in Environmental Education. *The Journal of Environmental Education,* 1980, *12,* 13–16.

Bandura, A. *Principles of Behavior Modification.* New York: Holt, Rinehart, and Winston, 1969.

Becker, E. *The Denial of Death.* New York: Free Press, 1973.

Becker, E. *Escape from Evil.* New York: Free Press, 1975.

Bennett, W. J., & Delattre, E. J. Moral Education in the Schools. *Public Interest,* 1978, *50,* 81–98.

Bergin, A. E. Psychotherapy and Religious Values. *Journal of Consulting & Clinical Psychology,* 1980, *48,* 95–105.

Berne, L. *Games People Play.* New York: Grove, 1964.

Blakeslee, T. R. *The Right Brain.* Garden City, NY: Anchor/Doubleday, 1980.

Bobgan, M. & Bobgan, D. *The Psychological Way/the Spiritual Way.* Minneapolis: Bethany Fellowship, 1979.

Bowlby, John. *Attachment and Loss, Volume I: Attachment.* New York: Basic Books, 1969.

Bowlby, John. *Attachment and Loss, Volume II: Separation, Anxiety, and Anger.* New York: Basic Books, 1973.

Bowlby, John. *Attachment and Loss, Volume III: Loss, Sadness and Depression.* New York: Basic Books, 1980.

Bufford, R. K. *The Human Reflex: Behavioral Psychology in Biblical Perspective.* San Francisco: Harper & Row, 1981.

Buss, A. H., Plomin, R., & Willerman, L. The Inheritance of Temperaments. *Journal of Personality,* 1973, *41,* 513–524.

Coan, Richard W. *Hero, Artist, Sage or Saint? A Survey of Views of What is Variously Called Mental Health, Normality, Maturity, Self-actualization and Human Fulfillment.* New York: Columbia University Press, 1977.

Collins, G. R. *The Rebuilding of Psychology.* Wheaton, Ill.: Tyndale, 1977.

Cooper, J. R., & Bloom, F. E. *Biochemical Basis of Neuropharmacology.* Fourth Edition. New York: Oxford, 1982.

Crabb, L. J. Biblical Counseling: A Basic View. *The CAPS Bulletin,* 1978, *4,* 1–6.

Davidson, R. J., & Fox, N. A. Asymmetrical Brain Activity Discriminates Between Positive and Negative Affective Stimuli in Human Infants. *Science,* 1982, *218,* 1235–1237.

Dawkins, R. *The Selfish Gene.* New York: Oxford, 1976.

Eger, M. The Conflict in Moral Education. *Public Interest,* 1981, *63,* 62–80.

Farber, S. L. *Identical Twins Reared Apart: A Reanalysis.* New York: Basic Books, 1981.

Festinger, L. *A Theory of Cognitive Dissonance.* Evanston, Ill: Row, Peterson, 1957.

Fleck, J. R., & Carter, J. D. *Psychology and Christianity: Integrative Readings.* Nashville, Tenn.: Abingdon, 1981.

Fromm, E. *Man for Himself.* New York: Rinehart, 1947.

Fromm, E. *The Sane Society.* New York: Rinehart, 1955.

Fromm, E. *You Shall be as Gods.* New York: Holt, Rinehart, & Winston, 1966.

Gilligan, C. In a Different Voice: Women's Conception of the Self and of Morality. *Harvard Educational Review,* 1977, *47,* 481–517.

Gilligan, C. *In a Different Voice: Psychology Theory and Women's Development.* Cambridge, Mass.: Harvard University Press, 1982.

Goodwin, D. W., Schulsinger, F., Hermansen, K., Guze, S. B., & Winokur, G. Alcohol Problems in Adoptees Raised Apart from Alcoholic Biological Parents. *Archives of General Psychiatry,* 1973, *28,* 238–243.

Gottesman, I. I., & Shields, J. *Schizophrenia and Genetics: A Twin Study Vantage Point.* New York: Academic Press, 1972.

Gow, K. M. *Yes, Virginia, There is a Right and Wrong.* Rexdale, Ontario: John Wiley, 1980.

Goy, R. W., & McEwen, B. S. *Sexual Differentiation of the Brain.* Cambridge, Mass.: MIT Press, 1980.

Groeschel, B. *Spiritual Passages: The Psychology of Spiritual Development.* New York: Crossroads, 1983.

Gross, M. *The Psychological Society.* New York: Random House, 1978.

Hamburg, B., & McGown, E. (Eds.). *The Great Apes.* Menlo Park, CA: Benjamin Cummings, 1979.

Harris, T. A. *I'm OK—You're OK.* New York, Avon, 1969.

Hartmann, H. *Ego Psychology and the Problem of Adaptation.* New York: International Universitites Press, 1958.

Hogan, R. T. Theoretical Ego Centrism and the Problem of Compliance. *American Psychologist,* 1975, *30,* 533–540.

Hogan, R. T., & Emler, N. P. The Biases in Contemporary Social Psychology. *Social Research,* 1978, *45,* 478–534.

Hogan, R. T., & Schroeder, D. The Joy of Sex for Children and Other Modern Fables. *Character,* 1980, *1,* 1–8.

Hudson, L. *The Cult of the Fact.* London: Cape, 1972.

Kilpatrick, W. K. *Psychological Seduction.* Nashville, Tenn.: Nelson, 1983.

Koch, S. (Ed.). *Psychology: A Study of a Science.* New York: McGraw-Hill, 1959–1963.

Koch, S. Psychology Cannot be a Coherent Science. *Psychology Today,* September 1969, p. 66.

Kohlberg, L. Stages of Moral Development as a Basis for Moral Education. In Beck, Crittenden, & Sullivan (Eds.), *Moral Education: Interdisciplinary Approaches.* Toronto: University of Toronto Press, 1971.

Kohlberg, L. *Essays on Moral Development, Volume One: The Philosophy of Moral Development.* New York: Harper & Row, 1981.

Kuhl, P. K., & Meltzoff, A. N. The Bimodal Perception of Speech in Infancy. *Science,* 1982, *218,* 1138–1141.

Kurtines, W., & Greif, E. B. The development of Moral Thought: A Review and Evaluation of Kohlberg's Approach. *Psychological Bulletin,* 1974, *81,* 455–460.

Lacoste-Utamsing, C. & Halloway, R. L. Sexual Dimorphism in the Human Corpus Callosum, *Science, 216,* 1982, 1431–1432.

Lamb, M. E., & Campos, J. J. *Infancy.* New York: Random House, 1982.

Lasch, C. *Haven in a Heartless World: The Family Besieged.* New York: Basic Books, 1975.

Lasch, C. *The Culture of Narcissism.* New York: Norton, 1979.

Levin, M. The Stages of Man? *Commentary,* 1982, *73,* 84–86.

Lipton, M., Camascio, A., & Killan, K. *Psychopharmacology: A Generation of Progress.* New York: Raven, 1978.

Lockwood, A. L. Values, Education and the Right to Privacy. *Journal of Moral Education,* October 1977, 9–26.

Lockwood, A. L. The Effects of Values Clarification and Moral Development Curricula on School-age Subjects. A Critical Review of Recent Research. *Review of Educational Research,* 1978, *48,* 325–364.

211

Maddi, S. R. *Personality Theories: A Comparative Analysis.* 3rd Edition. Homewood, Ill.: Dorsey, 1976.

Maritain, J. *The Person and the Common Good.* Notre Dame, Indiana: Notre Dame Press, 1966 (First published 1947 by Scribners, New York)

Marx, J. Research News: Autoimmunity in left-handers. *Science,* 1982, *217,* 141–144.

Maslow, A. *Motivation and Personality* (2nd Edition). New York: Harper & Row, 1970.

Maslow, A. *Toward a Psychology of Being* (2nd Edition). New York: Van Nostrand Reinhold, 1968.

May, Robert. *Sex and Fantasy: Patterns of Male and Female Development.* New York: Norton, 1980.

May, Rollo. *Man's Search for Himself.* New York: Norton, 1953.

May, Rollo, Angle, E., & Ellenberger, H. F. (Eds.), *Existence: A New Dimension in Psychiatry and Psychology.* New York: Basic Books, 1958.

McDonagh, J. M. *Christian Psychology.* New York: Crossroad, 1982.

McLemore, O. W. *The Scandal of Psychotherapy.* Wheaton, Ill.: Tyndale, 1982.

Michel, W. *Personality and Assessment.* New York: Wiley, 1968.

Michel, W. *Introduction to Personality.* New York: Holt, Rinehart, & Winston, 1971.

Müller, M. & Hadler, A. Person Concept. In *Sacramentum Mundi,* vol. 4. New York: Herder and Herder, 1969.

Myers, D. *The Human Puzzle: Psychological Research & Christian Belief.* New York: Harper & Row, 1978.

Myers, D. *The Inflated Self.* New York: Seabury, 1981.

Osofsky, J. (Ed.). *Handbook of Infant Development.* New York: Wiley, 1979.

Perls, F. S. *Gestalt Therapy Verbatim.* Lafayette, Calif.: Real People Press, 1969.

Polyani, M. *Personal Knowledge.* New York: Harper & Row, 1964.

Rieff, P. *The Triumph of the Therapeutic.* New York: Harper & Row, 1966.

Raths, L., Merrill, H., Simon, S. *Values and Teaching.* Columbus, Ohio: Merrill, 1966.

Rogers, C. *Client-Centered Therapy.* Boston: Houghton-Mifflin, 1951.

Rogers, C. *On Becoming a Person.* Boston: Houghton-Mifflin, 1961.

Rogers, C. Some Issues Concerning the Control of Human Behavior (Symposium with B. F. Skinner). *Science,* 1956, *124,* 1057–1066.

Shields, J. Heredity and Environment. In H. J. Eysenck & G. D. Wilson (Eds.), *A Testbook of Human Psychology.* Baltimore: University Park Press, 1976.

Simon, S. B., Howe, L. W., Kirschenbaum, H. *Values Clarification* (rev. ed.). New York: Hart, 1978.

Solomon, L. R. *The Rejection Syndrome.* Wheaton, Ill.: Tyndale, 1982.

Sperry, R. Hemisphere Deconnection and Unity in Conscious Awareness. *American Psychologist,* 1968, *23,* 723–733.

Strong, Stanley (Ed.). Christian Counseling. *Counseling and Values,* 1977, *21,* 75–128.

Symons, D. *The Evolution of Human Sexuality.* New York: Oxford, 1979.

Synder, S. H. *Madness and the Brain.* New York: McGraw-Hill, 1975.

Szasz, T. *The Myth of Mental Illness* (rev. ed.). New York: Harper & Row, 1974. (First published 1961, New York: Hoeber & Harper)

Szasz, T. *The Myth of Psychotherapy.* Garden City, NY: Anchor/Doubleday, 1978.

Tournier, P. *Grace and Guilt.* New York: Harper & Row, 1962.

Tournier, P. *The Healing of Persons.* New York: Harper & Row, 1965.

Vitz, P. C. *Psychology as Religion: The Cult of Self-Worship.* Grand Rapids, Mich.: Eerdmans, 1977.

Vitz, P. C. Values Clarification in the Schools. *New Oxford Review,* 1981, *48,* 15–20. (a)

Vitz, P. C. Secular Humanism and Morality: Against Kohlberg. *New Oxford Review,* 1981, *48,* 20–22. (b)

Vitz, P. C. Moral Education: A Comparison of Secular and Religious Models. In *Cathechetical Instruction and the Catholic Faithful.* Boston: St. Paul Editions, 1982.

Wallerstein, J. S., & Kelly, J. B. *Surviving the Breakup: How Children and Parents Cope with Divorce.* New York: Basic Books, 1980.

Wilson, E. O. *Sociobiology: The New Synthesis.* Cambridge, Mass.: Harvard (Belknap), 1975.

Chapter 8

The Person and the Human Significance of Life

Anna-Teresa Tymieniecka, Ph.D.

Editorial Preface

Modern thought has brought out the marvelous complexity of man, who is viewed as having a "place" and "role" within the entire system of life. At the same time, this contemporary appreciation points out vividly how precarious man's existence within the current of life is. The expression, "the human person," is used in everyday parlance to refer (often implicitly) to what is unique about man in the world, what makes him "special." The major question addressed here by Dr. Tymieniecka refers to this problem: How can the human being be conceived so as to give an adequate account of both the "naturalness" of life with which he "fits" into the entire life-system, and his role within the life-world in a manner unlike that of any other "animal"?

Dr. Tymieniecka begins her inquiry by showing the paradox which exists regarding the notion of the "human person" in contemporary culture: at the level of principles the "dignity" of the human person is acknowledged universally as

213

fully warranting the greatest of respect by man and his social institutions; in practice, the human person is abused in various ways, and its acknowledged rights are manipulated by fellowmen and social institutions with a view to the achievement of varying goals. She then expounds four "models" of the human person operant in people's minds and theories today, and discusses the underlying bases for each. The basis common to all of the models discussed is that of the person being the systematic articulation of the individual's "functioning." After a phenomenological look at the human person "in itself," undertaken in the third part of the essay, Dr. Tymieniecka is able to affirm that any adequate conception of the person must take into consideration a "virtual faculty" present in the human condition which she denominates "the Moral Sense." The latter is shown to be a more substantial basis for establishing the uniqueness of the human person than the more current basis of "values," since the rational calculus of values lends itself to the problem of the manipulation of the person, pointed out at the beginning of her inquiry, fails to provide a univocal basis for the mutual comprehension of man valid among all cultures, and paves the way for an excessive individualism. Dr. Tymieniecka then traces the workings of the Moral Sense in human functioning in the fourth part of her essay, depicting it as a key component for our understanding of the unique situation of the human person among living beings, amidst which it is man's essential contribution to give human meaning to the world of life and to his own actions, and to be the bearer of custodianship for the existential balance of "everything-there-is-alive."

An Overview of the Issue

At the recent symposium held in France to commemorate the origin of the personalist movement, it was remarked that, among the various concepts with which philosophers have attempted to grasp the specificity of the human being, only one has has remained unchallenged, and even gained in importance, namely, the concept of "person." Concepts like "human nature," "ego," "human subject," "consciousness," etc., which have in the past been used to express this specificity of man have now, in the light of recent insights into the situation of the human being obtained by scientific and scholarly inquiry, proved themselves unsatisfactory.

The scientific inquiry has clearly transformed our view of the living individual and of his circumambient world. From the static conception of the world as a box within which things and beings are "placed," we have moved to view the world as a relatively stable system in process of becoming, whose structure is projected by individual beings. The individual being is no longer seen as growing and developing according to a pre-established pattern of "humanness" from a prefabricated, miniature *homunculus* but as crystallizing from a germinal stage in a self-constructive process.[1] Last, and most significantly, the self-constructive progress of the individual appears to begin with an elementary conjunction of some simple elements within a life-context upon which it constantly draws and in response to which it shapes itself; and its progress is as much as integration into the circumambient life-conditions as a shaping of these conditions themselves. Modern science and philosophy have brought the investigation of nature, man, and the world from abstract speculation down into this concrete flux itself. We have become more attentive to the enormous variety of types of human individuals, to the life-conditions which have shaped them, and to the stages in the history of mankind during which the actually existing types of human beings have evolved. Having become aware of the transforming dynamics of life in which the progress of human beings is caught, we can ask: How far can the transformation of the human individual proceed without man's losing his "humanness"?[2]

The key intuition in the sciences of man consists of an emphasis upon the flexibility, variety, transformability, and vulnerability of the specifically human being who emerges from, and is sustained by, innumerable exterior conditions. This intuition pervades our approach to social and public issues; it underlies our sentiment of "cultural crisis" and "foreboding doom."

The groping for an adequate approach to the human being finds its expression in the search for an adequate conception of the human person. In philosophy, sociology, psychiatry, anthropology, public life or politics, reference to the human person in arguments concerning the crucial issues confronting man, the social world, or culture is identical with the recognition of man's specifically human status.[3] This reference is made to point out those uniquely human features which give man a special right to be considered in a special way by fellowmen and by man's collective institutions. It seems that today we could more than ever approve of Mounier's statement expressed several decades ago, that our civilization affirms the primacy of the human person over both the material necessities of life and the mechanisms of collective life. Last and most importantly, the value of the human person is such that it retains its prerogative, even an obligation, to reject the imposition of manipulating ideologies, tendencies, etc., that could be used to suppress its self-expression and decision-making. This means that to man as a person is attributed a special kind of prerogative precisely on account of the specific humanness which he exhibits. We may reaffirm with Mounier that in this sense contemporary culture — and not only in the Occident — exemplifies a strong personalistic tendency.

However, no single definition of the concept of "person" has yet been accepted. Conceptions of the person abound, and vary so widely that they suggest different, even opposed, attitudes toward man. The human person is, in fact, currently approached in terms of values. Since values are the product of specific cultures, they are themselves conditioned by the tendencies and biases of a particular cultural period. Hence, the concept of person, conceived on the basis of values, fails as a point-of-reference toward mutual understanding; different societies, social groups, and individuals subscribe to different sets of values. At the same time, an overemphasis on the values of the person, or on the status of the human individual, leads to an extreme individualism. Indeed, present-day Occidental culture has produced, in the name of the extraordinary value of the human individual/person, claims which menace the existential equilibrium of humanity itself. This suggests that the approach to the human person is not such a simple matter as it might seem. It is indispensable that we clarify the problem of the person before proceeding to some constructive ideas toward a proper understanding.

To this end, I will raise two sets of questions, which open a twofold perspective on the inquiry into the human person. First, we must look into man's current understanding of his basic existential conditions. Second, we must ask how this view of man's existential conditions (within nature as well as within his life-world) accounts for the varieties of notions of the person. The paramount question, however, which I will attempt to answer at the end of my investigation is: How should we conceive of the human person such that we can draw a definite line of demarcation between human beings and the animals, on the one hand, and indicate an adequate way for man to understand himself, on the other? I propose, in fact, that it is "moral sense" as a unique virtuality of the "human condition" within the system of life and the world, which is the decisive factor in man's specificity, the meaning of his life and of his destiny. It is also the sole valid indicator or man's responsibility in private and social matters. Most importantly, however, the moral sense is, in my view, the decisive factor in making man aware of his situation and role within the *existential* unity of everything-there-is-alive.

PART I

The Paradoxical Situation of the Human Individual as Revealed by Contemporary Science

a. Conditioning Versus Autonomy

Contemporary psychology, anthropolgy, and sociology have made us aware of the extraordinary precariousness of man's life and social situation — a situation precarious to the point that, in investigating the innumerable contingencies of the individual's life-course, the line of pursuit loses track of the crucial factors which direct his differentiation from the rest of life. When viewed within the multitude of existential ramifications impinging on it, human life seems to dissolve into the fabric of both natural life and societal existence.

On the one hand, in the face of the vital forces which constitute the unbroken network of existential conditions, the very reality of man's "autonomy" appears questionable. On the other hand, the precariousness of man's autonomy — whatever preliminary meaning we may attribute to it — would have to be wrung out by him from such an absorbing tissue of essential dependencies and interdependencies within this fabric of life, that the traditional ontologies and philosophies of human nature, in the anthropocentric emphasis, offer little more than ideal speculation. Indeed, in view of the innumerable factors shaping the individual life-course, and man's decisions and actions, we cannot assume without examination that any of his social manifestations, his likes and dislikes, aims and ambitions, even his will, are his "own." That is, concurrently with seeking whether he has any say about his course, we must discover what his "own" course would mean.

And yet, the same fabric of life and of the world, which ever seems to be absorbing the human being, is not chaotic. Existence means order. And strangely — but significantly — in the attempts to grasp this order, attempts in which we oscillate between the "infinitely great" and the "infinitely small" as the starting point, the greatest emphasis falls upon the individual as the cornerstone of universal world-order. The human individual is the core of the preoccupations of human science, morality, and the socio-civic laws, regulations, and structures; paradoxically, they are all founded on the assumption of the very thing which they puzzle over in their investigations: man's autonomy with respect to his circumambient conditions.

That is, all human interests and endeavors which are objects of inquiry (practical, philosophical, scientific) — and which ultimately reveal the nature of man — are distributed around the axis of this paradoxical nature of man: his existential selfhood measured over against the power of forces which keep him in existence.

In fact, our renewed phenomenological inquiry into the nature of *man and the human condition* shows that, in spite of the fact that the human individual might be "thrown" into the life-world (as Heidegger points out) without having a choice, he "individualizes" himself nevertheless in various phases which unfold his faculties within the circumambient life-conditions. In contradistinction to all other types of living beings, the human individual appears, in fact, as the only one who takes into his own hands the individualizing course and balances out his tendencies toward selfhood and the conditioning determinants. Moreover, he turns the second to the advantage of the first. Lastly, he deploys his virtualities for existential connectedness into the intersubjective commerce with other human beings from which, in a common effort, he elicits the personal significance of his own existence.

b. The Glorification of the Individual Versus Contempt for His Rights

It is at this juncture that the foundation of morality — morality operative in the intersubjective circuit of man's self-individualization — is to be found. In the present stage of Western culture, in which man's "selfhood" attempts to exercise an inventive control, even over the intersubjective, that is, social conditions, we witness a striking and absurd phenomenon. On the one hand, there is great progress in recognizing human individuality; there is a stress upon and call for the highest possible autonomy and independence of the self (in freedom of choice, direction, respect for individual needs, etc.) in the intersubjective, social life-world. This concern with the individual is expressed by recognition of man's rights and of the need for suitable conditions in

218

which to exercise them. Further, these rights are being protected by elaborate, rationally formulated, legal measures: principles, laws, rules, regulations, and precepts support their recognition. These rights form the operative "nervous system" of social life: individual transactions, corporations, societal institutions (educational, practical, political, religious) have pledged to honor them, and pride themselves on their attempts to incarnate their validity. These rationally devised measures designed to protect man's individualized selfhood — which is proclaimed to be an inalienable right — has been increasingly corroborated and developed. Again, paradoxically, as if to challenge the moral validity of this specifically human prerogative, the inventive meaning-bestowing as actually put into practice in modern Occidental culture characterizes itself by a well-founded suspicion on the part of individuals toward those social institutions which, while pretending to implement these laws, are in fact intent on ignoring, abusing, and violating them; that is, there is a widespread effort to neglect the *moral axis* upon which the very essence of intersubjective sociability is suspended.

c. Overrationalization resulting in the Loss of Balance in Vitally Significant Estimations

1. *Injustice*

A few decades ago, Husserl diagnosed the crisis of Occidental culture as involving the estrangement of the Western human being and of his lived-world from his existential soil — which he called the "life-world" of natural human deployment. Husserl attributed this estrangement to the excessive, and inadequately interpreted, development of human reason (intellect). His denunciation of reason was, however, restricted to the cognitive experience.[4]

Can it be that Husserl meant to defend an unadumbrated and automatically assumed sovereignty of reason, which is in a specific way responsible for this seemingly insoluble paradox? Is man not much more than a cognizing being? Is the cognitive experience constitutive of the life-world not essentially intertwined with the "moral experience"? The question of paramount importance is then: What is playing the crucial role in the foundation of the life-world in its social, that is specifically human, phase? What is the relation of the cognitive experience to the moral experience? Certainly, in modern culture — in the objective regulations of the social order, the sphere of the implementation of law and of the distribution of social justice and morality, etc. — it is held to be reason (intellect) which is the sole arbiter of the "objective" understanding, deliberation, decision-making, and implementing of law. Law, which is rooted in morality, is meant to enable the human being to delineate his own life-course in the midst of social "conditioning" upon the unfolding selfhood. In practice, however, the social institutions which implement laws often jeopardize this selfhood and violate man's sense of justice, his rights, and his very conscience by submitting it to the unyielding "conditioning" of social forces.

Is not the intellect, which interprets social laws in their implementation, responsible for this unfortunate development? Does its priority not confound the proper moral postulate of objectivity — to "give everyone his own" — with the false assumption that moral significance is the fruit of a morally neutral "objectivity" of things and of a life-survival system? Indeed, we entrust to reason the differentiation, discrimination, and appreciation of social situations in which moral significance is at stake. The logical conclusion is clear concerning the social appropriateness of this moral significance. Yet, since it is the faculty of the intellect, infinitely dissecting, adumbrating, inductively or speculatively concluding, and projecting new possibilities, which is recognized as the arbiter, then the understanding and appreciation of the social situation and the final decision depend upon the sharpness with which the intellect is exercised. In its infinite possibilities, the abstracting intellect is always capable of turning things to its own advantage. Short of logical contradiction, everything can be plausibly established and justified by reason. That is, there are infinite ways and means for achieving the social "conditioning" of the individual.

2.   The Abuse of Life

The superiority of reason over all the other functions of the human being is assumed obviously on the grounds of its capacity to estimate and calculate the elements of life-conditions. Yet, this calculation is performed with reference to values, which are themselves partly the fruit of rational estimation. Values may be situated in relation to each other; regulated, not according to their "natural" role, but by the respective importance attributed to them. Not only does this importance vary from culture and from one historical situation to another, but another, but it is itself subject to the rational calculus. With the growing faith in the sovereign values of human rational self-consciousness as the specific prerogative of the living human individual, his essential "ingrownness" in the life-system of all living creatures and nature (with the specific life-conditions) has been slowly forgotten. The person, identified with the intellectually suggested conveniences of the rationalized modes of existence, has lost consciousness of its life-community with everything there is alive. To pursue its so-called human prerogatives (privacy, independence, self-decision, etc., etc.) the human individual of today is alienating himself from his innermost grounding in the system of life. Moreover, stressing his unique self-importance, contemporary man has, due to the shortsighted pursuing of his individual interest, broken the equilibrium of his existential balance within the web of the unity of all living beings. The preference given to values serving uniquely his overblown importance endangers his very existence (ecology, arms race, use of natural resources, etc.).

It is apparent that the "rational calculus" of values is blind to the facts, laws, and prospects of life.[5] It is also obvious that reason alone is a misleading guide in matters of such crucial significance. I suggest that all matters of life are ultimately of "moral significance."

d. The "Moral Significance" of Life

To conclude, the crucial issue remains: If it is reason which, overreaching itself, becomes instrumental in the abuses of moral practice, what is it that is being abused? In other words: What is essential to the moral significance of human life? The precariousness of the human sociobiological condition points to the overwhelming role of the "natural" spontaneities (reactions, instincts, feelings, emotions, etc.) and to the limited power of reason in dealing with the opposing forces, competitive situations, conflicts of interests, etc. And yet, not only does the individual delineate his life-course, but in addition he manages to cooperate with others in ways which respect their various interests. The modalities of this "transactional" understanding establishes the social world, which brings a new "meaningfulness" of life into the natural orbit. In the light of what we have just observed, it could not be in virtue of the rational faculty alone.

What is significant in fact for this inquiry is the search for the origin of moral meaningfulness in human feelings and actions. The fact that communication within human life and the social world is suffused with a "moral language" (concepts, judgments, values, etc.) is obvious. It is equally obvious that this language is not the "language of objects."

Currently in philosophy it is assumed to be the "language of values." In my own contributions I am challenging this priority of values. I submit that this priority is the real culprit in the current moral disarray: the discrepancy between the striving for freedom of the human conscience (against social conditioning) as the guarantee of the highest accomplishment of human beingness (guaranteed by laws), and the cunningly subversive coercion of this very individual into submission to the practical ineffectiveness of the laws and social conditions. This submission deprives man even of the "freedom of conscience." Its effects impinge even upon the self-interpretative meaningfulness of his life, his very selfhood!

Indeed, the moral significance of our intersubjective relations with other beings neither stems from, nor remains protected by, the jurisdiction of reason alone. We have to seek the origin of the moral significance of man's self-interpretation in existence in the autonomous faculty of the *Moral Sense!*[6]

PART II

The Notion of the "Human Person" at the Crossroads of the Understanding of Man Within the Life-World Process

a. The Notion of "Person" as the Point of Reference for the Understanding of Man Within his Life-Conditions

As mentioned above, in contemporary thought the notion of the "human person" plays the role of a point of reference for understanding the human being. The human being is in our times viewed in concrete terms, that is, not as an abstract model of an entity, but as a living individual struggling for survival with the organic life-conditions on the one hand, and the world-conditions on the other. Concreteness and flexibility in the notion of "human person" appear to be most appropriate to account for various features of the human individual, which are approached from different perspectives. Fundamentally, this notion is meant: first, to grasp and indicate the distinctiveness of the human being with respect to other living individuals and things, and the modalities of organic and social life; second, in appreciation of man's conduct, aims, rights with respect to the perspectives of his innermost nature. I would venture to say that, in general, too much stress is placed upon the unique accomplishments of the human being and not enough upon his role among other living beings which this uniqueness compels him to play. That is, in articulating the notion of the "person," we seek to establish a new *meaningfulness* (understanding) *of the specificity of the human being with respect to his organic conditions as well as to conditions which the world within which he delineates his life-course sets upon it.* In our times, in which little is taken for granted, we seek for an ever more adequate understanding of the world and of our place in it. Significantly, we have come to discover that not only the "brute" organic/cosmic/vital facts have no "meaning" unless we ourselves as sentient beings turn them into the conditions of our existence, but also that we might even transform these conditions by our own inventiveness. Therein lies the greatness and the peril of our age.

To establish the significance of the human being within his *vital*[a] conditions, within nature and his lived world, the notion of person is instrumental from various perspectives. First, it appears at the center of the investigations conducted by human science (psychiatry, psychology, the social sciences, etc.).[7] Second, it serves as a center of gravitation in the public debates on cultural, social, and political matters. Third, it remains a crucial notion in personal and religious practices. Although it is conceived in a great number of ways, and in terms of various approaches, we may distinguish in all of them one of the following three functions attributed to it.

First, the person always appears as a system of organization (or articulation) of the functioning of the living individual within his life-conditions. Second, it is taken as a pattern centralizing the fundamental faculties and virtualities operative in the individual's life-progress. Third, the notion of the "person" expresses through its structure and virtualities a specific phase of the individual's developmental achievement. The epitome of this third model, which includes the other two, is, or culminates in, man's self-conscious functioning. It pinpoints the specifically sociopolitical[b] significance of life.

---

[a]The term 'vital' is used here to denote the fully developed phase of life and of its conditions.
[b]By 'political' is meant here, in the Greek tradition, the specific feature of man's social nature consisting of constructing a "polis," a state orchestration of social life.

b. The First Two Basic Models for the Conception of the Person

We may see the *first function* of the notion of the person as basic to psychiatry. Introduced into psychiatry by Freud and Jung,[8] the person plays an increasingly central role in diagnosis and therapy. It is intuited as a specific functional pattern by means of which the human being organizes his vital operations at the level of the life-world. Starting with organic processes, the individual unfolds a network of processes relating him to his circumambient world, by means of which, beyond strictly organic growth and subsistence, he projects around him a spatio-temporal dimension. Within this network he himself acquires a meaning as a living being and his circumambient conditions acquire the meaning of a "life-world." This projection by the living individual of interworldly relations with other living beings, things, events, and processes, endows them with a significance that reaches beyond that of the brute organic survival that is attributed to a *specific functional system:* the "person" (Binswanger).[9] Through his interrelations with other living beings, persons, events, and processes, the individual and his life-world are simultaneously sustained in existence, grow, and expand. Mental illness is here viewed as the dissipation of this functional system: the person — the central functional pattern of the interworldly relations — is disturbed; its functional ties disintegrate (Henri Eye).[10] With any degree of disintegration of the person some corresponding dimension of the life-world loses its significance. The mentally ill person becomes "confused" or "disturbed" but does not leave this world; the physical and social world "is there" for the others as it was before. Yet for the mentally ill it is reduced to its bare physicality. The significance of interworldly relationships which previously sustained the person within this world now vanishes.

The specific role of the person in giving meaning to the world within which the human individual pursues his existence is equally obvious in the *second type* of role attributed to the person. Indeed, from a sociocultural perspective, we attribute to the person a set of faculties, which accounts not only for the organic existence of the human individual but also for his sociocultural forms. These are organized in a coherent pattern comprising constant as well as variable features. Intelligence, imagination, will are the faculties which all human individuals are assumed to possess. They are the constants. Yet the industry with which individuals use them, capacities to apply them to different circumstances, adaptability to life-conditions, etc., seem to account for the vast variety of cultural and social differentiations which distinguish humanity as such. Moreover, the various "gifts," "talents," "virtual propensities," etc., which belong to this pattern, are distributed unequally and in their respective development account for the uniquely different "personalities" of individual human beings. The meaningfulness of life, which as a result of human creativity, inventiveness, etc., takes different cultural forms — as well as different forms of interpersonal and social relations — is the result of the person so understood.

We see, then, that in the process-like views of the world (and of the step-wise unfolding of life) to the notion of the person is attributed those functions that allow the individual to establish and pursue a coherent, meaningful existence within the flux of changing conditions.

c. The Third Model of the Person as a Subject/Agent Within the Social World

The radical shift from the assumption concerning the stable situation of man in the cosmos maintained in antiquity and the Middle Ages, to that of a fluctuating role which man develops for himself within the social world (an approach that began with modern philosophy and finds its culmination in present-day thought), motivates the third model of the conception of person. In fact, when it comes to the issue of public life, we find that philosophy, social science, political thinking, etc., almost unanimously refer to the person as to the *relatively stable system of self-conscious manifestation:* an "agent" from whom the initiatives and their realization within the social world stem; as the "subject," who is the direct or indirect recipient, victim, beneficiary, etc., of these actions. Seen simultaneously as agent and subject, the person is the cornerstone of public life: the bearer of responsibility toward others as well as of individual rights. Whether it be responsibility or rights in the private, legislative, judicial, political, or religious sectors, in all of them it is assumed that these are responsibilities or rights of the human person.

Both as the agent and as the subject, the person is assumed to be a concrete, fully developed, and self-conscious being.[11] "Self-consciousness" means, in the first place, *the capacity to relate the significance of circumambient conditions to one's own vital needs.* Second, it means to endow one's vital course with specific meaningfulness of existence.

Third, and foremost, it means *the capacity to rise above the concrete acts of achieving one's vital development toward the principles, evaluation, and planning of those acts, and to invent new means and ways to advance that development.* In this sense we talk about the person as "transcending" man's biological, social, and political conditions: as a self-conscious agent, the person may encompass their singular, concrete significance, accept or reject it; or, invent and propose a new one. It is the conception of the person as the actor within the social world that gives rise to the enigmatic question: To what degree is man sharing his life-course and his life-world, and to what degree is he shaped by them? The stand on this matter inspires different formulations of the notion of the 'person'. The conception of Karol Wojtyla of the person as "self-determined" stems from the juncture of the above. [12]

The three abstract models of the person as distinguished above are operative in the conception of the person as an agent/subject. We cannot fail to see that all three of them fulfill this special task in man's functioning as a living being. Contemporary philosophy unanimously agrees that the specifically human feature is to be able to establish the web of meaningfulness accounting for the self-conscious entity of man, as well as for the meaningfulness of others and of the common life-world. However, in the appreciation of the faculties of man which enter into his meaning-bestowing, priority has so far been given to the intellect. To the work of the intellect alone is attributed not only the orchestration for all other faculties and the establishment through an intentional network of consciousness of the objectivity of life and world existence (Husserl, Max Scheler), but to intellect is also attributed the highest adjudicating role.

Although it is also universally accepted among contemporary philosophers of various persuasions that it is the *ethical significance* of actions and reactions, feelings and reactions, feelings and decisions which marks the unique threshold between the vital meaningfulness of life and the specifically human, cultural significance of life, yet this ethical turn in man's self-interpretation is also attributed, in the final analysis, to his rational faculties. [13] In the introductory remarks I have denounced the abuses of reason; this denunciation makes the understanding of the human being an open question. In light of the foregoing analysis of the notion of the person as used in contemporary thought, the question about the specifically human feature of the living individual boils down to this: What is the origin of the significance which marks a

226

turning point in human development? This passage is indicated by the passage from the *vital meaningfulness* of circumambient conditions to the *sociocultural* one. But what the specific sense-factor that brings it about is, has to be clarified. We have also to ask how does this "sense" originate.[c] In my attempt to answer this question, I will challenge the sovereignty of reason in three respects. First, I will propose that the decisive factor in the specifically human significance of life (in the *vital, social* and *cultural* world) is not the intellect, but the *Moral Sense*. Second, the essential feature of the human individual — of his humanness — does not reside in his highest rational self-consciousness, but in his *consciousness of the universal life-conditions*. Third, in view of man's awareness of them, his individual rights have to be balanced against the interests of *all other living beings*. The human person *indeed* crystallizes the works of the moral sense and thereby becomes the *custodian of life*.

PART III

The Phenomenology of the Human Person in its Essential Manifestation

In the preceding discussion I have emphasized, first, the crucial role attributed in contemporary thought to the notion of the "person" and clarified the reason for this; second, I have emphasized that this role culminates in its "meaning-establishing" function; and third, I have proposed that it is the "moral meaningfulness," which the human person alone unfolds, that leads a living being to become truly human. In brief, to be "human" is to see life in moral terms.

Last, I have claimed that this moral significance stems from a unique factor. That factor — the moral sense — is, in my view, a "virtual factor" of the "Human Condition", which is decisive for human "Nature." It is not a ready-made code of moral conduct to be applied in action. On the contrary, it unfolds together with the vital, psychological, intellectual, and spiritual development of the individual: an unfold-

---

[c]By 'sense' is meant here that which "infuses" the linguistic forms with significance so that they may present meanings (it should not be understood in relation to senses, sensory, sensuous etc. referring to sensory organs).

ing, which culminates in the emergence of the person. It is within the person that the moral sense functions. It imbues the actions of the person with its quality. Through the person it spreads into the social world and life. It is my claim that the life of the spirit which lifts the human being above the strictly human confines and Nature, surges and develops as an inner stream of the moral life. It is by means of the moral exercise that the soul weaves the thread for the "radical leap," to use Kierkegaard's expression, toward the encounter with the Divine.

It is now time to give a succinct phenomenological view of the person as it, sustaining the forces of life, invents the social world and, turning its back upon Nature, weaves the thread of the "transnatural destiny of man," aspiring thereby to enter directly into the great game of creation and redemption.

a. The Phenomenology of the Human Person in a Fourfold Perspective

When we want to give a succinct phenomenological account of the human person, we have to distinguish three main perspectives. In the first place, the human being appears in its concrete "manifestation," first as an organized, stable core, marking by its substantial persistence a "place" in space and time, as the *sense-giver* and as the *moral agent*. It is manifested, first, in the "substantial persistence" of its "presence" within the world of life and of human interaction: as the "body."[d] Second, the person manifests within the life-world the human being in his "self-identity." This self-identity is partly manifested in the role which the person assumes, namely, in maintaining an identical center from within which man's interaction with other living beings in the external life-world is consistently organized and from within which they spring forth. The person as the identical center reveals itself also through the "forces," "powers," and strivings, which lurk behind the interactions and signal the existence of an invisible realm of the person, which reposes in itself. Indeed, although caught in the incessant turmoil of *actio et passio* within the circumambient world, on one hand, and within the irreversible course of an inner transformability of its own capacities, on the other, the person still remains the "same." This

---

[d]By "substantial persistence" is meant here the way in which the living being "appears" to our senses as a cogent, self-reposing, stable and perduring factor of life and to our actions as a responsive and autonomous partner.

self-identity reveals itself indirectly through the persisting pattern of sameness in the external interactions within the world of life. Through these, however, appears an equally "substantial persistence" of the person's "invisible," "inner" life of passions, emotions, feelings, drives, nostalgias, etc. In this perspective, the person appears as the psyche/the soul.

The third perspective upon man opens when, focusing upon this identical pattern of the person ascertaining itself most powerfully, although in an indirectly "visible" way, through life-participation, we witness it in the role of an "ordering factor." The human being through his cognitive and inventive powers assumes in fact the role of an architect of the life-world and of the social world. Through congnitive means he projects a system of articulations into the otherwise indissociable, opaque maze of forces. He discerns and measures their intergenerative powers and calculates their effects; he plans and projects. He basically projects the meaningfulness of life.

In fact, in this perspective the person is conceived as a cognitive and inventive apparatus: mind or reason. With the faculty of the intellect at its center, a vertiginous living system of rational ordering, applied to man's individual life-course as well as to that of his circumambient milieu, springs forth. This meaningful system reposes in the scheme of consciousness which spreads over the person's entire realm and penetrates all through the rational articulations of intentional interconnectedness. Thus the person "embodies" the system of the conscious mechanism which generates the *rational meaningfulness of the life-subservient sense.*

But the question arises: Is the person a "sense-giver" of only one — the rational — sense?

From the above-described self-identical center of the human being made visible through the substantial persistence within the dynamics of life through which the body and the soul are present within the world, there opens up the fourth perspective in which the person — or its humanness — asserts itself within the interactions of the life-world. Indeed, the person asserts itself by the *self-enactment* of its life-course. Not only are all the vital operations, by means of which its physical, organic, and psychic faculties are unveiled, the very expression of the person, but their modalities, directions and aims are the person's "choice." The person acts; the person is an *agent.* Although most of the vital choices are situated within the play of conditioning forces, yet in the midst of this conditioning the *personal agent* not only deciphers the possible choices from the life-situations, but he also introduces *his own distinctive sense into the evaluation of alternatives:* the *moral sense.* It is as the *moral agent* that the person stands out as "human" within the business of life.

Let us now envisage how the body, the soul, the conscious mechanism and the moral agent manifest together the nature of the human person.

b. The Person in its Manifestation

1. *The Body-Complex*

In approaching the human being from the standpoint of his process-like nature we may appear to go against common sense. Do we not experience the human being, whether as another man or ourselves, as a "being" that is a consistent entity, reposing in itself and "occupying" a position in space as well as centralizing the passage of temporal phases of the past and future in a presence? We experience man, indeed, as the cornerstone of life and as continuously "present" in life's flux — not only participating in it, but, as it were, challenging it by its own life-directions, devices, etc. Hence we experience ourselves and others in what has always been considered a "substantial" persistence. The person representing the human being is then accountable for the ways in which it is experienced and manifests itself in the progress of life. It is credited then with accounting for *stability of self-enaction, and "substantiality" in manifestation.* These two attributes of the person manifest themselves through the body.

In principle, we distinguish in our experience of the body between (1) the body as an object (whether it be someone else's or our own body); (2) our body as experienced by ourselves: the organs in their functioning that we experience as our own, e.g., sight, hearing, etc.;[14] (3) our body as "ourselves," that is, our originary (basic) feeling of ourselves as extending through our organs (e.g., movements which we command by *our* will, and which make us an integral segment of life in acting and "suffering"). Considered as such an experienced complex of functions, our body (or the body of another man that we experience through the impact of his bodily manifestation) as an automatized highly complex functional system "carries" the human person; the body is the "ground" in which the person lives and through which it manifests itself. How is this intimate interweaving of the "dumb" life-mechanism of Nature with the sentient expression of the psyche to be accounted for? In fact, the body as an organism is interwoven with the vital, psychic, "substantial" system of the soul.

2. Mute Performance Versus Sentient Interiorizing: the "Voice" of the Body

Not only do scientific observation and experimentation of the way in which our body — the human body as such — is carried on by innumerable operational circuits show how the so-called "inorganic elements" take part in the organic life-carrying mechanisms and operations, but we experience it in a direct observation (e.g., medicinal treatment of our vital organs by inorganic substances, etc.). This cooperative interplay of both occurs under the aegis of the individual's life-process.

The organic processes which carry our bodily stability and sustain us as an entity (in contrast to a process which consists merely of a series of transformations), are themselves so automatized — as Bergson already emphasized — that experiencing ourselves as "our body" we remain completely oblivious to them. Only when their automatic circuits break down (e.g., illness or bodily injury) do we become aware of their role. And yet they seem to "carry" this being of ours and to establish and maintain in existence the outward appearance of ourselves, which we call "our body." They carry also the movements of our organs which we experience as ours and under our command; which organs themselves are established and carried on by these mute processes. Each and every one of these operations is "ours." In this sense, our body is a result of each and every operation, which constitutes an integral link in the circuits of a person's life and manifestation.

In fact, the functional circuits organize the vital operations and lead them to unfold organs; these latter play the role of establishing constructive centers. They all enter fully into the enactment of the life-process of the individual.

Contrary to misleading appearances, nothing just happens to us in an "anonymous" way; each functional segment participates fully in our progress and we, as a self-individualizing living beingness, stretch in it and through it. Here it suffices to note how some of the operations we remain totally unaware of, breaking down in efficiency, disrupt the entire functional balance and we are thrown off our usual unawareness of our organs to feel a pain so acutely "localized" in one single area of our vital operations, that we feel our entire being concentrated in this one segment, hitherto ignored (e.g., the toothache). We may distinguish, however, within a vast spectrum of their differentiation, "organically significant operations" and "vitally significant acts." The first ones are "mute." Their emergence and mechanic performance is so automatized and repetitive that they do not "stand out" to make themselves "see," "hear," etc. They raise a "voice" only when the regularity breaks down and upsets the entire system. Their coming together occurs on the basis of a constructive need that "need" not affirm itself, i.e., make itself known. But in contrast with this type of operations, are the *vitally significant* acts which supplement them.

The life process in its spreading calls for operations which release *vitally significant* reaction/responses to circumambient conditions. The release of the responses is not rigidly repetitive and uniformly established; they surge with respect to the ever-varying elements of the flux of life from which the human being differentiates his own course from the one in which he himself progresses.

The operations surging "in response," in reaction, to the elements of circumambient conditions, emerge from the already established organs "on behalf of which" they "respond" by signals of alarm, signs of satisfaction, calls of need, etc. Thus, the nature of these operations is more complex; we call them in general "acts." Whether we talk about the most elementary "acts" (e.g., recoiling from a life-threatening contact, as in the lowest, pluricellular organisms), or pulsations within our more complex being of joy, forcefulness, like or dislike, etc., we mean operations endowed with expressiveness, standing out, attracting our attention; that is, uttering a "voice." With the development of its expressiveness, the voice of the vital acts intensifies into a coherent unity. The field upon which this unity of expression manifests itself — its ground — is what we experience as the "body." Indeed, what we experience as the body is the unity of a life-sustaining complex which spreads in space and time. As such it is the primary manifestation of the basic identity of man. It also maintains man's self-sameness. In its operation, as well as in its manifestation, the body establishes and sustains the spatio-temporal continuity of the "presence" of the human being within the world.

From the substantial but mute manifestation of the body in space, we have, with the vocal presence of the body, proceeded to its temporal spread. However, in moving from the mute organic operations to the "vocal" physiologico-psychic acts, we have almost imperceptibly pene-

232

trated into the middle-ground territory of sensing, feeling, desiring, etc., which the body shares with the psychic, or the empirical realm of the soul.[15]

c. The Body/Soul Manifestation of the Person

The body is indeed neither experienced nor externally manifested as a "neutral" or inanimate "thing." Unless we see it, lifeless as a corpse (which does not maintain its form in space and time), the living body is not only "animated" in the sense of reacting, moving, but above all, it is "animated" as expressing a surplus over what it merely appears to be. "Hidden" behind its frame appears an "invisible" concentrated "agency" which feels, desires, strives, decides, etc.[16] This hidden, invisible, and yet "substantial" complex of powers and forces constitutes a forceful "inward" presence. It is manifested by the bodily acts and motions as an equally, although differently "substantial," driving force. In fact, the human person is *experienced* most prominently in its "inward" presence. Our superficial experience of the overt activeness of the individual shows us already that it is organized and oriented from a "center." We become aware of the person through the experience of some or other strikingly individual act of a living being; this overt, bodily act enables us to glimpse the inward agency from which it stems; the act in its quality manifests the inwardness of the person. The multiplicity of acts sketches the field of this inwardness. With it we are moving upon the common territory of body and psyche.

Psyche, however, belongs also to the "intimate" dominion of the soul, which constitutes the nature of this inwardness. We have now to describe the soul itself in its essential nature.

d. The Essential Nature of the Soul

Let us now consider the essential nature of the soul as it manifests itself.[17] Edmund Husserl, the founder of phenomenology, has explored in unparalleled depth the pre-eminent significance of the spirit in human life. He has also emphasized the crucial role of the soul in the mediation between the body-complex and the spirit. There are in his thought three different functional realms that are interwoven but distinctive: the body, the soul and the spirit. At the borderline of the bodily functions emerge those of the soul, while at the borderline of the functions of the soul emerge those of the spirit. This diffusion of all three of them as if along one continuous axis occurs because Husserl (and later phenomenologists, e.g., Scheler) place themselves on one, single plane: That of the ordering function of the intellect. Although I fully recognize the indispensable role of the cognitive/constitutive apparatus (consciousness with its faculties), still I approach these functional complexes (including the rational apparatus) from a more fundamental point of view than that of rational ordering; namely, from the point of view of their role with respect to *man's unfolding from within the Human Condition.*[18] Only in its perspective may the nature of the soul appear in its fullness.

In agreement with Husserl, I see the soul, first, as the passional ground of forces nourishing the bodily mechanisms; second, as the center of the self-identity of the individual. I agree with Husserl, that the crucial role of the soul lies in being the middle ground between the body in its vital and passional (passions and strivings) resources and the spirit. Yet — and here I part radically with him — although it is this natural, empirical wealth of the soul that makes it the middle ground of the human make-up, its nature, its resources and its role have to be interpreted differently from Husserl: although Husserl is right in seeing in the soul the ground of the spirit, yet in contrast to his view, it is not at the *borderline* of the soul that the spirit originates; rather, it surges from its *center.*

a) The soul gathers into itself, like into an experiential receptacle, all the life-operations of the living body, the organism; from the soul, as from a center, spring the prompting forces and powers that galvanize the entire living psyche. In this fashion, the soul is the "substantial ground" of powers. Concretized in these powers, the soul reposes in itself; however, the soul is not — as Leibniz, Husserl, and Ingarden after them, thought — self-enclosed by its substantial content, like the Leibnizian "monad," which had "no windows" nor "doors."

b) On the contrary, while the body is open to the influx of externally conditioned energies and substances, so the soul is opened to stirrings, nostalgias, strivings, longings, revelations, which do not belong to its natural ground; they stem from the abysmal realms of prelife-conditions. They do not remain encapsulated within the soul or merely pass through it. In fact, they galvanize and stir the most essential resources of the soul; through them they ignite the entire apparatus of man's functioning. This functioning, which is, in the vital course of things, oriented rationally for the sole sake of survival — for the propagation of the designs of the animal nature — is by their influence prompted to enter the workings of nature itself and to invent new avenues of life. This inventive work leads to a specifically human meaningfulness of life.

Indeed, it is through the crevasses of the otherwise opaque passional ground of the soul that there enters the "initial spontaneity," that has originated life as such, with all its resources. [19]

c) It is with the Initial Spontaneity that there enter into the code of the natural life of the individual — its *entelechial* code (to be rationally "deciphered") of natural unfolding — the "virtualities of the Human Condition," of which the most significant for making life "human" — for endowing it with a "human significance" — is the *Moral Sense*. [20]

d) The soul is the battlefield upon which, in the turmoil of life-energies and influxes of the Initial Spontaneity, the human condition concretizes itself within an individual, concrete, living human being. Beyond that, the soul provides the ground and the field for an extraordinary, "extranatural" turn within the unfolding of the human condition: the turn toward the birth of the personal spirit.

In fact, as I have attempted to show elsewhere, the life of the spirit, that is, of grace, is not offered ready-made, floating within the human cultural realm ready to be taught, absorbed, and participated in. On the contrary, as mystics have shown in their autobiographies, in order that it may emerge within a human psyche a tortuous and long road of a concrete, personal transformation is necessary. [21] This transformation occurs within the empirical soul as the response to its nostalgia, longings, stirrings, etc. prompting it to seek ways and means in order to surpass the aims of life. Furthermore, it is an outcome of a specific concentration of all the powers of the soul which occurs by its becoming progressively "disabused" of the natural life-values and of the "business" of life. The powers of the psyche/soul, so far engaged in the business of life, now turn back upon life's aims and their validity. There is initiated a *quest* oriented by the moral sense in which the soul calls for a "witness" of its plight of being "lost" in the vanities of life and seeks an "ultimate" evaluation of its earthly aims. [22] In the moral-evaluative confrontation between the soul and its "inward witness" a thread is spun which no longer conducts to life-subservient interests, but rather to the "Transnatural Significance of Life." If we follow the progress of this unfolding of the "life of grace" with Teresa of Avila, *(The Mansions)*, we see how the soul in its empirical, vital, and personal identity becomes the very substance from which is spun this thread of the Transnatural

Destiny of man. In the moral evaluation vis-a-vis the "witness," the soul despoils itself like an artichoke, leaf by leaf, of its earthly concerns. The "leaves" of the soul's concerns with the natural life all fall in succession until the very center of the soul is revealed, and the soul's thus liberated and purified dynamisms of grace are ready for a "radical leap" to meet the Divine Witness face to face. The soul is thus revealed as the inward receptacle of the unearthly significance of the sacred within which it meets face to face the Ultimate Witness.[23]

To summarize: (1) The soul appears as an empirical life-promoting and sustaining factor; (2) The soul, which is orchestrated through the intellectual apparatus of the intentional consciousness — with the self as its axis — appears as the factor of the self-identity of the human being. In this sense, we as human beings identify ourselves with the totality of our experience. (3) The soul appears with respect to the Human Condition as the "middle-ground" into which the decisive virtualities of man flow and within which their individualizing unfolding generates and develops. That is, the soul appears as the ground for the origin of *all the types of meaning* by which man endows neutral and anonymous nature with *his own* meaningfulness, with *his own* sense. (4) Finally, although it seems that the soul extends and remains in an intimate interplay with the body, on the one hand, and with the life of the mind or intellect, on the other — articulating and animating the one, and being informed and processing its dynamisms through the filters of the other — thus encompassing the entire human person, it is far from enclosing it within itself. Although the human person might be self-enclosed like a "monad," the soul — contrary to the views of some phenomenologists — is not. It is, at one extreme, recipient of the ungraspable, inexplicable Initial Spontaneity, and at the other, processor of the existential thread breaking through all its natural frontiers toward the Transnatural.

And yet, it is through the vehicle of the moral agent that both the specifically human significance of life and the Transnatural Destiny of man are worked out. To understand the specifically human person, we must then investigate the moral sense from which its meaningfulness stems.

Now, it remains for us to bring together our presentation of the person in its substantial manifestation. It appears that the person is manifested: first, in the self-sustaining, "animated" bodily complex; second, through the substantial self-identity of the soul; and, third, as

236

an agent presenting the person as we experience it in the "real" self; all three of these complexes are informed by the mind. This analysis of its modes of manifestations shows "what" and "how" the person is. Nevertheless, if we want both to understand what makes the individual specifically human and to account for its humanity, we must approach the person from the point of view of the various types of *functioning through which it becomes and unfolds as a living being and accomplishes its human telos.*

The reason for this priority is clear: the human being becomes human through the introduction of *his* type of meaningfulness of life into an otherwise anonymous, "pre-human" nature. He does it as the "Creator of his own Interpretation of Existence."[24] The sense of this interpretation and of its unfolding emerge from and through his functional system. The modes of the manifestation of the person in reality, in life, and in the world are but the result of its meaning-unfolding functions.

Among them, the one which constitutes the instrument through which all lines of his constructive meaning-bestowing upon brute facts proceed, is the moral sense.

It has to be emphasized at this point that the crux of the present conception of the human person lies in its being the moral agent. *Yet it is a moral agent only insofar as its life-enactment is, throughout all the "vocal" circuits of its functioning, informed by the moral sense.* We have now to attempt to trace the origin of the moral sense and its role in constituting the human person.

PART IV

The Moral Sense of Life as Constitutive of the Human Person

a. The Person as the Subject/Agent Within the Life-world

We have so far emphasized the role of the person in the living individual's organizing, articulating and acting; that is, in his functioning through which he unfolds by delineating his individual life-course. When it comes, however, to asserting the point at which this life-course takes a turn of a specifically human sort, it seems most difficult to single out from among the factors entering into human functioning an element that would account for the specificity of this turn which both differentiates man from other living beings, and maintains the line of continuity with other functional circuits. When we ask: What accounts for the specificity of the human being, we cannot consider the human being in an abstract set of features by means of which he "presents" himself; we have to seek this specificity in the network of functioning by means of which his manifestations occur. That is, we have to seek it within the life-world which he establishes as the system of meaningfulness of his existence. We have to seek it in the various types of interrelations, meanings and corresponding "languages" (e.g., the language of art, the moral language, the religious language, etc.) which serve as means of communication within the human world. Furthermore, as is obvious from the first two models of the person presented above, the person draws upon and participates in the entire system of life and nature. Unlike the notions of the "subject," "consciousness," or "ego," which stress the separation from concrete nature, the abstraction of human thought, the person emphasizes the *unity of all living factors within man.*

Although we could say that contemporary philosophy in general agrees that it is the ethical factor or the spirit that accounts for the specificity of the human manifestation (Husserl, Scheler, etc.), the problem is far from being solved in a satisfactory way. It depends on, first, how we conceive of the origin and nature of morality, and second, how much validity we attribute to it. The question of the specifically human factor within the life-world remains an open question. We have prepared the ground for taking it up afresh. First, we will pursue it as the question concerning the *origin and nature of the uniquely human meaningfulness of the human existence and of the world.* Second, we will approach it as the question concerning the *specific meaning-bestowing function of the person as the subject/agent within the social world.* It will appear from our analysis that it is up to the human person to introduce the moral sense into the understanding of the *life-world* as the *social world.* Man's self-consciousness, thereby established, entails *consciousness of the conditions of its progress,* i.e., man's *responsibility for life's survival.*

b. Man Self-Interpretative Individualization[25]

In fact, we may seek for the source of morality by retracing the phases of *man's self-interpretative indivdualizing life-course.* In my previous work on the self-individualizing (interpretative) progress of the real

238

individual I have distinguished the following phases: (1) the "pre-life" virtualities coming together in the life-individualizing process; (2) the *entelechial-oriented organic/vital phase;* (3) the *vital sentient phase;* (4) the *sentient/psychic phase;* and (5) the *psychic/conscious phase,* initiated by the "source experience," in which *all* of man's "virtualities" unfold.[e] In each of these phases of the dynamic constructive progress of the individual, that is, in the unfolding complexity of the functional mechanisms and systems, the following, crucial issues arise: first, the various types of ways and means of coordinating the elements entering into the operative and generative systems; second, the principles of these coordinations; third, the potentialities of the elements (and of the operational segments) to unfold their functioning and to assume their respective roles in the constructive advance of the self-interpretative process. I have maintained that it is by these various types of articulations of processes, by which the individual differentiates himself from the circumambient conditions — while benefitting from the otherwise neutral elements, but which he may turn into essential resources of his own progress — that he establishes the meaningfulness of this progress, and creates the meaningfulness of the circumambient conditions with respect to their relevance to his needs. It is the element of constructive differentiation from his life-conditions while transforming them into *his conditions* of the "life-world." In the first phase of the pre-life conditions, we may consider this coordination of needs and means as an automatic response of virtually loaded pre-life-elements coming together in trial and error or seemingly haphazardly.[26] There is no valuation present there, not even in a germinal form.

We can, however, talk about a principle of "fitness" according to which the coordinates will occur. It begins, as it seems, with the origin of the individualizing process of beingness at its *organic/vital* phase. There we are dealing with a solicitation/response situation, in which the "need" of the emerging complex of living individualizing elements — under the aegis of the entelechial principle intrinsic to it — seeks and "solicits" other elements for their "satisfaction" toward the further progress of life in its unfolding.

---

[e]The term "source-experience" — in contradistinction to the classic phenomenological term 'originary experience' — has been introduced by the present author precisely to pinpoint the crucial moment within the unfolding of individualizing life at which from the animal action/reaction agency a transition occurs to the specifically human experience originating simultaneously the human subjéct.

239

With the phase of the *vital/sentient* self-individualizing complex of processes there enters the acquiescence/rejection principle of the constructive discrimination of vitally significant elements — a far more complex significance. Here life's need for further life-prompting elements is not automatically and mechanically satisfied: it is qualified by the sentient discrimination on the side of the individual, who qualifies the elements of his circumambient world by distinguishing those which may satisfy, or are congenial with, his needs, and those which are not. It is, however, only upon reaching the complexity of the *sentient/psychic* phase of man's self-differentiation in the constructing process that we witness a specific significance brought in by the *acquiescence/rejection* principle of articulation. Indeed, beyond the mechanical functionality present in the individual's sentient/vital seeking for, and "recognition of," the elements needed for his organic functions up to the point where satisfaction occurs — observed in the second and third phase of the constructive differentiation of life — we find in the sentient/psychic functionality brought in by now a more complex existential interaction. It involves an evaluative complex of *recognition/estimation/appreciation* on the one hand, and a responsive acceptance or qualified refusal, on the other.

The discrimination/fitness system proceeds in a pluri-directional "sensitivity," and establishes "significance" consisting in "psychic" relations to elements of the virtual fulfillment of the individual's existential needs. This need/satisfaction system crystallizes in the network of existential gregariousness of the higher living beings. Its existential significance lies in communicating by protective reflexes, signals, single and chain-acts of care (belonging to the instinctual/ psychic life-protective set) the same existential "life-interests" shared by individuals. It is rooted, however, exclusively in the *self-interest* of each member of the group, with the addition of an existential-affective reliance upon the affective presence of other individuals.

The above-mentioned types of coordination of life-promoting elements, operational segments and functions establish the distributing order of the individualizing progress. At each of the phases they establish the *meaningfulness* of the elements which enter into the individualizing process. Each type functions by establishing sense-giving. Yet, its sense comes from, first, the *vital,* and second, the *gregarious* life-significance of the life-serving process. In its coalescent/fusional/ organic way it functions as sense-giver; as vital sense-giver in the vital/psychic selecting mechanisms; as *vital/gregarious* sense-giver in the sentient/psychic appreciative and interest-sharing selectiveness. At each of these phases there emerges an appropriate significant *novum* that has been released from the progressing complexity in functioning, which stimulates the virtualities intrinsic to its components.

The previously enumerated coordination principles carry on the life-progress in all types of selectiveness which they serve, whether by response, acquiescence, or even by an individual initiative. For their being they merely need to put into operation an *"existing" reason*. But even the touching "devotion" to the care of little ones shown in animal behavior has its *reasons* in instinct and affectivity which *"excite"* the functional system and prompt its operational and direct the "actions" of the animal towards these goals. Exciting reason is applied in its full extent in the use of affectivity and instinct as specific life-prompting functional complexes.

With the emergence of the full-fledged conscious functioning of the individual, the exciting reason, which prompts his selective mechanism toward acquiescence or rejection, does not suffice by itself. Full consciousness means not only the instinctive sharing of self-interest with other individuals, but also the propensity of *expand one's own individual meaningfulness into transactions with other individuals*. The dominant limitation by the *universal scheme of life* — identical for each species — is broken down and recedes before the *inventive function* by which the individual devises his own way of existential self-expansion. This expansion may be accomplished only in transaction with others.

In *transactions* among individuals we deal with multiple and partly conflicting interests; each of them demands its own; each of them is prompted by *individual life-interests;* each of them seeks to promote the new significance of *his* devices for his own self-interpretation in existence; each of them is, by his own spontaneous impetus in this *existential expansiveness* — and even while encroaching upon those of others — going in directions that are naturally prompted to intrepret the transactional components according to his own life-interests "carried" by his *expanding spontaneities*. Thus, he is prompted to interpret his own significance upon the transactional network: the transindividual social world, which is nevertheless common to all of them. Were we left with the coordination principles of the exciting reason, hitherto valid, in which the decisive factor is the drive toward one's own life-interest — even already significantly expanded into that of sharing in the *preserva-*

tion and *propagation-of-life-significance* with other individuals — the expansiveness would have, in the first place, remained limited to the functional circumference of vital/sensibility. The individual would share with the other beings in the "law of the jungle," as penetratingly analyzed by Kipling. In his analysis the gregarious order appears partly as a "law" based upon the instinctive/vital/sentient/psychic/operational circuit, in which the sharing of common vital interest, survival and progagation instincts, the affective needs, etc., establishes a vital-interest circuit which harmonizes with the overall system of life. With the advent of full-fledged conscious experience within which emerges the *intellectual sense,* marking a new individualizing phase of the individual life-progress, an *objective order* of the life-progress is released. The *inventive function* of consciousness — and cooperation with it — being added to it, a *communication* among individuals is instigated and spontaneously unfolds.[27] The emergence into operation of the inventive function of the human being not only explodes the life-subservient directional scheme for the coordination of functional operations, but it gives them a new focus, an imaginatively *self-enlarging inventory of possible ways* to unfold and stretch *one's own meaningful existential script* over the intersubjective life network. The release of these factors would certainly prompt attempts at transactional undertakings by individuals in concert. Yet, would the available coordination principles be adequate to such a common effort?

The operative-coordinating principles which give significance to the life-promoting operations — *organic, vital, gregarious* — are geared to the self-interest of each of them alone. They establish in the individual's self-interpretation its *vital sense.* The objectifying reason (intellect) releases a new sense — *the objective Sense.* This latter is altogether neutral to individual survival interests. The rational deliberation which it allows for the sake of estimating purposes, means, circumstances for action and undertakings in common appreciates the individual approval toward an "agreement" or an individual decision to commit oneself to its implementation. In such an agreement, the life-interest of the individual would be, necessarily, as much satisfied as curbed or renounced. The "exciting reasons" which serve individual striving and express its needs recorded by instinct and affectivity toward life-preservation would fall short of the mark. In the striving of individual interests could a transactional agreement ever take place? The "law" of the strong or of the cunning would prevail.

242

c. The Moral Sense in the Intersubjective Interpretation of Life Affairs

Seeking for a new factor which, in the face of the neutrality of the intellectual sense versus the individual aggressivity of a pre-transactional situation, appears indispensable for entering upon a neutral deliberative analysis and for inspiring an interpretative turn toward mutual agreement, consensus, and commitment to implement its terms, we discover the *Moral Sense*. In fact, the surging of the *Benevolent Sentiment* of the Moral Sense endows the interpretation of the transactional component variants with a *justifying reason*.[28] Justifying reason, as Lord Shaftesbury so penetratingly saw, demands the "sense of right and wrong." This sense is presupposed by the cognitive function of deliberative operations; it is also independent of other extraneous sources (e.g., religious). It is by the working of the Moral Sense that the benevolent sentiment applies itself to the interpretation of conflictual situations. It surges from, and differentiates qualitatively in, the self-interpretative progress of the individual himself. Its effect manifests itself primordially on the significance of the transaction. The transactional self-interpretation goes together with the "neutral" informative and cognitively objectified set of elements for deliberation. The benevolent sentiment being brought in, the *valuability* of these elements for the significance of the purposive end of the transaction has to be established, not strictly individually but in common; not for the sake of any one of the partners alone, but transgressing their strictly self-centered interests. This *valuability* resides in the threefold relevance of the transactional interests of the involved individuals. It resides, first, in the relevance of the given transaction to each unfolded individual interpretative script and in the prospect (with an implied necessity) of promoting in full or in part the life-significance of each individual. Second, it resides in the valuability of the elements of this expanding striving/adjusting/surrendering "negotiating" complex with reference to the given circumambient life-world situation (ecology, social system, etc.) of each partner in the negotiation. Lastly, it resides in the valuability of the elements for selection to the *universal life-system,* which the selection might serve, simply accommodate, or jeopardize in some respect.

However, the switch from the existentially significant coordination category of mere "fitness" in the automatic or "exciting" phases of the self-individualizing complexity, to that of valuative significance in the selective process of coordination is a further indication of the radical transformation within this process. Here we are hitting the threshold of the passage through which — as a discrete and progressively extended phase in the spontaneous self-interpretative progress of the living individual — from the merely life-promoting meaningfulness of self-individualizing life, we cross to the *human significance* of life. The sharpness of this threshold is marked by the question: On what basis does an individual make a deliberate selection of alternatives which are against, in conflict with, or simply a surrender of, his own *life-interests* for the sake of those of others? In other words, what gives "valuability" to the alternatives that oppose self-interest and in terms of what may we justify our selection? If the threshold to the human significance of life is marked by the new relevance of life-promoting deliberations to the significance-axis of "right" and "wrong," how does this axis originate in the Moral Sense? As the basic significant factor in the deliberation and valuation context, the right/wrong axis elevates this significance from the level of the strictly "exciting" mechanisms — serving the self-interest drive of the self-enclosed individual — to that of the inter-subjective "justification."

It is the Benevolent Sentiment at work, introducing the ultimately *moral* axis of *right/wrong,* that establishes the intersubjective life-sharing. It allows the balancing out of the conflicting self-interests.

The justifying reason which directs the decision of the transactive significance cannot indeed be founded on the automatized relevancies; it is rather the result of, and a conclusive step in, a deliberative process. Although deliberation involves all of the conscious faculties — which have to be released in the source-experience — none of them is capable of bringing in this *novum.* Where does it make its original appearance? I suggest that we discover its presence first in the *valuative process.* The principles of selectiveness along the line *valuable/unvaluable,* operating in the valuation process, with respect to the components of transactional deliberation — that is concerning basically our relation to the Other — are conduits of the Moral Sentiment. The selective decision is not a mere calculus of convenience but conveys the moral sentiment by means of conscious moral acts of *approbation* or *disapprobation.*

Approbation/disapprobation, conscious acts, as the manifestation and carrier of this *significant novum* we are concerned with, are neither based upon, nor consist in, an intuitive instance of the cognition of values. They are judgments which manifest the new up-lifting sense-giving factor: the *Moral Sense*. It is the vehicle of man's social significance, of his self-interpretation in existence: of the *social world*.

d. Valuation and Moral Sense

In fact, the moral sense enters the valuative progress in man's self-interpretation in existence as a specific and irreducible *novum* of the spontaneous *Benevolent Sentiment* that surges from the full-grown complexity of the evolutive significance in the individualizing (and through the individualizing) progress of life. Nevertheless, we cannot assume either that it is due to this progress that the moral sense, as a meaning-giving factor, in its crucially significant sentiment of benevolence toward the Other, operating in intersubjective interactions within the life-world, is released from the functional vital complexity, nor can it be reduced to the latter at any stage of its unfolding. It must have been "lying there in waiting" as the virtual element of the *Human Condition* — a virtual element for the *specifically human meaningfulness of the life-progress* and of the life-world.

With the recognition of the moral sense as the new meaning-bestowing factor we can at last "exfoliate" properly the nature of valuation, understood as a morally significant, selective experience. In contrast to the ethical emotivists who see moral valuation as the expression of feelings, it appears that valuation emerges together with its own form, the *moral context,* in which the "factual" components appear virtually in a moral perspective. Although imbedded in a network of sentient, instinctive, affective, intellectual and other life-promoting factors, these elements, with the concrete emergence in this complex of the valuative process of the Moral Sense, appear fraught with *virtual* moral aspects.

In opposition to the intellectualism in ethical theory which assumes that all evaluation in the field of ethical action goes back ultimately to the intellectual/estimative (deliberation and choice) rationalism represented so forcefully by Leibniz, we see from our analysis that the intellect could never account for the specific effects of the intrusion of benevolence. Would a moral act of approbation/disapprobation be possible without the benevolent sentiment introducing a basis for the differentiation, along the axis right/wrong? Leibniz' fallacy lies in his erroneous stress on the strictly personal/subjective significance of "morality." We have, on the contrary, seen that morality surges into the interpretation's subjective realm as an *interpersonal* affair.

As for the "affective intuitionism" represented by Max Scheler and his followers, the controversy with the moral sense position is more nuanced. The distinction of the "states of mind" and the "intuition of values" does not free the intuitionistic position from the essential fallacy of attributing an undue role to cognition in the morally valid estimation. The undue role attributed to cognition enters via the direct relating of moral experience to values. In contrast, the foregoing analysis has transferred the crux of the nature of moral experience from the role of value to valuation and shown that the moral elements reside in the valuative process. It has thus moved it from the direct reference to values to that of the direct emergence into valuation of the Moral Sense.

By these differentiations within the nature of the basic moral experience identified with the valuative experience, we have also found a middle way between conceiving moral experience as either an intellectual or an affective perception. The intuitive factor which gives to valuative experience its specific moral significance has been identified with the spontaneous sentiment of benevolence brought in by the Moral Sense. It is not *related* to this intuition; it is this intuition itself!

e. The Meaning-Bestowing Proficiency of the Moral Sense

We have attributed to the moral sense a specific sense-giving and promoting function which is responsible for the meaningfulness of "moral life," "moral conduct," and "moral language." We must now try to analyze it directly as it manifests itself within the self-interpretative *system* of the individual. These analyses lead us to contest the identification of the moral sense with a psychic faculty or with any faculty for that matter. On the contrary, the moral sense using *all* the conscious faculties is a *unique* type of spontaneous function, which is virtually present in the *Human Condition,* in which the psychic faculties in their mature form also crystallize. It actualizes in its functional proficiency in the *source-experience.* It works out its modes and its way with and through the psychic faculties; yet in itself it is and remains a unique *operative* spontaneity, a "subliminal spontaneity" insofar as it belongs virtually in the Human Condition.

The moral sense is, indeed, not an innate or ready-made *functionl factor,* but a virtual *sense-giver.* It is released within the individual's evolutive progress marking the threshold from the gregarious to the specifically human life; it unfolds its meaning-bestowing role when the faculties to promote its proficiency are ready for it. Once unfolded, it does not develop or remain at one and the same stage automatically. Due to the potential for deviation in the valuative processes and their interpretative application to the individual's conduct, it may weaken to the point of losing its strength and interpretative proficiency.

f. Moral sense and "human nature"

With traditional ethicists, we may raise the question whether the moral sense, as the source of morality, belongs to "human nature." This question leads to some instructive distinctions. It all depends on what we understand by "human nature." In the first place, it certainly does not belong to human nature if identified with the basic phase of man's self-interpretation in existence. As I have suggested elsewhere, in its vital (organic/psychic) phase individualization is controlled by an intrinsic *entelechial* principle. Thus the moral sense does not belong to "human nature" if we understand by it the entire individualizing complex, which the entelechial principle unfolds through its operational ramifications. That is, the moral sense does not manifest itself through and in the "animal nature" of the human being. It belongs, however, to the essential factors through which the human being unfolds his *specific beingness.* It is the key factor in founding the individual's *social significance of life* in a specific quality of his commerce with other human subjects; furthermore, it belongs to these factors insofar as this commerce concerns the essentially human interpretation of life-significant interaction: distribution of goods, opportunities, services for further self-individualization of human beings. Nevertheless, we could envisage the moral sense as belonging to "human nature" if we understand the latter from the perspective of our inquiry, namely, as *the set of virtualities to be unfolded in the conscious development of the living individual into guideposts of moral significance for his self-interpretative progress in intersubjective interaction with others.*

To conclude this argument: insofar as we conceive of "human nature" as a conundrum of virtualities necessary to initiate and promote the dynamic intersubjective progress of individualized existence, human nature contains the moral sense as its essential and decisive factor.

g. Perception of "Good" and "Evil"

As pointed out above, in its qualitative complex the Benevolent Sentiment contains, on the one hand, a "directive" from its "center," a "center of qualitative orientation" which resides in its *sense*. On the other hand, this *sense* is not an instance of a neutral awakening comparable to the sensuous "senses" (e.g., "instinct," stirrings, feelings, etc., which are being consumed in their spontaneity). On the contrary, this type of sense has a *prompting* impluse and bears in its nature, a "prompting for . . ." moment, a germinally meaning-bestowing significance. This significance resides qualitatively in "benevolence" (for the sake of the Other). Although the benevolent sentiment lacks an explicit indication of that in which its "benevolence for the sake of the Other" principally consists, yet it bears it germinally as a proficiency to be crystallized in the experiential exercise. In this exercise it also reveals a universal principle. In fact, in the ever-recurring centers of reference within the infinite variations in which benevolence is subjectively experienced and applied to actions concerning intersubjective reciprocity (as well as in the transactive interpretation of the life-world), we find an ever-repeated residual sense: the "good" of the Other. Hence, with the use of our aesthetic contemplation and intellectual objectification functions, we arrive at the intellectual fixation of the *Good* as the ultimate directedness of the moral sense. In extreme opposition, the deviation from the positive "for . . ." of the *benevolent,* to the negative "against" of the *malefic* valuation, leads us in its infinitely extended and varying spectrum of instances in moral praxis to posit cognitively moral *Evil* as the opposed final sense-direction.[29]

With these elucidations of the moral sense we have paved the way to an adequate approach toward the explication of the origin, nature, and role of moral values. However, before we come to this central point of our investigation, we must first consider how the exercise of the moral sense on behalf of the Other "flashes back" upon the interacting subject.

h. The origin of moral conscience

The "fulfillment" of the moral sense within the subject involves, however, more than just attentiveness to the promptings of the moral sense. Its ground-laying moment lies in moral valuation; its central agency is the moral *conscience;* its proper implementation lies in the authenticity of the moral script: the existential script of the moral subject.

In the first place, the moral sense reaches the self-interpretative process in its surge only if it is adequately acknowledged in the valuation, that is, if, in the transactional complex of conflicting interests, the Benevolent Sentiment prevails over the life-tendencies of self-interest. That it may gain this upper hand, however, a deliberation of its role is needed. The deliberation comprising the moral sense as one of its valuative principles unfolds a specific *valuative-preference mode:* to attribute to each of the conflicting elements its *due.* Thus its exercise prompts the unfolding within the interpreting subject of the corresponding *valuative-attributing* modes, the basic one being *righteousness.* The next mode of valuative-attributing concerns the appropriate "recognition" of the respective "merits of the case," which prompted by the moral sense for the good of the Other, in spite of all misgivings which one might otherwise incur, and in spite of all emotional resistance on the side of the appreciating subject — yet taking them all into account — has to express *his own* stand, *his own* perspective: it calls for the *mode of appreciative sincerity.* Moreover, the stirrings of self-interest which hinder "impartiality" in decision-making, bending the tendencies of decision-making functions, stay under the promptings of the moral sense, which moves the pendulum toward a golden middle in the conclusive act toward the *probity of judgment.*

Thus complete moral valuation brings together a full-fledged appreciative and deliberating apparatus: *moral conscience.* The above enumerated modalities of (valuative) moral appreciation constitute the axis of conscience essential to the proper implementation of the moral sense in our moral self-interpretative system.

Finally, we cannot forget the significance of the *transactional modality* with which the moral judgment prompts its implementation in the interworldly situation. In fact, in its prompting spontaneity the moral sense indicates its own criterion to be applied to the application of the moral judgment in action. This criterion, which we recognize in current life practice under the name of *fairness,* prescribes that the active implementor should follow all the appreciative aspects of the moral judgment with detachment from all circumstantial pressures. This model axis of appreciation/valuation/judgment/(decision-making), which constitutes the basis for the deliberating moral conscience, is at the same time the vehicle of our social interaction as the guaranty for our self-fulfillment. Sincerity of recognition, righteousness of appreciative attribution, and probity in meting out judgment, pave the way for the self-devised, self-interpretative *authenticity* of human existence in intersubjective relatedness. Regarding the genesis of conscience as a morally deliberating and judging agency, a further point is to be observed.

In the actual exercise of moral sense in transactional deliberations, we do not reassemble our valuative and deliberative system of principles, etc., each time anew, bringing in the moral sense directly and spontaneously into significance-molding operations. It is left to the initially unfolded conscious agency, with its indispensable moral orientation — if not an "ideal" model of moral "probity" — to repeat the modal moral "attitudes" in repetitive kinds of situations. In current usage we understand by "moral conscience" a conscious agency that represents a previously acquired set of attitudes.

i. Some fallacies concerning the origin, cognition, and role of moral values in moral valuation and experience

A paradoxical question emerges at the start: How can we explain that, in a cultural period like our own, which distinguishes itself from previous periods of Western culture by a highly refined conception of moral values and by sophisticated institutional (legal, etc.) methods to implement them in current interpretations of human transactions, we still witness in social practice the violation, abuse, neglect, ignorance, or outright contempt of them? This issue, which I stated at the outset of my inquiry, will now be explained by way of a contrast between the origin and role of values in moral practice and the moral sense.

First, we must draw a succinct conclusion from the previous analysis to the effect that, apparently, values do not function as *a priori* points of reference for moral valuation, but conversely, they emerge from the valuative process. In fact, values as objectively graspable "entities" or "objects" are — and in this we disagree with most phenomenological ethicists — the fruit of the constitutive function of congnitive consciousness under the aegis of the intellect. Yet, it is not as such that they functionally contribute to promote, or to direct, the implementation of the moral sense in action. It is true that we refer to values in our cognitive deliberations of transactional situations as points of reference. Yet had values been the decisive moral factor, how could we explain the current phenomenon of moral life, that in spite of our awareness of all the moral aspects which they offer us for evaluative and elective judgment, we may still choose to ignore or to circumvent their practical moral implications and decide not for the right but for the wrong; not for a benevolent stance but for self-interest. Having made this decision how could we have found a satisfactorily justifying "moral" reason for it? Although we might "know" perfectly well all the moral aspects, implications, and subtle nuances of the values involved, yet we might remain as if "blind" — Max Scheler would say — to the moral significance of the transaction, in the interpretation of which we would be applying said values.

We may return here to the previously mentioned role of reason. If we conceive of moral practice as related essentially to the "intuition," emotive or intellectual, of values — that is to their cognition — we surrender ourselves to the power of either reason or emotions or both conjoined. There is, in fact, no end to the objective strategies which the intellect may invent in the rational estimation of the transactional situation. They may be such "devious" strategic interpretations, that the "objective content" of the values involved may be by one or the other side used to serve self-interest. By applying values as points of reference to interpret our self-interest, we confer upon our judgments, decisions, and actions a seeming "moral" justification. Yet doing so, we may totally abuse the "authentic" *moral significance* of the transactional situation. Indeed, when we refer to the cognition of the previously intellectually constituted values as points of reference of moral action, we naturally may presume that by our cognitive attention we may revive within our evaluative process the moral sense which they are meant to represent. That is, it is not just a revival of emotions which this moral content of ideal pure subjectivity may entail. However, such an expectation is fallacious, a *non sequitur*. It is not in the power of reason to conjure up the moral sense, which, being intimately "subjective," nevertheless possesses a strictly universal validity of its own: its own *"sense,"* a sense most universally valid because valid for man as such. To conclude, the cognition of values is morally proficient *only insofar* as the "moral actor" is in a position to *revive* through them the corresponding modal form of the moral sense. The awakening is not necessarily in the power of values themselves.

The moral experience, as well as the cognition of values, possesses an ambivalent significance due to the *aesthetic sense/aesthetic taste*. The subject's enjoyment accompanies not only the experiential crystallization of the moral sentiment on the side of spontaneity, but also the cognition of values on the side of constitutive structuralization. No doubt we enjoy our good, virtuous, benevolent feelings, attitudes, actions. We have recognized in this enjoyment one of the spontaneities prompting the exercise of the moral sense: its major force. The cognition of values, because they express the benevolent/malefic sentiments in *objective* forms of the moral sense, proportionately manifests the *aesthetic* load of "enjoyment virtualities."

We find indeed a gratifying and uplifting aesthetic enjoyment of *positive* moral values in contemplating them rationally — as much as we find morally "destructive" the enjoyment of *negative* (malefic) moral values. And yet this contemplation does not entail — or necessitate — the *lived spontaneity* of the benevolent/malevolent sentiments, nor of the moral sense in general. Hence the well-known fallacy of moral practice: we take our uplifting enjoyment in the contemplation of moral values for the moral state of our conscience and our subjective beingness. This contemplation should "naturally" animate the moral sense's spontaneities by stimulating the multiple aesthetic, intellectual, and sentient chords of the psychic functional system, in which these spontaneities find their resources and which carry it as a psychic phenomenon. Yet, this natural direction might be, and too often is, diverted by self-reflective concentration (narcissism) on the benefit of the enjoyment. Thus, to modulate our functioning "morally" remains the exclusive task of the practical exercise of benevolence and of the moral sense in its fullness.

Hence: Let us stop talking about values and revive the moral sense!

Conclusion

The Moral Person as the Custodian of the Existential Balance Within the "Unity of Everything-There-Is-Alive"

In the above inquiry I have not attempted to establish in the first place the "essence" or "nature" of man, as has been customary in traditional philosophy. I do not deny that the "essentialistic" approach possesses considerable merit; undoubtedly the human mind seeks to "understand"; it delights in universal principles and concepts which give intellectual enjoyment and satisfaction. Moreover, such principles and concepts leave the impression that man's understanding encompasses the entire universe of his concerns and that he can easily locate his own place in it. Lastly, universal forms, fixated in the fluid and elusive progress of the life-experience, and principles offer an — illusory — support to fall back on. However, man's life scheme, which clings to certitudes that are unwarranted by concrete events, is invariably shattered by the unfolding course of affairs; and man's expectations are then disappointed. In short, called to the task of bridging the gap between the abstract explanations of the speculative intellect and the concreteness of the ever-changing life-progress, traditional philosophy, as well as classic phenomenology, becomes hopelessly entangled in controversial generalities. It fails to shed light upon concrete facts through which human life and man's destiny advances and delineates its course. A philosophy which offers universal explanations that fail to enlighten man in concrete life issues and to give him direction toward solving them is a mere game of the intellect.

Instead of aiming at an abstract theory of the essential nature of man, I have approached man from the perspective of the *Human Condition*. In this perspective the gap between the more or less concrete phases of unfolding life (brute nature-bios-mind) is overcome by pursuing its becoming in terms of *conditions* from within which the living individual and the human person unfold. The human person emerges as the source of the life-significance of "brute facts," in enacting this significance on the one hand, and on the other hand, inventing it as self-conscious agent. Although we have differentiated the specifically human person by his crucial meaning-bestowing role in introducing the moral significance of life, this specific role does not distance itself from, but merely expands, deepens and renders more flexible the life-significance brought about by the "natural person" proper to all higher types of living individuals. In this respect two crucial points must be emphasized. First, in delineating his meaningful life-course the person manifests himself in his inventive role as an outstanding type of beingness from among the entire chain of living beings. The human person in its role of self-conscious giver — receiving, giving and promoting agent — manifests on the one hand, a *universal consciousness of life-conditions,* and on the other hand, its self-consciousness culminates in the capacity to appreciate, calculate, and plan them.

It is not only in virtue of reason that this self-consciousness emerges, but equally — and most importantly — in virtue of the moral sense. While reason and imagination open up possibilities for unfolding and growth, the moral sense opens the perspective of the moral accomplishment and of the spirit. This accounts for the unique autonomy of the human being and his "transcending" the narrow limits of natural life-significance.

Second, we must emphasize that it is in view of the universal self-consciousness of the human person that its ties with the "great chain of living beings" acquire a new significance.[30] From a mute and matter-of-fact participation it is transformed into a conscious and moral *unity-of-everything-there-is-alive*. Indeed, the moral sense brings into the natural unity of life a benevolent sentiment toward all living things. The human being does not rise from the natural anonymity of life for the sake of aiming at an ever greater autonomy and self-awareness. The moral sense reminds him that he is an integral part of living nature. Moreover, in his universal self-consciousness of the life-conditions he is intimately united to *everything alive*.

Lastly, the moral awareness of the universal life-conditions prompts the person toward responsibility for the progress and well-being of all living things. Our approach steers the middle course between the extremes of naturalism and spiritualism, but remains open to both. Our conception of the person emphasizes, indeed, man's integral participation in and his unique role with respect to the unity of life.

The specificity of this uniquely human role consists in three points: (1) The human person is self-conscious of the universal life-conditions and capable of appreciating, inventing and planning the routes of life. (2) In virtue of the moral sense, the human person is capable of making judgments and decisions for conduct and action. (3) The human person manifests benevolence and moral responsibility for the well-being of all living beings.

It is on account of our self-consciousness (developed in *these* respects) that the human person originates the consciousness of its unique "human dignity." It is also in its name that we claim a singular respect for human dignity.[31]

In the perspective of the human condition the human person emerges in its highest significance as being THE CUSTODIAN OF THE EXISTENTIAL BALANCE OF EVERYTHING-THERE-IS-ALIVE!

Notes

1. Cf. Anna-Teresa Tymienecka, *Leibniz' Cosmological Synthesis* (Assen: Royal Van Gorcum 1971).
2. Cf. Anna-Teresa Tymienecka, "The initial spontaneity: The pessimism-optimism controversy concerning the human condition," in *The Crisis of Culture,* ANALECTA HUSSERLIANA, Vol. V (Dordrecht/Boston: D. Reidel Publ. Co. 1976). In this volume we have turned away from the historical approach which from Spengler's *Der Untergang des Abendlandes,* through Toynbee, Husserl, and Weber, has been emphasizing the transformations within Occidental culture, to focus upon the disintegration of the human being himself, as it manifests itself in literature, the arts, and social life, etc.
3. In my early book, *Phenomenology and Science in Contemporary European Thought* (New York: Farrar, Strauss and Giraux 1960), I have shown how phenomenology, stemming from Husserl, Heidegger, Ingarden and Jaspers, has deeply transformed the approach to the human being in numerous realms of scholarly pursuit as well as in the human sciences (sociology, anthropology, psychiatry, etc.), by an attempt to rescue the specifically human element in human nature from the scientific reductionism to which it had been subjected.
4. Edmund Husserl, *The Crisis of the European Sciences and Transcendental Phenomenology* tr. by David Carr (Evanston, Illinois: Northwestern University Press 1970). Although the conception of 'science' has in the last decades greatly changed from the one which Husserl inherited from the 19th century, still the depth of his philosophical insights makes this treatise a classic to which reference must be made in any serious philosophical consideration of our present-day "crisis."
5. I have attempted to show the "nature" of life in a succinct study: "The praise of life: Metaphysics of the human condition and of life," in *Phenomenology Information Bulletin, A review of phenomenological ideas and trends,* Issue 6 (Belmont, MA: World Phenomenological Institute 1983). Cf. also: "Initial Spontaneity and Self-Individualization of Life," ANALECTA HUSSERLIANA, Vol. XVII.
6. Two sections of this study, pp. 33–48, have appeared in my introductory study to *Foundations of Morality, Human Rights and Human Sciences,* ANALECTA HUSSERLIANA, Vol. XV (Dordrecht/Boston: D. Reidel Publ. Co. 1983).
7. Cf. the section on Karl Jaspers and Gabriel Marcel, as well as the entire part on phenomenological psychiatry, in my book cited above in note 3.
8. Cf. Calvin S. Hall and Gardner Lindzey, *Theories of Personality* (3rd ed., New York: John Wiley and Sons 1978).
9. Cf. Ludwig Binswanger, *Grundformen und Erkenntnis menschlichen Daseins* (Zurich: Niehans 1953). Ludwig Binswanger, the celebrated Swiss psychiatrist, inspired by Husserl and Heidegger, has developed a psychiatric conception of the human being within the "life-world" in which, in contrast to Freudian views, no priority is attributed to a unique driving force within man. Rather, man's entire experiential system as expanded by his interactions with other men within the world becomes the pattern with reference to which psychiatric methods are devised. Binswanger has found numerous followers in several branches of what has become known as "phenomenological psychiatry."
10. In recent times, a highly developed conception of the specifically human person has come from the famous French psychiatrist, Henri Eye. Eye and his school have brought to a culminating point the phenomenological tendency of Binswanger, Bujtendyjk, E. Minkowski, E. Strauss and many others, in vindication of the belief that psychiatric diagnosis and therapy should deal with human nature as a whole. In his famous book, *Consciousness, a Phenomenological Study of Being Conscious and becoming Conscious,* tr. by John H. Flodstrom (Bloomington, IN: Indiana University Press 1978), Henri Eye presents, in its full expanse, the source and the experiential compass of the uniquely human conscious self as a person. Eye, and following him, Lanteri Laura, devise methods of psychiatric diagnosis with reference to the "disintegration of consciousness," i.e., of the person.
11. It is Max Scheler who has stressed particularly the significance of acting in the understanding of the human person. While emphasizing the autonomy of the person and the differentiation of the person from the individual, Scheler has highlighted particularly the

social participation of the "intimate person," endowing it with a special form of the "social person." Cf. Max Scheler, *Gesamtwerke*, Bd. 2, *Der Formalismus in der Ethik und die Materiale Wertethik* (Bern: franke Verlag 1966), and by the same author, Bd. 8, *Erkenntnis und Arbeit* (Bern: Franke Verlag 1960).

12. Karol Wojtyla, *The Acting Person*, ANALECTA HUSSERLIANA, Vol. X (Dordrecht/ Boston: D. Reidel Publ. Co. 1979). (This is the definitive text established in collaboration with the author by Anna-Teresa Tymieniecka).

13. Although Max Scheler attempts an inversion of this approach by seeking to show the origin of values in emotions, nevertheless values ultimately emerge in an already constituted form; this could not have occurred without the work of the intellect. Cf. the present writer's monograph, "The moral sense at the foundations of the social world," in *Foundations of Morality, Human Rights and the Human Sciences*, cited in note 6.

14. Cf. Anna-Teresa Tymieniecka, "Die phänomenologische Selbstbesinnung, Der Leib and die Transzendentalität in der gegenwärtigen phänomenologischen und psychiatrischen Forschung," ANALECTA HUSSERLIANA, Vol. I (Dordrecht/Boston: D. Reidel Publ. Co. 1971).

15. The distinction between our body as an object and our body as experienced stems from Edmund Husserl. Cf. his *Ideas Pertaining to a Pure Phenomenology and a Phenomenological Philosophy*, Book II (den Haag: Martinus Nijhoff 1982), Part I.

16. For Husserl's most careful and masterful analysis of the relationship between our body as experienced and the psyche (or empirical soul), cf. *Ibid.*, Part I.

17. I have attempted an investigation of the soul in its "essential manifestation" in my book, *The Three Movements of the Soul*, to appear in Vol. XIX of ANALECTA HUSSERLIANA.

18. Regarding the concept of the 'human condition,' cf. the present author's monograph, *Poetica Nova . . . a Treatise in the Metaphysics of the Human Condition and of Art*, ANALECTA HUSSERLIANA, Vol. XII (Dordrecht/Boston: D. Reidel Publ. Co. 1982).

19. Cf. Anna-Teresa Tymieniecka, "The initial spontaneity," ANALECTA HUSSERLIANA, Vol. V (Dordrecht/Boston: D. Reidel Publ. Co. 1976).

20. In the above study, I have also indicated that from the very beginning of the individual unfolding of the human being, moral "virtualities" are present.

21. I have succinctly analyzed this progress, terming it the forging of the "Transnatural Destiny of the Soul" in several of my writings. Cf. "Hope and the Present Instant," in S. Matczak, ed., *God in Contemporary Thought* (New York/Louvain: Learned Publications/ Nauvelearts 1977).

22. This progress of spiritual unfolding with reference to the Other, the other self — the "inward witness" — has been the subject of my attention in *The Three Movements of the Soul*, cited in note 17.

23. The specific "mechanism" of this quest after the ultimate significance of human existence, as conducted with respect to another self, has been shown by the present writer in "Man the creator and his threefold telos," ANALECTA HUSSERLIANA, Vol. IX (Dordrecht/ Boston: D. Reidel Publ. Co. 1979). It appears that whoever the Other is, the concrete "encounter" with him or her *in* the significance of life is ever-elusive, because the Other functions merely as a concrete reference point, while it is the "inward witness" that is being consulted by the soul in its innermost depths. I am showing in this study how this comes to light when every supposed "communication" between the soul and the other self necessarily breaks down. With this break, however, the soul is ready for the face-to-face meeting with the Ultimate Witness, who "has been there hidden in the intimate center of the soul all along" (as Teresa of Avila shows also).

24. Concerning "man's self-interpretation in existence" cf. Anna-Teresa Tymieniecka, "The creative self and the other in man's self-interpretation in existence," ANALECTA HUS-SERLIANA, Vol. VI (Dordrecht/Boston: D. Reidel Publ. Co. 1977).

25. The following analyses have appeared in my monograph, "The moral sense at the foundation of the social world," cited in note 6.

26. I have outlined the life-progress from the pre-life conditions accomplished by means of the individualisation of the living being in "Natural spontaneity in the translating continuity of beingness," in *The Phenomenology of Man and of the Human Condition: Individualisation of*

Nature and the Human Being, ANALECTA HUSSERLIANA, Vol. XIV (Dordrecht/Boston: D. Reidel Publ. Co. 1983); and in "Spontaneity, individualisation and life," in *Phenomenology of Life: A Dialogue between Chinese and Occidental Philosophy, loc. cit.,* 1983, Vol. XVII.

27. The indispensable role of man's inventive/creative function within the virtualities of the Human Condition as the vehicle of specifically human "orchestration" of all man's faculties, has been stressed by me in a series of published works. Beginning with my book *Eros et Logos* (Louvain: Nauwelearts 1972), I have been developing the phenomenology of creativity in a series of writings. Cf. "Imagination creatrix," ANALECTA HUSSERLIANA, Vol. III; "The prototype of action: Ethical or creative?," *Ibid.,* Vol. VII; and "Man the creator and his threefold telos," *Ibid.,* Vol. IX.

28. Although I did arrive at the present views independently, they are, nevertheless, in agreement substantially with those of the British moralists of the 17th century. Cf. Anthony, Earl of Shaftesbury, "The Moralists," in *The Characteristics of Men*, Vol. 2; and *An Inquiry Concerning Virtue and Merit*, Vol. 2.

29. Francis Hutchison asserts that the moral sense is a direct intuition of the Good. That is, he considers the moral sense as the source of the recognition of good and evil in an immediate perceptive evidence. Cf. Francis Hutchsion, *A System of Moral Philosophy*, Vol. I (London 1755). Although I basically agree with him, because, as Aristotle (*Magna Moralia*, Lib. 2, c. 10, 6a2, chap. 10) says, in discussing "right reason," unless a man bears within himself the sense to distinguish the good from the bad, there is nothing to be done; yet to say that the moral sense is a direct perception of the good or bad is a misleading shortcut through the complexity of human functioning. Hutchison's view is, however, understandable: he did not investigate the workings of the moral sense within a full-fledged analysis of the genesis of moral evaluation, nor within the moral orchestration of transactional intersubjectivity of man. In the present work, this analysis is supplied and the conception of the "moral sense" is expanded.

30. It has been for the present writer a marvellous surprise to "discover" at the heart of the phenomenological enterprise (as undertaken by Husserl, Hedwig Conrad-Martius, Edith Stein, Roman Ingarden, Max Scheler, etc.) an underlying remnant of the classic philosophical architectonic design, common to Aristotelian and Medieval thought in general, which Emmanuel Kant — borrowing the expression from the poet Alexander Pope — has called "the great chain of Being." Cf. Anna-Teresa Tymieniecka, *Beyond Ingarden's Idealism/Realism Controversy with Husserl,* ANALECTA HUSSERLIANA, Vol. IV; and Eugene Kaelin, "Man the creator and the prototype of action," *Ibid.,* Vol. XI, where he is presenting the conception of the "great chain of being" proposed by me. Lately, however, I have found a parallel to the conception of the "great chain of being" (which I have elaborated as having its source in man's creative faculties), in the realm of the life of Nature. I have seen it in the phenomenon of the "Unity-of-Everything-there-is-alive." Cf. my essay, "The praise of life: Metaphysics of the human condition and of life," cited in note 5.

31. For an investigation of the nowadays so popular concept of "human dignity," cf. the present writer's monograph, "The moral sense at the foundations of the social world," Part II: Human Rights and Moral Sense, cited in note 13.

Chapter 9

The Human Person
in Sacred Scripture

The Reverend Donald Senior, C.P., S.T.D.

Editorial Preface

What does it mean to be a human person?

The Bible answers this question differently from the way one would find in a unified philosophic system or a scientific analysis. The difference is due partly to the way the Bible was composed: gradually across centuries, with the many writers involved, and out of a great variety of historical situations.

But the Biblical way of answering the question is determined even more by its unique threefold focus on the human person:

1. *A religious focus. The Bible does not treat explicitly of questions raised, for instance, by pantheism: Is the human person an entity which exists as an individual in itself, rather than existing as an aspect of some other being (in se et non in alio)? However great minds might eventually and explicitly face and formulate the issue of human individuality, the sacred writers bend themselves instead to the task of insisting that the human person and his race have no existence,*

*meaning, or fulfillment except in the Lord God Who revealed Himself
to Abraham.*

2. A communitarian focus. *The Bible refuses to treat the human person
simply as an individual standing alone in his relationship to his God.
To the contrary, the Biblical writers insist that the individual person
is joined to a vast multitude of human beings, and indeed to all of
God's material creation, whose origin, story, and destiny the individual profoundly shares.*

3. A holistic focus. *The Bible by-passes any scientific or philosophical
analysis of the various parts, functions, or dimensions which constitute
the human person. The sacred writers mention some of these diverse
aspects of the human person, but primarily as symbolic and representative of the* whole person.

*Thus, the Biblical writers take note of man's "flesh," not in order to say
something about the structure, dynamisms, or teleology of human organs and
tissues, but in order to say something about* the whole person: *that he or she is as
earthy as the earth itself, is in solidarity with the human community, and would
be condemned to a futile existence were it not for the presence, promises, and power
of the Lord. Other Biblical terms — "body," "heart," "breath," "blood,"
"spirit" — are used in much the same way: to say something, not about any of
these individual components, but about the* whole human person *as bound to
the Creator, to the human community, and to the material creation.*

*The fact that there is this three-fold Biblical focus on the human person does
not, of course, imply that the focus is perfect in any particular book of the Bible or
era of Hebrew history. Especially "in the fullness of time," the teachings of the
Lord Jesus, without at all undermining the communitarian focus of the Jewish
Scriptures, clarify further the unique responsibility of each individual before
God. Even more did Jesus emphasize that the present world could be neither a
kingdom for God nor a home for the human person without a radical, even
apocalyptic, liberating transformation, a transformation rooted in the power of
His own risen body.*

*The Biblical message does not rule out rational and scientific consideration
of human individuality, human responsibility, or human physiology. Indeed,
the Biblical accent on the religious, communitarian, and holistic realities of the
human person can both inspire such systematic analyses and their syntheses, and
correct hasty and destructive conclusions and projects to which human beings are
prone in purely humanistic approaches. The inspirations and correctives which
the Bible offers to "the proper study of mankind," the Church, with full
confidence in the Spirit, can expect to offer in her authentic magisterium.*

259

Introduction

Questions about the nature of the human person usually become acute when we are in crisis. The technological issues which are the object of this assembly put critical questions to us as human beings: Is an essential aspect of our humanity in jeopardy by our rapidly expanding capacity to alter or control reproductive capacities? Does a commitment to nuclear energy threaten humanity's relationship to creation itself?

It is not surprising that in the face of such staggering human and ethical questions thoughtful Christians should reexamine the fundamental sources of our faith tradition. What I hope to achieve in this paper is at least a partial synthesis of the biblical portrayal of the human person.

The biblical canvas is so vast that I can only point to some of the decisive brushstrokes. Lest the Scriptures be exploited in a less than responsible fashion, it is important at the outset to sketch as clearly as possible some of the guidelines that should direct our approach.

First of all, we should not expect from the biblical materials a clear, systematic and homogeneous portrayal of the essential components of the human person. The Bible itself is neither systematic, homogeneous nor consistently clear. It is a pluralistic collection of materials, spanning many centuries, emerging from developing and varied cultures, from many different authors, and expressed in a wide variety of literary forms, few if any of which could be called philosophical or systematic. The Scriptures have meaning in relation to the questions we are posing, but the biblical response must be taken on its own terms. While revered as the Word of God, the Bible is at the same time a human word, and therefore time-bound, culturally conditioned and in need of interpretation.

Secondly, even when the task of biblical interpretation has been responsibly carried out, we cannot apply the Bible's portrayal of the human person to contemporary issues in isolated fashion. Such, at least, is not the way Scripture is understood within Roman Catholic tradition. The written Word must be understood in the context of the Word as articulated and interpreted by the Christian community and its legitimate teaching authority. Placing Scripture within this framework means that the biblical vision must interact with accumulated Christian wisdom and with the workings of the Spirit of God within our contemporary cultures and history. Therefore the biblical vision of the human person is, in a genuine sense, only a partial vision. The agenda of your program which includes inputs from the empirical sciences, contemporary theology and philosophy, reflects this Catholic perspective.

Finally, I want to spell out as clearly as I can what I understand the nature of our *question* to be, at least as it applies to Scripture. By the "nature of the human person" I understand not some immutable, timeless constant hidden somewhere within the vital components of humanity which, if discovered, could serve as an evaluative grid upon which all basic ethical issues could be pre-determined. Such a conception would overlook the staggering impact of time and culture on human awareness. There is no clearcut blueprint of the human person that can be determined with rational precision. Humanity is in process of becoming; this is not only a discovery of twentieth century thinkers, but, I would submit, an instinct of biblical tradition.

What we seek in looking for the "nature of the human person" is therefore something more modest. As Edward Schillebeeckx suggests, "what we have at our disposal is no more than a set of *anthropological constants,* rather than a positivistic outline, or a pre-existing definition of 'human nature' in philosophical terms. . . . In other words, in very general terms these anthropological constants point to *permanent* human impulses and orientations, values and spheres of value . . . they present us with constitutive conditions (given the analysis and interpretation of any particular contemporary situation) which must always be presupposed in any human action, if man, his culture and his society are not to be vitiated and made unlivable."[1]

Such a descriptive approach, I believe, fits better into the nature of the biblical data. The Bible may not offer a fully articulated and immutable blueprint of essential humanity, but it does witness to a set of instincts and fundamental convictions, drawn from experience and the constant reflection on humanity's relationship to God and to creation, that results in certain values and conditions which define authentic humanness. This biblical vision of humanity is surely an essential component of any truly Christian ethical reflection.

I. A First Sounding: Some Biblical Terms for Constitutive Elements of the Human Person

Perhaps the quickest and most effective way to plunge into the biblical mode of thinking about the human person is to sample some of the most common vocabulary used in Old and New Testaments to describe the human person. In ordinary speech patterns a culture reveals some of its anthropological assumptions, just as we do in such expressions as "you had no heart" or in speaking of "food for the soul".

A commonplace and essentially true assertion about the biblical worldview is that it is holistic. While various "faculties" and aspects of the human person are differentiated, these seem to intertwine within the corporate whole that makes up the human person. The peculiar language of the Bible, particularly the Old Testament, illustrates this. Often a *part will be used to identify the whole,* as seen from a particular vantage point. As we will indicate, the feet or the throat or the heart or the neck are often used not as a mere reference to one part or organ of the human body but as metaphorical language for the human person itself.

Let us move to some examples.[2] One of the most important terms used to describe the human person in the Hebrew Scriptures is *nepesh;* it is often translated as "soul." But such a translation overlooks the connotations of the word and tends to impose later, dualistic concepts on the biblical text. The word *nepesh,* in fact, has a variety of meanings. In Isaiah 5:14, for example, the word seems to mean *throat* or *jaws* ("The underworld wrenches wide its *nepesh,* and opens its mouth beyond measure"; cf. also Hab 2:5). In Psalm 107 the word speaks more widely of the organ that takes in food and drink: "the hungry and thirsty whose *nepesh* fainted within them" (Ps. 107:5); "for he (God) satisfies the thirsty *nepesh* and the hungry *nepesh* he fills with good things" (Ps. 107:9). Proverbs 27:7 observes: "A sated *nepesh* stamps on honey with his feet but to a hungry *nepesh* everything bitter is sweet". Other texts speak of the *nepesh* as the organ for breathing (e.g. Jer 15:9).

Such connotations of hunger, thirst, longing help identify the more generic meanings of this rich term. In Genesis 2:7 we are told "Yahweh God formed man of dust from the ground, and breathed into his nostrils the breath of life; and man became a living *nepesh*". As Wolff points out the text does not say man has a *nepesh* but he *is* a *nepesh.*[3] He is, in other words, a breathing, hungering, thirsting, needy being. *Nepesh* is, therefore, synonymous with an aspect of human life that describes the human person in its totality.

The word *bashar,* "flesh", is another illuminating term. This term is frequently applied to the human person and to animals; it is never used of God (of 273 times in the Bible, 104 are applied to animals). This notion of "meat", palpable flesh, is basic to the term, as in Isaiah 22:13:

"Behold, joy and gladness, slaying oxen and killing sheep, eating *bashar* and drinking wine. 'Let us eat and drink for tomorrow we die' ". The term is also used of the human body as in Lamentations 3:4, "He has made my *bashar* and my skin waste away, and broken my bones."

But the term takes on wider meaning. It can refer to the human body as a whole, not just the flesh or meat in distinction from bones or blood, as in Psalm 38:3, "There is no soundness in my *bashar* because of your indignation". or in Psalm 119:120, "My *bashar* trembles for fear of thee and I am afraid of your judgments". From here the connotations can move from a designation of the human person as a whole to the human person *in relationship,* as in Genesis 2:24 where the union of Adam and Eve is described as "becoming our flesh," or in a frequent idiom which describes blood relationships as "our own flesh" (cf. Gen 37:27; Neh 5:5, etc.).

The fact that the term *bashar* or flesh takes its basic meaning from literally the meat or bodiliness of animals or humans leads to a final and pervasive connotation of this term, that of *weakness* or *limit.* Job asks God, "Do you have eyes of flesh *(bashar)?* Do you see as man sees?" (10:4) Deuteronomy emphasizes the consistent contrast between God (to whom the term *bashar* can never be applied) and humanity (which is essentially flesh or *bashar*): "For who is there of all flesh *(bashar)*, that has heard the voice of the living God speaking out of the midst of the fire, as we have, and has still lived?" (Deut 5:26).

Thus "flesh" describes the human person in its totality as essentially corporeal, at one with other non-human creatures, limited, mortal, finite, weak. Note this same connotation for the term "flesh" (= *sarx* in Greek) is used by Paul; more on this later.

Other terms describing essential components or dimensions of human person need to be cited. The term *leb* or *lebab* is usually translated "heart", but again some cautions must be raised. *Leb* seems to have a wider meaning than the heart organ, and when it is used metaphorically it does not mean primarily the seat of feelings or emotion as "heart" is used in our culture.

Leb and the alternate form *lebab* are used some 858 times, the most common anthropological term in the Bible. It is rarely used of animals (in distinction to the term *bashar*). A text of I Samuel 25:37-38, describing the death of Nabal, is most illuminating for discovering the true meaning of *leb*: "His heart *(leb)* died within him, and he turned to stone. About ten days later Yahweh smote Nabal; and he died".

Obviously something different than the organ of the heart is meant by *leb* in such a text! Nabal probably died of a stroke; therefore the term *leb* means that center of his being which kept Nabal conscious and rational prior to his stroke. The *leb* was believed to be in the innermost recesses of the chest cavity, the source of movement and consciousness, similar in some degree to what moderns would identify with the functions of the brain.

From this anatomical base, the term *leb* or heart can be used to describe essential aspects of the human person as a whole. The "heart" is equivalent to the hidden, inaccessible aspects of the human person: ". . . man looks on the outward appearance, but Yahweh looks on the heart" (II Sam 18:14); "He knows the secrets of the heart" (Ps. 44:21). To the heart are ascribed basic emotions and feelings: "A tranquil heart is the life of the flesh, but passion makes the bones rot". (Prov 14:30); "Let not your heart be stirred up over sinners but continue in the fear of Yahweh all the day" (Prov. 23:17). In the heart is determined the essential orientations of the human person to good or evil, something equivalent to our notion of conscience, the heart experiences "joy" or "sadness". But the heart is even more basically the source of *desire:* "Thou has given him his heart's desire . . ." (Ps. 21:2), and of *reason* itself. In fact, this latter function is the most frequent metaphorical use of the word heart: "They teach you, and speak to you, and utter sayings out of their heart" (Job 8:10); "A heart of insight acquires knowledge and the wise ear seeks knowledge" (Prov. 18:15). The heart also *decides:* "May he grant you your heart's desire, and fulfill all your plans!" (Ps. 20:4). Yahweh is said to hate "a heart that devises wicked plans" (Prov 6:18).

The term "heart" has, therefore, exceptionally broad and important usage. The Bible, as Wolff notes, "views the heart as the centre of the consciously living man. The essential characteristic that, broadly speaking, dominates the concept, is that the heart is called to reason, and especially to hear the word of God."[4] Note that the biblical conception of the human person does not minimize the role of the intellect. By means of the term "heart" the biblical literature asserts that thought and desire and feeling stand at the very core of the human person as distinct from the rest of creation. And it is precisely "in the heart" that the human person encounters God.

A few other examples can round out our survey of anthropological terms in the Hebrew Scriptures. Certainly the term *ruah* or "spirit" needs to be considered. In contrast to the other terms we have discussed, *ruah* does not take its root meaning from some part or aspect of the human anatomy, and the term is applied to God more than it is to human beings (136 times applied to God; 129 to humans, animals and false gods). The root meaning of *ruah* seems to be that of wind (cf Gen. 1:2; Isaiah 7:2), a forceful power of nature at God's disposal. By extension the term comes to mean the life-breath that God gives to the human person (cf. Job 34:14-15: "If he (God) should take back his *ruah* to himself and gather to himself his breath *(neshama)* all flesh would perish together and man would return to dust;" or Ps. 104:29, "You send forth your *ruah,* they are created."). Thus the wider connotation of *ruah* means the vital power or force that gives life and authority to the human person, as in English we might use the term "spirit".

Note that the term *ruah* does not lose its basic *theological* dimension. While the human person is endowed with *ruah,* this is essentially a gift of God. Here, as we shall note later, is a basic anthropological and theological conviction of the Bible: what distinguishes the human person and circumscribes its autonomy is precisely this vital dependence on God for life force — here is the basis of the essential relationship between God and humanity.

A similar but distinguishable term is that of *neshama* or "breath". At times this term seems synonymous with *ruah,* e.g., "Thus says Yahweh. . . who spread forth the earth . . . who gives breath *(neshama)* to the people who walk upon it and spirit *(ruah)* to those who walk in it" (Is. 42:5). However, this term is more physiologically rooted and does not have the consistent theological connotation that *ruah* does.

Finally, we have the term *dam,* "blood". Life, in Hebrew thought patterns, is "essentially manifested in the breath and, incomparably more often, in the blood."[5] Blood as manifestation of human life is sacred; from this conviction comes the terminology of designating crimes as "crimes sgainst blood." The cultic laws also stem from this conviction: to taste blood in the eating of meat is absolutely forbidden (Gen 9:4; Lev. 3:17, etc.) The *bashar* of the animal, its "flesh", is designated as food for the human person, but the blood as manifestation of life, belongs only to God. As Wolff states: "Everything that is said about breath and blood in the anthropology of the Old Testament is instruction in an ultimate reverence for life. But this reverence is not derived from the manifestations of life itself; it is based on the fact that the breath and the blood belong to Yahweh, and therefore life without a steady bond with him and an ultimate tending toward him is not really life at all".[6]

This spectrum of terms, by no means comprehensive, gives us an initial insight into the anthropological suppositions of much of the Old Testament. Rather than segmenting the human person into distinguishable components or faculties as later western thought would do, the biblical viewpoint sees the human person as a corporeal whole. Like lenses or filters on a microscope, specific organs, or qualities of this corporeal whole are used to describe vital and essential aspects of the entire human person: thinking, feeling, willing, of the earth yet invested with a divine life force, in essential relationship to the earth yet made human by the vital life force of God. We will gather up these dimensions into more comprehensive form in the next section of our paper.

Before concluding this section, however, we need to consider briefly how this Old Testament view is retained or altered in New Testament terminology. Of all the New Testament writings, only the letters of Paul come close to setting forth an explicit anthropology, and even for Paul this is not a conscious goal.

The New Testament authors in general are much more acutely influenced by Greek culture and thought patterns than most of the Old Testament writings (with the possible exception of such "late" Old Testament works such as the book of Wisdom where the Greek term "immortality" first appears). However, even though the speech patterns of the New Testament texts are necessarily expressed in Greek, it is obvious that semitic and biblical assumptions about the human person are still operative. The text of Mark 14:38 — "the spirit *(pneuma)* is willing but the flesh *(sarx)* is weak" — is probably best understood not in terms of the Greek body/soul dichotomy, but with the semitic *bashar* (the human as limited), vs. *nepesh* (human as living, desiring being), or *ruah* (human as infused with divine life force) distinctions. The close connection between spiritual illness and bodily illness apparent in many of the healing stories in the Gospels (for example, the healing of the paralytic as sign of forgiveness of sin in Mark 2:1-12), illustrates this same mentality. It is not a matter of asserting that bodily illness is a punishment for, or immediate consequence of, personal sin. Rather, body and spirit are one; therefore both manifest the human person's vulnerability to evil. In Matthew 15:18 the statement, "But what comes out of the mouth proceeds from the heart, and this defiles a person. For out of the heart come evil thoughts, murder, adultery, fornication, theft, false witness, slander", can only be understood when heart is conceived as equivalent to volition and conscience as it is in semitic culture, not the seat of emotions, as it is in western thought.

The reflective nature of Paul's writings reveals more directly his anthropological assumptions than do the narrative forms of the Gospels.[7] But even in Paul no systematic or consistent use of terms is apparent, and, while he uses Hellenistic terminology for faculties of the human person, it is likely that his semitic background is much more influential on his basic conceptions than his exposure to Hellenistic culture.

At first blush, Paul seems to speak of the human person in body/soul terms (cf., for example, I Cor. 5:3, "though absent in body I am present in spirit"), but closer examination shows that this is not the Apostle's basic conception. The human person *is soma* (body); the *soma* is equivalent to the human person as such, understood in its corporeal sense (e.g., "Let not sin therefore reign in your mortal bodies, to make you obey their passions" (Rom. 6:12; cf. also Phil. 1:20; I Cor. 6:15, etc.). Paul occasionally speaks of *soma* in a pejorative sense (Rom. 6:6 "body of sin"); here it is equivalent to the Semitic notion of *bashar* ("flesh"), that is, the human person as weak, limited, mortal.

More commonly, Paul uses an entirely different term, *sarx* ("flesh") to express humanity in this pejorative sense. *Sarx* is very similar in Paul's terminology to the function of *bashar* in the Old Testament; it refers to the human person in its entirety, but viewed from its corporeal, earth-bound, limited dimension. Thus Paul can list the "deeds of the flesh" (as in Gal. 5:19-21) and mean not simply sensuality (as our Western conception might lead us to suppose), but sin in general, whether or not an abuse of human sensuality in sexual and other ways.

Paul also refers to the *psyche* of the human person. Sometimes he seems to mean the "self" (cf. Rom. 2:9) but more often it refers to the vital principle of the human person, his or her consciousness. As such, it is very similar to the Hebrew word *nepesh*. In no sense is *psyche* to be understood as "spirit" or "soul" in the sense of an entirely non-material entity, distant from the body. For example, Paul uses the word *psychicos* to indicate the individual who is as yet untouched *in his totality* — physical and rational — by the Spirit of God (I Cor. 2:14).

Paul also uses the term *pneuma* ("spirit"), which is close to the

267

Hebrew word *ruah*. At times it is very difficult to distinguish in Paul's writings between *pneuma* and *psyche*. However the term *pneuma* is also used of the Spirit of God and, in some texts where the term is applied to the human person, it seems to designate that God-given knowing, desiring, willing aspect of the human entity that makes it apt for communion with God (cf. for example, Rom. 8:16).

A final example is the practically synonymous use of the terms *kardia* (heart) and *nous* (mind) in Paul. Both terms, with little apparent distinction, apply to the entire human person as a knowing, desiring, willing, judging self.

Thus Paul's terms for the human person do not offer a systematic analysis of separate, essential faculties: soul, body, mind, will, emotions. Instead, Paul conceives of the human person as a whole that is *at once* corporeal, weak, limited, mortal (the human as "body", as "flesh"), conscious, willing, judging, desiring (the human as "mind", "heart", as *psyche*), and as capable of conscious, willing communion with God (the human as "spiritual" or *pneumatikos*). A concept, in other words, quite similar to that which was traced in the Hebrew Scriptures.

II. Anthropological Constants Across the Biblical Witness.

The terminology we have considered by no means exhausts the anthropology of the Bible. None of these terms directly addresses categories of time and relationship which are also crucial to any understanding of the nature of the human person. But the distinctive vocabulary of the biblical literature first of all cautions us that the Bible comes from a culture different from our own. And, secondly, this terminology, limited as it is, points to broader conceptions of the human person contained in the Scriptures than are contained in literature of other culture, e.g., of Hellenism. In this latter half of my paper I would like to cast in "thesis" form what I consider the "anthropological constants" of the Bible. The list could, I am sure, be refined and extended. But I believe that the basic theses are defensible as at least a preliminary description of the nature of the human person dominant across the diverse traditions of the Old and New Testaments.

1. Human existence is rooted in, dependent on, and oriented to God. In searching for the biblical view of the human person, it would be difficult to overstress the fact that the Bible takes an essentially *religious* perspective. All aspects of human life and human history are defined in the context of humanity's relationship to God. This is not to say that the Bible is *theological* in the strictest sense of that term; it is not dominated by explicit reflection on the nature of God as such. The focus remains on the human arena: the stories of the Patriarchs, the agonies of Israel, the treasuries of proverbial wisdom, the mission of Jesus and the disciples, the struggles of Paul's churches. But the determining reason for all of this material, indeed the very reason for the existence of the Bible at all, is that in these stories, sayings, and reflections, the biblical peoples articulated their convictions about how God's life intertwined with human destiny.

This becomes, therefore, the most basic fact about the nature of the human person in the Bible. The origin, sustaining force and ultimate meaning of the human person are found in God, not in creation or human history. The human person, to be sure, is *earth bound* and *world-oriented* (as we shall note below); the human is *bashar, sarx*. But the specific, distinguishing mark of the human is precisely this bond with the divine.

A variety of images and themes of the biblical traditions illustrate this fundamental assertion about the human person. One of the basic messages of the creation accounts in Genesis is to underline the divine origin of the human person. All life is created by God, including the animals, birds, plants, and the earth and its universe. But with the human person, male and female, a particular relationship is established. The account in Genesis 2 uses the metaphor of divine inspiration: "The Lord God . . . breathed into his nostrils the breath of life *(neshmat hayiim)* and the man became a living being *(nepesh)*" (Gen. 2:7). In vivid metaphor, the biblical account roots the origin of human life-breath in the creative suscitation of the Lord God. Although other living things already exist, none have this bond with the Creator.

Genesis 1 uses the intriguing and mysterious "image of God" metaphor. The Priestly account has the builder God muse, "Let us make *Adam* in our image, after our likeness . . ." (Gen. 1:26). The decision to create the complementary sexuality of the human person as male and female also is a part of this same decision to make the human race in the "image of God": "So God created the human person in His own image, in the image of God he created him; male and female He created them" (Gen. 1:27). The precise meaning of this phrase "image of God" has been much discussed, but the most probable meaning in the context of

Genesis 1 is the power given to the human person to have dominion over the rest of creation (cf. 1:26b; 1:28-30). The human person is viewed in this biblical tradition as the center of the created world, sharing in the life-giving exercise of God's own care over it. Later biblical traditions such as Psalm 8:6-8 and Eccles. 17:3-4 reinforce this conviction.

The human person's essential bond with God is expressed in a variety of other biblical images, narratives and metaphors across the length of the Scriptures. The covenant between Yahweh and Israel, while limited to Israel and its ancestors and originating within historical circumstances and not the primeval act of creation, still reflects this conviction of an essential link between Yahweh and humanity. The covenant with Noah (cf. Genesis 9) reinforces Yahweh's special relationship to humanity; never again will all flesh be destroyed. It is significant that the covenant with Noah extends beyond humanity to all living creatures (cf. Gen. 9:10, 12, 15), but it is apparent that humanity in the person of Noah is the principal object of Yahweh's attention. The covenants with Abraham (Genesis 17) and Moses (Exodus 19) restrict the arena to Israel. But even though less mythic in scope, and to that degree less indicative of Israel's conception of the essential anthropological components of humanity, the covenant is so pervasive and fundamental a theological symbol in biblical thought that it becomes, in effect, one of humanity's (viewed narrowly as Israel) vital and defining relationships. Cut off from the covenant bond, Israel or the individual Jew is "non-existent", dead; faithful to the covenant, Israel is able to be itself.

Other sacred institutions and symbols reflect this special, defining bond. The Land, from which Israel draws its sustenance and identity, is gift, a sign of God's covenant promise. The Monarchy evolves into a sacral institution, sign of God's care for the people, with the King as vicegerent of Yahweh and responsible for the life-needs of the people. The Temple not only glorifies David's Jerusalem but it comes to symbolize, as the ark had done earlier, the living presence and therefore the defining bond of God with his people.

The New Testament radically re-interprets many of these basic defining symbols of God's relationship to Israel in terms of Jesus. The Risen Christ inaugurates the new and eschatological covenant (Mt. 26:28); he is the New Temple, not made by hands (Mk. 14:58, Jn. 2:19), he is the agent of salvation whose redeeming act creates a new "land", a "new heavens and a new earth" (Rev. 21:1); he is, especially in

270

Pauline theology, the one who enables humanity to be truly the "image of God" (Rom. 8:29).

This assertion of a peculiar bond between God and the human person which underlies these varied symbols and images is both the glory of biblical anthropology and an important source for its sense of boundaries. Because of this relationship to God, the human person is inherently sacred, unique within the created world. But, at the same time, the human person is not autonomous or self-sustaining. The destiny of the human person cannot be discerned simply on the basis of its own plans or apparent capabilities. Humanity, in the view of the biblical drama, is always dependent upon God's sovereignty, whose ways remain mysterious, even whimsical. Humanity's true destiny will not be determined by the empirical.

2. **The human person is a created being, destined to live in the world, essentially corporeal and finite.** Assertions about divine communion with the human person need to be counterbalanced with another firm biblical conviction; the human person is earthbound.

The creation stories and their echoes in other biblical traditions make this point clear. The human person is not a fallen God draped in an earthen cloak. Nor is there some component of the human frame which is essentially spiritual, immortal or not of the earth, as is the case in most variations of Greek and classical western anthropologies. Even though God breathes into clay to make the human person, that breath becomes *human* breath, in communion with the divine, but able to make no claims upon it.

This is an immensely important emphasis of the biblical materials, and one not easily appreciated by later Christian and Greco-Roman minds. Humanity's place is *in* the world: man and woman are to "be fruitful and multiply", to "fill the earth" (Gen. 1:28). Earth is their place because they, too, are of earth.

For almost its entire history, Israel had no clear conception of life beyond death. Its redemptive hopes were for long life, good vineyards, safe homes and many children to insure the continuity of the clan (Is. 25, 65). Burial rites which seemed to imply immortality were discouraged.[8] Only under the impact of Persian and Greek thought, and only in the latest books of the Old Testament Canon (cf. Wisdom and Maccabees) do ideas of life beyond death or of immortality come to the fore.

Thus death and mortality are taken very seriously by the biblical writers. Only the living belong to God; the dead are finished, unable to praise Yahweh, which is the most vivid sign of truly human activity (see, for example, Ps. 115:7). Death and its incipient symptoms of sickness, sorrow, poverty and limitation, are the "enemies of God" (I Cor. 15:25-26), to be avoided and feared. Humanity's allegiance is not beyond earth but *to* the earth, and to the Living God that created it and sustains it, and gives humans dominion over it.

Modifications are brought to this viewpoint by the New Testament, of course, but they are modifications, not a complete revision. The Gospels portray Jesus' own ministry as a fierce commitment to bodies. The presence of God's rule is demonstrated in his healing activity (Mt. 12:28; Lk. 11:20). He makes withered arms whole and drives out demons from tortured bodies (Mark 5:1-20), and from vital organs (Mark 9:14–20). Redemption is thereby illustrated as essentially world-oriented, not as rescue out of the world. New Testament traditions about the death and resurrection of Jesus, and through him of all humanity, are only comprehensible against the backdrop of the creation-centered anthropology of the Hebrew Scriptures. Resurrection is not to be understood as the retrieval or survival of an essentially immortal component of the human persòn, but as God's triumph over death, which had the capacity to utterly destroy the totality of the human person. Resurrection is, in effect, a creative, redeeming act of God which brings new human life from the midst of death. The stories of the Maccabees, where some of the earliest references to resurrection are to be found, think of it in vivid bodily terms. The martyr Razis hurls his entrails to the crowd, "calling upon the Lord of life and spirit to give them back to him again" at the resurrection (cf. 2 Mac. 14:46). The courageous Jewish mother who must watch her seven sons being tortured and executed by the Greeks exhorts them to remain steadfast, because the God who gave them life in her womb will restore them in the final day (2 Mac. 7).

Resurrection is viewed here as a kind of glorious resuscitation of the human body/person. New Testament reflections on resurrection are more subtle, emphasizing continuity with the bodily existence of humanity along with radical transformation. Thus the Risen Christ can eat broiled fish, but he is also unrecognizable to his disciples (Lk. 24:36-43; Jn. 21:4-14). Paul states that the body which is sown in death "is not the body which is to be, but a bare kernel (of it)" (I Cor. 15:37). What is "sown" is a "physical" (*psychicon,* that is a body that is

272

earthbound, historical, limited, almost the same connotation as *sarx*), whereas the resurrected body is "spiritual" (*pneumaticon,* that is, a body completely animated by the divine impulse, free from the limitations of sin and death). Paul's terminology here (cf. I Cor. 15:35-50) shows the sophistication and refinement that resurrection concepts underwent in Hellenistic Judaism and Christianity. Yet even here the essentially corporeal viewpoint of biblical anthropology is present. The human person, dead or resurrected, "physical" or "spiritual" remains a *soma,* that is, a *body.*

This aspect of the biblical portrayal implies for humanity an intrinsic, even desperate relationship to the created world that has often been blunted by the more "other-worldly" orientations of post-biblical Christian theologies, heavily influenced at times by neo-Platonic thought. Here, too, one can see the rationale for some of the biblical terminology for the human person described above.

3. Human existence is historical: the human person remembers the past, is aware of the present, and looks toward an evolving future. The whole "project" of the Scriptures is predicated on "memory" as an essential component of the human person. The experiences of the past give meaning to the present and provide hope for the future. As Wolff points out in a striking image, the biblical person moves through history in the posture of a rower.[9] The rower faces where he or she has already been; from that "past" the progression of the voyage can be measured and there too are signals for direction in the present and future. In fact, some biblical texts speak of the future as "behind" (Jer. 29:11), and the past as "in front" (cf. Ps. 143:5), the exact opposite of our own way of speaking.

Much of the Scriptures, Old and New, are expressions of the "memory" of Israel and the early church. Not "memory" in the sense of accumulated reports of events as such, but "memory" as the human person and the human community (again reduced in the Biblical drama to Israel and the Christian communities), reflecting on the significance of their story in which God has shaped human destiny. Israel can only understand who it is by remembering the acts of God in exile and exodus, in the wandering of the Patriarchs or in the origins of creation. The Christians only know who they are in the stories of Jesus and the disciples, in the narration of his death and resurrection, in the missions of Peter and Paul. Only by searching the past does Israel and the church understand the present and project hopes on the future.

The crucial role of memory in human identity implies that there is continuity in history. The human person is not an isolated individual but is "in time," dependent upon and defined by a past. Likewise, the individual is also dependent upon and defined by the future. Who Israel truly is will not be fully expessed until the future has dawned; only then will the promises given to her be realized. The same powerful future orientation or eschatology, is present in the New Testament. While basic elements of the Christian vision of humanity can be drawn from the past — God's acts in the history of Israel, Jesus and the early community — "what will be" is yet to be revealed. This "mystery" will be known only at the end of time, when God's plan of redemption is fully realized (cf. this conception in Ephesians 1:3-10). Therefore humanity is defined "in time"; the human person is in process of becoming.

This emphasis upon history and time as essential components of the human person has its limits, too. While Israel's sense of history and epic narrative seems to imply a strong sense of continuity within history, its experience and its theodicy brought important qualifications to this sense of continuity. Apocalyptic patterns of thought emphasized the element of *discontinuity* within history. This world experiences death and is in need of radical re-creation. The things past are "no more". It is never clear whether biblical apocalyptic means complete discontinuity or is using such language as a rhetoric to stress the need for reform and transformation. But Apocalyptic notions of history do show that for all of biblical thought, the element of continuity within human history is not to be found within the capacity of the human person. Ultimately, the biblical mind sees *God* as the only basis of continuity within human history itself. It is God that assures the next generation; it is God's generative power which allows the future. It is God's acts that make up the significant past. And only the mysterious designs of God determine the turns in humanity's story.

Therefore the essentially religious vantage point of the Bible once again impinges upon its anthropology. The human person is essentially historical, living and defined in time. Even though the creation stories portray a "paradise lost" drama with the perfection of the human person situated in the past, this is not the fundamental vantage point of the Bible. Humanity's real potential has not yet been revealed; the glory of human destiny is future, not past. The eschaton exerts a tremendous magnetism on the biblical vision, particularly within the New Testament. But the controlling force behind this unfolding history is neither evolutionary dynamics intrinsic to creation, nor the random alternations of chance, nor mere human ingenuity, but the purposeful intent of God.

4. Human Existence is essentially Social and Communal. This emphasis in the biblical view of the human person is, I believe, well known. The creation story once again reveals basic assumptions: "it is not good for man to be alone . . ." (Gen. 2:18). The human person is essentially relational: ". . . male and female he created them" (Gen. 1:27). The whole backdrop to the biblical saga is the family or household, the clan, the tribe, the nation; the individual has existence only in relation to these. [10] The Torah and all of the major institutions of Israel reflect this corporate and communal vantage point.

By contrast, isolation is seen as a de-humanizing experience. The sojourner, the orphan, the widow — those who by definition stand outside the clan and family structure — are the classical examples of those who are vulnerable and in need of aid. They are the special wards of the King. To be alone is an affliction and a curse; from the depths of such aloneness the Psalmist cries out for Yahweh's help (cf. Ps. 22, 69, 102).

It is, of course, not only in relationship with other human beings of family and clan that one finds life; Israel's relationship with God is also considered an essential component of life, as we noted above. Therefore, death is seen as the ultimate isolation; the dead are unable to praise or communicate with God and are, therefore, non-existent (Psalm 115:7; Ps. 88:10-12).

This "corporate personality" of the biblical peoples is what gives meaning to so many of its religious symbols. The King represents all of Israel, and can be declared "the son of God" just as the Israelites themselves through the covenant are "sons and daughters of God." The failures of one person can lead to dire consequences for the nation or his descendants. [11] The sufferings of the Servant atone for the guilt of the community (Is. 53). Such symbols have meaning only if they derive from experience of an essentially communal life in which the individual does not truly exist except in relationship.

Under the impact of Greek thought, the role of the individual becomes more pronounced within biblical tradition. Some would even consider this an important contribution of Jesus to biblical religion. From the inner circle of the community, Jesus reached out to the single lost sheep, to the single coin, the individual wandering son, the banned toll collector or shunned Samaritan woman. Jesus' interpretation of law often seemed to relativise Pharisaic emphasis on communal identity in favor of individual need (Lk. 13:10-17). In his teaching about God's care for Israel, the love of God for the individual Israelite is emphasized: each hair of the head is numbered, not a single sparrow falls to the ground unnoticed.

However, this must be seen as a corrective or emphasis which operates out of an essentially corporate perspective. The controlling symbol for Jesus' ministry is the "coming Kingdom of God", an essentially social image; he establishes some of his disciples as the "Twelve" an evident reference to eschatological hopes for restoring the nation Israel, and his ministry of healing usually results in the restoration of the isolated individual to family and village (Mk. 5:19; 1:44). Thus Jesus' perspective and that of the New Testament in general was in strong continuity with the essentially communal viewpoint of the Hebrew Scriptures. For New Testament theology, too, few if any of the symbols and images used to describe redemption can be understood unless it is assumed that the human person is by nature not autonomous but an essentially social being: "body of Christ," "New Adam," "baptised in his death and resurrection," "church," "people of God", "atonement", are examples of this perspective.

The intuition of western thought has been to highlight the dignity and autonomy of the individual. This, too, is an insight worthy of respect. But, as we have become increasingly aware, it is very difficult to have the biblical symbols, which continue to be the heart of our theology, make ultimate sense when the human person is viewed atomistically.

5. **The human person is responsible.** In biblical descriptions of the human body, the "ear" has special significance. The ear was to be adorned with jewelry. The submission of slave to master was signified by a hole bored through the earlobe. Such attention to the ear is symptomatic of a stress on the importance of "hearing". In the biblical view, one of the essential characteristics of being human was to be able to hear and to respond. Thus Solomon was blessed for asking of God a "hearing heart" before anything else (I Kgs. 3:9-12). For the deaf to hear was considered a sign of the endtime when humanity is brought to its full potential (Is. 35:5). Jesus' own miracles bear this symbolism (Mk. 7:31-37).

Such emphasis on hearing and responding is linked, as so many other traits are, to the fundamentally religious perspective of the Bible. God speaks and humanity is to "hear" and "respond." This is the ultimate definition of authentic human life. God's word creates all life (e.g., Gen. 1; Is. 55:10-11) but only the human person is able to hear it and respond to it. To so hear God's word is genuine wisdom; to respond to God's word is to find life. Metaphors of perception and response characterize biblical language for faith or lack of it in both Old and New Testaments:

> Go, and say to this people: 'Hear and hear, but do not understand; see and see, but do not perceive.' Make the heart of this people fat, and their ears heavy, and shut their eyes; else they will see with their eyes, and hear with their ears, and understand with their hearts, and turn and be healed (Is. 6:9-10).

This text is cited or alluded to on several occasions in connection with disbelief in Jesus on the part of his opponents or disciples (cf., for example, Mark 4:12; 8:17-18; John 12:40, etc.).

Attentiveness to the Torah or Mosaic Law becomes the dominant impulse of religious fidelity within Jewish biblical tradition. The Law is ultimately God's revealing word to his people; therefore, to "hear" and "obey" is to be responsive to God, the constant bedrock of authentic human life. In several New Testament traditions, basic symbols of God's revealing word or Torah are re-interpreted and applied to the exalted Christ. In Johannine theology, for example, Jesus is the "Word" sent from God who makes him known (Jn. 1:1-18); the supreme expectation of the human person in Johannine categories is that one must come out of the darkness and "hear" the Word that is Jesus (Jn. 3:16-21). Thus for John's Gospel "hearing" is "believing" (cf. Jn. 8:42-47). And in biblical categories, to "believe" never means mere notional assent to truth, but the total commitment of heart and mind that leads to obedience. So here, too, the human person is being defined as most human in the act of "hearing" and responding. In Matthew's Gospel, symbols applied to the Torah in Judaism are now applied to Jesus himself: in 11:28-30, for example, the disciple is invited to take Jesus' easy yoke, an image previously used of the Torah. Wisdom imagery applied in Judaism to Torah as the revealing word of God and the keeping of Torah as true knowledge are applied in both Matthew and John, as well as Pauline theology, to the Risen Christ.[12]

In most instances this vital human component of hearing and

responding to God refers to the people of Israel or to the followers of Jesus, thus seeming to imply a confessional context rather than an essential component of the human person as such. But as we have noted before, the Bible's viewpoint is always religious and it seldom speculated about the nature or plight of those outside of Israel or the church. When the nations or the non-believers are spoken of, it is often in negative terms. However, there are important texts where the dimension of human responsibility, the ability to perceive reality and to act on those perceptions, is explicitly extended to "outsiders", thereby revealing that the biblical authors considered this an essential human quality, and not just a consequence of faith. John, for example, speaks of those "in darkness" as having access to the light, but *choosing* not to come into the light (Jn. 3:16-21). In Romans 1-2, Paul speaks at length on the Gentiles who had the capacity to find God in the order of the universe or in the "Torah" written in the instincts of their hearts. Their own weakness left them in "ignorance," just as sin stood in the way of Jewish response to God's word in the revealed law of Moses. Yet "hearing" and responding were part of humanity's God-given endowments. The Gospels' protrayal of the mission of Jesus also makes this assumption. His keynote message: "The Kingdom of God is at hand, repent (*metanoiete,* literally "change your mind or perspective), and believe in the good news" (Mark 1:14-15), is offered to those "inside" the boundaries of the Jewish religious community, but also to "outsiders" such as the Gerasene (i.e., Gentile) demoniac, the Syro-Phoenician woman, the toll collector, and the Roman Centurion. Eventually the early church would come to understand that in fact every human person had the capacity to respond to the Gospel, and in so doing would find authentic fulfillment of their personhood. The judgment texts of the Gospels also imply human responsibility: one is able to hear the Gospel and may respond or turn away. The human person is ethically responsible.

Our discussion of the next component, that of sin and death, will bring significant qualification to human freedom. Nevertheless, it is clear that despite the lack of parameters of God's sovereignty, or the limitations of human flesh and the confinements of the clan, and the powers of the cosmos or of death itself, the human person is responsible: able to perceive reality, called to act in response to it, and accountable for the consequences. Not only is the human person responsible, but in so being is most characteristically human. No other creature in the Biblical menagerie has this power.

The objects of this responsibility are expressed in countless ways, but the major chords are constant. The human person is responsible for the earth. As made in the "image of God" the human person has "dominion" over the rest of creation, is called to exercise bountiful care towards it, as God himself does. The human person is also responsible to and for his brothers and sisters. The entire sweep of the Torah and the message of Jesus (which is deeply instilled with the spirit of the Torah) presumes that one owes care, protection, and respect for other human beings. The violation of any living thing is an offense; but the violation of a human life or human property is viewed as a breaking of one's fidelity to the covenant, as disobedience to the word and as an act for which not only the individual, but the family, the clan, the tribe; and indeed, the nation bears the consequences. Nothing in the New Testament in any way blunts this biblical sense of responsibility.

6. **Humanity and the created world are beset by evil, sin and death.** Despite the transcendent dimensions of humanity noted in some of the preceding characteristics, the Bible never flinches from sober awareness of the *limits* of the human person. Some of that limitation has been noted under the category of the created nature of humanity; the human person is of the earth, flesh, and thus limited to this world.

Another aspect of human limitation is more sinister and more mysterious, namely that of sin and its consequence, "death". Despite the presence of a God-inclined spirit within the human person, there is also the tendency to rebel, to disobey, to violate one's responsibility to the earth, to living things, and to other human beings. It might be argued that such moral limits are not intrinsic to the human person as such. Sin is not part of the God-intended scenario for Eden. Wisdom 1:12-16 affirms that whatever God made was wholesome and without destructive tendency, but the human person made a covenant with death and invited it into human history.

But the Bible is not a philosophical text. Its efforts to determine the origin of sin and death do not imply that the human person left to itself would be akin to Rousseau's noble savage. Sin and moral death are part of the human story, from the failure in the Garden and the death blow to Abel through the murmurings in the desert and the deadly lust of David to the murder of Jesus. Humanity is weak, capable of rebellion, in desperate need of purification and liberation.

In this aspect, too, the Bible's communal perspective is important. While the transgressions of individuals are certainly catalogued, sin is also seen as a "force" all its own, a sphere of power which exerts its dominion on the human scene and holds human destiny in its grip. Later biblical traditions, probably under the influence of Persian thought, would identify the source of Sin's power as Satan. This is clear in the New Testament texts, especially the Synoptic Gospels. Jesus' mission is described as active combat against the demonic forces who infest human bodies and human lives. This mysterious power of evil is manifested in illness, in isolation from village and family, in self-destructive tendencies. Jesus liberates human persons from this power and restores them to life. In these stories an important anthropological conviction is being expressed: human life is blunted by evil that transcends the moral will of the individual.

Pauline theology has a similar conception, even though Paul does not describe exorcisms. Individuals are capable of "transgressions *(parabasis)*," Paul recognizes, but in most instances he speaks of sin *(hamartia)* in the singular, as a power or force that grips humanity and which can be shattered only through the redemptive power of Christ's death and resurrection. The metaphor of Christ as the "New Adam" expresses this most explicitly: through Adam, sin and death "enter" the world and hold it captive; through Jesus, life floods back to humanity (cf. Rom. 5:17).

When death is linked to sin it is seen as the inevitable consequence of the destructive power of evil. In some texts death is viewed in more neutral terms as the relentless conclusion to human life, the outcome of the human person's fleshly nature (e.g., Psalm 103:15). Death at the end of a long life is no curse, even though it is not welcomed (Gen. 25:8; Job 5:26).

But in other texts and perhaps from another vantage point, death is no mere conclusion; it is a destructive force, God's "last enemy" as Paul will refer to it in I Corinthians (15:25-26). Death is the "wages of sin" (Rom. 6:23), that dissolution of human life symbolic of alienation from God.

Even though the Bible speaks warily of "Sin" and "Death" as powers which hold humanity in their relentless grip, this description remains existential rather than fully metaphysical. In the final analysis there is no real dualism in the biblical world view. Sin and death and the demonic are not God's peers. The drama of apocalyptic as found in Judaism and in a New Testament text such as the book of Revelation seems, at first blush, to conjure up a cosmic duel between good and evil, between Christ, God's champion, and the deadly beast of Satan. But at no moment is the outcome in doubt. God's sovereignty, even over sin and death, is never questioned within the Bible.

III. Observations and Implications

No doubt the anthropological constants we have described could be augmented by other considerations, but I believe these at least are basic and consistent affirmations of the Scriptures about essential characteristics of the human person.

It must be apparent that these components are interrelated. In fact, most of them stand in a kind of dynamic tension. The human person has a close bond with the divine, animated by God's Spirit, sharing in God's dominion over creation; yet that same person is earthbound, limited, mortal. The human person is responsible, able to hear and perceive reality and respond to it; yet the human person is checked by evil and death, seemingly doomed by its "body of death" (cf. Paul's lament in Romans 7:24). The human person is individual, unique, yet made to cling to other "flesh", finding meaning and fulfillment only in relationship to family, clan, nation. The human person is endowed with historical consciousness, aware of the past, standing in the present, evolving toward the future; yet humanity experiences profound discontinuity, with the past serving as little warning or preparation. Human destiny is not totally in human hands.

Often it is at the intersection of these forces and tensions that the biblical drama comes into play. The human person find its moments of hope when the full span of defining components are acknowledged; falsehood, illusion and tragedy come when one dimension is ignored or whirls out of balance. Thus humanity has dominion over the land as part of its heritage in being God-imaged, but such dominion is limited or qualified by other dimensions of human existence. The very term "dominion," while correctly translating the Hebrew verbs *kabash* and *radah* found in Gen. 1:28, can connote to a modern reader oppression and exploitation of the powerful over the weak. Feminist theologians have rightly criticized Christian theologians for unqualified appropriation of such modes of thought and expression deeply ingrained in patriarchal cultures, including the biblical. The proper meaning of humanity's God-given "dominion" over creation can only be a responsibility exercised in the fashion of God's own care for his world; therefore, it must not be exploitive, but life-giving, caring and nourishing. As social beings, humans had to share the land; as religious beings ownership could not become idolatry; as corporeal beings and therefore earth-dependent, the land had to be cared for. Biblical stories such as the story of Ahab and Jezebel and their violation of the rights of Naboth (I Kgs. 21) or Jesus' parable about the man and his barns (Lk 12:15-21), all flow from these assumptions about the human person. Or, to use another type of example, the human person was indeed responsible and capable of being endowed in a special way with God's spirit, but the human person is also beset with evil and the seeds of death. The human person can dream of the future, but there are continuing checks on unbridled dreams through the realities of social obligation and God's mysterious providence. So David the King has a special portion of God's Spirit, and is promised a long-lived dynasty, but his murderous lust shatters his dream and brings an unexpected future (2 Sam. 11-12). Paul's famous lament expressed this baffling intersection of the transcendent and the mortal: "For I delight in the law of God, in my inmost self, but I see in my members another law at war with the law of my mind, and making me captive to the law of sin which dwells in my members. Wretched man that I am! Who will deliver me from this body of death?" (Rom. 7:22-25). Recent scholarship sees this passage not as an autobiographical expression of Paul's frustrations as a Jew under the law, but as Paul's first-person dramatization of humanity or perhaps of Judaism itself prior to liberation by Christ.

So the Bible testifies to the need for a process of reflection that keeps soberly and honestly in view the many dimensions of the human person. When an essential component is overlooked or exaggerated, then disorientation besets humanity. Although it is never stated in so many words, it is clear that for the New Testament Jesus is the complete human person. All of the components we have described above find their illustration in the Gospels' portrayal of Jesus, in the Christ figure of Pauline theology, and in the appeals to Jesus in other New Testament texts such as I Peter or the Apocalpyse. Thus Jesus' communion with God is more evident and more privileged than that of any other Israelite. He "becomes flesh" taking on himself a body and a human history (Jn. 1:14). He catches up the great moments of Israel's past (the glory of David, the pain of exile, the martyrdom of the prophets, the revelation to Moses), and is a sign of the new creation yet to dawn. He is one with Israel, sensitive to the needs of the poor and the sick and the outcasts. He identifies with the "least." He exerts power over creation, stilling the seas and the wind. The demons obey him. Even the component of humanity's sinfulness find "fulfillment" in the New Testament portrayal of Jesus. Through crucifixion he experiences death; he becomes "sin" (2 Cor. 5:11); he is cursed under the law (Gal. 3:13). By his ministry and death Jesus is portrayed as fulfilling the atoning role of the Servant (Mk. 10:45), absorbing into himself the sin and guilt of the community. By his resurrection Jesus breaks through the limits of the past and discloses humanity's future with God.

Jesus, therefore, is the "New Adam", the representative human being (I Cor. 15:45). The entire gospel project can be understood in this perspective. The story of Jesus is retold so that later generations of believers could rekindle their vision of what God intends humanity to be.

We have yet to ask what all of this reflection on the Bible and its portrayal of the human person might mean for the staggering issues posed by modern technologies. Although that is not my specific task, allow me to conclude this paper by attempting to illustrate how I see that the biblical material might have some relationship to the ethical dilemmas posed for the believing Christian in the 20th century.

First of all, let us admit frankly that the Bible has nothing *explicit* to say to either reproductive technologies or nuclear energy per se. The Bible, of course, knows nothing at all about the molecular structure of matter or about nuclear energy. It knows nothing about modern technology nor about the peculiar economic, social, political and environmental problems it poses for us. The same, I contend, is true about reproductive issues. Obviously, the Bible knows nothing about technological parenting or the stages in the development of a human fetus. For the whole span of biblical cultures from Moses to Jesus, scientific knowledge in these areas advanced hardly at all.

Some passages speak in poetic style of the origin of human life in the womb. Psalm 139, for example:

> For Thou didst form my inward parts, thou didst knit me
>   together in my mother's womb.
> I praise thee, for thou art fearful and wonderful . . .
> Thou knowest me right well; my frame was not hidden from thee,
>   when I was being made in secret, intricately wrought
>   in the depths of the earth.

Thy eyes beheld my unformed substance; in thy book were written,
every one of them, the days that were formed for me,
when as yet there was none of them. (Psalm 139:13-18)

Here Yahweh is compared to a weaver, knitting together the vital parts of the human person in the depths of the womb. Note, too, that the womb itself is compared to the "depths of the earth," reminiscent of ancient conceptions which considered the human person to sprout from the earth "like an ear of corn." The point of the Psalm is to assert God's initiative in the formation of human life: "you formed my inward parts (literally, "my kidney")." "Your eyes beheld my unformed substance. . . ." It is not a commentary on the biological process forming the embryo. This in fact is hidden from human eyes and only metaphors —weaving, germination of plants — can be used to image it. But here is the point; what is hidden from humanity is not hidden from God, and He alone is the author and controlling force of all life.

A similar mix of archaic biological knowledge and profound theological assertion about the origin of human life is found in Job 10:8-12:

Thy hands fashioned and made me; and now thou dost turn about
and destroy me.
Remember that thou has made me of clay; and will thou turn me to
dust again?
Didst thou not pour me out like milk and curdle me like cheese?
Thou didst clothe me with skin and flesh, and knit me together with
bones and sinews.
Thou has granted me life and steadfast love; and thy care has
preserved my spirit.

Here a variety of metaphors are used to assert God's initiative and creative force at the origin of human life: God is the potter, fashioning the human being from clay; God is the weaver (as in Psalm 139), knitting together skin, flesh, bones and sinews; and God is the dairy farmer forming a body as the farmer makes cheese. The last image again reveals the scientific ignorance at work here; as commentators have suggested, the author of Job is probably thinking of the injection of the milky seminal fluid into the vagina. Like milk curdling into cheese so the semen is thought to congeal and be transformed into a firm body. In every instance the metaphors illumine, not the actual biological process, but a theological conviction: God is ultimate source of human life — *he* is the weaver, the potter, the one who pours the milk and makes the cheese.

This conviction is expressed in many other references to life in the womb. Another set of examples would be the experience of vocation or call within the womb. Paul insists that his apostolic commission is of divine not human origin, God "had set me apart before I was born" (Gal. 1:15) — the quotation is from Isaiah (Is. 49:1; see a similar thought in Jer. 1:5) who speaks of his prophetic call in the same vein. A similar motif may be at work in Luke 1:44 when Elizabeth reports that John the Baptist leaped for joy in her womb at the sound of Mary's greeting. This incident, found only in Luke, fulfills the promise of the angel to Zechariah in 1:15: "he will be filled with the Holy Spirit, even from his mother's womb." John, in other words, is destined by God to be a prophet, and he begins to exercise this God-given role from the very beginning of his existence when he jumps with gladness at the approach of the Messiah.

These texts on the origin of prophetic vocations in Isaiah, Paul, and John the Baptist are obviously not meant to comment on the process of conception or the origin of the human fetus; they are ways of expressing the Bible's conviction about God's actions in the history of significant human beings.

The Bible, then, has little to offer us in the question of when human life begins, just as it could offer little help about when death really occurs. In both instances, its horizon was understandably bound by the primitive state of its scientific knowledge.

Acknowledgment of these limits within the Scriptures does not mean, however, that the Bible is irrelevant to the moral dilemmas facing us in such issues as nuclear and reproductive technologies. The Scriptures, responsibly interpreted within the context of the Christian community, thrust into our consciousness a vision of humanity's relationship to God and to our earthly environment that cannot be ignored in any decision that has the potential to substantially affect the human person.

The "anthropological constants" we have noted above, and their dynamic interrelationhips, are an important part of that vision. Some of these constants appear not incompatible with the very technology that seems to create our problems. The biblical commission to "have dominion over the earth" is the ultimate demythologization of the world and the revelation of its secularness. The world is not some demi-god with an alien and potentially threatening soul. The human person belongs in the world. God has commissioned men and women to be "his image", to exercise creative care towards the earth, bringing, as God had done, light from darkness, life from chaos, fertility from barrenness. As Ludwig Köhler describes it, this biblical commission is the establishment and endorsement of civilization itself. [13] There may well be, as some have suggested, an intrinsic connection between the fact that western civilization was partially brewed in a biblical culture and the fact that technology developed more rapidly in the West. Experimentation, the gathering of data, projection through hypothesis, and planning — all crucial steps in scientific and technological methodologies — seem in harmony with the biblical vision of the human person who alone of all creation is endowed by God with memory and intelligence, with a sense of time, with the warrant to take responsiblity for the future.

But there are other constants at stake and humanity's exercise of responsibility cannot ignore them. As citizens of the twentieth century who have seen nuclear technology honed for the mass destruction of human life and have witnessed the global economic inequities that at times seem a necessary product of modern industrialization, we cannot afford to rhapsodize about the genius of human enterprise or to suppose that technology has only a benign spirit. If that technology threatens the earth, then humanity is ignoring its own earthboundedness, its "flesh." If a spin-off of that technology should be an exploitation or destruction of the bonds among human persons, or between humanity and its God, then the limits and evils of technology must be acknowledged and challenged. The religious sense of the Bible warns against allowing technology and progress to become idols.

Reflections in this vein, incomplete as they are, perhaps illustrate the Bible's function. The Bible's portrayal of the human person and the story of humanity's relationship to God and world offer no recipe for solutions to ethical problems. The decisions are ours, not the Bible's. But the Bible does remind us who we are, what are our glories and our limitations. Across the saga of the Bible are displayed values of justice, of reverence for life, of awe for the creator and his creation, of the human person as bodily whole with spirit and heart, of the intrinsically social nature of humanity — male and female, family, clan and tribe, of awareness of our sinfulness and the need for transformation. The biblical wisdom affirms again and again that these values make us what we are. Many, if not all of these intuitions occurred to thoughtful people outside of the biblical traditions. But for us the authority of the Scriptures as God's revealed word makes this wisdom sacred. That sacred wisdom, recalled and re-interpreted, is an irreplaceable part of any vital judgments the people of God must make.

Notes

1. Edward Schillebeeckx, *Christ: The Experience of Jesus as Lord* (New York: The Seabury Press, 1980), p. 733.
2. I depend in this section on the excellent work of H. W. Wolff, *Anthropology of the Old Testament* (Philadelphia: Fortress, 1974). Another important resource for anthropological aspects of the Hebrew Scriptures would be the now classic work of J. Pedersen, *Israel: Its Life and Culture* (New York: Oxford, 1927) I-II. No comparable work exists for the New Testament materials. W. G. Kümmel, *Man in the New Testament* (Philadelphia: Westminster, 1963) attempts some comprehensiveness but not on the scope of Wolff.
3. H. W. Wolff, *Anthropology*, p. 4.
4. Ibid., p. 55.
5. Ibid., p. 59.
6. Ibid., p. 62.
7. On Pauline anthropology, cf. J. Fitzmyer, S.J., "Pauline Theology," in *The Jerome Biblical Commentary* (Englewood Cliffs, NJ: Prentice-Hall, 1968), Vol. II, pp. 818–825; and E. Käsemann, *Perspectives on Paul* (Philadelphia: Fortress, 1971), pp. 1–31.
8. Cf. H. Wolff, *Anthropology*, pp. 99–118; and W. Eichrodt, *Theology of the Old Testament* (Philadelphia: Westminster, 1967), Vol. II, pp. 426–529.
9. H. Wolff, *Anthropology*, pp. 88.
10. Cf. G. Robinson, "The Biblical View of Man," *Indian Journal of Theology* 27 (1978), pp. 144–145.
11. This is especially evident in the law codes of Israel describing procedures to be used to redress serious wrongs such as the taking of an innocent life: see, for example, Deut. 21:1-9.
12. See the discussion in J. D. G. Dunn, *Christology in the Making* (Philadlephia: Westminster, 1980), pp. 163–212.
13. L. Köhler, *Hebrew Man* (London: SCM, 1956), pp. 126–217.

Chapter 10

The Human Person
in Contemporary Theology:
From Human Nature to
Authentic Subjectivity

The Reverend Michael J. Himes, Ph.D.

Editorial Preface

Around the year 1700, many cosmological and historical views which had been taken as "true" 100 years earlier were completely rejected, even by "the man in the street." With this thought revolution, rooted largely in scientific advances, came also a scepticism as to whether any generation of human beings can adequately grasp the meaning of any phenomenon beyond the place which it has in their own age. Indeed, any given phenomenon might have no significance except as a transitory event in a historical process of evolution which the human mind cannot, in the final analysis, comprehend. This modesty of claims for, if not outright cynicism about, the capacity of the human mind to grasp a transcendent and universal meaning for earthly experiences came to be known as "historical consciousness."

Scientific theories from the 18th century, such as Darwin's, to the 20th century, such as Heisenberg's, confirmed and epitomized in the popular mind the new "historical consciousness" which has now become an irradicable element of the modern mind. George Hegel's philosophy categorized man's most abstract thinking as, ultimately, in essence, a developing process.

Faced with the almost universal rise of "historical consciousness," a number of 20th century theologians, Protestants first and later some Catholics, advocated a new expression of Christianity which would abandon use of classical concepts which seemed to connote a static and abiding meaning. While the anti-modernist activities of St. Pius X and, shortly later, the Neo-Orthodox theology of Karl Barth temporarily blocked such efforts, Christian thinkers of the past 30 or more years have turned again to face as inescapable the challenge of "historical consciousness" as it has rooted itself in the mentality of 20th century western civilization.

Many Catholic theologians today, such as Bernard Lonergan, are convinced that: 1) contemporary "historical consciousness" allows, at best, only probable conclusions from a scientific hermeneutic of Scripture and tradition; 2) the theologian has from this hermeneutic, therefore, no absolutely certain premises from which to draw absolutely certain conclusions; and 3) that a whole new conceptual framework and vocabulary must be found for the Christian message.

All of this affects our efforts to speak in adequate theological terms about the human person. For "historical consciousness" excludes any changeless concept of "human nature" and therefore eliminates "claims which pose illegitimately as natural law" 'Rahner). In moral issues, what theology can do is to enter into dialogue with other formal anthropological disciplines by bringing to such a dialogue the interpretative power of the doctrinal symbols which express the Christian experience of agape, God's all pervasive love. These symbols, yet unfulfilled in old Israel's history and complete in Christ and the apostolic Church, not only give an understanding of the meaning of contemporary human experiences, but also are themselves expanded in light of those experiences.

There is a danger that this emphasis on developing experiences, both in secular life and within the on-going life of the Church, will lead to a neglect of speculative theology. Such is not necessarily the case, however, for "historical consciousness" points to the typically human ability to transcend history, that is, intellectually to recognize it for what it is and freely to influence its direction. The writer holds, indeed, that the speculative theology which is embued with "historical consciousness" will ground an authentic moral theology rooted in man's "subjectivity." He sees the content of a genuine natural law as adequately stated in Lonergan's six conditions for true subjectivity: "Be attentive. Be intelligent. Be reasonable. Be responsible. Evaluate. And, if necessary, change." Only Christ as the perfect human being possessed this subjectivity in its fullness. This fullness is constituted in Him alone as the one full expression of divinity in all of creation. We ourselves also become expressions of divinity in the measure that we live our own subjectivity.

The Church must give moral guidance in questions of enormous complexity today. Yet it seems that one of the traditional starting points of moral theological reflection, the notion of a universal human nature, is seriously questioned today even by contemporary theologians. Why is this so? How does contemporary theology understand the human person? And how is that helpful in responding to the pressing ethical issues of our time? These are, as I understand my task at this Workshop, the questions before me.

Clearly, one must be very rash to attempt to answer them! And so I begin by carefully indicating what I am about in this paper. If I am to speak of *contemporary* theology, I must indicate what the characteristics are of being contemporary. Therefore, I first intend to examine, however briefly, what I understand to be the hallmark of modernity, namely, historical consciousness, and to note its effects on our (presuming that we are all instances of modernity) idea of humanity. Then recognizing that within this historically-minded and so pluralist context there is no such thing as one theology, but there are rather many theologies, I will attempt to suggest an important concern underlying a great many major streams of contemporary theological thought with regard to the meaning of the human person. I will further suggest a way in which many theologians today, either implicitly or explicitly, have responded to that concern. Finally, I will offer a suggestion about the relationship of our question to the area which has become more and more the chief focus of contemporary theologizing, Christology.

At the end of the last century, the great Protestant theologian Ernst Troeltsch wrote of the ever increasing tension between Christianity and modernity. Far too perceptive and honest to trivialize this friction by ascribing it to some one or two causes, Troeltsch concluded:

> This conflict arises not merely from the insubordination of
> natural reason but clearly and above all from the complete
> and multifaceted change in modern thought in the last two

centuries and its contrast with the thought-forms and perspectives within which Christianity arose in its time and which its ecclesiastical institution has preserved.[1]

Troeltsch's placing of this sweeping change in the ways in which westerners thought about themselves and their universe two centuries before, puts the beginning of this intellectual transformation at the close of the seventeenth century. This corresponds to the period from 1680 to 1715, which Paul Hazard called the age of the crisis of European consciousness.[2] The seventeenth century was an era of scientific and philosophical revolution, a time which saw "the infinitization of the universe," in Alexandre Koyré's words; and the destruction of the cosmos, understood as "a finite, closed, and hierarchically ordered whole."[3]

I wish to suggest a far-reaching aspect of this extraordinary period which too much attention to the giants of the seventeenth century[4] — Bacon, Galileo, Kepler, Harvey, Pascal, Descartes, Locke, Newton, *et al.*, may obscure: the increased speed at which scientific and philosophical ideas become "common sense."

In 1600, the "man in the street" in London or Paris, Frankfurt or Amsterdam, knew that the earth on which he stood was the center of the cosmos and that the sun, moon, planets and stars moved around it. He knew from the Bible that this whole arrangement had come into existence 5604 years before, give or take a year. He knew that his physical well-being depended on the proper balance of four humors within him, each produced by a different organ of his body. "Everyone" knew this. But by 1700, the great-grandson of this "man in the street" knew that the earth was one of the planets revolving about the sun, that the universe containing this solar system was both far larger and far older than had been thought, and that his body was a kind of machine centered about his heart which acted like a pump. And this was what "everyone" then knew. But there was another point which the "man in the street" in 1700 knew: his predecessor in 1600 had not known what he knew now.

It was this last which was truly revolutionary. If the common sense of a generation or two before seemed hopelessly wrong-headed and antiquated, then the intervening years had made a great difference. A new way of understanding oneself and one's world had appeared. But then could not the passage of more time yield more remarkable discoveries which might make our vision of reality seem as quaint as that of our grandparents? The increased rate of scientific and technological change in the seventeenth century made it possible to observe significant differences in common sense from one generation to another or from the beginning of a lifetime to its end. The possibility of the significantly and radically *new* appeared in the western experience. Simultaneously, the past became distant, other, remote from the present and therefore both more interesting and more difficult to fathom; and the future became, in principle, open. For if today is so very different from yesterday, why should tomorrow not be even more different from today? The end of the seventeenth century produced a crisis in consciousness not because it was an age of scientific revolution, but because the people of the time *recognized* that theirs was an age of scientific revolution. They discovered the possibility of revolution, of radical newness.

The discovery of time is the hallmark of modernity. Every aspect of human life and thought, familial and social relations, politics, economics, the human and natural sciences, have been historicized. By this I mean that in all these spheres of activity the principle is now generally accepted that to gain an adequate understanding of any phenomenon or adequately to assess its value, it must be considered in terms of the place which it occupies and the role which it plays within a process of development.[5]

Thus, by the end of the eighteenth century, the historicization of the natural sciences began with geology, a process which became fully accepted in the next century with the work of Sir Charles Lyell. As early as 1778 in *The Epochs of Nature,* a work whose very title would have astonished the generation of Isaac Newton, the Comte de Buffon wrote:

> The surface of the earth has taken different forms in succession. Even the heavens have changed, and all the objects in the physical world are, like those of the moral world, caught up in a continual process of successive variations.[6]

In the nineteenth century, the name of Charles Darwin has come to symbolize the historicization of nature and the natural sciences, and *The Origin of Species* to be the trumpet-call heralding the abandonment of the idea of a static nature. The notion of biological evolution, in the words of R. G. Collingwood, is only one expression of a tendency which may work, and has in fact worked, in a much wider field: the tendency to resolve the very ancient dualism between changing and unchanging elements in a world of nature by maintaining that what had hitherto been regarded as unchanging was itself in reality subject to change.[7]

The extraordinary hold which the idea of evolution took on the imagination of so many in such diverse fields in the nineteenth century was due to its having combined the two most powerful intellectual currents of that century, science and history. By the beginning of this century, it seemed that almost all the sciences had accepted Buffon's dictum that "Nature's great workman is time."[8]

Indeed, our own century has witnessed the extension of the historicization of the sciences to the final bastion of a static mathematicized scientific understanding, physics. From Einstein through Heisenberg to Paul Dirac, the cosmological theories of contemporary physics have moved steadily away from the unchanging and eternal laws of Newtonian physics. So astute and knowledgeable a philosopher of science as Stephen Toulmin can now claim that "at a theoretical level, a Universe whose laws are changing from epoch to epoch is no longer an idle fantasy."[9]

Perhaps as Darwin is the figure who has come to represent the historicization of nature in the nineteenth century, Hegel is the name which represents the historicization of thought. Hegel is so subtle a thinker that any characterization of his work is likely to be a caricature. One might claim that, rather than historicize philosophy, Hegel attempted to philosophize history. "History in general is therefore the development of Spirit in *Time,* as Nature is the development of the Idea in *Space.*"[10] But there is certainly no doubt that, by making philosophy the history of philosophy, Hegel moved from an eternally static to an eternally developing notion of truth.[11]

Thus the claim made by Lord Acton, although it seems almost to make history the queen of the sciences, was, by the time it was written in the 1890's, largely true: history, he wrote,

is not only a particular branch of knowledge but a particular mode and method of knowledge in other branches. [It] determines their influence on society. It embraces other sciences, records their progress and the tests by which truth has been ascertained. Historic thinking is more than historical knowledge.[12]

And yet, in the latter half of the nineteenth century, even as the historicization of every area of life seemed complete and the emergence of "historic thinking" or historical consciousness an undeniable fact, a concern about the effect of this massive change in western consciousness began to be voiced. Wilhelm Dilthey was one of the most perceptive of those who recognized the ultimate effect of the emergence of historical consciousness.

The historical thinking of the Greeks and the Romans mainly presupposes a definite human species equipped with definite characteristics. The Christian doctrine of the first and second Adam and of the Son of Man presupposed the same. The natural system of the sixteenth century was still sustained by the same presupposition. In Christianity, it discovered an abstract, permanent paradigm of religion, natural theology; it abstracted the doctrine of natural law from Roman jurisprudence, and a model of taste from Greek artistic activity. According to this natural system all historical differences contained basic constant and universal forms of social and legal arrangements, of religious faith and of morality. This method of deducing common features from the comparison of historical forms of life by using the idea of supreme types, abstracting natural law, natural theology and rational morality from the varied customs, laws and theologies, still dominated the century of constructive philosophy.[13]

But this world-view had disintegrated by his day, Dilthey believed:

So the point of view of developmental history could be applied to the study of the whole natural and historical development of man and man as a type dissolved in this process. The evolutionary theory which thus originated is necessarily linked to the knowledge of the relativity of every historical form of life. In the vision which encompasses the earth and its whole past the absolute validity of any individual form of life, constitution, religion or philosophy vanishes. So, more drastically than awareness of conflicting systems, the development of historical consciousness destroys faith in the universal validity of any philosophy which attempts to express world order cogently through a system of concepts. [14]

Or as Dilthey's contemporary, Lord Acton, wrote, "History defeats metaphysics." [15]

This was the alarming result of the shift to historical consciousness in the west, a relativism leading to nihilism. If every world-view, every philosophical system, every moral code, is the product of a particular age with its particular advantages and problems and can make no claim to universal validity, then are we not reduced to organizing our individual lives and our societies, making choices, and evaluating alternatives on the basis of personal preference, advantage, or groundless tradition? What prevents religious indifferentism, philosophical skepticism, moral and political opportunism? Truth, it might well seem, is what the victors decide, and right is what succeeds.

This was the crisis of the intellectual world which began to grip all fields of thought at the end of the last century and the beginning of this. Clearly theology could not refuse to face this challenge without accepting the alternative of irrelevance and incredibility to modernity. Creative and courageous scholars with profound religious concerns dealt forthrightly with the issues raised by historical consciousness. In Protestant circles perhaps the most distinguished such figure is Troeltsch; within Catholicism at that time the names which readily come to mind are Maurice Blondel, Friedrich von Hügel, and Lucien Laberthonnière. Unfortunately their efforts were unable to have their full due effect. On the Protestant side, Barthian Neo-orthodoxy emerged after the First World War with its own agenda and so thorough a rejection of the nineteenth century and all its works that not responding to the exigencies of modern consciousness became virtually the hallmark of truth. On the Catholic side, the Integralist reaction to Modernism led to a doctrinal positivism and theological conformism which relegated the pressing questions of modernity to the status of "contemporary errors" to be refuted, but not taken seriously.

The flowering of Catholic theology in the middle of the century and the passing of the "Barthian interlude" in Protestant theology have brought the questions posed by historical consciousness to the fore once again. Walter Kasper has written that Troeltsch's warning has been proven accurate, that the conflict between theology and science, which seemed so pressing to so many at the turn of the century, would turn out to be merely a symptom of the deeper divorce between theology and history. He cites the judgment of the contemporary philosopher Gerhard Krüger that "history is today our greatest problem. It is so in the threefold sense that it is simultaneously our most pressing, most encompassing, and most serious problem."

Langdon Gilkey has skillfully analyzed the modern context of religious thought in its many aspects. Historicity and relativity are inextricably intertwined, and their combined effect is judged by him to be "central to all we mean by the secular spirit" which is modernity.

> For this modern view, all that is is pinioned within the flux of passage or of history, determined in large part by all that lies behind it, shaped by all that surrounds it, and to be replaced by what follows. Nothing in nature or history, and so by implication nothing at all that is, is thus *"a se"*, an unchanging and self-sufficient substance, capable of existing in and by itself and thus exhibiting an essence underived from and so unrelated to the other things that surround it. Nothing anywhere in experience, space, time, or any mode of being is, in that sense, absolute; all is relative to all else and so essentially conditioned by its relevant environment. [17]

The ontological expression of this historical relativity is the philosophical concept of "internal relations", i.e. every existent is formed by its concrete relations to its context. This principle dominates every form of modern philosophy, according to Gilkey, whether idealistic or naturalistic, existentialist or phenomenological. It is presupposed by the natural, social and psychological sciences. Gilkey, like Kasper, proclaims the fulfillment of Troeltsch's and Dilthey's prediction: "The sense of the relativity of all things to one another in the passage of time — of the forms of the cosmos itself, of natural life, of our own species, of political and social structures, of the most significant historical events, the noblest of ideas, the most sacred of scriptures, institutions or creeds — practically defines our era." [18]

This is the context in which all truly contemporary theology must be carried on. The emergence of historical consciousness is the central characteristic of modernity. The meaning of that fact for theology has been very helpfully explored by Bernard Lonergan.[19]

Lonergan has referred to three points which must be recognized if one is to understand contemporary theology. First, whereas theology was at one time understood as a deductive science, it is now largely empirical. In that earlier understanding, conclusions were reached with varying clear degrees of certitude from premises derived from Scripture and tradition. In contemporary theology within the context of historical consciousness, the data of Scripture and tradition are interpreted by the best available hermeneutical procedures and yield results which are, at best, probable.

> An empirical science does not demonstrate. It accumulates information, develops understanding, masters ever more of its materials, but it does not preclude the uncovering of further relevant data, the emergence of new insights, the attainment of a more comprehensive view.[20]

Second, the move from a deductive to an empirical understanding of theology is irreversible because the shift from classical to historical consciousness is irreversible. Although Lonergan does not mention this, I suggest that this irreversibility is seen in the fact that historical consciousness can adequately account for the emergence and dominance of classical consciousness and for its replacement, while classical consciousness has no way to account for the emergence and dominance of historical consciousness, save perhaps in the purely negative category of a mistake. Lonergan notes that one fruit of this irreversible move into a new context is the need for a reorganization of the theological field into specializations, a task which he has attempted in his influential *Method in Theology*.

> Where once the dogmatic theologian was supposed to range over centuries, now Scripture, patristics, medieval and modern studies are divided and subdivided among classes of specialists. Where once the dogmatic theologian could lay down an overall view that echoed the conciliar *tenet atque semper tenuit sancta mater Ecclesia,* now an overall view tends to be either a tentative summary of the present state of research,

or a popular simplification of issues that are really not simple at all.[21]

Third, the movement of theology into the context of historical consciousness requires a new conceptual framework and a new vocabulary. The language of Aristotle, so useful for so long within the world of classical consciousness, is inadequate to the new demands. The new framework and language may be derived from a great many possible sources, not least of all, Scripture; personalist, phenomenological, and existential categories are frequent sources.

> Religion is concerned with man's relations to God and to his fellow man, so that any deepening or enriching of our apprehension of man possesses religious significance and relevance. But the new conceptual apparatus does make available such a deepening and enriching. Without denying human nature, it adds the quite distinctive categories of man as an historical being. Without repudiating the analysis of man into body and soul, it adds the richer and more concrete apprehension of man as incarnate subject.[22]

It is noteworthy that understanding man as an historical being does not deny the category of nature. This is because, within the context of history, one recognizes the usefulness of that category at certain times for certain purposes. Lonergan has described the shift from a classical to an historically conscious world-view, happily for our purposes, employing the understanding of man as an example.

The classicist begins by abstracting from all the differences distinguishing one man from another and so is left with a residue called human nature. Obviously, on the basis of this procedure this human nature will be always and everywhere the same.

> One may fit out the identity, human nature, with a natural law. One may complete it with the principles for the erection of positive law. One may hearken to divine revelation to acknowledge a supernatural order, a divine law, and a positive ecclesiastical law. So one may work methodically from the abstract and universal towards the more concrete and particular, and the more one does so, the more one is involved

in the casuistry of applying a variety of universals to concrete singularity.[23]

In such a procedure one will never arrive at a demand for a change of law or form or method because abstract universals do not change. Like mathematical principles, they are what they are defined to be and so cannot alter.

The starting point for a consideration of the human person in the context of historical consciousness is quite different.

> One can begin from people as they are. One can note that, apart from times of dreamless sleep, they are performing intentional acts. They are experiencing, imagining, desiring, fearing; they wonder, come to understand, conceive; they reflect, weigh the evidence, judge; they deliberate, decide, act. If dreamless sleep may be compared to death, human living is being awake; it is a matter of performing intentional acts; in short, such acts informed by meaning are precisely what gives significance to human living and, conversely, to deny all meaning to human life is nihilism.[24]

A similar approach can be applied to human communities. Within a common field of experience, shared ways of understanding complement one another and create a community of mind. The common judgments arrived at within such a community create a consensus to which common commitments are given which enables the community to affirm its destiny and its faith in providence.

But, as Lonergan notes, these individual intentional acts and communal meetings are not timeless abstractions.

> They are the hard-won fruit of man's advancing knowledge of nature, of the gradual evolution of his social forms and of his cultural achievements. There is such a thing as historical process, but it is to be known only by the difficult art of acquiring historical perspective, of coming to understand how the patterns of living, the institutions, the common meaning of one place and time differ from those of another.

The difficult art of acquiring historical perspective has been the work of every generation since the seventeenth century discovery of the remoteness of the past, the openness of the future, and the possibility of newness. Historical consciousness has become the common sense of modernity which has altered the procedures, standards, and goals of all the sciences. Modernity is conscious of being modernity, of being different from the past. "So to modern man it seems self-evident that he has made his own modern world and, no less, that other peoples at other times either have done the same or else have made do with a world fashioned by bolder ancestors and inertly handed on."[26]

The contrast then is between two ways of trying to understand the human being, one "abstractly through a definition that applies *omni et soli* and through properties verifiable in every man", the other "as a concrete aggregate developing over time, where the locus of development and, so to speak, the synthetic bond is the emergence, expansion, differentiation, dialectic of meaning and of meaningful performance."[27] Since abstractions do not change, the first view will never find within itself either a demand or even a possibility for change. Intentionality and meaning are, by contrast, never static, always dynamic, always developing, sometimes declining, constantly capable of reformation. Thus not merely the possibility of change but the insistence upon it is built into the second method of apprehending human being. And not only is this second approach in harmony with contemporary consciousness, as the first is not, but it is also in far greater consonance with the normative foundational witness of the Christian tradition. In Lonergan's judgment, the abstractness which is at the heart of the understanding of human nature within a classicist worldview

> is not theological; it is grounded simply upon a certain conception of scientific or philosophic method; that conception is no longer the only conception or the commonly received conception; and I think our Scripture scholars would agree that its abstractness, and the omissions due to abstraction, have no foundation in the revealed world of God.[28]

Clearly one of the salient features of the historically-minded approach to the study of the human being is its insistence that such study be multi-dimensional and inter-disciplinary. Thus, while theology can and must add a necessary element to our understanding of the human being, it cannot pretend to speak the full or only word on the human person. Nor can it, on the basis of its own resources, respond to every question which may be raised about the human person. Thus the theologian cannot respond to the question of the precise beginning or end of humán life purely and simply as a theologian. He *can* and *must* participate in the response to such a question by reflecting theologically on the data supplied by other sciences. This is, I believe, a major implication of theologizing in an historically-minded context. David Tracy has noted that while a major strength of a theologian operating in an essentially classicist world-view is the ability "to develop sophisticated models for providing systematic understanding of the basic beliefs of his church community", the principal weakness of such a theologian is "his inability to make intrinsic (i.e., inner-theological) use of the other scholarly disciplines."[29] Questions regarding genetic manipulation consequently impel the theologian into conversation with the fields of medicine, sociology, and public policy, a conversation in which the theologian does not "lay down the law" in advance, but makes the contributions of these other disciplines an "inner-theological" element in his own reflection.

But the question must be raised: what does theology itself bring to this conversation? There must be some uniquely theological contribution to this inter-disciplinary dialogue, else why should the theologian be admitted as a partner in the conversation? Only the very, very rash and the astonishingly out-of-touch would maintain the ability of theology to answer the moral questions posed by genetic engineering, reproductive technology, and surrogate parenting or those raised by the arms race, the threat of nuclear war, and the policy of deterrence by terror. But surely theology has *something* to add to the discussion which is peculiarly its own.

The theological task is to bring the interpretive power and insight of the symbols of the Christian tradition to the inter-disciplinary dialogue, thus giving form and meaning to the data supplied by other disciplines and simultaneously allowing that data to expand our understanding of the meaning of those symbols. This is the perennial work of theology: the mutual interpretation of the symbols drawn from tradition (with Scripture as the normative record of the originating stages of the tradition) and contemporary experience. These symbols are the powerful persons, events, objects, ceremonies, images and stories in which the Christian community, and Israel before it, has understood its mission and the divine self-gift which it has received. Among the most important of these symbols are God, Christ, Spirit, Trinity, incarnation, redemption, resurrection, Church, eucharist, grace, Mary, baptism, sacrifice, atonement, etc. The Church has to protect these meaning-giving symbols, and thus has translated many of the most important ones into credal statements, normative doctrines, and laws. But certainly no one — under pain of idolatry — can claim that such translations are exhaustive. The symbols always remain richer than their doctrinal formulations, which is why they have traditionally been referred to as "mysteries."[30]

These inexhaustibly rich symbols have arisen from the history of the Old and New Israel's experience of God's self-gift, his revelation. Thus all the symbols of the Christian tradition, from the most central to the most peripheral, are expressions of the God-man relationship, the human experience of the *Agape* which surrounds and grounds all that exists. Christian theology has always proceeded on this assumption even though unacknowledged at some points in its history. Its explicit recognition is at the very heart of all the various streams of modern theology and has been since the beginning of the nineteenth century when it received deliberate avowal by Schleiermacher in Protestantism and Möhler and the Tübingen school in Catholicism.

But there is a great problem here. If the theological contribution to the discussion of the ethical problems confronting us as we move into the last years of the twentieth century is the interpretation of the experience, formulated by the natural and social sciences, in light of the symbols of the Christian tradition, and those symbols are the expressions of the Christian experience of revelation, the God-man relationship, is not this entire project undercut by the radical historicization of all thought and experience which we have described as the chief characteristic of modernity? The responses to the pressing ethical issues of our time must affirm and protect the value of the human person. Moral theology operating in the classicist world-view described by Lonergan rooted its answer to moral dilemmas in a universal human nature. But the existence of such a nature, or at very least its knowability, is precisely what is denied by the scientific and philosophical understanding of historically conscious modernity. Does this not reduce the possible responses to ethical questions to prudential judgments as to what may work for the moment? Indeed, does not the entire theological enterprise come into question? For, if the symbols of the Christian tradition are expressions of the God-man relation, the thorough historicization of the understanding of human being must make that relation so fluid that no total or unsurpassable symbol of that relation can exist. What does this do to the incarnation, the atonement, or the resurrection?

Edward Schillebeeckx has raised this question of the status of Christian theology in historically conscious modernity with great sharpness and clarity. He notes that theologians' attempts to enter creatively into the context of historical-mindedness have introduced the term "salvation history" which was virtually unknown prior to the Second World War. This has radically altered the plan of content in every theological treatise.

> God accomplishes in history his intentions with regard to man. God's activity is history in that it reveals itself, and it reveals itself by becoming history. Revelation is a growing historical process set in motion anonymously in the concrete life of every human being in the world. It acquired a more concrete form in Israel and finally reached the constitutive phase of its maturity in Christ and in the early apostolic Church. Whenever a present-day theologian wishes to enquire about the content of divine revelation in connection, for example, with faith in creation, he turns first of all to Israel, to see how this people — and they precisely as the people of God — experienced the reality of creation and interpreted it in the religious sense. Then he considers Christ and how he, conscious of his Sonship, actively experienced this reality. Finally, he investigates the way in which the earliest Christians, as the people of God redeemed in Christ, concretely experienced and interpreted this same reality of creation.[31]

Furthermore, theology, which once had philosophy as its primary dialogue partner, now has entered into a conversation with history which has opened new insights into the implications of Christian faith. "Not only is eschatology, for example, actively forming the basis for a *theology* of Church history — a similar development is also taking place in the creation of a theology of earthly values, of history, of work, of the physical cosmos as the environment of man, and so on."[32]

But, Schillebeeckx observes, there is a danger in this new theological orientation. Whereas the theological manuals of an earlier day presented theology apart from the economy of salvation, there can be today too often the presentation of the economy without any properly speculative theology.

> Phenomenology, which correctly stresses the historical character of all human life, has not always appreciated the fact that this historical character in man is accompanied by a *consciousness* of time in the strict sense of the word. And a consciousness of time implies a rising above time. This does not mean that we somehow come to stand outside time and the world, but that there is a *transhistorical orientation* in the historical character of our human life.[33]

Here Schillebeeckx raises a point of enormous significance: historical consciousness is *consciousness* not only within but *of* history. Any analysis of historical process which reduces human agency to the product of historical forces, whether social or economic, psychological or physical, fails as historical explanation because it cannot account for the historian. For the historian maintains that he *knows* the truth, in however limited a degree, about the events which he studies. What he thinks about the past he seeks to justify by historical data; the judgments which he makes he supports by properly historical warrants. He does not accept that his reconstruction of the past is the product of external forces determining this judgment so that his historical conclusions are those which he must draw given his own historical circumstances. To some extent, however limited, he maintains that he transcends his present so that he may, in some measure however small, know the past. He cannot be merely the product of history, for he knows history.

Thus the historical consciousness of modernity with its sweeping claims of universal relativization still rests, often tacitly as Schillebeeckx observed, on a claim to transcendence. This permits me to suggest an understanding of the human person which must emerge from any self-reflective and consistent historical consciousness: the human being is, first and foremost, a creative participant in history. Humanity, understood within modern historical consciousness which does not lapse into the outmoded historicism of the turn of the century, is the ability to respond to one's circumstances by grasping one's past, determining one's present, and shaping one's future. The distinctively human mode of existence is an interplay of given factors — biological, psychological, social, economic, political, linguistic, geographical, etc. — and intentions, goals, purposes, understanding, misunderstanding, determination and courage, weakness and cowardice, altruism and selfishness. The human being is both product and producer, creature and creator. Obviously there is a given into which we come or, better, out of which we come, but there is also our response which has some greater or less degree of spontaneity. We are both in history and transcendent to it.

Langdon Gilkey, one of the most perceptive analysts of the theological implications of our historical being, has described this interaction in human experience as the relationship of freedom to destiny, which in its distorted form becomes fate. Although in sinfully fated situations, freedom is inexorably driven toward the extreme of determinism, it is never totally extinguished.

> At best so-called determining factors provide conditions *for* and so set limits *to* human actions. Human beings, and so their groups as well, for example, are in truth driven by hunger and by insecurity, but how and how far they are so driven is never determined finally by the conditions. What humans in fact *do,* which alone is causative of historical events, is determined only within the mysterious interaction of these given limits and conditions with their own needs, desires, intelligent judgments, intentions, norms, goals and resulting decisions. Thus there are always alternatives in history; and events are historical in that until they happen, they *need* not have occurred. All here is finally contingent. Put another way, nothing is a *cause* in history unless it evokes a human response. And no situation merely in itself is determinative; only the way people "take" it, i.e., the way they understand it, interpret its meaning for themselves and their future, and so deal with it. Thus are modes of interpretation (social symbol systems, norms and goals), desires, motives, purposes, intelligence and comprehension, and finally the mystery of decision and of enaction, all significant, not to say basic, factors in historical events. These "inner" factors alone mediate into event the effects of what might seem in retrospect to be necessary trends and conditions. As

in individual existence, the fundamental ontological structure for groups and so for historical passage is the polarity of destiny and freedom, the inherited "given" from the past on the one hand, and the present human response in the light of possibilities for the future on the other.[34]

This fundamental characteristic of being human, namely, the ability creatively to participate in historical process, shifts the category for understanding what is permanent in the human person from human nature to subjectivity. Human nature is a static, because abstract, concept; subjectivity is a center of intelligence, decision, and action, and so presupposes change, growth, and development. The turn to the subject is a study of the human being in so far as he is conscious. Such a study

> attends to operations and to their centre and source which is the self. It discerns the different levels of consciousness, the consciousness of the dream, of the waking subject, of the intelligently inquiring subject, of the rationally reflective subject, of the responsibly deliberating subject. It examines the different operations on the several levels and their relations to one another.[35]

Such study cannot procede by abstraction, because abstraction prescinds from the concrete, and it is only in the concrete that the operations of the subject, i.e. inquiry, reflection, deliberation, action, occur. It is precisely by setting such concrete operations aside that classical consciousness arrived at the abstraction "human nature." In order to turn to the concrete subject, one must employ a transcendental reflection.

The use of the term "transcendental" in this context began with Kant, who thus designated "all knowledge which is occupied not so much with objects as with the mode of our knowledge of objects in so far as this mode of knowledge is to be possible *a priori*."[36] The transcendental method is closely identified in philosophy and Catholic theology today with the school of thought which traces its origin to Joseph Maréchal and has included Joseph de Finance, André Hayen, André Marc, Emerich Coreth, Bernard Lonergan, and Karl Rahner.[37] In fact, however, while these scholars do represent a quite consistent and recognizable intellectual tradition, transcendental reflection in a broader sense has been employed by a vast array of quite diverse philosophers and theologians from Maurice Blondel to David Tracy, from John Henry Newman to Johannes Baptist Metz. This broader sense is, in Rahner's description, the examination of an issue "according to the necessary conditions given by the possibility of knowledge and action on the part of the subject himself."[38] For example, when I speak of this sheet of paper before me, I am speaking of this paper *as I perceive it*. To speak of anything outside of me is also implicitly to speak of me. Transcendental reflection turns our attention to what must be true of me if I can perceive and speak of this sheet of paper at all. It asks what the conditions of my being must be if I can perform these operations.

Thus, if the context of modern historical consciousness presupposes tacitly or explicitly the human person's transcendence to history and so necessarily understands man as capable of creative participation in history, transcendental reflection on man must inquire what conditions hold within human being which allow such creative participation. What must be true of the human subject if he is able to grasp the past and shape his future and, to do so, is able to enter into political, social, and economic co-operation with other subjects?

It is by such a transcendental reflection as this on the concrete historical subject that we arrive at the concrete operations which we call, when taken together, authentic human existence. Our capacity for these operations makes us human. Our fulfillment of these capacities is an obligation which calls us to be moral beings. Lonergan has formulated this obligation to be human by performing these operations in imperatives which he names "the transcendental precepts": Be attentive, Be intelligent, Be reasonable, Be responsible, Evaluate and, if necessary, change.[39] Thus the human being is no longer understood by reference to faculties, qualities, or obligations, but rather by the operations of intentionality which render him a subject capable of performing those operations and so entering into the specifically human world of shared meaning. It is here that we discover the permanent dimension of human being. Rahner observes that we have here the possibility of recovering what has been traditionally called "natural law."

> Irrespective of how we are to determine the precise relationship between this natural law and grace, in any case it is only possible to justify natural law from within, by means of

307

transcendental deduction of the nature of man and — furthermore — of his fundamental setting in his historical situation with its unique claims on him. It cannot be done by a purely *a posteriori* collating of factual particulars and conditions of man's individual and social existence, even if they are ascertained to be of 'general' occurrence. For not everything that *is,* nor even everything that is or seems to be *general,* is automatically what *must be.* Particularly in moral theology a transcendental anthropological theology would be able to gain insights of considerable practical importance, especially (though not exclusively!) in the matter of eliminating claims which pose illegitimately as natural law.[40]

The content of this natural law is, I suggest, well stated in Lonergan's transcendental precepts.

It is noteworthy in this connection that in recent decades the language of the Church's social teaching has shifted from the nature of man to human rights guaranteeing the exercise of true subjectivity. This change began with John XXIII's *Pacem in terris* and can be seen in such Vatican II documents as *Gaudium et Spes* and *Dignitatis Humanae.* From the time of Leo XIII, Catholic social teaching based in classically understood natural law emphasized the values of justice and order. While seeking to preserve those values, more recent teaching, especially in the statements of Paul VI and John Paul II, has emphasized the freedom necessary for authentic human existence and sought to guarantee those political, social, and economic conditions, both national and international, in which this freedom can be exercised.

Notable also is the fact that when considering the ethical issues raised by genetic technology we must, within our historically conscious context, recognize that man does take charge of himself. As a subject, not merely an instance of some abstract human nature, the human being always "makes" himself. "According to Christian anthropology man really is the being who manipulates himself. Naturally, on account of the genuine historicity of his being and of his apprehension of truth, this fact has entered even into the Christian's awareness of faith in a quite new and penetrating way."[41] Thus the pressing questions which the possibilities of genetic and reproductive technology raise for us today merely underscore in a strikingly new way the self-creative capacity of man. Now, however, it is no longer confined to the intellectual, moral, social, and political realms; now it is biologically expressed. The human subject is taking charge of evolution.

The response of moral theology to this fact cannot be based on a timeless human nature if it is to be intelligible and therefore applicable to modernity radically and irreversibly marked by historical consciousness. Being neither a moral theologian nor knowledgeable in genetic and reproductive technology, I cannot say concretely what the moral theological response may or should be to the many questions which now confront us, or the many more which soon will. But I do suggest what the basis of any response must be in the context of modernity. That which is in accord with and furthers authentic subjectivity, i.e. which makes us more attentive, intelligent, reasonable, and responsible, is morally acceptable. That which violates such authentic subjectivity, i.e. which inhibits attentiveness, intelligence, reason, and responsibility, is immoral. This is, in the context of contemporary theology, the principle which holds universally and grounds all our moral theological judgments.

This paper is in danger of exceeding the limits set by the requirements of this conference, yet there remains an obvious and extremely important question which may well be posed at this point, and to which thus far I have given no attention. Is there a specifically Christian contribution to this discussion? Transcendental reflection on man as creative participant in history as described here is a philosophical reflection which forms an intrinsic moment in contemporary theology. But, in itself, it is not a theological reflection, if theology is, as I have described it, mutual interpretation of the symbols of the Christian tradition and contemporary experience. The theologian must ask himself, in Rahner's words,

> What does his own anthropology really tell him about man? That he is the being who loses himself in God. Otherwise nothing. For only what is implied in *this* statement or can be said about man in *this* connection is a genuinely *theological* affirmation of his anthropology. Any other statement about man is only of theological significance provided that it can be referred back to this one, and provided that it is made clear (in whatever way, whether transcendentally or otherwise) that its denial would destroy man's being-in-reference-to God. [42]

The project of a theological anthropology is truly theological only if human subjectivity is shown to be intelligible as an openness to and receptivity for the ground of subjectivity. To show that this is the case and that it does not compromise the gratuity of God's self-communication has been a major theme in Rahner's work. It is possible, however, only in light of the unsurpassable act of divine self-gift which we call the Incarnation. That act of divine self-gift in its fullest expression coincides with the perfection of human subjectivity and spontaneity, the ultimate act of self-transcendence, i.e. fullness of divinity is expressible in creation only as and with fullness of humanity (not, please notice once again, as a complete human nature, but as ultimate subjectivity). Thus Christ is the measure of authentic human subjectivity and, as such, the theologian must always make his affirmations about man, implicitly or explicitly, within a Christological context. The Christian moral theologian works within this context as well, of course. Indeed, understanding moral decision-making not as the application of timeless principles derived from a natural law based on a static concept of human nature most clearly seen when it is assumed by the Son; but rather as an exercise of concrete historical subjectivity, the fullest exercise of which is the occasion for the perfect self-expression of God in incarnation, allows, in my judgment, moral-theology today to be more radically *Christian* than before.

The nineteenth century and first decades of the twentieth century were the age of ecclesiology; the Church was the focus of theological attention, and almost all other issues were treated in such a way that their ecclesiological reference became apparent. That period climaxed with the Second Vatican Council. The questions which we have inherited from that great event in the Church's history have tended and will, I think, tend increasingly to center attention on Christology. The language and thought-forms of the Chalcedonian formulas are those of the classical world-view. We need to re-examine the intention of that formula in order to re-express it in the historically conscious context of modernity. As we do so, the Christian community's understanding of personhood will develop and be enriched, affecting everything from our doctrine on sin to our styles of Church polity. At the same time, the moral theological response to issues like genetic control, the possibility of nuclear war, environmental threats, the equitable distribution of human and material resources on a global scale, and — perhaps — the movement of the human race off the planet, will further enlarge our appreciation of the possibilities of being human, and so deepen our insight into the humanity of God in Jesus. What questions we have to ask! And how privileged we are to ask them!

Notes

1. Ernst Troeltsch, "Die christliche Weltanschauung und ihre Gegenströmungen," *Gesammelte Schriften,* 4 vols. (1922; reprint ed., Aalen: Scientia Verlag, 1962), 2:325.
2. Paul Hazard, *La Crise de la Conscience Européenne* (Paris: Boivin, 1935); Eng. trans., *The European Mind,* 1680–1715 (New York: New American Library, 1963).
3. Alexandre Koyré, *From the Closed World to the Infinite Universe* (Baltimore: Johns Hopkins University Press, 1957), p. 2.
4. Bernard Lonergan mentions Hazard's judgment and Herbert Butterfield's placement of the birth of modern science in this period, as well as Yves Congar's opinion that dogmatic theology finds its beginning at this same time; see Bernard Lonergan, "Theology in Its New Context," *A Second Collection,* ed. William F. J. Ryan and Bernard J. Tyrrell (Philadelphia: Westminster Press, 1974), p. 55.
5. This meaning of historicization of thought and evaluation is derived from Maurice Mandelbaum's definition of historicism, although I am obviously applying it more widely than he does; see Maurice Mandelbaum, *History, Man, and Reason: A Study in Nineteenth-Century Thought* (Baltimore: Johns Hopkins University Press, 1971), p. 42.
6. Georges Louis Leclerc Comte de Buffon, quoted in Stephen Toulmin and June Goodfield, *The Discovery of Time* (Chicago: University of Chicago Press, 1982), p. 145.
7. R. G. Collingwood, *The Idea of Nature* (Oxford: Oxford University Press, 1960), p. 10.
8. Buffon, quoted in Loren Eiseley, *Darwin's Century: Evolution and the Men Who Discovered It* (Garden City, New York: Doubleday and Co., Anchor Books, 1961), p. 41.
9. Toulmin and Goodfield, p. 265; see also Ginestra Amaldi, *The Nature of Matter: Physical Theory from Thales to Fermi* (Chicago: University of Chicago Press, Phoenix Books, 1982); Werner Heisenberg, *Physics and Philosophy: The Revolution in Modern Science* (New York: Harper and Row, Harper Torchbooks, 1962); and Jagjit Singh, *Great Ideas and Theories of Modern Cosmology* (London: Constable, 1961).
10. G. W. F. Hegel, *The Philosophy of History,* trans. J. Sibree (New York: Dover Publications, 1956), p. 72.
11. See G. W. F. Hegel, *Lectures on the History of Philosophy,* 3 vols., trans. E. S. Haldane and Frances H. Simson (London: Routledge and Kegan Paul, 1955), 1:27: "It is only the living and spirtual which internally bestirs and develops itself. Thus the Idea as concrete in itself, and self-developing, is an organic system and a totality which contains a multitude of stages and of moments in development. Philosophy has now become for itself the apprehension of this development, and as conceiving Thought, is itself this development in Thought. The more progress made in this development, the more perfect is the Philosophy."
12. Lord Acton, Cambridge University Library, Add. 5011, 340, quoted in Herbert Butterfield, *Man on His Past: The Study of the History of Historical Scholarship* (Cambridge: Cambridge University Press, 1969), p. 97.
13. Wilhelm Dilthey, *W. Dilthey: Selected Writings,* ed. and trans. H. P. Rickman (Cambridge: Cambridge University Press, 1976), p. 134.
14. Ibid., p. 135.
15. Lord Acton, Cambridge University Library, Add. 5011, quoted in Butterfield, p. 97.
16. Walter Kasper, "Kirche und Theologie unter dem Gesetz der Geschichte?" in *Glaube und Geschichte* (Mainz: Matthias-Grünewald-Verlag, 1970), p. 49.
17. Langdon Gilkey, *Naming the Whirlwind: The Renewal of God-Language* (Indianapolis: Bobbs-Merrill Co., 1969), p. 48. See also the same author's discussion of the contemporary context for theology in his *Religion and the Scientific Future* (New York: Harper and Row,

1970); *Catholicism Confronts Modernity: A Protestant View* (New York: Seabury Press, 1975); *Reaping the Whirlwind: A Christian Interpretation of History* (New York: Seabury Press, 1976), esp. pp. 188–208; and *Society and the Sacred: Toward A Theology of Culture in Decline* (New York: Crossroad Publishing Co., 1981).

18. Gilkey, *Naming the Whirlwind*, p. 48.
19. The references in Lonergan's work are numerous. Especially pertinent are: "The Transition from a Classicist World-View to Historical-Mindedness," "The Future of Thomism," "Theology in Its New Context," and "Revolution in Catholic Theology," in *A Second Collection;* "Time and Meaning," and "Healing and Creating in History," in *Bernard Lonergan: 3 Lectures,* ed. R. Eric O'Connor, Thomas More Institute Papers/75 (Montreal: Thomas More Institute for Adult Education, 1975); and *Method in Theology* (New York: Herder and Herder, 1972), esp. pp. 175–234.
20. Lonergan, "Theology in Its New Context," in *A Second Collection,* p. 59.
21. Ibid., p. 60.
22. Ibid., p. 60f.
23. Lonergan, "The Transition from a Classicist World-View to Historical-Mindedness," in *A Second Collection,* p. 3.
24. Ibid., p. 3f.
25. Ibid., p. 4.
26. Ibid., p. 5.
27. Ibid., p. 5f.
28. Ibid., p. 5.
29. David Tracy, *Blessed Rage for Order: The New Pluralism in Theology* (New York: Seabury Press, 1975), p. 25.
30. See the important article by Karl Rahner, "The Concept of Mystery in Catholic Theology," *Theological Investigations* IV (Baltimore: Helicon Press, 1966), pp. 36–73. For a brief but useful statement of the major points of this article, see Rahner's entry, "Mystery" in *Encyclopedia of Theology: The Concise Sacramentum Mundi* (New York: Seabury Press, 1975), pp. 1000–1004.
31. E. Schillebeeckx, *Revelation and Theology,* 2 vols. (New York: Sheed and Ward, 1967–68), 2:141.
32. Ibid., 2:143.
33. Ibid., 2:144.
34. Langdon Gilkey, *Reaping the Whirlwind,* p. 43.
35. Bernard Lonergan, "The Subject," in *A Second Collection,* p. 73.
36. Immanuel Kant, *Critique of Pure Reason,* trans. Norman Kemp Smith (New York: St. Martin's Press, 1965), p. 59.
37. A general study of this "transcendental school" in Catholic thought is Otto Muck, *The Transcendental Method,* trans. William D. Seidensticker (New York: Herder and Herder, 1968). A brief but good presentation of the school is given by Helen James John, *The Thomist Spectrum* (New York: Fordham University Press, 1966), pp. 139–192.
38. Karl Rahner, "Theology and Anthropology," in *Theological Investigations* IX (New York: Herder and Herder, 1972), p. 29.
39. The references to the transcendental precepts are frequent in Lonergan's work. For their introduction in the context of method, see *Method in Theology,* p. 20.
40. Rahner, "Theology and Anthropology," in *Theological Investigations* IX, p. 44f.
41. Karl Rahner, "The Experiment with Man: Theological Observations on Man's Self-Manipulation," in *Theological Investigations* IX, p. 212. See also in this same volume, "The Problem of Genetic Manipulation."
42. Karl Rahner, "Christian Humanism," in *Theological Investigations* IX, p. 192f. See also, Rahner, "The Theological Dimension of the Question about Man," in *Theological Investigations* XVII (New York: Crossroad, 1981), pp. 53–70.
43. The references are very many in the Rahnerian corpus, but preeminent is his *Hearers of the Word,* trans. Michael Richards (New York: Herder and Herder, 1969); see also his *Foundations of Christian Faith: An Introduction to the Idea of Christianity,* trans. William V. Dych (New York: Seabury Press, 1978), esp. pp. 24–175.

Chapter 11

An Integrated
Christian View of
The Human Person

The Reverend Benedict Ashley, O. P., Ph.D.

Editorial Preface

In this contribution to the Workshop, Fr. Ashley tries to incorporate the main points of the earlier papers into an integrated Christian view of the human person. In the first part of his essay, he expounds what he considers to be important insights into the concept of the person, as well as certain cautions about abusing the concept, from the areas of psychology and other social sciences, phenomenological philosophy, biblical scholarship, and historical theology. With these in mind, he then works progressively toward an updated theological description of the human person. He begins with a concise exposition of the distinction between person and nature as that between "who acts" and "by what" he or she acts. He then develops the notion of human person as an analogy with the Divine Persons, whereby the perfections of knowledge and love are realized in the human being according to a mode proper to itself. The Model of such a human person is Jesus Christ, whose divine *Person is manifested to us through His human nature. Father Ashley then adds to this analytical framework a consideration of the three modern themes of historicity, subjectivity, and freedom of the human being and their relationship to the human person. He makes an assessment regarding the extent to which their impact on modern life and morals should be taken into account in pastoral work. He concludes with a* descriptive *definition of a human person as "a being modeled after Jesus Christ, as a living body created by God through parents like itself, with the capacity to grow into an adult which can transcend its spatial and historical limitations through spiritual knowledge and morally responsible love of God and other created persons, and who is entrusted by God with co-creative stewardship over the subhuman world."*

In the first part of this paper I will briefly compare the reflections on human personhood which have been presented to this workshop by a biblical theologian, a systematic theologian, a philosopher, and a psychologist, attempting to identify the common elements which need to be included in any attempt to formulate a synthetic Christian view of the human person. In the second part I will attempt to formulate such a view. Of course, the other speakers are in no way responsible for what I am going to say, although I have greatly profited from their papers.

Part I: An Interdisciplinary Comparison

The Bible, as clearly shown by Donald Senior, does not present us with a systematic definition of the human person. Rather it balances insights derived from different perspectives. Human existence is limited by its earthly and mortal character; but is a gift of the God in whose image we are created. Because we are made in His image we share His lordship over the earth; but are responsible for this stewardship to the Creator and to each other. Our existence is historical, a struggle with evil and death; yet we hope confidently for the coming Reign of God, for the transformation of the Resurrection, and for eternal life. As individual persons we each are precious in God's sight; but we can live fully only in and for the human community. If we are to look to the Bible for some way to unify these antitheses it will not be found in an abstract definition of human personhood but in the person of Jesus

314

Christ, the New Adam, who by His all-embracing love of every human being, has most clearly revealed to us what it is to be truly human.

When we compare this biblical view of two thousand years ago with what Paul Vitz tells us about the understanding of the human person provided by today's behavioral science, we again find that there still is no generally accepted synthesis. As recently as 1970 it seemed that there was a widely accepted model which emphasized that the human person is primarily the product of learning and that when this learning leads to an integrated personality the result is a high degree of individuation, autonomy, and freedom. More recent research, however, seems to have shaken this consensus by stressing the biological and social limitations of human autonomy and freedom and has exposed the great difficulty of achieving an objective description of the human person because of the biases which result from human subjectivity and the pluralism of ideologies and interests in our times. Dr. Vitz has recommended that we look not to psychology but to Christian theology for a true view of the human person, since the very concept itself is of Christian origin. It was in the Christological and Trinitarian controversies of the patristic period that this emphasis on the notion of personhood first appeared.

Before turning to Christian theology, however, it is necessary to ask about the ideological factors which, as Dr. Vitz has indicated, confront and color the Christian view today and of which theology must be critically aware. Dr. Tymieniecka has incisively analyzed these tendencies of modern thought, and has shown the dilemma into which we have fallen because on the one hand modern society so promotes the autonomy of the self-conscious individual and on the other undermines this autonomy by using every kind of political, economic, and technological pressure to manipulate the individual and force conformity with the culture and its institutions.

Dr. Tymieniecka points out that this dilemma characterizes the whole history of modern thought and is the consequence of the shift which occurred with Descartes from the classical and medieval way of looking at the human person in an objective, ontological way to looking at the human person from the viewpoint of subjectivity and historicity. She proposes as a solution to this dilemma that the human person is constituted not by mere self-consciousness, nor by absolutes and to set us adrift in a sea of cultural and moral relativism. The way out, as Fr. Himes indicates, cannot be to canonize a single theological system as

Leo XIII did with Thomism. We must live somehow with theological and philosophical pluralism if we are to take human historicity seriously. Nor can the way out be to return to a time when human historicity and subjectivity were not thematic concerns. Rather we must honestly face this modern problematic, as Karol Wojtyla has done, while remaining true to the continuity of reason and faith without which history itself would be a meaningless string of incidents, the human subject would be without personal identity, and the human community, especially the Catholic community, would be hopelessly divided.

Fr. Himes proposes, as a theology which has dealt honestly with this problem, Transcendental Thomism which defines human personhood as "the ability to participate creatively in history", and which has shown how such a definition can ground the language of "human rights" which the Church today so often uses in support of her moral teachings. But his chief point, it seems to me, is to underline the truth stressed by Donald Senior on the basis of his biblical analysis, that the fullness of humanity has been manifest to us historically in Jesus Christ.

From this brief review it is apparent that there is a general agreement among our speakers that today no account of the human person is acceptable which does not take very seriously the historicity, subjectivity, and freedom of that person. Dr. Vitz has also warned us that while modern psychology has cast a great deal of light on these themes, at the present time it does not provide a generally agreed upon model by which they can be integrated with other aspects of the person. Dr. Tymieniecka, reinforced by Terence Brinkman's account of the philosophical work of our present Pope, which has also been reflected in his encyclicals and pastoral discourses, has made it clear that philosophy today has focused the discussion of the human person in its historicity, subjectivity, and freedom, not merely on self-consciousness, but on the *moral act* through which the person constructs itself in itself and in relation to other reason as objective cognition, but by "the moral sense" through which the human person constructs itself as it judges the good or the evil and commits itself to one or the other. Moreover, this moral sense is directed not merely to the good of the subject but benevolently responds to the good of other persons and the world which environs all persons in common.

In Dr. Tymieniecka's profound analysis there is a basic agreement with the more politically oriented views of the philosopher Karol Wojtyla in his remarkable book *The Acting Person*[1] which Terry Brinkman will discuss in our Workshop. How significant it is that today Wojtyla has been called to be Chief Shepherd of the Church, one who is not only a distinguished philosopher, but a philosopher who ·does not flinch from dealing with the hardest problems of modern thought, especially those of the historicity, subjectivity, and freedom of the human person, not merely by traditional metaphysical methods, but by the characteristically modern approach of phenomenology! In *The Acting Person* Wojtyla, having in mind the problem of the person living under a totalitarian regime, sought to identify phenomenologically that experience in which the human person most specifically reveals itself. He came to the conclusion that it is not in the purely cognitive act of self-consciousness that we come to know who we are, but in the free moral act *(actus humanus)* by which we come into full possession of ourselves. Such an act results not merely in the attainment of some value extrinsic to the person who acts but first of all to the development of the person as such for good or ill, and this not merely in itself but in relation to other persons. Wojtyla has also shown phenomenologically that it is only by the will to recognize other persons as persons, and not merely as human, that we can overcome that "alienation" which so many thinkers find characteristic of modern man, and enter into real *participation* in the human community.[2]

Our historical theologian, Fr. Himes, has reinforced the emphasis of all the other speakers on the centrality for understanding the human person of the themes of historicity, subjectivity, and freedom. Theology today must take full account of these aspects of the human person, even though at first sight their acknowledgement seems to destroy the grounds for all moral and theological persons.

Father Himes' proposal of Transcendental Thomism as a promising approach to these problems, and the advocacy of others of Process or Liberation Theologies all have their merits. As long as a theology respects the data of Scripture and Tradition as these are interpreted by the Magisterium, as well as the solid achievements of the human sciences and the precision and consistency demanded of all thought by philosophy, it deserves a hearing. Therefore, I also claim respect for a Thomistic, but not Transcendental, account of the human person, which I believe fulfills the requirements of modernity as well or better than other approaches, provided that we do not try to absolutize Thomism but understand it historically, that is, as an investigation of reality which has continued to develop to our own times, not only as to its details but as to the problems it treats and the methods by which it treats them.

II: What is the Human Person?

Method

It is a foolish mistake to try to define what is well known by what is less well known. Modern philosophers of the analytic school have shown that all technical language must ultimately be defined by ordinary language in the terms of the daily experiences which we all share. Only through such a reduction is communication possible. In ordinary English "person" refers to the "I" and to the "you" who enter into dialogue, and then to the "we," the "he" and the "she" who also speak, but it does not refer to the "it," the subhuman being that acts but does not speak, unless we imaginatively "personify" that it. The "person" is that which answers the question, "*Who* is it?" We answer that question by substituting for the "it" the *name* or a pronoun: "It is Mary" or "It is she," or perhaps some common noun such as, "It is the postman."

This last case indicates that when we cannot call a person by his name, we have to use a description. "He is tall, pleasant, and a postman." But when we do that we have shifted from answering the question "Who is it?" directly to another question, "What is it?" or "What is he?" This shift is responsible for a great deal of the vagueness in current talk about the human person. We need to distinguish "the person" which answers the question "Who?" from the "nature" possessed by the person which answers the question "What?" The reason for this confusion is that not a few philosophers deny that we know *substances,* as the late and beloved Fr. Ambrose McNicholl so clearly showed us in a previous workshop.[3] According to these thinkers we know the *phenomenal* but not the *noumenal.* We can describe human beings but we do not know that they are substances, autonomous existents, behind the flux of phenomena. Fortunately, the phenomenologists to whom I have previously referred attempt to overcome this difficulty by a modification of the phenomenological method. It suffices here to observe with them that substances, including the human person, are not known directly but as they are manifested in their acts through which they are really related to other substances in the world. These acts are not the person as such, but they manifest the person in relation to other persons, and furthermore they modify and develop the person.

What is the relation, then, between the person as an autonomous existent and its "nature", between my "I" and my "humanity"? From one point of view they are simply identical, "I am human." But other "I's" are also human. We must, therefore distinguish between the common humanity which I share with others, and my unique individual humanity. My individual concrete humanity seems to be identical with my "I," yet, even here we need to maintain a distinction between the "Who" and the "What." I am an individual human, but my individual humanity *by which* I am able to perform the various acts through which you know me as that by which *I* am, is not simply that "I."

Thus we come to the conclusion that in what follows, we must keep straight in our thinking several senses of "human person:" (1) most properly it refers to the autonomously existing beings or substances which have a claim to say "I" and which we address as "you"; (2) we mean the description or nature which answers the question, "What is he" as an individual; (3) we mean the description or nature which answers the question "What are human beings" as a class; and (4), we mean all these taken together.

Most discussions today are not about "person" in the first strict sense just defined, but about the description or nature of human persons. Moreover, the stress on historicity, subjectivity, and freedom as aspects of this description tends to ignore or neglect sense 3, namely, what all human beings have in common, in order to emphasize what is individual and unique. It is this individuality of a person in a particular historical time and place, with a unique subjectivity or way of seeing and feeling we call "personality." The notion of "human person", therefore, is that of an autonomously existing being who is an individual member of the class who are described as "human". We now have to ask in what that "humanity" consists.

What we know about *humanity* fills thousands of books of biology, anthropology, psychology and many other disciplines. But we are not interested merely in collecting this information. What we want to know is what ties all these facets of human personality into a unified nature which makes us a human community with equal rights and which gives to each member of that community in his or her individuality the ability to participate in that community. In short we want to form a concept of human nature both as it is common and as it is individuated so that we will know how to relate to the persons who possess that nature.

In order to arrive at a description of the human nature by which the human person is human, it is necessary to choose to follow one or another of the disciplines already proposed to us. I have chosen to follow the line laid out by our biblical and systematic theologian as most appropriate to our present purposes. Consequently, I am not going to begin with what psychology has to tell us, nor with the philosophical effort to locate what is specific to our experience of humanity; but with the suggestions given us by the Scriptures and theology. This means starting not with the human person's humanity but with God and His divinity, since we are in His image, and the image must be understood and evaluated from the original. Thus I will first look at the Divine Persons, then at created persons who are purely spiritual, then at the human person which is embodied. I will show why that embodied person is necessarily a subjective, free, and historical being and what implications this has for pastoral ministry.

II: The Human Person

Let us first review what traditional Thomism said about the human person, then discuss what the themes of historicity, subjectivity, and freedom add to this account, and finally attempt an integration of the new and old.[4] I will also attempt to indicate some of the pastoral applications in the course of the discussion.

First, Thomism emphasizes that the *prime analogate* of "person" is not to be found in the human person, but in the personal God. God is said to be personal because He is all-knowing and all-loving.[5] Although He infinitely transcends His creation, this very transcendence of every limitation brings Him into the most intimate contact with His creatures. Because He is the God who made us and who continually sustains us in being, and because He has chosen to call us by His grace from within the very interior depths of our being, we can pray to One who hears us.

Jesus Christ is a human being like us in everything but sin, but He has revealed to us by His life, death, and resurrection that He is in the fullest sense of the word the Son of God. This implies that in God there are two divine Persons, the Father and the Son, who are personally distinct. Jesus has also promised that the Father would send us the Spirit who is from the Father through the Son, and who is thus the Third distinct Person in God. God is personal, therefore, because the one Divine Nature, one being, life, and power is eternally communicated to Three distinct Persons. The best way we can resolve the seeming paradox of this Triunity is to understand that these Persons are identical with the One Divine Nature of the Godhead, yet distinguished from each other as three distinct "I"'s by the *relations* by which this One Being is communicated to each.[6] The Father is the Person who totally gives His Divinity to the Son, and the Son is the Person who totally receives that Divinity, while the Spirit is the Person who totally receives that same Divinity from the Father through the Son, and in doing so, unites them in the absolute Divinity of Love.

From this contemplation of the mystery of the Triune God we come to see three things. First, that the term "person" answers the question, "Who is it?", because it refers to a subsistent being, i.e., a being that exists in itself as an "I", and not merely as an aspect of something else or as a figment of the mind. Second, that the term "nature" answers the question, "What is it?", i.e., that *by which* this subsistent being is the kind of being it is. Third, that in God, "person" signifies a relation between subsistent beings by which their being is not three beings (as it is in three human persons who share one common nature), but is one identical Being which all three Persons possess through their different relations to one another.[7]

This mysterious Triune God has freely chosen to create a universe in which there are both persons and non-persons; but the persons are created for their own sake since they can share in God's conscious life, while the non-persons are created for the sake of the created persons.[8] The persons are made in God's own image in that they are also capable of knowledge and of free choice, although they differ infinitely from Him in that they have their existence and life in a relation of complete dependency on Him, and thus have limited knowledge and freedom. God created them to share in the happiness of the community of the Trinity if they freely choose to do so, and He empowers them to do so by His grace. Their personhood, therefore, is manifested fully only in this act of choice, especially as that is expressed in faith, hope, and love, by which the Trinity becomes the indwelling life of their total persons.[9]

Some of these created persons, namely the angels, are like God in being purely spiritual beings; that is, they possess knowledge innately and they exercise their freedom without undergoing change in turn from the things they act on. Unlike God, however, each angel according to its own specific nature has a limited vision and they need the rest of the universe as a mirror in which they gain some better notion of the Creator and commit themselves to Him in faith before they are admitted to contemplate Him with clear vision.

God has also created human persons who are also made in His image and in some measure spiritual, yet who lack *innate* knowledge and therefore require, as an essential component of their personhood, a material body through which they can acquire knowledge of the universe by sensation. From sense knowledge they can then derive spiritual understanding of the world and the existence of their Creator, but without their bodies they could learn and do nothing.[10] Because they have some spiritual understanding, they are also in a limited way capable of free choice; but they can exercise their freedom only by acting bodily upon other material objects and thus undergo alteration from this reaction. Nevertheless, although human beings have a knowledge and freedom beset by such limitations, we truly possess a spiritual capacity to know and choose freely, and thus are persons, possessing a personhood analogous to that of the angels, and even of the Divine Persons.[11]

Because created persons (both the pure spirits and the bodily human persons) have sinned, the world no longer exhibits the perfect order and beauty intended by the Creator. Consequently, we human beings do not see ourselves clearly as we really are in our essential nature.[12] Yet that true human nature has been manifested to us in Jesus of Nazareth, who is the Son of God become personally present in our material world by becoming one of our race through His taking to His Divine Person a human nature, which is as truly His as His Divine Nature. Thus both the Divine and the human nature of Jesus Christ exist in a single Person. While in Him His Divine *Nature* is identical with His Divine *Person* (since as we have seen, the Divine Persons, although distinct from one another, are identical with the Divine Being), His human nature exists not in a human person but in His one Divine Person. This does not imply that Jesus Christ lacks anything that a human person possesses, namely anything of humanity; but that He is a Divine Person who possesses that complete humanity.[13] If it were not so, then God would not be present with us as Emmanuel in our visible, historical world.

Thus for Aquinas the term "person" implies: First, that the human person is a subsistent, autonomous being, so that each of us can say, "I am." Second, this subsistent being possesses a human individuated nature, which answers the question, "What are you?". Third, all members of the human family, because they have one essentially similar nature with the same basic needs and capacities, have the same basic rights and obligations to each other and to the whole community. It is apparent also that it is a caricature to describe this traditional view, as we sometimes hear, as "static" and "abstract". For Aquinas, the human person is a concrete existent which exists and manifests its existence through activity, an activity which is, within limits, free and developmental. Nevertheless, his understanding certainly falls short of taking full account of human historicity, subjectivity, and freedom to which modern thought is so sensitive.

Historicity

Let us now ask how it might be possible to expand this classical account of the human person so as to do justice to the modern awareness of the historicity of the human person. [14] The medieval world in which Aquinas lived was a relatively uniform world. People were all at least nominally Catholics; there was one learned language. The barbarians and infidels were beyond the border. Moreover, the knowledge of history was very vague and largely based on the Bible and a few classical authors. To the contrary, in our times we are acutely conscious of the long history of our human race, of the immense variety of cultures and customs in which humans have lived, and even today the vast range of religions, nations, and classes. Our scientific outlook is based on the discovery that the universe and life have evolved, that future is unpredictable, but certain to be very different from the past.

This means that there are not only many points-of-view, many "worlds" depending on where you stand, but that each of these is undergoing constant development, and that there is a "war of worlds," the confrontation of many different world-views and value systems which clash and interpenetrate. The life of the individual is also a continual process of change. We can trace the life of each person from a single cell to adult maturity and on to decay and death, and in this life-drama every step we take, every decision we make shapes us into a new reality.

We become aware, if we are Catholics, what a small part of the human race in the past and present we are, and that in the course of history our Church has undergone great changes. Christianity as a concrete way of life has taken on many different forms, and at no time has the Church existed as a perfectly unified whole, perfectly one in government, faith, and worship, but has always had to live in controversy, faction and schism. This undeniable fact of the historicity of what we always supposed was the most stable reality in our life, our faith, threatens us with religious and moral relativism.

If each of us is limited, not only by our personal subjectivity, but also by the horizons, of our culture and our age, what sense is there in talking about "human nature" as if we were talking about one permanent reality? The world of the Bible is not our world. The language and symbols which must have been so meaningful to the Jews, living in a largely rural Israel in the epoch from 1000 B.C. to 100 A.D., are so different from those of 20th century Americans that on Sunday morning when the Scriptures are read in the liturgy, few are really listening. Even the preacher is often at a loss as to how to translate the ancient message into terms that mean something to him or to his people. What is even more dangerous is that we read into those words our own literal-minded prejudices as if they were the word of God. The creeds and canons of the Church also are couched in formulae whose real meaning is often very difficult for modern people to understand. They recite the Nicean Creed on Sunday, but lacking a knowledge of the history of the questions it was formulated to answer, what can the man in the pew make of it?

Once we have the courage to face this problem of human historicity for the very real and practical problem it is for evangelization, what pastoral applications can we draw from it? Three points, at least, seem to be clear. First, it means that in our teaching and preaching we must ourselves be able to discriminate between what is essential to faith, and what is the product of particular historical conditions. We must not confuse the Gospel with the American way of life; nor with the style of piety in which we were raised. God is Lord of history and He certainly has given us in the Gospel a message which transcends the vicissitudes of history; but it requires deep insight for us to uncover this continuity of truth.

Second, the essential historicity of human existence means that it is an illusion to suppose that mere conservatism will conserve the perennial truth. Trying to freeze the past in a world in flux can only result in killing and crushing the past. You can keep your old hat when the fashion has changed, but it no longer looks the same to anybody but yourself. To preserve the living truth, it must constantly be re-translated into a new language that can convey its meaning to a world that no longer understands and even misunderstands the old language. Moreover, the living truth, like a growing child, must grow or it will become a dwarf or die.

Third, if we are to know the people we serve, we must know them in their historical context, not as if they were specimens in a museum. These human persons are not just what they are, but what they have been and may be. Our ministry cannot be so much directed to a judgment on their present status as Catholics, as to the growth that will be possible for them in the future if the groundwork is laid now. Jesus saw in people not so much their actualities as their possibilities.

Thus it is important for us to make our own the vision of history given by Vatican II in *The Church in the Modern World*. The Council, in telling us to look for "the signs of the times" was not asking us to be "conformed to the spirit of this world" (Romans 12:2), but to open ourselves to prophetic discernment. The prophets see signs both of doom and of promise, but they read these in a very different way than most of their contemporaries. We should not just lament the evils of the time, but should see the hand of God at work, not only in religious affairs but also in the advances of science, technology and the arts. Whatever gives humankind power to cultivate and improve the world that God has given us, is a gift of God enabling us to be co-creators with Himself, and to carry out the command to Adam "to possess the earth" and to cultivate it (Genesis 1:28). This same power, however, can be abused to destroy the earth and humankind with it. We need prophetic historical insight to be able to distinguish between construction and destruction.

Subjectivity

Historical humanity is subjective in both a positive and negative sense. Positively, the subjectivity of every person, including the Divine Persons, is self-consciousness.[15] Negatively, human subjectivity, be-cause of our finite and bodily being, is enclosure within ourselves. *Cogito ergo sum;* but I soon discover that my existence is limited by the world of flux in which I am carried along and isolated from other persons. Our consciousness reveals not only a timeless world of truth, but a stream of images, feelings, moods, impulses, plans and projects, memories and novel insights. Furthermore, we have discovered within ourselves a deep well of subconscious and unconscious life, the effects of which are powerful, but whose operations are secret and only symptomatically evident. We become aware that our self-consciousness is inextricably bound up with a body that is opaque to consciousness and with a world alien to the self, standing in objective facticity over against us. Does this world of objects have meaning for us, or must we give it meaning?

Thus, if we take the classical statement that "man is a rational animal" as true, we must also admit that "rational" covers only a small part of what we are, and that most of what we are must be "animal", below the level of clear consciousness and freedom. Yet the animal part of us is not the animality of any other kind of animal; it is peculiarly a human animality which penetrates and is penetrated by our subjectivity. Hence we cannot reduce the complexity of the human person to a mind which coolly observes the world and records it in a set of neat concepts which governs the world with serene freedom, and uses the body as a convenient and docile servant. Nor is each of us individually just an instance of a common "human nature" which we can adequately define. Rather, each of us is unique, and each of us looks out on the world from the perspective of a unique experience gained not just by looking at the world, but by struggling with it.

Our relation to this world is never static. We are recipients of gifts from the world and are wounded by its violences. We are oppressed and restricted and find that our freedom is often reduced to a very narrow compass. Yet we also find that we have an amazing mastery over the world. In our subjectivity, we discover an amazing creative capacity for transcendence. We can reach out to explore the vastness of the world, and pass over the horizons of our present point-of-view to wider vistas. Modern science and technology seem to give to humanity the power to recreate the world and even to change human nature itself by genetic engineering. Most astonishing of all is our power to transcend our subjectivity and enter into inter-subjective relations with other persons, so that our different worlds fuse and we participate in a new and richer shared world. In this way the whole history of the human family and its opening future can become the possession of each one of us.

This understanding of the "rational animal" as a being whose nature is not closed by a fixed definition, but open to an unending process of growth and development to perpetual self-transcendence, has important spiritual and pastoral implications. As Wojtyla says[16] It requires an act of our will to recognize in other people that they are not only human, but that they are persons; that is, that each of them is an "I" just as I am, and thus we accept them on their own terms. Modern psychology has reinforced this insight by showing that we cannot help another person to really change until we have been able to establish this "I-Thou" relation with them. To many, the Church appears as an impersonal bureaucracy which may be interested in helping humanity, but which is unable to meet human beings as persons, as other "I's" who have to live their own lives on their own terms.

One of the reasons today that so many otherwise humane persons cannot recognize the evil of abortion, is because they have not made that act of the will which is necessary to accept the unborn child, not just as a human being, but as a person, as another "I." They are acutely aware of the personhood of the mother and of others in the visible world of human relations because they can imaginatively identify with them as conscious persons. But to people who favor so-called "free choice" of abortion, the unborn child, because it is hidden, unconscious, unable to communicate, cannot be imagined as a person, while its troubled mother is easy to sympathize with. Hence in our educational pro-life work, we need not only to reason with people, but first of all to help them *imagine* and *feel* the unborn as a personal being.

For pastoral ministry, therefore, it is essential that we recognize in those to whom we minister their *moral identity* as persons who have each been created by God to play a unique role in human history, and who deserve from us the help they need to fulfill that role as responsible agents who have an important contribution to make to the life of the Church and the world. In each of them we must see Christ manifesting Himself in a special way needed to complete the Father's plan, and hence we must see each as gifted by the Spirit. This requires on our part a reverence for persons and a hope in their possibilities, which is not easy to maintain in a world that reduces persons to a Social Security number.

Freedom

Our speakers have described the paradox of the modern world which is so conscious and so proud of the vast power of human freedom and creativity; but which seems bent on undermining that freedom by

327

using this same power to manipulate and pressure individuals into slavish conformity. Dr. Vitz has shown how modern psychology wavers between glorifying human freedom and denying its possibility in the face of biological and social determinism. The truth is that the human person has free will, but within a very narrow compass.

In our culture freedom is publicly glorified, but usually identified with the absence of external coercion, the freedom to do what I please. The liberation theologians of the Third World have rightly stressed the fact that for most people social injustice and deprivation not only make it difficult or impossible for most people to do what they please, but even to do what they believe to be right. We must admit, however, that even when people are free to do what they please, they can still be slaves to their own ignorance and compulsions which eventually destroy them and others. Thus, along with the questions of social liberation go the still deeper problems of personal liberation. We look to the Church to bring us the Good News of genuine freedom from sin, personal and social; but we know also that some people experience the Church as unjust, and accuse it of enslaving the faithful in narrow-mindedness and neurotic guilt.

When we consider that freedom expresses the subjectivity of the human person who becomes self-transcendent by his or her free decisions, and when we consider that the historicity of the person means that those decisions must be made in particular circumstances and on the basis of a limited understanding of the world, we begin to see why it is difficult to bind the individual to moral norms for all persons, at all times, and in all places and circumstances.

The pastoral implications of all this make relevant the thesis of Dr. Tymieniecka concerning the moral sense as constitutive of the person, and the work of Karol Wojtyla in maintaining that the human person is best revealed and comes to completion in the *moral act*. This act is not merely the cognition of facts, but is the evaluation of facts, the discernment and decision about right and wrong. The moral act cannot be such unless it is free; and in it alone is true freedom found, which is not the freedom to do what I please, but to do freely what I see to be right.

Yet if we are realistic, and if we listen to the findings of psychology, we must admit that most acts of human beings have the character of free acts only very imperfectly. Not only are people limited in their psychological power to choose alternatives, but they often are not aware of their responsibility to evaluate alternatives. They do what they are told to do, or what others are doing. Moral education must be a liberating process by which people are prepared and enabled to act in moral freedom.

Historically, the Church has no doubt been forced to recognize the herdlike character of most human activity. Did not even the Lord compare the people to sheep? But sometimes we have been almost cynically tolerant of their sheeplike passivity and have often exploited it to insure conformity to public norms. We have sometimes failed to have confidence in the intrinsic capacity of human persons to develop into free beings. We do not see, as the Lord saw, that simple fishermen can become apostles who will sit on thrones and judge the Angels, if only these men are called forth to discipleship. The problem of freedom in the Church is not just one of relaxing rules and regulations, but of the inspiration and education of people to be free by giving them new responsibilities.

This education in freedom, however, does not mean that we must give place to cultural and moral relativism. Human historicity and subjectivity limit and condition our understanding of what is good and bad for human persons; that is, what furthers or hinders their development into true images of God. Human persons are themselves limited by the basic needs and capacities which all members of our species have in common, and which explain our striving for survival as a global community which constantly interbreeds and carries on cultural exchange. Historically, the human family is growing closer together and into a more complex network of relationships, but not separating into new species. The exceptions to cross-cultural generalizations which anthropologists love to cite to prove cultural relativism are, significantly, usually taken from small marginal tribes.

Some moral theologians have complained that certain magisterial documents seem to have forgotten the Vatican II statement that moral norms must be established in view of "the nature of the human person and its acts", and to have reverted to a biologism which considers only the organic parts of the human person and their biological functions. Some have defended a consequentialist mode of moral judgement; and others have attempted to establish a methodology which rejects the traditional concept that some acts are intrinsically immoral under all circumstances, in favor of the view that the morality of an act is determined exclusively by the proportion of premoral values and disvalues involved. [17] Some have even mistakenly accused the publications of the Pope John Center of favoring (or at least not clearly opposing) this proportionalist position. Undoubtedly, the controversy on this difficult technical (yet extremely important) question of moral norms needs to be pursued in a spirit of truth and charity until the issues are resolved.

Let me only say here as a Senior Fellow of the Center that once we accept the view that the human person is manifested in his acts (which after all is only a philosophical way of saying what Our Lord said, "By their fruits you will know them."), then it becomes clear that the morality of a human act involves the whole person, and not merely a part. But it also means that no act can be moral which is contradictory to the basic functions out of which the human person as a whole is integrated. There is no good for the *totality* of the human person that does not respect the good of its essential parts.

Furthermore, it becomes clear that in judging the morality of an act the first consideration must be the good or evil which redounds to the integrity of the human person from the relation of the act in its intrinsic character to the nature of the person who performs it. If the act by this character is contradictory to basic human needs, rights and obligations, then it is *intrinsically* evil and cannot be rectified by any intention or circumstances. Finally, it is apparent that this intrinsic character of the act cannot be exclusively determined by its external consequences, nor by the proportion of premoral values and disvalues (although these may be *signs* of its character). Rather, an act's intrinsic character must first of all be determined by whether it enhances human nature or distorts it.

Thus a lie is always wrong, whatever the circumstances or purpose of the liar, and whatever the foreseen consequences, because the one who lies contradicts his own human personhood, not merely by misusing the organ of the tongue, but because human persons become more truly human by speaking the truth. They contradict the basic need of human beings for trust in communication by acting against this need. As Karol Wojtyla emphasized in his analysis of the acting human person to which I have referred, we make ourselves by our acts, so that the one who lies makes himself a living lie, whatever his excuses.

Freedom and moral responsibility are thus at the heart of personhood, and our pastoral guidance needs to be directed to helping people understand morality, not merely as the observance of external laws, nor as a calculus of gains and losses, but first of all as living in a way that manifests the humanity of the human person in conformity to its intrinsic body-soul structure, and develops that structure to its full flowering as an image of God.

This conception of a freedom that is cooperation with God in the completion of His creation and its history, is directly applicable to the problems this work-shop is considering. God has given us great power over His creation, but it is the power of *stewardship*. We can and should use the power locked in the atom, but only to cultivate our garden-world, not to reduce it to a desert. We can and should use technology to control and perfect the marvelous power of human reproduction by which the human family is expanded, but only to complete God's predestination of the human community, not to make an idol of our sexual powers, or to usurp His lordship over life and death.

III: A Definition of the Human Person

To sum up the reflections, I will suggest a descriptive definition of the human person:[18]

A human person is a being

(1) modeled after Jesus Christ;
(2) As a living body created by God through parents like himself;
(3) with the capacity to grow into an adult which can transcend his spatial and historical limitations;
(4) through spiritual knowledge and morally responsible love of God and other created persons;
(5) and who is entrusted by God with co-creative stewardship over the subhuman world.

The first clause follows the insistence of several of our workshop speakers, and especially by Father Donald Senior, that an adequate notion of human nature cannot be derived from our present fallen human condition, but only from the New Adam, Jesus Christ, in whom alone human nature has been perfectly fulfilled. It could be added that the feminine side of human nature is perfectly exemplified in His mother Mary. The second clause corrects that Platonic dualism which too often has distorted Christian spirituality. As Dr. Vitz showed in his talk, we differ from other kinds of persons because we are bodies, part of the physical world of nature and evolution. We are members of the human race not merely in form, but by the actual community of flesh and blood. Although our model Jesus Christ had a Divine Father, He too had a human mother and is bone of our bone, flesh of our flesh (Genesis 2:23).

The third clause indicates that although we are mortal bodies that need the Resurrection, yet we are, again like Jesus Christ, made in God's image as spiritual beings capable of knowledge and love. Through this spiritual transcendence we can transcend the past, the present, and the future and enter the infinite realm of the spirit. This capacity is actually and virtually, not merely potentially, ours even before we can exercise it, before birth and in childhood, because the unborn child from the moment of conception *develops itself* to adulthood by its own intrinsic powers, provided it has the sufficient physical and social environment to nurture it. Father Himes in his paper has shown that human historicity has a positive significance, since by our capacity to "participate creatively in history", we transcend it.

The fourth clause indicates that this capacity for knowledge and love enables us not only to know our physical world in its vastness, but to enter into communication with other persons past, present and future, and thus to form that community of created persons which God has graciously chosen to admit to His own Kingdom, the Community of the Trinity. As Dr. Tymieniecka showed in her paper, this is the flowering of what is most personal in us, namely our "moral sense" or capacity not only to know, but to love others.

The final clause returns us to the theme which Christopher Derrick proposed for our whole conference: reverence for the sacredness of God's creation over which we have been given stewardship. We are called to complete God's creation as the New Paradise in which God will dwell with His people; no longer a desert, nor an untended garden, nor a ruined Babel, but a New Jerusalem.

Notes

1. Karol Wojtyla, *The Acting Person* in collaboration with Anna-Teresa Tymieniescka, trans. by Andrzej Ptooki, vol. x, *Analecta Husserliana*, Dordrecht, Netherlands, D. Reidel, 1979. See also, "The Intentional Act and the Human Act that is Act and Experience, *Analecta Husserliana*, vol. v, 1976, pp. 269–80.
2. "Participation or Alienation", ibid. vol. vi, pp. 68–74.
3. "Person, Sex, Marriage, and Actual Trends of Thought", *Human Sexuality and Personhood*, Pope John Center, St. Louis, 1981, pp. 138–168.
4. A very useful collection and analysis of the texts of St. Thomas Aquinas dealing with the concept of *persona* will be found in Charles De Koninck, "In Defense of St. Thomas Aquinas", *Laval Theologique et Philosophique* 1 (2), 1945, pp. 1–103. On the theology of "persona" in the Trinity, see William Hill *The Three- Personed God*, Washington, D.C.: Catholic University of America Press, 1981.

5. *Summa Theologiae,* I, q. 29, aa. 1–4.
6. *Ibid.* q. 28, aa. 1–4.
7. *Ibid.* q. 39, a. 1.
8. *Ibid.* q. 65, a. 2 c. These topics are treated at length in my unpublished dissertation, *Contemplation and Society,* Aquinas Institute, St. Louis, 1949.
9. *Ibid.* a. 93 a. 7. On this subject see the thorough treatise of L. B. Cunningham, *The Indwelling of the Holy Trinity,* Dubuque, Priory Press: 1955.
10. *Ibid.* q. 75, aa. 14.
11. *Ibid.* q. 93.
12. *Ibid.* I–II, qq. 82–86.
13. *Ibid.* III, aa. 2–5. On recent discussions of the hypostatic union see Jean Galot, *Who is Christ?,* Chicago: Franciscan Herald Press, 1981.
14. Martin Heidegger, *Being and Time,* translated by J. Macquarrie and E. Robinson, New York: Harper and Row, 1962, pp. 424–455.
15. See Wilhelmus A. M. Luijpen, *Phenomenology and Metaphysics.* Pittsburgh: Duquesne University Press, 1965.
16. "Participation and Alienation" (note 2 above).
17. See Benedict M. Ashley and Kevin D. O'Rourke, *Health Care Ethics,* St. Louis: Catholic Health Association, 1982, pp. 160–175, for a discussion and evaluation of Proportionalism.
18. Note that this is a "descriptive," not an essential definition.

Chapter 12

Pastoral Concerns
Regarding the Person

*This chapter presents the morning and afternoon
plenary discussions between the bishops attending the
workshop and the speakers of the day: Dr. Tymieniecka,
Dr. Vitz, Fr. Senior, Fr. Ashley and Fr. Himes (the
authors of chapters seven through eleven). The dialogue
has been slightly edited for brevity from tape recordings of
the proceedings.*

Morning Plenary Discussion
February 2, 1983

Bishop: My question is aimed at trying to form some criterion of
judgment in the matters we are studying here; that is, I want to
obtain some standards with which to judge the situation of nuclear
energy and reproductive technologies. The "person" can only be
understood in a harmonic perspective. Thus, we understand the
person from its conditionings on the biological, economic, social,
political and ideological planes. In a cultural-dynamism sense we

understand it in relation to the world where the sense of benevolence prevails as a value. If one understands "value," from the psychological and philosophical points of view, as a relation between my real — or, better, my ideal ego and what gives it satisfaction, how can the sense of benevolence (or any other "directive" value, in the psychological meaning of the term) be concretized in our circumstances, so as to acquire a reference from which to discriminate what is good, and what bad, regarding the nuclear problem and the reproductive technologies?

Dr. Tymieniecka: Yours is a very complex question. It is perhaps difficult to see the notion of the "person" in direct, immediate relation to concrete practical problems of nuclear energy, society, biology, etc. In fact, it seems virtually impossible. However, what seems more promising to me is establishing a way, an approach, toward viewing the person as the very *basis* for addressing the question you ask. What I have developed in my study is, precisely, a notion of the person which fully takes into account the dilemma between the person as society's prevalent "value"-referrent, the source and object of benevolent sentiment, and the notion of the "person" as a guide for resolving the types of problems being studied here in these days.

Since time is short, I can only summarize my position by saying that what I have tried to show, really, is that it is necessary to invert the orientation we give to personal and social life, and all the practical problems we are facing, from the currently dominant Cartesian view of man as "master of nature" (a rationalistic, intellectualistic viewpoint), to a view where man is seen in the first place, as a moral person, endowed with, and directed by, a *moral sense* which is not one of domination, but of *custodianship.* In such a view, we will consider ourselves as morally responsible for helping other living beings first of all; we will think of ourselves only in last place.

Bishop: Some of us would like to direct a question to Dr. Vitz. In your presentation today, you spoke of the breakdown of the consensus that has obtained in psychology for the last 60 or 70 years about the understanding of the human person. Fr. Senior, in his presentation, spoke of the constants that one can find in understanding the human person in Scripture. Our question is rather broad. We would like to know if you see any relationship between the biblical

335

constants Fr. Senior spoke about in the understanding of the human person, and the breakdown of the former consensus in psychology?

Dr. Vitz: I think many of the constants that were mentioned by Fr. Senior are actually being, in many respects, rediscovered by psychology. For example, the classic emphasis in the consensus was on the individual as the *autonomous person,* severing relationships with others. It is almost as though the ideal person in that consensus were somebody like James Bond, of movie fame, who was — ironically — a man without any bonds. He had no family, no real girlfriends even; he was just an isolated autonomous unit. And the consequences of that ideal for the destruction of one's personality and living is now one of the things that is occasioning the change in the consensus. I mentioned, as well, that the economic assumptions supporting the consensus were part of the factors; another way of putting it is to say that it's very hard to self-actualize at today's prices.

Psychology has either explicitly or implicitly rejected any consideration of the relationship that we have to God. What I have called the new "Christian psychology" is trying to consider this relationship explicitly. If there is a Christian understanding of personality, one of the concepts it must elaborate is the idea that a person comes into existence and fulfills himself not through autonomy, not through separating, but through *commitment.* It should be a *covenant* psychology, a covenant concept of personality. And it would also be biblical; the first covenant would be the commitment that each of has to God, a return of His commitment to us. The second covenant of our commitment would be to others. This is, in many respects, the exact *opposite* of what Carl Rogers, and people like him, are talking about. In other words, the notion of becoming an autonomous individual, a type of "James Bond," if you will, is really an antistructure to the biblical concept of a person, and antithetical to what I think a fundamental Christian notion of the person would be.

But, a Christian kind of psychology remains to be developed. It would essentially say that as a person, we come into existence through committed relationships to others. This commitment begins with our commitment to God, and then, to others; and that is how we become a person. In fact, I think that we became a

336

person to begin with, very likely, due to our mothers' commitment to us, as well as our father's, and our families', etc. Such a concept would fit well with the constants of Scripture outlined by Fr. Senior, as well as with the growing disillusionment with what I have spoken about as "the old consensus." I think there would be other congruencies also, but I hope that what I have said answers your question clearly enough.

Bishop: My question is addressed to Dr. Vitz. In your description of the consensus of the 1970's, which I frankly admired and appreciated, the second point you made was that human nature is considered by the consensus as intrinsically *good.* In the critique of that consensus, is any consideration given to original sin as part of the human condition and situation, and if so, how is it taken into consideration?

Dr. Vitz: Yes, in some sense, this is occurring. Many of the non-Christian scientists do not, of course, speak in terms of "original sin." They speak about the intrinsic capacities of human beings toward aggression, exploitation, hurting others, etc. Sociobiology has no problem stating that man has natural tendencies which a theologian, and most normal people, would call evil. That much, therefore, is being accepted, and it gets us right back to the constants of Fr. Senior, and of biblical psychology or anthropology. The notion is there, and Christian psychologists are addressing it explicitly, that we have a problem, that human *nature* has a problem.

Bishop: Does it get to the point where psychology as such is arriving at the conclusion that mankind needs a saviour at the natural level as well, or is it going too far to say that?

Dr. Vitz: I don't think it is going too *far;* I think it is going to *fast* for us psychologists. That is where I believe we are headed and, in some small way, that is what I am trying to point out. But the field is not there yet. It is, perhaps, of some interest that Freud himself — who, in his major ideas, was not part of the consensus, although he did help start some of it — described what he called "Oedipal human nature," which is intrinsically rebellious, wanting to kill the father, sexually possess the mother, and supposed to be characteristic of all of us. He described Oedipal human nature with the words "original sin," which is very interesting. So, there are some very sound psychologists, at least in limited ways (I am not giving a blanket endorsement to Freud), who were not part of the consensus and who recognized this aspect of human nature which has not received any consideration in American psychology for the last 30 or 40 years. Those psychologists, along with the biologists and the ethologists and, I hope, the Christian psychologists, will bring the *nature* of our problem back into focus, at which point it will become clear that, in view of our problem, Christ is the only answer.

Bishop: We would like to ask Dr. Vitz two questions. First of all, would you place the encounter movements, for example "Marriage Encounter," within the old consensus, or as flowing out of that consensus? And would you comment on the value of such movements, as you perceive them, for the development of the human person? The second question is, would you clarify whether you think that psychiatric drug therapy is a positive or negative development?

Dr. Vitz: Encounter groups were part of the old consensus, part of the humanistic self-oriented psychology of Carl Rogers and Fritz Perls. I have never participated in a Marriage Encounter group, nor have I ever had a conversation with anyone about it. But as I understand it, Marriage Encounter arose in Spain and was an activity where couples participated in encounters on weekend retreats, in discussions and so on. That, it seems to me, is a different phenomenon, at least in its origins. It seems to have originated in Spain as a very sensible and different kind of phenomenon which, over here, got moved toward — and sometimes transformed into — the psychology of encounter groups, partly because of its name, partly because when it came here encounter groups were very important here in the secular world. But I cannot say anything more about it than that.

Secondly, you asked about the new kind of drug therapy and whether I thought it was good or bad. Actually, I was trying not to say! I do not wish to pass judgment on the technique. In some, in fact many cases, such therapy seems to be very good in controlling the psychiatric problem, and that is what the drugs are used for. Potentially, of course, such drugs are subject to real abuse, and it is probable that some individuals are misdirected toward this kind of therapy.

I can give you one example, that of a woman who came to me and told me about her situation. She had been seeing pastors for counseling for 10 or 12 years, most of whom had "bought into" the self-oriented psychological techniques. She found their guidance superficial and unhelpful. It even aggravated the problem because constantly she would leave thinking how good she was, only to wake up the next morning with a temporary psychological high which would deteriorate as she got back into the "real" world, leaving her feeling even worse. Subsequently, she found out that her problem was a cyclical manic-depressive mood problem that went through regular cycles, no matter what. Now she takes lithium, and is quite positive about its consequences, and quite negative about the therapeutic and pastoral misdiagnosis of those who had been unaware of this kind of therapy. However, I would not want to make too much of this anecdote; other examples, I'm sure, could be found in support of the contrary problem, and we can all understand how such drugs might be abused politically, and in other ways. I would say that it is something to be aware of and requires prudence in seeking expert help.

Bishop: Fr. Senior, would you say that, according to the Bible, the person is for society or the group, or is society for the person; and, in this, is there a difference between the Old Testament and the New Testament?

Fr. Senior: Your question reminds me of a saying of Jesus: Is the Sabbath for the human person, or the person for the Sabbath? I think that the conception of the human person is, itself, social in the Bible. In other words, the individual is not pitted over against the social.

The Bible is not a systematic analysis. I think of it as a slice, a *long* and *deep* slice, of life presented from a perspective open to God, so there is accumulated there a lot of wisdom and life-experience over a long expanse of cultures within one large *line* of culture, still wide enough and deep enough to collect a lot of wisdom. The roots of the Biblical peoples were nomadic and clannish; and that type of existence "clings." They live in a type of social organization in which to be alone is to die, so that for them the human person is necessarily social. The society cannot be over against the person.

The group's interests, however, might become too rigid; its social institutions could lose the values in which they were inspired. This happens, for instance, with the institution of the monarchy. The monarchy is a stage in the social organization of Israel. But, at a certain point, the monarchy itself becomes so oppressive of the very group for which it has been formed that the kings become agents of social repression, rather than agents of nurturing the human beings in their care. The prophetic movement begins to critique the institution of the monarchy, at this point.

If Jesus brings a corrective, it is not by pitting the individual over against the group, but by bringing the group to its full awareness. A year ago, at the Hebrew Union College in Jerusalem, I heard a Jewish Biblical scholar give a very interesting talk on this very theme. He acknowledged that the traditions of the New Testament, Jesus's own ministry, seem to have brought a corrective to a rather rigid structure of society. But that was only possible, according to the scholar, because Jesus could presume a very strong *communal base*. The scholar raised a very interesting point: If Jesus had undertaken His ministry in a society in which there was a great emphasis on the *autonomy* of the individual, perhaps His prophetic call would have been directed at forming a core, a center, of commonality, instead of appealing so much, as He did, to the outcasts.

So, I see no dramatic differences between the New and the Old Testaments such that the Old Testament would be "social," whereas the New Testament would be "individual." I think that all along throughout Israel's history there was a tradeoff, a tension, between the entity, the people, the wholesomeness of the people, and the individuals comprising it. At times, the common aspects became too rigid or overlooked certain values. But the prophetic movement, or like movements, corrected these false tangents. Jesus represents one important phase of this corrective. I hope with this to have responded to the main point of your question.

Bishop: I would like to express my gratitude for all that has been said so far about the human person. What has been focused on up to now seems to be various manifestations of what a person is *like*. A person has a moral sense, he is made in the image and likeness of God, with intellect and free-will, and the notion of the person certainly does have a historical development. I would like to ask, aside from all these manifestations about the person, if someone could explain more exactly what a person essentially *is?*

Dr. Tymieniecka: It is a very difficult question to answer, but I like a challenge. In my opinion, in view of the enormous changes in the way in which we consider the nature of the world, life and human beings, we cannot approach "personhood" adequately from the point of view of "what" a person is. Nor can we approach the question of what "man" is adequately, because, as I mentioned before, "man" and, specifically, the "person," is tied up within a complete process of becoming, constructive becoming, with the rest of living beings. Consequently, both "men" and human beings specifically, the nucleus of man, the person, is in a perpetual process of transformation. Therefore, we can enumerate features which we attribute to man as he *manifests* himself, from various perspectives. But, as to what he *is,* he is perpetually in process: our bodies, our flesh, undergo perpetual exchanges of substances, cellular changes, etc., from the time we enter this world until the time we die; we are in perpetual change of all our physical properties, of all our physical content. And the same is true with regard to our psyche, or our instincts, or our feelings, or our attitudes; it is even true with regard to the way we exercise common sense and reason. The point is, then, in the light of all these enormous transformations, that we can approach the "person" most adequately from the point of view of what the person's *function* is within the totality of life, i.e., what *man's* function is within the totality of life. In my paper I try to show that not only in psychiatry, psychology, sociology and cultural studies, but also in *religious* studies, we assign to the word "person" at least three different *functions.* I will mention only two at the moment.

The first of these is the function of *orchestrating* all our faculties which establish the meaning of the world and of life. The person is viewed, let us say, as the orchestrating *nucleus* of all our faculties, and this we see especially in psychiatry and psychology. For example, at a recent Conference on Mounier held in Paris it was pointed out that of such psychiatric notions as the "ego," "consciousness," the "subconscious," and so forth, which have been used to represent the human being, even "psyche" for that matter, of all these concepts the only one to truly survive has been the concept of the "person." It was introduced to psychiatry, of course, by Freud and Jung. But its *functional* role in articulating, orchestrating, all the other functions was most significantly developed by the psychiatrist, Ludwig Bindswanger, early this century, who took his inspiration from phenomenology and existentialism. In putting special emphasis on the person as orchestrating all its other faculties, Binswanger has called attention to the fact that this orchestration is carried out within the *world,* that is, while the person is orchestrating them, the "life-world" emerges. When I speak of the "world" here, I am referring to the "human world," not the world of "nature." This function seems to view the person still at the biological, psychic level, which pertains equally to the higher animals, as well as to man.

The second, and most significant, function of the person as a specifically *human* person, is that of being an *agent.* In the specifically human realm — which, in my theory, is constituted by the possession of the *moral sense* — the person is orchestrating all our functions in such a way that we can ponder not only our functional values, but also, once having pondered and evaluated them, we can choose as a free agent the course of action we are going to take, as a consequence of the moral sense. This second, specifically human, function of the person, then, makes us the moral agent.

I believe that, in the light of the enormous changes in our outlook stemming from our new insights into life and man, everyone in science and cultural life would agree that such is what the human person *is.*

Bishop: My question is directed to Dr. Vitz. You indicated the possibility of a "Christian psychology." My question is one of methodology, epistemology. Assuming that psychology is an experimental science, how can it be Christian; how can the *science* be Christian?

Dr. Vitz: Two things. First, at the level of "psychology of personality," I do not think you can meaningfully call it a *science* even as it exists today. Part of the purpose of my ideological critique is to point out the extent to which psychology, by implying that it is fundamentally scientific when it is talking about "self-actualization," or "ids," "egos" and "super-egos," is not really — in any useful and sensible sense — a science. It is an intellectual discipline, but it should no longer attempt to use the term "science" to describe itself if *by that term* is meant some notion of impartial objective knowledge in the traditional sense of natural science and its methodology. Therefore, I do not think that the great majority of what is called "psychology of personality" can be usefully described any longer as science, except perhaps in the old sense of *scientia,* but it has a context today of objectivity that I think is not correct. That is where the ideological critique is having its impact; slowly but surely it is cutting psychology away from this assumption that it is a science, and placing it into the context of social, philosophical, ethical, and, ultimately, religious frameworks.

How, then, can one speak of a "Christian psychology"? Well, I am simply mentioning that the attempt is being made, and since it is something that is in the process of taking place, I cannot describe it with much detail, much less defend it. Also, just as with anything else, some attempts are better than others. Let me just try to describe a couple of the features which ought to be present in the work of a Christian counselor or psychotherapist.

On the theoretical level. The moral system, the ethical system from which such psychologists are operating is much more clearly explicit than that of the secular psychologists, who usually do not tell you what their moral or ethical system is; in many cases, they haven't actually given it a great deal of thought.

On the practical level. Christian psychologists are introducing explicitly Christian concepts and techniques into the therapeutic process. Sometimes this involves such familiar things as prayer, praying for their clients at the beginning, or even during therapy. It may involve fasting as a suggested technique for the client as a way of, shall we say, developing self-control. But it would also involve such basic things as forgiveness. One of the great healing concepts, or healing experiences, is forgiveness. We all know that it is one way to finally get rid of old hatreds, grudges and anxieties (new ones as well, for that matter). Forgiveness as a notion so central to healing relationships between people, is not found in any of the existing secular psychologies. For them, you can only forget, you cannot forgive. Forgiveness involves intrinsically a kind of moral/ethical outlook, and though other religions embrace the notion as well, I'm sure — it is certainly a very basic Christian idea.

Those are some of the ways in which it is beginning to develop; there are others, but we are getting short on time, so I will leave it at that.

Bishop: I was pleased to discover that my parents were forerunners and practitioners of the new realism, since they frequently reminded me that I was not totally and intrinsically *good,* and certainly that I was not *autonomous.* Therefore, I feel very comfortable with most of the directions in which the new realism is going. The concern that I have centers around the statement which I believe you made, that personhood is rooted in the biological. Is *this* a cause for apprehension for those of us who might worry that through exaggeration this might emphasize the *soma* and neglect the *psyche,* neglect the spiritual? Is it a concern?

Dr. Vitz: Eventually, I think it is of concern. I think I also mentioned it is of concern because of its political and social implications as well. The balance that was mentioned by Fr. Senior with respect to our rootedness, our earthliness, and at the same time, our transcendent relationship; and, of course, the possibility of transformation through a spiritual reality, through Christ living in us — *that* obviously has to be kept alive, be kept strong, in the faith. But, at the same time, I think that the new biology gives us a more realistic basis for *starting,* for knowing the depth of the problem to which Christianity is really the answer. We cannot *just* concentrate on the problem and on our biological nature; for a deeper understanding of man, we must be cognizant of the ways in which we are called to spiritual life and to holiness, and in some sense, to transcendence.

Afternoon Plenary Discussion

February 2, 1983

Bishop: In the Mexican bishops' Puebla document, and in *Familiaris Consortio,* the deepest understanding of the person is posited in the totality of self-giving, following the analogy with the self-giving of the Trinity and of the historical Incarnation. This is taken to be the decisive point regarding personhood, which defines it; it is summarized in the Love of God, or better, in God-who-is-Love. Could we not also say that, in accord with the deepest teachings of St. Thomas Aquinas regarding exemplarity, that this "self-giving" is what is most profound about personhood? If so, then openness, relation, is something essential to the person. And if this is so, then a person can only reach fulfillment by giving "of self" to others. In this case, then, can we not say that the formation of a person culturally, and his or her cultural task (for example, in the area we are studying here, technology) is valid only insofar as it opens up to, and defines itself by, giving itself to others, and not remaining closed-up inside the individual or the particular group, the same being true with regard to nations, as well?

Fr. Ashley: Well, I don't think it would be fair to say that, textually, St. Thomas ever draws those conclusions; but I was trying to indicate that there is a foundation in St. Thomas for that way of thinking. First of all, that is why I emphasized that *only* in God is personhood fully realized. And God's personhood is one of relation, is *essentially* relative, and that relation is always one of giving and receiving; giving in love and receiving in love; the Divine persons *give* themselves to each other. I think that current thought has begun to see that and bring it out more clearly. When we compare the human person to God we fall very far short of that way of seeing the matter. We tend to think of personhood as that which makes us individual, and therefore as that which *isolates* us. But the deeper view would be to see that what is really the important point about personhood, is not that human limitation, but the divine *likeness* by which we open ourself to other persons and donate ourself to other persons. And that gives a very profound ground, then, for the social character of man.

You know, St. Thomas *does* make the point that when we say we are creatures that know and love, what we know and love are *persons*, first of all. We only know other things secondarily, and incidentally. What we are primarily interested in knowing and loving is other persons.

Bishop: My question is directed to Fr. Himes. Lonergan's transcendental precepts which you outlined for us make *some* sense in making moral judgments; however, they are not very helpful in terms of handing down — in the sense of Tradition — what underlies the faith, for example, the Trinitarian dogma. You pointed out that there are two ways of viewing the faith today, one classical-minded, the other historical-minded, and that many younger Catholics share the latter view. If there is going to be a synthesis, if we are going to pull this thing together regardless of the evolution of it, then it seems to me that *somehow* we have to establish a basis for revealed truths as being unchangeable. At the same time, we must allow for this historical consciousness to deal with the *cultural* tradition, which is in flux; and if there is a gap, we must bridge it. Isn't that primarily the role of the historical theologian at this point, to try to work out a synthesis?

Fr. Himes: I think, Bishop, what you are describing is indeed a crucial role for theology, but I think it is primarily the role of a *systematic* theologian to be doing that at the moment. I think the *historical* theologian's primary task is to try to do the systematics of previous times. So, the primary task for the historical theologian *should be,* for example, to say what is the extraordinary achievement that is given to us in a figure like a St. Augustine, a St. Thomas Aquinas. What is the extraordinary achievement of the Counter-Reformation, of the age of somebody like St. Robert Bellarmine, for example. He must deal constructively with the central issues that faith posed for the time of these people, and that their time posed to the faith. I think the person who has to try and do that now is the systematician. I think what the historical theologian does *may be* to say that you can see where a current idea or practice is a change, a development, an alteration, a shifting of emphases, etc., as compared to the past. But that is not first and foremost, I think, the historical theologian's task.

Secondly, and very briefly, let me address that question of revealed truth. Fr. Senior could probably speak to this better than I because this is a view which, I think, flows directly out of Scripture. One of the things that the tradition *seems* to have held is that revealed truth is given to us precisely in terms of historical experience. It is not, in other words, Israel's *doctrine* which is revealed. It is Israel's *history,* and from that comes Israel's doctrine. It understands its history and from that comes its doctrinal positions. The same thing is true, I think, of our experience within the Christian tradition. It is not first and foremost Christian *doctrine* which is given us, it is the *person of Jesus*. And from that we try to state what that experience *is* in normative fashion in doctrine and in creedal statements. The experience is once, for-all, and forever: Jesus Christ, yesterday, today and forever. The way in which we are able to *express* that experience and to have new elements of that experience reflected and refracted through our experience at the moment, *that* is something that shifts and grows constantly. But the experience, the *given* which is unchangeable is the person of Jesus Christ; that's the given.

Bishop: One of our concerns dealt with Fr. Himes's statement that he was discussing the *normative* human person. On our part, there is a concern that perhaps the normative might also become the *minimal*. We are concerned about the minimals, and we would like someone to boldly confront that issue, because we feel that the minimals are the ones that are under attack now, and the most vulnerable, and we would not want the normative to become the minimal.

Fr. Ashley: I have often met in just ordinary public debate the person who says the fetus is *potentially* human, but not human. And that is, I think, the hardest popular debating point to cover, because the word "potential" means a lot of different things to different people. I have tried to use an illustration to distinguish between two cases.

If we had a block of marble here in front of us or some clay, that substance is potentially a statue, but it requires a sculptor, a Michelangelo, to turn it into a statue. That is the metaphor that these people have in mind when they think of the fetus: it is potentially something that can be *made* into a human, but it is not yet a human. It is partially formed, but it is not complete. But, then, one must ask, *who* is going to *form* the fetus into the complete statue? *That* is the point they have not thought about, because the biological fact is, it is the fetus that *forms itself* into the complete human being. It is as if the marble were Michelangelo; the fetus makes itself, that is what is peculiar about the fetus. Our sculptor, Michelangelo, must be *actual* to form the statue; likewise, it has to be an actual human being who is forming itself into a fully differentiated mature human being. (We can see that in the case of the child. Nobody is turning the child into an adult except the child. People are *helping* the child grow into an adult, but *it* has the intrinsic capacity to turn into an adult, and so does the fetus to turn into a child.)

As to the case of an extremely deformed infant. . . . I was saying earlier to someone that if it can be *established* that there *are* fetuses that have a radical genetic defect such that they have *no* capacity to form themselves into human beings, perhaps then we could say that they are not human. For example, there is the really difficult case of the anencephalic child who has no brain, and no head, at all, and apparently it is due to a genetic defect. There are many of those. It is just possible that such a child is not a human being. However, we do not *know*. It is also possible that they *do* have the radical capacity to be human, but that one stage of development has been missed, and the rest could not follow. The position of the Holy See on abortion does *not* depend on proving that the fetus is a human being; the Church has taken the position that the fetus *may be* a human being. So, I would say we would still have to treat such a case as human, unless someday science *proved* that this is truly not human, has no capacity to be human. It's hard to see how science could prove it, but maybe it could.

Bishop: Fr. Himes, as you have described the task of the historical theologian you seem to be using the word "history" in a very traditional way. The historical theologian studies the history of theology. . . .

Fr. Himes: Well, I'm very traditional.

Bishop: But when you speak of "historical consciousness" as the mark of our times, I think that is a *very* different use of that word. I also am concerned that we be able to differentiate the changeable from the constant in our tradition. Msgr. John Tracy Ellis seems to think that our time is a period when the study of history is at a very low ebb, and that we are very uninformed historically. Perhaps using the word in different ways is undermining our efforts to communicate about these matters. Do you think the word "history" is getting in our way when we use it in both the traditional sense, and in the sense understood in the phrase "historical consciousness"?

Fr. Himes: Certainly, Msgr. Ellis is the dean *par excellence* of American Church historians, and I could not agree more, Bishop, with your pointing out, as Msgr. Ellis so frequently does, indeed, as everybody in the field of history laments all the time, that Americans are a people who are rather *careless* of history, by and large. Dr. Vitz mentioned, for example, that among young students there is a kind of return to the eternal values, to permanence. That is typically American. Emerson thought the same thing was happening in his generation. Sydney Mead, who I believe to have been one of the most perceptive analysts of American religious culture, often said that if you want to understand American fundamentalism, you have to understand that it is Christianity without history. It is an attempt to say that I don't need the intervening nineteen centuries, because it's just Jesus and me, and I get Him through the Book. That's all I need, it's the Book and me. It's a history-less Christianity. Certainly it is true that what has happened in American life is a denigration of history: Henry Ford's, "History is bunk!"

On the other hand, what is missing, it seems to me, is the realization that there is a kind of historical "subconsciousness" still permeating American life because, oddly enough, we are a culture that prides itself on being revolutionary. At the same time, we are kind of fundamentalist about our revolution. You know, a lot of American conservative thought is "Thomas Jefferson and me," just as a lot of American religious fundamentalism is "Jesus and me." You just change the book, from New Testament to the Declaration of Independence, but in either case we can skip the intervening histories. I think there is a deep rift in American life between the historical consciousness which has permeated our value system, and our *denigration* of history in our political thinking, our conscious social structures, and — very often — the way in which we express ourselves religiously.

An image of that which comes quickly to mind for us Catholics — certainly, when I was growing up, one of the *words* that was extremely important in my upbringing as a Catholic was "Tradition." But, precisely what tradition meant was that "nothing had changed." Oddly enough, Tradition was not the story of "how we passed it on for nineteen centuries;" it was the story of "how nothing really changed importantly in nineteen centuries." One of the reasons why people had such enormous problems, for example, with liturgical change, is because somehow or other, there was a kind of subliminal image that Jesus wore vestments and used the Sacramentary in *Latin,* the *Ordo Missalis,* at the Last Supper, and that He gave the Roman Ritual to the Twelve at the Ascension. So then, oddly enough, and I think that was typical of us as American Catholics, we talked about the enormous value of History, *and,* at the same time, said that "however, it hasn't really affected anything at all." There is, I think, a great rift between these two points of view and it is necessary to sort them out. I think you are *exactly* right, the two ways in which we use the word "history" have created a great deal of confusion.

Fr. Ashley: I would like to ask Fr. Himes this question, though. I think that, in a way, you are selling history, or the historian's work, short. History is not only to show that things have changed, but also to show what has not changed. You know, the historical approach to the Scripture is not only concerned to show that the Biblical people thought very differently than we do, but to *communicate* with the past so that what they knew makes sense to us. So, the worry I think is on the Bishop's mind is how do we recover the words of Our Lord in their real sense for us. And history is absolutely necessary for this.

Fr. Himes: Oh, absolutely. But I would also suggest that *perhaps* that gets us into a discussion of the present hermeneutical concerns, of people like Gaddamer, for example. The whole question of literary criticism becomes *centrally* important in that question, because to ask, "how do we recover the words of the Lord, the *sense* of the words of the Lord"? (though obviously of *infinitely* more importance to us, infinitely more), is still the same *sort* of question as asking "How do I know what Shakespeare meant when he wrote *Hamlet?*" It is really the same sort of question, a profoundly *difficult* one, which I think leads us into questions of esthetics and hermeneutics.

Fr. Ashley: And isn't that the real sense of what Schillebeecx says, though: that we have to *transcend* history by making the past ours? We are the same Church that was there in the first century; in spite of all the changes, we form one community.

Fr. Himes: As Louis Carroll said, "To stay where you are you've got to run all the time."

PART IV

Reproductive Technologies

An Overview

The next six chapters present a crucial medical-ethical issue of this century from a variety of perspectives. The issue arises because human persons are gifted with sexual complementarity, "male and female He created them." In that capacity a man and woman can become two in one flesh, and this act of intercourse can lead to the fertilization of a new human person within the body of the woman.

In the twentieth century science has learned new chemical, mechanical, and surgical techniques to prevent this fertilization of new life which would otherwise occur in fertile couples. The Catholic tradition since the apostolic age of the Church has opposed contraception as an attack on the procreative act which violates it and destroys its life-giving significance. These techniques of contraception are not discussed in this volume.

Instead, these chapters examine contemporary uses of technology to offer the marvelous life-giving achievement to couples who are

351

otherwise infertile. Despite the obviously desirable outcome of such new technical procedures, Pope Pius XII in the mid-20th century firmly and repeatedly opposed artificial insemination and even condemned *in vitro* fertilization, though he did not live to see the latter procedure result in successful pregnancies.

Chapter 13, although citing the position of Pope Pius XII, focuses primarily upon the work of the present philosopher-Pope, John Paul II. The author writes from his profound knowledge of the way Karol Wojtyla has used the phenomenological method to analyze human experience and the human moral act as self-creating in a personalist sense. Against this background the human act of conjugal intercourse expresses the marriage itself, and through that act the man becomes husband and father while the woman becomes wife and mother. The substitution of a technological procedure to accomplish fertilization produces a child, but the child issues from laboratory activites, not from human, moral, marital acts. The author finds that Pope John Paul II would base his opposition to these laboratory activities on the radical separation of being and acting, the circumventing of the existential relations and the *communio personarum,* in which sexual persons find their subjectivity fulfilled.

Chapters 14 and 15, in sharp contrast, picture technology actually at work in studying infertility and performing *in vitro* fertilization or artificial insemination. Chapter 14 reviews current scientific knowledge of male and female causes of infertility with special attention to diagnosis, semen analysis, and tubal microsurgery to restore fertility.

In chapter 15, the author presents scientific descriptive data on technological aids for the infertile couple. He explains the steps in *in vitro* fertilization, from artificial stimulation of ovulatory function to replacement of a scientifically fertilized human embryo in the *woman's* uterus. The author of chapter 13 would probably prefer at this point not to speak of the "mother's" uterus since the woman has not expressed her gifted being in act as wife to become mother.

Chapter 15 maintains a technological perspective, moving on to discuss artificial insemination from a husband or a donor. The use of a donor offers an anxious couple at least triple the hope of success compared to that found in insemination from the husband. The practical procedures of selecting the donor and securing free and informed consent from the woman to be inseminated and her husband are briefly described in this chapter.

Chapter 16 moves into an entirely new kind of technique for by-passing infertility. It describes legal aspects of surrogate parenting where a couple in which the wife cannot or will not bear a child arrange for the husband to donate semen for another woman to achieve pregnancy. She then relinquishes her newborn child to the husband-donor of semen and his wife.

To assure successful fulfillment of responsibilities by the parties involved in surrogate parenting a legal contract is made prior to insemination, the surrogate mother then relinquishes her parental rights after the birth, the natural father takes custody, and his wife adopts the child. In the various states these arrangements might violate statutes which control adoption arrangements and which prohibit the exchange of money for the adoption of a baby. States which have adopted Section 5 of the Uniform Parentage Act treat the husband of a woman who has been inseminated from a donor as the father of her child — another difficulty for surrogate parenting.

Hence civil law at present does not protect or regulate surrogate parenting. Chapter 17 explores the impact of the new Code of Canon Law in the Catholic Church upon reproductive technologies. Canon 1055 describes marriage as a covenant between a man and woman "ordered by its natural purpose to the good of the spouses and the generation and education of children." The ends of marriage can be stated in terms of the "good of the spouses" and the "good of the child."

Church teaching prohibits artificial intervention to remove fertility from marital acts. It likewise has prohibited artificial insemination to generate children. One might argue that the "good of the spouses" demands acceptance of technological parenting, but one might equally argue that the "good of the child" prohibits it. The Code itself does not address these questions but its new description of marriage will stimulate further expressions of Church teaching in the years ahead.

The final chapter of this section, chapter 18, captures the dialogue between the authors of the previous five chapters and the Bishops at the Workshop. The Bishops, as teachers in the contemporary Church, probe deeply for the practical and pastoral implications of the new reproductive technologies in the light of the Judeo-Christian tradition and Catholic teaching about marriage and the family.

The Editors

Chapter 13

John Paul II's Theology of the Human Person and Technologized Parenting

The Reverend Terence P. Brinkman, S.T.D.

Editorial Preface

Pope John Paul II, as the philosopher Karol Wojtyla, sought to visualize the human person in a manner which both encompassed the cosmological involvement of the person in the world and the irreducibility of the person to the level of the world of nature. He focuses on man as conscious subject, as a being-in-the-world who reveals himself in acting.

Wojtyla sees the unity of the "experience of man" and the "experience of moral action." Looking at the interiority of man as a person he sees that the "I" is found in the moral act as the person defines his humanity and his goodness or badness. The identity of man is established as the "I" reveals its "self" in self-determination. A vertical transcendence is found in the way the subject freely directs himself toward his own "self" as a goal, determining himself through various objects of action and choice of values.

As philosopher, Wojtyla appeals to the subjective participation in human-
ity as the basis of the I-other relationship and of an interior role of duty flowing
from the structure of humanity. The "I," in choosing itself, participates in the
humanity of the "other," and chooses him in its own "I."

The "I-you" relation is a particular expression of transcendence proper to
man specifically as a person; the "I" chooses self-fulfillment in the acceptance of the
"you," another "I" like my own, for myself. Because of the interior intentional-
ity and orientation to value of persons, the "I" is faced with the gift of another
like itself as a help to self-fulfillment. The intentional relation of sexuality thus
involves the personal and moral structure to which it offers fulfillment in a certain
respect. The "we" complexus also enters the understanding of marriage and
sexuality since a married couple bond together in a communion of life and love and
a form of transcendence in support of society. The basis for sexual communication
is in the communio personarum *by which subjectivity is objectively experi-*
enced and communicated as a disinterested self-gift.

Hence Pius XII opposed artificial insemination because, while it produced
fertility, it did not express the fruitfulness of the spouses which comes from the
structure of self-determination by which fulfillment is found in acting *since it*
alone explains self-modification. Karol Wojtyla's approach to the person inten-
sifies this insight. For him "technologized parenting" leaves out the very structure
of the mode of personal unity through affirmation specific to human acting that
explains the relation of being and acting, its fruitfulness and its unity.

An authentic ethical analysis of "technologized parenting" demands
understanding of "person-in-existence" and not simply of person as a "thing."
Marriage, also, is not a "thing," it is a cooperation of persons and its reality is
in the realm of action, the action of persons. *The core issue which Pope John*
Paul II has raised is the interconnection of the human act and the moral act in the
interpersonal communion of marriage.

In a certain sense the title of this chapter is somewhat deceptive. It
is obvious that what is desired is a further clarification of the ethical
norms governing human reproduction through their function of guiding and limiting the moral good of human acts. But, the title itself
carries a variety of incongruities. For example, why must one speak of a
"theology" of the human person when, in fact, a philosophical analysis
would suffice at least if one is convinced of the legitimacy of reason's
capacity to find the truth? Then again, why does one desire to enter into
a question of the human person, which is in essence the domain of

anthropology, in order to find the "normative" about which anthropology as a science might be agnostic?

Further still, from an impressionistic view of the title there is the implication that from this strategy of starting with a "theology of the human person" one has, in fact, simply translated an "is" to an "ought," i.e., moved a naturalistic image to an ethical imperative. Semantically, there is the problem of both the words "technologized" and "parenting" individually and as a couple. Neither word in their root is a verb, and yet, both are used as verbals — as participles or gerunds. In short, one wonders if in these words a host of intentional structures have not been collapsed into their present form that imply a philosophical substructure of considerable complexity. Finally, one must wonder, given this audacious title, if it is possible in such a short essay to explicate the thinking of John Paul II, and do so lucidly, especially for an audience who may not be well acquainted with his writings? But, despite its deceptiveness and the pitfalls that harass such an endeavor, the attempt will be made to make what is seemingly incongruent in the title indeed consistent in fact.

The More Classical Visualization

To enter into the philosophy that underpins the convictions of the philosopher Wojtyla is a first step to decoding his theological objectives. It seems obvious that his intellectual drive has been to explain, and hence not only to be creative but also faithful to the tradition of the Church concering her care for man. In a sense, in this essay we will attempt to "follow along" that intellectual journey. It is unfortunate indeed that we will (because of the brevity that the genre of the essay demands) not be able to explore certain connected links that more fully illustrate the realism of his attempt, and thus we will have to remain content with a somewhat esoteric exposition. Nonetheless, enough can be discerned to provide for a more fruitful discussion at a later time.

We can approach the question of the human person in the philosopher Wojtyla's visualization by seeing in what sense his explanation is contradistinct from the anthropological constructions that had preceded him.

For Wojtyla the philosophical attempt to define man has been nothing other than an attempt to establish his identity.[1] He classifies the history of this effort into three moments.

The first moment is to visualize man through the Aristotelian definition, man is a rational animal. Wojtyla maintains that while the definition satisfies the Aristotelian terms of classification concerning the species (man) as known through his nearest genus (animal) by the factor differentiating the species in the genus (rational nature), this definition is such that it carries the *conviction* of the reducibility of man to the world.[2] Thus, man is always understood within the external cosmos in which he exists. Wojtyla calls this type of understanding cosmological since man is seen as an object — one of the objects of the world to which visually and physically he belongs. In his opinion, objectivity thus conceived means nothing other than explaining human reality with the primary analogate of man's reducibility to the world. Wojtyla's own comments are relevant on this point:

> The whole scientific tradition of the complexity of human nature, of the spiritual and bodily *compositum humanum,* which through scholasticism passed from the Greeks to Descartes, moves within the limits of this definition, that is, on the basis of the conviction as to the essential reducibility to the level of the world of that which is essentially human.[3]

A second moment in the history of the visualization of the identity of man by philosophers is founded on the conviction of the primordial originality of human being and hence of his irreducibility to the level of the world of nature. This attempt to visualize man, according to Wojtyla, is as old as that of Aristotle, and it is found precisely in the attempt to see man as a person as carried in Boethius' definition — an individual substance of a rational nature. At this point in his analysis, Wojtyla makes a subtle distinction between the *conviction* of the irreducibility of man and the actual historical *understanding* of man as a person in classical metaphysics. The conviction is based on the fact that the visualization of the subject *(suppositum)* or the essential subjectivity that signifies man cannot be reduced to or adequately explained by the nearest genus and the specific difference. In Wojtyla's opinion subjectivity is a synonym of all that is irreducible in man.[4] On the other hand, the historical understanding of the person in traditional metaphysics accented the *individuality* of the substantial being, man, as a possessor of a rational or spiritual nature rather than the whole specificity of subjectivity essential to man as a person. This accent on individualism in effect

357

drove a further wedge in the attempt to unify conceptually the dyads subject-object and soul-body which situate the "human" of humanity.

The third moment that Wojtyla enunciates is that of a further explication of the definition of person from its metaphysical "site." The definition already constitutes a statement of a *suppositum* (a specific subjectivity of existing and acting) and an affirmation of man's being a *persona* (a subject objectivized).[5] This attempt at visualizing the reality of man does not depend upon comparing man to objects, nor directly from seeing man as an individuated being, but through the specificity of that being's own subjectivity given directly in experience, namely, from the *interior experience of man's own selfness in consciousness,* hence as someone. Thus, in explicating the term "subjective" and hence in conserving the conviction of man's irreducibility, Wojtyla feels that the word "human" can be defined by the concept "conscious subject," and this, in turn, gives us a more objective vision of man who is object and subject, the person, as being-in-the-world.[6]

As a philosopher had Wojtyla simply desired to break down the dichotomy between objectivity and subjectivity alone? While it is undeniably true that this was part of his philosophical endeavor, it would seem that the tack he took was rather a methodological one of concentrating on the specifically human (the irreducible) that was passed over in the more cosmological visualization. This "specifically human" is given in the intuition of man's being a person but the mode of analysis in traditional metaphysics concerning the concept of person tended to visualize it as a monad and hence statically. There was, on the other hand, in viewing man's being from this metaphysical "site" an opening to seeing man's being as dynamic in the further concepts of *agere* and *pati.* But, this too was reductionistic for it left out the concrete specific structure and human mode of operation irreducible to man by which "acting" and "happening" connected him to existence as a whole. This irreducible element Wojtyla deems as the "experience lived through," and its further concreteness is an "I," who, as a subject, "lives himself." In other words, the experience of "man" cannot be exhausted by way of cosmological reduction because this experience is given in one's own experience of interiority as "man" and hence as he is an eyewitness of himself, of his humanity, and of his person.[7] It is to this indispensable way to the cognition of man in view of his personal subjectivity that Wojtyla turned to define "man" by allowing him to *reveal* himself in acting. This had two ramifications: 1) methodological,

2) the quest to identify the intrinsic union of the words "human act" as the moral act, and their mutual interpenetration in the personalistic dimension especially in regards to the specific moment of transcendence proper to the personal "I."

Methodological Considerations

Given that it is the irreducible that the philosopher Wojtyla wished to uncover in its operative and constituent elements, the method he used was phenomenological. This assertion, however, needs to be qualified.

The philosopher Wojtyla by his methodological bias for the phenomenological had moved in this direction not so much as a rejection of his scholastic, or more precisely, Thomistic background, but because of the reality he wished to analyze, i.e., *the human experience*. He sees a phenomenological analysis as a complement to the Thomistic, and still further, as "unpacking" the density in the Thomistic intuition of the human act as the moral act. Thus, his choice of a phenomenological methodology was to have an instrument that could trace and grasp the structural tie of human subjectivity with the "experience lived through."

While it is possible to see this approach as giving methodological preference to the notion *operari sequitur esse* in that the action is the foremost cognitive approach to explicating being, he uses a phenomenological mode of analysis for two reasons: 1) one must enter the question of consciousness, and 2) this method allowed for a penetration of the subject free from preconceptions and, in this sense, makes an understanding possible by letting the subject reveal itself.

However, he made two provisos in his acceptance of this methodology. First, he did not accept the theory of cognition understood phenomenalistically, that is, viewing the inherent division of knowledge into an organizational unity. For him experience is already an understanding, and this showed the organic unity of human cognition which presumes a metaphysical base — *percipi* $\neq$ *esse*. Second, while accepting the intentional structure of human existence, he felt the phenomenological approach, as also scholastic methods, fell short of seeing man as a unity of operation and unified by his operation since phenomenologists tend to identify the *suppositum* with consciousness (phenomenological) or attribute it to a power (intellect or will) separate from the person.

Seeing the Unity of the "Experience of Man" and the "Experience of Moral Action"

The "experience of man," that is, that which explicates him from the moment of his action, has been given traditionally in the term, "the human act," in which the experiencing of what is morally good and bad is included as an essential and especially significant moment — moral experience. This reveals three things: first, that while anthropology is not ethics nor ethics anthropology, they are inextricably connected when one starts from the basis of human experience. Second, it explicates the intuition that human character always and at every moment is connected to the moral act, e.g., the virtues. And further, it is specifically the moral act that identifies man not simply as good or bad in the abstract but as good or bad *as man (ut homo)*. Third, but given that this is a rather generalistic notion (for example, "man" as a word is an abstraction), in the profile of Wojtyla's approach by dwelling on the interiority of man as a person, it is the "I" that yields up its contents and objectifies the structures that construct a self in act. More specifically, the "I" is found in the moral act by which it defines its humanity and itself as good and bad precisely through the moral values of the act which form the person, not just in its character but in its being.

Why had Wojtyla taken this turn to experience? There are three reasons. First, it was based upon a judgment of realism that any approach to man and specifically to ethics must be based *a posteriori*. In part, as a philosopher, his approach was a rejection of the *a priori* approach begun with Kant and continued in Scheler. Second, he felt that the scholastic approach that too rigidly identified the *human* act with being solely the *rational* act left unspecified the deeper dynamic of the interior drama that yields the personal formation of man's character and being. In part, this was the beginning of his rejection of utilitarianism. Third, he saw that the dynamic unity of person and act had been separated, and that this visualization made two separate somethings when, in experience, what is found is a someone, a personality, formed from and by a specific action of its self called self-determination.

The Question of Transcendence and the "Moment of Truth"

For Wojtyla the philosopher, the question of the identity of "man" is therefore inextricably drawn as to its specificity from the very way "I" reveal my "self" in self-determination. In the linguistic expression "I do," which formalizes the experience of human acting, one can see immediately that there is a causal connection of the "I" as agent. In a sense, "I" am the efficient cause. In scholastic terminology this has been attributed to that faculty of the person known as the will. On the other hand, in a phenomenological analysis this is seen rather as a form of transcendence outward to an object from desire. Both modes of analysis, in a sense, correct the other. The phenomenological corrects the scholastic in asserting that it is the whole "I" involved in this "issuing forth." At the same time, desiring in the phenomenological sense is given a stasis or center in the will (or more appropriately, the rational will) in that it is a mode of choosing and deciding.

However, there are shortcomings in either methodology. Both understandings in this question of transcendence are centered too much on the object or end desired rather than on the subject in its concrete subjectivity. For in "willing" I do not simply choose an object and "intend it" in the phenomenological sense, nor do I simply make it an end of the desire in a scholastic sense. I also make as object/end my own self. In the fundamental experience of self-determination one does not simply relate the causal dependence of the act to the "I" alone (though this is quite important) but also the action specifically forms a "self" as the first object or end of human action, and this "autoteleology" remains in the subject and modifies that subjectivity.

This form of transcendence is not horizontal as is implied in the scholastic and phenomenological schools, but is vertical and is centered in the concrete mode of choosing and deciding that is the operational specificity of the subject (thus objectifying its constitutive elements) and the opening through which the subject is penetrated and modified. This "in selfness" is what is termed by Wojtyla the intransitive dimension of action to differentiate it from the transitive (e.g., the agent pushing the ball in which the action is transferred to the ball). In short, in conscious action the subject directs himself toward his own "self" as a goal, "for he cannot refer to various objects of action and choose various values without determining himself and his value, through which he becomes an object for himself as subject."[8]

If one understands this, one can see in what way Wojtyla has overcome the dichotomy of subject and object. More importantly he has uncovered the connection between anthropology and ethics, particularly the mode in which "is" and "ought" concur. Wojtyla has attempted to explain this relation in a variety of ways, always under the title, however, of the "moment of truth" that marks this form of transcendence, that is, personal.

At times he has explained this relation in a more scholastic sense in which the will is related not to the good simply, but rather to the movement of the intellect to truth in self-actuation. In this the "truth of the good" is the movement of the person dynamically realizing itself in the face of the object as good. In this more metaphysical sense the will is demonstrated not to be determined *ad unum* by the good of the object, but rather, by its organic union with the truth, it is given the freedom not to choose (I may, but I do not have to). On the one side of the desire "I want," but on the other side the will is also guided or directed by the truth to what I must do when I want an object as good. This transcendence to truth that the will normatively seeks is at the same moment that which not only reveals the personal structure but also is the moment of the formulation of duty. This submission to truth or perhaps more technically, the surrender to the truth of the good *in act* is not only self-expressive but is also at the heart of the experience of moral duty. This more metaphysical tack allows Wojtyla to assert that through the powers of the person (intellect and will) the being itself becomes good or bad through modifications of its being. In this sense, Wojtyla regrasps the notion of the *bonum honestum,* the true good.

He has, on the other hand, attempted to explain this relation more phenomenologically since there is a tendency, in thinking of intellects and wills in the abstract as separate and unconnected faculties, of betraying a primary instruction of Thomas that these are accidental to the *suppositum.*[9] The phenomenological explanation (when complemented by the metaphysical) does allow an entrance into the specific subjectivity of the person through the medium of consciousness and it helps to preserve the integrity and unity of the personal act which the metaphysical explanation may miss.

In consciousness, the act of self-determination reveals the deeper structures of self-possession and self-dominion. Freedom is seen as a part of the structure of self-possession and self-dominion and is, in fact, synonymous with these structures. It is the unique feature of this form of freedom to see it is bound to the experience of responsibility. The subject actualized through these structures in act is nothing other than that phenomenon called the self. But, is it the self in essence for which the act is aimed? It can be nothing other than the self but with a variant.

This variant comes in the question of fulfillment in which it is as if the subject "outgrows" itself in a particular directionality. Put simply, it is not that in accomplishing an act the experience of fulfillment emerges, but rather that I am fulfilled in accomplishing an act. This personal form of fulfillment can be more closely isolated in the particular value relations of the person, the experience of moral values in the act of the person. This comes from the analysis of conscience in which the moral values have the quality of good and bad in one's experience and it is likewise connected to specific contents of human realizations: prudence, justice, etc. What this particular schema also adds is the juridical aspect of the self obliged to the effect through its responsibility. Also this schema has the advantage of recognizing the difference between end and fulfillment in which the subject, perhaps in an a-conceptual manner, lives through its self and experiences fulfillment as happiness or peace in accomplishing an act. It is not simply in the efficiency of achieving the end, rather it is in the absorption, as it were, of the moral value of the accomplishment of the act that fulfillment is experienced. In this sense, happiness is always an end interiorly experienced of being truly good as man. This, however, is distinctive to itself and is not to be confused with the end as the object of choice. On the negative side the danger of the identification of the two leads to utilitarianism. On the positive side, it shows the very contingent and difficult struggle that the quest of self-fulfillment entails. [10]

Preliminary Conclusions on Personalism

It can now be seen that the experiential approach is that strategy to exfoliate the irreducible about the man as a person. One "experience lived through" is a question of a person's movement as seen interiorly, i.e., as the "I" experiences its own identity in acting and existing precisely in constructing the "self." The most decisive moment of self-realization is that of self-determination, as it presumes the necessary and therefore normative movement of vertical transcendence in response to horizontal intentionalities, and more particularly in the specifically human "surrender to truth" — the moral domain experienced in conscience. While this moral dimension does not inculcate the heart of every cognitive experience of value, it does reveal how intimately the words "human act" are connected to the moral act or conscious act. It further reveals man as the maker of himself (at least in a psychological or moral sense) and that his freedom is bound by the truth of his own humanity. It further reveals man's contingency because of his quest for fulfillment, and he finds this experientially in his existing and acting which is irreducible to any other explanation than through *his own act* and its structural dynamism. In short this philosophical project is nothing other than the manifestation of man as a spirit, and, at root, the fundamental axiological referrent is this specific dynamism of the person.

Wojtyla the Theologian: Preliminary Discussion

As a theologian Wojtyla asserts the congruence of his own philosophical thought to that which is revealed and further explained in Christian anthropology. He often quotes the text from *Gaudium et Spes* n. 24 to the effect that man, being the only creature on earth which God willed for his own sake, cannot reveal himself fully otherwise than by making a disinterested gift of himself. [11] His own conclusions from this text are varied but it remains a locus of his theological outlook. The "for his own sake" of the text is ambiguous. It can mean "for God's sake" or "for man himself." Wojtyla has interpreted it both ways, but the substance of his thought would indicate that man in being good for himself is being good for God. Or man in sinning against himself or his own good is sinning against God and His justice. Fundamentally, however, from this text Wojtyla wishes it to be seen that inherent to the relational image of the person the substantial aspect is indirectly revealed — the personal structure of self-determination. His most straightforward conclusion is that this structure which identifies the "self" is the "law of gift," not only operationally by which man is a person, but also ontologically. This inscription in the being of man, the person, is the only inscription that Wojtyla admits of. As a further consequence he wishes to bring out that it is this turning in toward one's self (for which consciousness and self-determination are working) which is the source of the most ample opening out of the subject toward reality.

Relationality

If we may sidetrack ourselves for a moment from the theological project and enter into the relational aspect of the subject "being for others," we may conclude the theological exposition in a manner that enlightens the Pope's talks on the theology of human love, and further, shows man's being an image of God not only as a concrete "self" but as an image in his personal relations particularly as those relations are a *communio personarum* (*Gaudium et Spes,* #12).

It has been the onus of philosophical thought through the ages to recognize that cognition as such, while it can explain in part the union of the knower and the known, must do so mediately. The "other" remains always other as subject. In the theory of knowledge it would seem that God alone can know us as we are, unmediated by the universals and generalizations that are necessary for our cognitional grasp. As useful as this is, it becomes problematic in the field of the relations of persons, who do not relate to one another as objects but as subjects. And, it is particularly quizzical that such relations assume an almost ontic status of importance for persons. This seemingly almost mystical union of persons creating a reality of themselves has formed the center of several philosophical anthropologies. In Averroes it would seem its explication would come from a single soul of which individuals are participants. With Hegel, and more explicitly in Marx, it marks the drive toward the "species man" with each individual a component. While these analogies are of an idealistic bent, it would seem that such an approach is operative in several thinkers in anthropology who identify the human with cultural embodiment.[12]

This has not been the only tack among philosophers. Such a reality as "community" has been explained in a reductionistic analogue concerning drives common to all creatures, particularly the higher animals. Such theories have attempted to view this reality through naturalistic explanations and a variety of determinisms that lead to the inexorable conclusion that physical processes are the heart of such relations. One need not look far to find such examples, particularly in the discussion of human sexual drives. It is quite noticeable in many anthropological and metaethical analyses particularly the Wolffian and, to some extent, those of Thomas. While it is true that such data are necessary to flesh out a more specific content to interhuman relations, these explanations do not explain the irreducible element of the interpersonal bond.

A rejection of the more naturalistic explanation of the "social nature" of the human was led by Herbert Doms in the late thirties. While we cannot go into an analysis here of the value of such a work, it was rejected because of the methodological difficulty inherent to some

365

phenomenological analyses of identifying the subject with consciousness (and hence excluding the dynamism of the will in consent). This view preferred to identify cognitive intentionality with its sometimes emotional preconceptions as the relational bond which, in turn, "swallowed up" the concrete subjectivities in their specific form of dynamism as the potentiality for the actualization of a relationship between persons.

Karol Wojtyla, through his analysis of Scheler, saw the shortcomings of this form of personalism,[13] and in turn has attempted to isolate the relation of "I-other" by which the paradox of interhuman unions is overcome. He has done this precisely by recognizing that human cognition is mediated by concepts, universals, and generalizations in the question of understanding the "other,"[14] and, at the same time, that consciousness does, in fact, limit our experience to one's own self (as non-transferrable), and thus a telepathic relation to the "other" is realistically impossible.[15] How then does he explain the relation?

Participation

Wojtyla begins his explanation through an analysis of participation. Rather than seeing the "other" as dense and impenetrable, that is, as an object, through the experience of one's own "I" in self-determination (the specifically human form of self-communication), one can recognize that this being is not simply "other" but rather a different "I" and constituted in its humanity by self-possession conditioned by self-consciousness as its own "I." Thus, despite the fact that self-determination (the relation I-self) is experientially non-transferrable, the recognition of the "other" (the relation self-I) opens up the possibility of understanding that it is on the basis of a subjective participation in humanity by which the relation I-other is confirmed. The affirmation of the other "I" is given not simply in recognizing that the other is "man," because I-other implies a more concrete participation, but rather on the basis of that mode of my being by which I accept and confirm myself. In this sense, I accept his "I" (I affirm the person) that is, I choose him for my "self" or in my "self" in the very manner in which I choose myself, for I have no other approach to another human being as an I,[16] even my own. Hence, I am called to participate in his humanity, concretized in his person, similarly as my humanity is in my person. While this "calling" is spontaneous, and not prescinding from emotional factors, it is experienced, but not always as a "choice" (and hence willed), but may be a simple "identification"[17] of the other as "another I." Being a choice in this sense (in which the "I" is bound to the "self") has both the ontological and axiological, and therefore ethical, relation as does the moment of self-determination. For Wojtyla, this is the personalization of the relation I-other and it is guided externally by the Christian commandment of the love of neighbor,[18] but obviously from his analysis it is an interior duty flowing from the structure of our humanity and bound from within. He feels that such experiences are captured in Kant's second categorical imperative of treating the person as an end and not as a means,[19] for this respects the nature of a subject.

Why had Wojtyla proceeded in this manner in which "I choose him in my I" or "on the basis of my I"? First, it is a drive toward realism which is not mediated by concepts but by the immediate experience of humanity. Second, it brings out the ethical significance of such an identification in the relation I-other. Third, it is consistent with his method of dwelling on the irreducible and posits the specifically human reality of personal relations prior to reductionistic theories. Fourth, it is profoundly personalistic without falling into the conceptual trap of identifying the *suppositum* with the relation while at the same time conserving the subjectivity of the "I" through which participation is potentially actualizable. Fifth, it points out concretely the form of personalism which Wojtyla accepts as viable and realistic. Finally, it demonstrates the dual aspect of community in which not only do I contribute to its reality but also I am fulfilled myself in this relation. Obviously, a conclusion of this interpretation is that alienation is the opposite dyad of participation, and it produces in the person not only the feeling of being a pariah in society but further the interior contradiction of one's ability to accept and affirm one's own self in existence.

I-You Complexus

Wojtyla has further classified this net of relations in the schema I-other into two further complexes which he deems the I-You (community relation) and the We (societal relation). In his view the I-you relation is profoundly personal and hence has an anterior status of priority in the interhuman complexus than does the "we."[20] It is the I-you relation that reveals the *communio personarum* appropriate to humans precisely as persons for which no naturalistic explanation can suffice.

The I-you is a specific moment where the freedom of non-determination is exposed as a choice for the affirmation of self-fulfillment in the acceptance of the "you" (another "I" like my own) for my self. To make this assertion a tiny bit more concrete (though the example given here is only one variant of the pattern, and not the only one) in the realm of sexually differentiated persons, one must see the intent of Wojtyla.

It has often occurred in the past that human sexuality was perceived purely as a biological determinism. Its purpose was objectively to propagate the species and subjectively to satisfy the tensions of the organism. The reaction to this visualization saw human sexuality being rather a spiritual consciousness prescinding from its biological rootedness and hence an ontological state of reciprocity bound by the intentional structure of love. In several theological analyses today this dualistic significance of human sexuality, particularly as it relates to the meaning of human sexual intercourse, is accepted as the definitive state of the question after Vatican II. The inherent contradiction of this construct is often noted, but more often than not, it is accepted as a paradox, or an ambiguity. The methodological differences that generate the two meanings often go unnoticed, and the presumption is made that these meanings are simply essences in any event. What binds these essences is the rationalist explanation which recombines them in the strategy of existential planning. The basis for planning begins not from the preferred significance (propagation or love) as such, but rather from the method of analysis that had led to one or another of the significances as determinative. In short, what is both ontological and normative is the question of planning. The plan is revealed to some by the simple observation of the biological mechanism; for others it is a function of the question of pure reason in useful construction of premoral values.

Wojtyla the philosopher has viewed this question differently precisely because of the unity of reference given in experience, especially the experience of self-determination in the light of the question of self-fulfillment. Self-fulfillment reveals both the contingent and intentional structure of human existence. But, despite the induction of elements that reveal the diverse contents of human existence as fulfilling in some regard, they are always bound to the foremost axiological referrent of self-realization through self-determination. In this sense, the content arising from the sexual realm (for example, masculinity) is always "for" the person. While it is possible to isolate such an element in abstraction, it does not indeed exist in this manner in personal experience. Rather, while it gives a particular directionality to human existence, its orientation is always a self-realization and hence bound to

368

that which is the mode by which a person specifically determines himself and fulfills himself in existence.

What Wojtyla has introduced as a novelty is that, because of this interior intentionality and orientation to value extant in persons, it is precisely this structure that stands at the center of interhuman relations. Thus, the primary perception is not simply that my masculinity is enhanced in the face of her femininity, but rather that I am faced by the gift of another like myself as a help to my self-fulfillment and esteem precisely in the same way that I would fulfill myself as a person through the structure of self-determination. Hence, my primary referent and participation is in the humanity of the other as a person. It is this referent that orients one to the truly good of being fulfilled as a self to which the experience of sexuality is bound. Thus, the intentional relation of sexuality is not simply to a particular content but always involves the personal structure (and hence the moral structure) to which it is a fulfillment in a certain respect. Further, and more importantly, this visualization makes participation the center of the relation of persons prior to that of reciprocity. This insight guards against a reductionistic analysis that would too quickly look at reciprocity as the bond of the relation (and thus at the "contents of the trade-off"), placing the justness of the trade-off outside of the experiential referent. In this visualization the fulfillment of the subject is recognized as central while at the same time the objectivity of the relation through participation is guided by the interior norm of self-determination.

For Wojtyla the *communio personarum* in the I-you relation is completed by reciprocity in which "I" am, in a sense, an object for their subject founded in participation and never separate from it or the realism of personal fulfillment would be lost. In this manner Wojtyla feels he has explicated the question of the "gift of self" apart from the visualization which comes from utilitarian balancing. What it fundamentally explains is the dynamism of finding a different *confirmation* of personal subjectivity and identity. It explains how dynamically the personal being can successively perceive his growing reality (and its inherent responsibility) as a man, a husband, and a father as a subject objectivized in self-determination that, in a sense, returns the various "contents" and integrates them in the person as a personality. It is not simply that the person knows he is a man, a husband, or a father, but rather that he *is* or "lives through" existentially being such and hence "knows" it in an experiential sense as his own acting and existing. This

369

visualization has the advantage of explaining the union of the spiritual-corporal existence of man and the form of integration proper to it, and, in relation to others, the mode of integration that affirm this union precisely through the process of transcendence that is the foundation of the personal reality. In Wojtyla's understanding, the *communio personarum* experienced in the constructs "I-you" and "we" is a particular expression of transcendence proper to man specifically as a person. This transcendence, sometimes deemed the "social nature" of man, allows the visualization by which the site of the proper dynamism specific to man as a person can be identified as normative as well as anthropologically realistic.

The We Complexus

According to Wojtyla the "we" schema is an interpersonal pattern which is the confirmation of the subject different from that of the I-you because it is directed differently. It begins in the experience "together with other I's" but is oriented to the common good. The word "common" explicates that action, together with the existence of those many I's as well, is in relation to some value. The common good is sometimes misunderstood. While it is abstract, it emphasizes not simply the material abundance shared in by all, but rather it also includes that which is produced through the common efforts of others which would not exist otherwise.

While this social aspect would not at first seem to enter into a discussion of marriage and sexuality (where the I-you schema seems to predominate), it is unquestionable that it does so. It is seen not only in the fact that we see married persons as a couple (hence, a "we" as a unified societal form) but it is further explicative of the exchange of their sexual values that forms the good and confirms their unity not simply as husbands and wives but potentially as mothers and fathers. In this sense, I am a father through her realization as a mother. In Wojtyla's opinon only this sense allows the realism of the action to be personal and realistic for marriage. It yields the following rubric: through the sharing of sexual values (and their potentiality) in common their diverse subjectivities are enhanced and confirmed and further integrated in a union of their persons that is a bond of a communion of life and love and a form of transcendence specific to human persons whose efforts are to the support of society.

Wojtyla the Theologian Reconsidered

If it is seen that transcendence is, in a sense, another name for person, in which being transcends itself as "truly good," or as one outgrows one's self in that direction in a specific form of intentional dynamism from the act of the person in self-fulfillment, one can begin to explicate the theology of John Paul II.

Theology permits John Paul II to take liberties with his philosophical definitions. As we had previously seen, his fundamental intuition concerning the reality of man comes from *Gaudium et Spes* #24 (and if we look closely, *Gaudium et Spes* #12). Biblical revelation, however, adds a specific nuance that escapes the concrete assertions of philosophy about the reality of man. Man is in the image of God. In saying this, it does not deny the reality of the human as Wojtyla visualizes it but rather it presumes it and further confirms the mode of man's recognition of his self-identity. This theological definition certainly affirms that the human reality is not reducible to the consideration that man is an object in the world of objects. The closest comparative is, in fact, the divine not only in its being but in its acting. Man exercises dominion and possession not simply over the world but over himself, that is, man is given the gift of freedom from determination except as he directs himself. In other words, the definition plants the human in the spiritual dominion proper to man as a being and in his operation. John Paul II points this out in his explication of Adam's test in which Adam himself differentiates his reality from that of the animal world (the world of objects) and demonstrates through *his own act of judgment his consciousness of his self-identity.* John Paul II is quite "adamant" that this theological definition is not extraneous and imposed from the outside but that it is intrinsic and explicated from the mode of operation proper to man as a person. In a sense, the Pope is saying that even God must await this revelation of self by man or he would not be man otherwise as an image, that is, free through self-direction. Thus it is that when man consciously chooses and directs himself and derives the truth of himself for his own good he fully explicates the plan of God as the fullness of his being. In this sense he is an image in that he can achieve in his fullness of operation

371

the existential modality by which God's being is the fullness of action.

It should be noted that being this image is not limited to the individual *communio personarum*. In short, the "datum" by which he comes to the insight of his own reality is the interior operation of transcendence that stands against the "datum" of the empirical information of the world around him as an object. Thus, in relation to the woman, despite being differentiated physiologically, Adam can still cry out (both as an evaluation and emotionally), "This one, at last, is bone of my bone and flesh of my flesh . . . ," hence recognizing that she is another "I" like his own. She is foremost a helpmate or partner in finding the significance of himself. It is important to note here the priority in the Pope's visualization. It follows his conviction that contingency and fulfillment as human reside in the question of self-identity and not simply sexuality. In fact, the woman is identified first as another person as a gift to myself prior to her recognition as a sexually differentiated being in Adam's experience. Thus, in the Pope's view, it is participation in the humanity of the other that is the basis of reciprocity that sets the significance of the relation prior to the exchange of sexual values.

At this point it would do us well to look at the notion of value in the understanding of Wojtyla. Value is that in which being erupts into existence, in short, a modality of the good conditioned under a specific content. When viewed cognitively value is an intentionality phenomenologically experienced.[21] In this can we say that sexual differentiation is a value of the being? The words used are important here. Sexual differentiation is most directly a value of the body. It participates in the same materiality as the body and is a specification thereof. However, in experience it is a value or an intentionality connected to self-fulfillment *for* the person *living* its existence. In this sense in which sexual differentiation is a value it is so as part of self-identification and self-construction which is guided by the form of vertical transcendence unique to persons. Sexuality is the essential concept we name the experience, but, in doing so, there is a tendency to isolate it from the main referent to which the experience is directed. This referent is the self and its specific form of modification under the truth of the good — a truth that identifies us not only as male and female but as masculine and feminine persons, that is, different experiences of incarnation of persons precisely as persons. Such an integral personalism is further explicated by Wojtyla as the metaphysic of modesty.

Modesty

The human person's eruption into existence comes anthropologically in the recognition that the body is the "sacramental" model by which personal existence is revealed. The body "reveals the person," not directly but mediately. It is the body also from which a variety of intentionalities flow that modify and condition personal existence, and, in this sense, subjective interiority can be touched directly. The mechanism of subjective existence which protects one's interior subjectivity as one's own is the experience of modesty. It is a kind of defense against improper intrusion into the personal realm which is inalienable, or better, *sui iuris*.

As we have already seen, sexuality is directed towards interior self-modification in the personal realm but sexual differentiation is known through the external object of the body. The experience however is integral, that is, that corporal existence is united with personal existence. The sexual values are not only a sign of differentiation but a sign of connection because they touch so immediately the person itself. Because the body is an object and can be perceived as such, and because sexual differentiation is part of that objective perception, this openness of being revealed before the gaze of another as object gives rise to the experience of one's own subjectivity and identity as a person as the full truth of a person's reality that must likewise be affirmed in the other's judgment. The "veiling" of our existence is nothing other than the protection of man's experience of being a subject from use or utility as an object. It is this experience of modesty which presumes the intimate connection between the person as subject (in a metaphysical sense) and the person as self (in a psychological sense). In either case, it is the word dignity that explicates the metaphysic or experience and connects them. Further, it is in the "must be affirmed" of the other's judgment of myself that this is an affirmation not only of cognitive realism (the adequation of the idea to the reality) but the foundation of the moral imperative of the good in its connection to truth. The basis then for sexual communication is in the interpersonal schema found in the *communio personarum* by which subjectivity is objectively experienced and communicated as a disinterested self-gift. What is concretely exchanged is the spiritual dynamism by which a self is formed in existence for the other in their full truth of subjective existence. In John Paul II's view this is nothing other than marriage guided by fidelity, permanence, and indissolubility as the *total self-gift*. Thus, the union of persons in marriage does not create a single being in the strictly metaphysical sense of the term, rather it is a creation of selves, a reality of persons, in subjective existence precisely through their action as persons in which their own existence is unified and fulfilled. Thus, while we call marriage a reality, it is not a thing; rather it is a cooperation of persons and its reality is in the realm of action, or more specifically, its contents are drawn from the act of the person for its basis. In this sense, *operari sequitur esse* and no other.

Technologized Parenting

The words "technologized parenting" are somewhat ambiguous in their intent. They could mean nothing more than the use of technology to promote the higher probability of conception by a married couple who experience problems in fertility. This would place the question in the realm of technique and a different evaluation of each technique ethically would be called for. More particularly, however, the words "technologized parenting" can mean asexual reproduction. In this case those techniques which presume as their basis the promotion of human conception other than through human sexual intercourse are the ones clearly meant by the words "technologized parenting." It is this latter significance that we take as the intent of the words.

The analysis of this question by theologians today revolves around the licitness of separating the unitive and procreative significances of sexual intercourse. There are those who find that such a separation of the significances of sexual intercourse would not be morally justified if for no other reason than it would be an admission of the possibility of the use of artificial contraception. There are those, on the other hand, who feel that the unitive significance ought to be tied to the question of the marital relation as the bond of its unity and that such an intervention biologically does not affect that bond but rather reenforces it. It is true that if fertility were simply a biological process of the organism and nothing more, the morality of the intervention into it would be no different than that of blood transfusion, organ transplants, or by-pass surgery. Strictly speaking, the moral tradition finds little problem with such medical interventions to correct the functioning of the process of fertility *within* the organism. The same cannot always be said when fertility is taken as part of the intentional relation of a married couple.

What specific union is involved in marriage between persons, and by what action through which fruitfulness in marriage is realistic and existential, that is, human? It is a question as old as Genesis — why does a man leave his father and mother and unite with his wife and how does this constitute an "in one flesh"?

The history of the conceptualization of this question, particularly in the least radical technique of artificial insemination,[22] is well known. The proponents on either side of the question of the licitness of such a question generally spoke from a perspective in which the union of persons was presupposed.[23] While their view was considerably more nuanced than we shall present here, one can note that those who found such an intervention to be morally viable generally emphasized the methodological premise that the couple as a unit were a single principle of reproduction. Cognitively, the transfer of sperm was neither moral nor immoral but rather a process of some ambiguity whose moral warrant came from marriage. Those who opposed the artificial process pointed out the lack of biological integrity when compared to the "natural act." In their opinion the couple had a direct right to acts apt for procreation and hence only an indirect right to a child.

An analysis of the argumentation of Pius XII in detail would exceed the scope of this paper, but the following can be noted briefly. Pius XII sought his solution through the reconsideration of how persons determine and fulfill themselves in marriage as a union in their actions specific to their being personal realities. In short, he turned to a theory of integral personalism, that is, to the unity given in personal experience through self-determination. This more psychological tack becomes quite evident in his 1956 allocution. In his view it was the *cooperative action of persons* and that specific *moment of transcendence of the person* that bound man and woman in unity and shared union *anthropologically*.[24] As he pointed out, the psychologists were correct in seeing the suffering of an infertile couple as debilitating. But did not this datum point to something else? Having a child does not make one father and mother simply; it only makes one a "parent." Are not the concepts father and mother a personal reality from their own being and acting as a desire for the fulfillment of their self?

Fertility was anthropologically part of the dynamism of personal fulfillment of their being and acting as incarnate persons, but the fruitfulness of their being comes from the structure of self-determination by which fulfillment as a person is found in acting because it alone explains self-modification. The marital act in this sense was an affirmation of the integral union of person and nature through a reciprocal exchange of sexual values as a self-gift and could not be seen simply as an exchange of life germs. [24] Fruitfulness in marriage is hence a wider concept than fertility in Pius XII's mind. [25] Fruitfulness is part of the question of self-determination (and the values derived therein from being a person) and hence fertility is a natural function *for* personal orientation and transcendence and not an end in itself. [26] The end of fertility as a natural process is a child. This is true whether one is married or not. However, marriage as the human reality of interpersonal communion of life and love is dependent for its explanation upon only one determinant: the freedom of self-determination for self-fulfillment by which a variety of intentional realities are integrated and are concretely the self both anthropologically and morally, as given through and for another self as an aid. Pius XII, therefore, resolved the question of artificial insemination by examining the existential relations of the marital partners carried out in the immediate personal cooperative action of the couple.

Has the philosophy of the human person in the thought of Wojtyla clarified the problematic? In the sense that he has not written on this specific topic of "technologized parenting," one cannot say he has. On the other hand, if one views his thesis on the human person as a clarification of the rather embryonic stage represented in the thought of Pius XII, one can affirm that he has.

If one is bound to the personal structure of self-determination for self-fulfillment, it is this moral site of anthropological fruitfulness that determines the correct moral site of fertility as human. Human fertility presumes as a moral condition the union of persons. Saying this means that the human body has a nuptial significance (through sexual differentiation and reproductive capacity) for the person. It is thus the dynamism of the person which is the site of human actuation and value orientation. While it is possible to speak of the body abstractly, in existence it is a personal reality and integrated in its intentionality as such not only through the consciousness but primarily through self-determination. So, too, while marriage can be thought of notionally, what escapes this visualization is the concrete subjectivities and their interaction through the action that creates the reality. We call this intersubjective reality the "gift of self." Again, there is a tendency to make of this action a notion which visualizes it as a thing. However, the gift of self is a specific actuation of the person precisely from the operative dynamism specific to persons that actually creates a self in existence. It is the shared affirmation of the persons in the very process by which they unify, integrate, identify, and live their existence that specifies the gift of self for another. Thus, the gift of self is nothing other than intersubjective participation, that is, a spiritual reality. In marriage this gift is "mediated" by the sexual values which are reciprocally exchanged.

Too often the gift of self has been identified too concretely as the reciprocal exchange. Rather, the reciprocal exchange of sexual values is first an anthropological affirmation of unity of the person and nature in the quadrant of self-fulfillment specific to the personal realm, and second a cooperative action of the subjects in the creation of the good specific to the values shared. While we distinguish as "first" and "second" the reciprocal exchange, we do so only notionally since, in fact, in existence such an affirmation is simultaneous. The ground of the distinction is, of course, one of directionality in the personal relations of "I-you" and "we." In this sense, the objectification of the self carried in the sexual value of masculinity is really a self-affirmation in which the person and nature is unified and given to the *affirmation* of the unity of person and nature of the feminine in her self-modification. In a sense, I complement her personal feminine self-fulfillment precisely through the mode in which I affirm my own self objectified in self-determination and self-fulfillment. In turn reciprocally, I "outgrow" myself not only in this respect but also in the affirmation of myself through her self-gift. At this moment when the I-you schema is realized there is simultaneously an affirmation of the cooperative action carried in the sexual values exchanged. I not only affirm the unity of her person and nature as feminine but her integrity as an incarnate spirituality and its dynamism, that is, her possible maternity through which I, in turn, find my paternity as a self. Here begins the we schema of the cooperative action, and while it has a different directionality it arises concretely from *the same affirmation of the person*. Hence, it is a single affirmation of different directionalities, and, in this sense, inseparable.

If it were simply a question of the organism being fulfilled, there would be no moral problem. The quadrant of actuation in this question of personal union, however, deals with self-fulfillment, which is always bound by the structure of self-determination. It is here that intentionality lies and is fulfilled as "man." It is only in the truth of this relation

377

that material significances (sexual differentiation and procreativity) are integrated and modify personal existence as the truly good in acting existentially.

In our opinion, this is how John Paul II would resolve the problematic of "technologized parenting." The specific form of transcendence of the person by which the self is communicable through self-determination is what creates the possibility of the personal transcendence experienced in communal and social relations. No other explanation suffices to elucidate the union or the experience of unity in the intersubjective dimension of human existence. No other explanation is existentially viable by which self-modification is realistic and adequates the experience "lived through" in concrete human subjectivity. If this is so, the integration of intentional significances arising from the multifold of human experiences, especially those that come from the corporal realm, cannot be explained except through this structure of personal transcendence and still conform to experience. While one can say objectivistically that all that is left out is sexual intercourse biologically, such is not the case when we examine the existential relation of persons. While one can say that ideally "technologized parenting" separates the unitive and procreative significance of intercourse, what is really left out is the very structure of the mode of personal unity through affirmation specific to human acting that explains the relation of being and acting, and further, its fruitfulness, its unity. In short, the "artificial" separation leaves out the concreteness of the *communio personarum* by which personal and hence existential relations are possible as a gift of subjectivity. In our opinion, John Paul II would reject any technical efforts to produce human life, even for married couples, except through sexual intercourse, since it alone explains the unitive mode of affirmation *in act* of the original unity of person and nature found in experience.

Conclusions

As a conclusion we pose the following question: will this form of argumentation be accepted as convincing? In response we propose something once said by G. E. Moore,

At all events, philosophers seem, in general, not to make the attempt; and, whether in consequence of this omission or not, they are constantly endeavoring to prove that "Yes" or

"No" will answer questions, to which *neither* answer is correct, owing to the fact that what they have before their minds is not one question, but several, to some of which the true answer is "No," to others "Yes."[27]

In effect, in our opinion, it is quite unlikely that the argumentation above will appeal to most ethicists in the field of medical ethics today. Many ethicists today are asking metaethical questions when they think they are proposing ethical solutions. A great many are meditating upon the *form* of ethical *discourse* as if it were the norm of the truly human and they leave the experience of morality an untouched data. In a certain respect, "experience" for some has come to mean the results of the positive data of the empirical sciences and nothing more. They are a relative content of organizational cognition; they are not seen as constitutive of the reality in which they inhere as a whole. In short, the "being" being explicated by today's modern schoolmen is that of the "object," "circumstances," and "end." But, is this derived "being" of the mind the human person in experience? It is doubtful that it is.

There has been a confusion in this, for the past few decades the word person has had little to add to the question of the word normative. In effect, person meant a "being" understood as a "thing." But is not the person a particular act of being which demonstrates itself as itself in act, and have we not reached a primary moment in the question of the "normative" that is specific to the question of person? All too often, in the recent past, we have allowed the word "rational" to explicate the meaning of person as if "rational" could stand alone in a void apart from the entire phenomena presented in experience, particularly the moral experience. Our first conclusion, then, is that there is a need to explore the metaethical basis of morality or we shall continue to be caught in a quasi-schoolboy argumentation that compares the differences of conclusions to our interpretation of the "proper" amalgam of the mix of the "object," "circumstances," and "end."

It must be admitted that for many today the most convincing argument against the use of certain techniques to promote conception "artificially" will be that of the so-called slippery slope. If it is allowable for a wife to conceive by her husband through some techniques because of psychological exigencies, why is it not also possible for a single woman to do so for the same reasons? Would she not have also an equal right to such fulfillment when it is shown that she is a stable and mature person, and certainly in light of the empirical evidence of nurturing of children by single parents, if she is fully capable of raising the child? The difference some would point out is that she lacks the warrant of marriage. But why is marriage decisive in the first instance and not the second when it would seem that "marriage" had little to play in the ethical argumentation that found the process morally licit? If "marriage" is presumed to be the ethical site for such a presumption, our second conclusion is that we must become quite clear in our discourse as to the reality of marriage that does in fact include or exclude the licitness of "artificial" techniques.

In one of those remarkable asides that St. Thomas is often noted for, he points out the ambiguity of physical actions having different moral values. His example is that of intercourse. How can precisely the same physical action have differing moral conclusions? He claims that moral determinations are not to be found in accidentals. But, in what sense is intercourse accidental? By accident does he mean "neutral"? In the interpretation of some this is what the word has been taken to mean. Does the word "accidental" mean "premoral"? For some this is precisely what it means. Much literature is available today on the question of the notion of value and disvalue in the word "premoral." Is intercourse then a value or a disvalue in a non-moral sense? But, at this point how are we to interpret the word "value" and by what criterion do we arrive to such an assessment? Our third conclusion is that the precision of our language often bespeaks a shifting in our philosophical bases. There is a need then not to be satisfied with what at first seems to have linguistic consonance when there is a considerable shifting in the philosophical assertions that underlie our mental constructs.

To conclude then, while it would seem to be beneficial pastorally to be able to present an argument so binding as to be conclusive in simple terms, we do ourselves and our tradition a disservice when we too quickly ask questions which correspond to "Yes" and "No." For, in fact, the linguistic cogency of the response may be the only cogency, and certainly not a moral one. What the question of "technological parenting" brings out is the necessity of the establishment of the interconnection of the human act and the moral act. If this is true, the Pope has given us a sufficient analysis to begin the penetration of this mystery, and, by his own example, the intellectual honesty not to reduce in a simplistic fashion the complexity of human, that is, moral existence.

Notes

1. The word "identity" is derived from the Latin *idem* meaning "the same." Hence, identity can mean the same on the basis of comparison. In the text which follows we will show how the intuition that man can be compared to his nearest genus opens up his identity on the basis of *comparability*. On the other hand, identity can mean to "identify and isolate" something in itself as to its own *individuality* that cannot be reduced to anything else. This also has been a philosophical intuition as will be brought out. However, there is a third sense to the word "identity" which is fundamentally psychological, and this speaks of the principle of unity in the dynamism of the process of becoming a person through personality formation, that is, a *self-identity*. As will be seen this too forms part of the philosophical visualization of "man."
2. Karol Wojtyla, "Subjectivity and the Irreducible in Man," *Analectica Husserliana*, 7, 1978, p. 108.
3. *Ibid.*, p. 109.
4. *Ibid.*
5. *Ibid.*
6. *Ibid.*
7. *Ibid.*, p. 111.
8. Karol Wojtyla, "The Personal Structure of Self-Determinaton," *Tommaso D'Aquino nel Suo VII Centenario*, Congresso Internazionale Roma-Napoli, 11–24 aprile, 1974, p. 382.
9. *Ibid.*, p. 383.
10. Karol Wojtyla, "The Person: Subject and Community," *The Review of Metaphysics*, 33, Dec. 1979, p. 287.
11. "Personal Structure" *op. cit.*, p. 388; also, *L'Amore Umano nel Piano Divino*, Città del Vaticano, Libreria Editrice Vaticana, 1980, p. 71.
12. See Thomas Beis, "Some Contributions of Anthropology to Ethics," *The Thomist*, 28, 1964, pp. 174–224.
13. See Karol Wojtyla, "The Intentional Act and the Human Act that is Act and Experience," *Analectica Husserliana*, 5, 1976, pp. 269–80; also *I Fondamenti dell'Ordine Etico*, Bologna, CSEO, 1980, pp. 79–86, pp. 116–128, pp. 167–174.
14. Karol Wojtyla, "Participation or Alienation," *Analectica Husserliana*, 6, 1977, p. 62.
15. *Ibid.*
16. *Ibid.*, p. 67.
17. *Ibid.*, p. 68.
18. *Ibid.*, see also, Karol Wojtyla, *Amore e Responsabilità*, Torino, Marietti, 1979, p. 29ff.
19. *Ibid.*
20. "The Person," *op. cit.*, p. 291.
21. "The Intentional Act," *op. cit.*, p. 273.
22. See John Wakefield, *Artful Childmaking: Artificial Insemination in Catholic Teaching*, The Pope John XXIII Medical-Moral Research and Education Center, St. Louis, MO, 1978; also Terence Brinkman, *The Anthropological and Moral Commitments in the Decision on Artificial Insemination*, Doctoral Dissertation, Rome, Angelicum, 1982.
23. Brinkman, p. 67ff.
24. *Ibid.*, p. 338f.
25. *Ibid.*, p. 353. It is certainly interesting to note the same distinction made by John Paul II in *Familiaris Consortio*, nn. 11, 16, 28, 41, 53.
26. Brinkman, *op. cit.*, p. 348ff. Such is the reasoning one finds in *Familiaris Consortio* particularly in n. 14 in speaking of the question of sterility.
27. G. E. Moore, *Principia Ethica*, London, Cambridge University Press, 1980, p. vii.

Chapter 14

Clinical Treatment
of the Infertile
Couple

Thomas Nabors, M.D.

Editorial Preface

Human infertility, the condition of a couple who have regular, uncontracepted intercourse for a year without achieving a pregnancy, affects approximately 10% of married couples in the United States. Female factors which can be identified and treated include failure of ovulation, inadequate luteal phase, and closed fallopian tubes. Male factors which can be identified and treated include abnormal semen, diabetes, ductal obstruction, and failure of semen to liquefy.

Diagnostic evaluation of the female tests for ovulation and tubal patency and semen analysis of the male can offer great assistance. But methods of sperm collection like use of a perforated condom, recommended by moral theologians who oppose masturbation as gravely wrong, may be clumsy or even practically useless. Tubal microsurgery for women with blocked fallopian tubes shows great promise of overcoming this kind of infertility.

From a clinical point of view, we define human infertility as that state existing in a couple having regular uncontracepted intercourse for one year without pregnancy occurring. Obviously, there are wide ranges of infertility, ranging all the way down to sterility. It is well known that the older a woman is, the less fertile she is, especially after the age of 35. The same is probably true of the male, but there are no clear cut data to show this. The natural history of fertility in "normal" couples having uncontracepted intercourse is that they will have a baby every two or three years until the mother is 35, and then every five or six years. Such was the case of my mother who was born in 1892. She had babies in 1909, 1912, 1914, 1917, 1918, 1920, 1922, 1924, 1926 (age 34), 1932 and 1938.

Incidence of Infertility

The incidence of infertility in the United States and Canada is approximately 10%[1]. Endometriosis is an important cause of infertility in the woman. Black people rarely have endometriosis. It is also of low incidence in those cultures whose people tend to marry and reproduce before and during their early twenties. It is classically a disease of caucasian white collar workers who postpone childbearing.

Speeroff, Glass and Kase[1] phrased their thoughts well when they wrote: "Perhaps of equal importance is a realization of what not to do. Too often therapeutic myths widely held by the laity receive explicit endorsement from the physician. Telling a woman that all she needs to do to achieve pregnancy is to be more relaxed is inaccurate. It also achieves an opposite effect by making her more upset at the the thought that she is in some way causing her own infertility. Barring severe anxiety, which can interfere with coital frequency or ovulation, there is no evidence that day to day emotional problems can cause infertility." They cite the report of Noyes and Chapnick[2]: "Despite many anecdotes to the contrary, adoption does not increase a couple's fertility." Rock, Tietze and McLaughlin were cited[3], decrying the use of thyroid extract as being useless in the euthyroid woman and citing Buston and Herrman[4] and Tyler[5].

Causes and Treatment of Infertility

Female Factors

1. Failure of ovulation (Stein Leventhal syndrome). This disorder is easily corrected by clomiphene citrate or Pergonal. Clomiphene is a weak estrogen having the ability to stimulate the pituitary and ovary, causing an increase in follicle-stimulating hormone which causes growth of the ovarian follicles, culminating in ovulation. Pergonal is human menopausal gonadotropin, extracted from the urine of post-menopausal women and contains 75 units of follicle stimulating hormone and 75 units of luteinizing hormone. When this is administered along with a boost of human chorionic gonadotropin, ovulation occurs. If the amenorrhea is associated with hyperprolactinemia, bromocryptine in addition to clomiphene is indicated. These so-called "fertility drugs" are fraught with the hazards of multiple pregnancies. Pergonal is commonly associated with those cases in which the mother has four or more infants. In the case of clomiphene, there are rarely more than twins. The twinning rate is about 12% and physicians are careful to point this out to the patient before prescribing it.

2. Endometriosis. Spangler et al[6] reported that 6 to 15% of infertile patients have endometriosis as the only factor responsible for the infertility. Surgical removal of the endometriotic lesions can be done, or they can be suppressed with a drug known as danocrine. However, the treatments do not improve fertility a significant amount, although important in relieving other symptoms.

3. Inadequate luteal phase is easily corrected by the use of progesterone.

4. Sperm allergy or build up of antibodies in the female causing sperm to agglutinate and rendering them useless for fertilization. The use of a condom for several weeks will allow the female to destroy her antibodies. They will recur, hopefully not before pregnancy occurs. When there are moral objections to the use of the condom, abstinence for several weeks is the solution.

5. Closed fallopian tubes as a result of infection, trauma, endometriosis and sterilizing operations. Microsurgery is the only solution.

6. Congenital malformations, Turner's Syndrome, congenital absence of vagina, uterus or ovaries. An artificial vagina can be constructed surgically, but these unfortunate people almost always have no

uterus. Uterine transplant is not yet on the scene. Turner's syndrome is not amenable to therapy.
7. Pituitary tumors. These should be removed surgically. If surgery fails, bromocriptine is helpful.
8. Cervical factors, infection, poor production of cervical mucus. Infections are treated with antibiotics and sometimes cryosurgery and cauterization. Cervical mucus can be improved with small doses of estrogen.

Male Factors

1. Abnormal semen. This may be related to a febrile illness of any kind, overheating of any kind — the wearing of tight fitting jockey shorts, prolonged periods of sitting as truck drivers do, even hot baths. Appropriate remedies are obvious. Abnormal semen following a febrile illness usually recovers in 3 or 4 months. The presence of a varicocele in the scrotum often produces abnormal semen. The mechanism is not entirely clear, but surgical removal will correct the problem.
2. Coital timing. A woman is fertile only a matter of hours each month and if the schedule of coitus is inappropriate, fertility will be reduced. Keeping a basal temperature chart is helpful.
3. Diabetes may cause impotence, rendering coitus difficult or impossible. More rigid control of the diabetes helps.
4. Endocrine. Failure of the pituitary-testicular axis that stimulates spermatogenesis. This can be helped with human chorionic gonadotropin or with clomiphene.
5. Ductal obstruction such as due to injury, infection or sterilizing operations. Re-anastomosis can be accomplished with microsurgery.
6. Failure of semen to liquify, trapping the sperm and disallowing transport of the sperm through the cervix into the uterus and tube. Mucolytic agents instilled in the vagina prior to coitus are helpful.
7. Hypospadias is a congenital condition whereby the urethral meatus is located along the shaft of the penis at various distances from the end of the penis. This condition as a cause of infertility must be rare, since most of these are corrected surgically in early childhood.
8. Kleinfelter's syndrome is congenital and genetic and is not amenable to therapy.

Diagnostic Evaluation

Everyone agrees that infertility should be considered the problem of a couple and not an individual. Therefore, the couple is evaluated as a unit. Diagnostic evaluation of the male includes general health, medical history, sexual history and semen analysis. Other tests to be performed are hormone tests, testicular biopsy and vasography.

In the female, we do a detailed history of sexual and reproductive past, menstrual pattern and general health. We test for ovulation by having her record her basal body temperature and by taking an endometrial biopsy. We examine the cervical mucus at the precise time of ovulation and do postcoital examinations of the cervical mucus to see if the sperm are penetrating it in adequate numbers. Tests for tubal patency include the hysterosalpingogram and the so-called Rubin's test in which carbon dioxide is passed through the cervix and the tubes. A three-way stopcock is used and on one end is a manometer. The carbon dioxide is applied under pressure which can be measured on the manometer. As the gas passes through the tube, the pressure drops. Following this, the patient is asked to sit, at which time the gas collects under the right diaphragm and causes a referred pain to the right shoulder. Look and see tests include laparoscopy, hysteroscopy and culdoscopy to search for such disorders as endometriosis and abnormalities of the tubes and ovaries.

Semen Analysis

Since 40% of infertility cases implicate a male factor, the semen analysis is vital. The manner of obtaining the semen specimen has always posed problems for moral theologians who view any masturbation as gravely wrong. That, of course, is the simplest and most direct method of obtaining semen. As an alternative, moral theologians in the past have recommended other indirect, clumsy and downright meaningless methods.

Some of the methods that have been described as licit by theologians[7,8] are:

1. Stripping the seminal vesicle by massaging this organ through the rectum. This is of no value since the seminal vesicles do not contain sperm, as was previously taught.
2. Removal of part of the semen after coitus. The pH of the vagina is

about 4.3 and is rapidly lethal to the sperm. For fertilization to occur, the sperm must immediately enter the cervix where the cervical mucus has a pH of 7.6. Another deterrent to this method is that vaginal secretions are mixed in and dilute the concentration. It also disallows fractionation which is important in pin pointing the trouble area.

3. Use of perforated condom, allowing most of the semen to be deposited naturally. Special condoms have to be obtained since the ordinary commercial condom contains spermicidal chemicals. The greatest deterrent is that the specimen cannot be fractionated and determining volume is not feasible.

4. Testicular biopsy. This is sometimes indicated for diagnostic purposes in determining why spermatogenesis is not taking place. It tells nothing about motility, which is critical in male infertility. Also, it requires a general anesthetic and the patient is subject to infection.

5. The cervical spoon (Doyle). This has no advantage over collection from the vaginal vault following normal coitus.

6. Needle aspirations. I doubt that any male would tolerate needle aspiration of any part of his testicle or vas deferens. This is not fractionable, motility cannot be assessed, and I do not know of anyone who has ever used this method.

In order to show you why these methods are inadequate, I will review the events in the process of ejaculation. (See Figure 1.) Sperm cells are formed by the germinal epithelium of the testis. They pass into the epididymis which is a convoluted duct that, when stretched out, would measure 12 to 15 feet. It takes about 12 days for this to occur. Maturation takes place in these 12 days, and by the time the sperm cells reach the caudal portion of the epididymis, they have some movement, but no forward motion. This is the reason that sampling sperm prior to their mixing with seminal vesicle fluid will not show their motility potential. The sperm are moved through the epididymus by ciliary action. They move up the vas deferens and are stored in the ampulla of the vas deferens, near the posterior urethra.

During sexual excitement, peristalsis of the vas occurs and pushes sperm into the urethra. At orgasm, contractions occur in the prostate and it empties its secretions into the urethra. The seminal vesicles contract to squeeze out their secretions. The bladder neck then closes as the urethral meatus opens up and the perineal and bulbourethral muscles contract spasmodically to force the semen from the posterior urethra through the meatus. Because of this series of events, the first portion of the semen has by far the majority of the spermatozoa. The first part of the fluid portion of the ejaculate comes from the prostate and the remainder from the seminal vesicles. This is the reason that fractionation of the semen into 2 or 3 portions is important. One can tell the area of malfunction. The semen clots immediately on exposure to the outside, and in 5 to 20 minutes, the clot liquifies and the seminal vesicle fluid then activates the sperm to their full moving potential, and allows them to make forward motion.[9]

In cases of male infertility in which an excessive volume of semen is produced, as in cases of chronic prostatitis and chronic seminal vesiculitis, the male can be advised to deposit the first portion of his semen in the vagina, withdraw to disallow dilution of the concentrated first portion by the poorer quality of semen that is in the last portion. Apparently, although only one sperm enters the egg, others must be present and in significant concentration.

One method of semen analysis is to collect the semen in three separate containers labeled and taped together for convenience. The patient manipulates himself to ejaculate, collecting the first portion in #1, the midportion in #2 etc. Errors of collection occur when the labeled container is mistaken.

In commenting on the obsolete morally licit methods of obtaining semen, Niedermeyer[10] wrote in 1961: "None of these methods fully satisfies the designated requirements. In cattle breeding, an electrophysical method of obtaining sperm for the purpose of artificial insemination has been applied very successfully. It has not yet been applied to man, but its theory seems applicable. The question is whether this can constitute the basis for a method that is morally unobjectionable."

By 1966, Amelar[11] had published his technique for obtaining an ejaculate from the human by using a simple hand electric vibrator. In two minutes or less, ejaculation occurs and the specimen can easily be fractionated. At times, an erection occurs and at other times ejaculation occurs without erection. Only a miniscule drop of semen is needed for analysis. If a man is concerned about wasting his semen, the remainder can be amassed in a syringe and placed in the vagina of the wife.

Tubal Microsurgery

In the past ten years newer techniques of microsurgery have been introduced and used rather widely. The operation is performed while viewing the operative site with a low powered microscope. An end to end anastomosis is usually done and, using very fine sutures, the various layers of the tube can be sutured to each other so as to create patency. The majority of patients seeking fallopian tube surgery are patients who have had a tubal ligation for sterilization and changed their minds. These cases get better results from re-anastomosis than those cases in which the tubes are closed as a result of infection. Victor Gomel[12] from the University of British Columbia and the Vancouver General Hospital reported on 118 of his operated cases. Reasons for wanting the operation reversed are found in Table 1.

Table 1.
Reason for Requesting Reversal of Sterilization (100 patients)

Reason	No. of patients
Change in marital status	63 (63%)
Crib death	17 (17%)
Desire for more children (marital status same)	10
Tragedy	4
Psychologic reason	6

Data from Gomel.[12]

Gomel[12] also reported the results of others using conventional surgical techniques and these are found in Table 2.

Gomel[12] also reported in 1980 his cases using microsurgery and these are found in Table 3.

From these data, it is clear that the microsurgery techniques are superior. Another item of progress lies in the fact that in the conventional techniques, it was necessary to use stents or hoods. These had to be subsequently removed, requiring a second operation.

Decherney and Kase[13] reported results of their own and others from the literature, cases of closed fimbriated ends of the tubes. These cases have resulted from infection, such as gonorrhea and are famous for their poor results. One of the problems is that in the disease process, the cilia lining the tube have been destroyed and there is no transport

Table 2.

Results of Tubo-Tubal Anastomosis for Reversal of Sterilization by Conventional Surgery

Author	Year	No. of cases	No. of intrauterine pregnancies	% Intrauterine pregnancies
Williams	1973	5	0	0
Umezaki et al.	1974	6	3	50
Siegler and Perez	1975	(17)	(4)	24
Seigler and Perez + literature	1975	46	14 + 3[a]	37
Hodari et al.	1977	14	3	21
Diamond	1977	12	3	25
Total		83	26	31

[a]Pregnancy reported, but outcome not stated.
Data from Gomel.[12]

Table 3.

Microsurgical Reversal of Sterilization

No. of patients	Minimum postoperative follow up period	No. of patients with uterine pregnancy	% Pregnant
118	Less than 1 week	76	64.4
47	More than 18 months	38	80.8

system for the fertilized egg. A high percentage of tubal pregnancies occur. Table 4 shows these results.

Our experience with microsurgery is relatively short and we can expect results to become even better.

The amount of the damaged tube that can be salvaged is important. The reason for this is that when sperm and egg unite, they remain in the fallopian tube for nearly a week, all the time developing. The fertilized ovum needs to reach a certain stage before implantation is physiologically possible. When the tube is too short, development of the embryo is not sufficient to implant when it reaches the uterus and it passes on out through the cervix and is lost. Silber and Cohen[14] reported on this subject and Table 5 is from their paper.

Table 4.
Comparison of Studies Utilizing Various Surgical Treatments To Correct Fimbrial Occlusion

Study	No. of patients	Patency rate	No. of patients conceiving	Term pregnancy rate	Ectopic pregnancy rate
Prosthetic device					
Young et al. (1970)					
Sovak technique	24		37.5%	25%	4%
Garcia and Aller					
(1974), hood	36	90%	26%	18.2%	0%
Roland and Leisten					
(1972), stent	130	95%	25%	23%	0%
Terminal salpingostomy (microsurgical technique)					
Swolin (1975)	33			24%	18%
Gomel (1978)	41		44%	27%	12%
DeCherneya (1981)	54	90%	44%	26%	17%

[a]Present study.
Data from DeCherney and Kase.[13]

Table 5.
Relationship of Total Tubal Length to Pregnancy

	Tubal length				
	0–2 cm	2–3 cm	3–4 cm	4–5 cm	5 cm
Total no. of patients	2	5	7	4	7
Pregnant	0	0	4	4	7
Not pregnant	2	5	3	0	0
Normal intrauterine pregnancy rate	0%	0%	43%	100%	100%

Data from Silber and Cohen.[14]

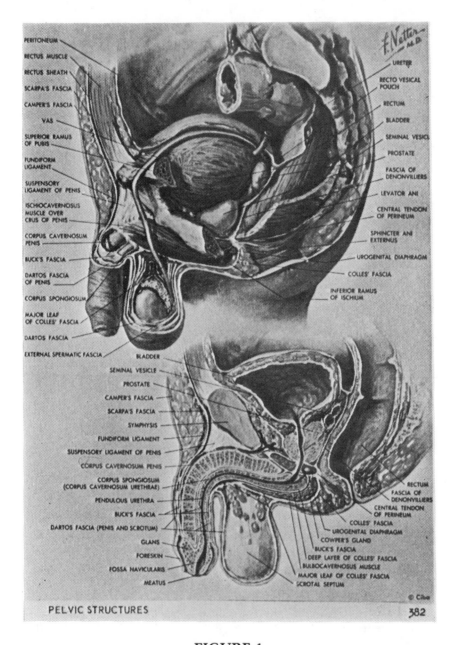

PERITONEUM
RECTUS MUSCLE
RECTUS SHEATH
SCARPA'S FASCIA
CAMPER'S FASCIA
VAS
SUPERIOR RAMUS OF PUBIS
FUNDIFORM LIGAMENT
SUSPENSORY LIGAMENT OF PENIS
ISCHIOCAVERNOSUS MUSCLE OVER CRUS OF PENIS
CORPUS CAVERNOSUM PENIS
BUCK'S FASCIA
DARTOS FASCIA OF PENIS
CORPUS SPONGIOSUM
MAJOR LEAF OF COLLES' FASCIA
DARTOS FASCIA
EXTERNAL SPERMATIC FASCIA

URETER
RECTO VESICAL POUCH
RECTUM
BLADDER
SEMINAL VESICLE
PROSTATE
FASCIA OF DENONVILLIERS
LEVATOR ANI
CENTRAL TENDON OF PERINEUM
SPHINCTER ANI EXTERNUS
UROGENITAL DIAPHRAGM
COLLES' FASCIA
INFERIOR RAMUS OF ISCHIUM

BLADDER
SEMINAL VESICLE
PROSTATE
CAMPER'S FASCIA
SCARPA'S FASCIA
SYMPHYSIS
FUNDIFORM LIGAMENT
SUSPENSORY LIGAMENT OF PENIS
CORPUS CAVERNOSUM PENIS
CORPUS SPONGIOSUM (CORPUS CAVERNOSUM URETHRAE)
PENDULOUS URETHRA
BUCK'S FASCIA
DARTOS FASCIA (PENIS AND SCROTUM)
GLANS
FORESKIN
FOSSA NAVICULARIS
MEATUS

RECTUM
FASCIA OF DENONVILLIERS
CENTRAL TENDON OF PERINEUM
COLLES' FASCIA
UROGENITAL DIAPHRAGM
COWPER'S GLAND
BUCK'S FASCIA
DEEP LAYER OF COLLES' FASCIA
BULBOCAVERNOSUS MUSCLE
MAJOR LEAF OF COLLES' FASCIA
SCROTAL SEPTUM

PELVIC STRUCTURES

382

FIGURE 1

Glossary

1. Basal body temperature — one taken on first waking when the body is at complete rest.
2. Culdoscope — an instrument for examining the space behind the uterus to visualize the tubes, ovaries and uterus.
3. Endometriosis — tissue of the lining of the uterus growing at ectopic areas. Gives rise to menstrual cramps, extra bleeding, and infertility.
4. Hyperprolactinemia — prolactin is a pituitary hormone that stimulates a woman to lactate, or produce milk.
5. Hysterosalpingogram — Xray studies made with contrast material in the uterus. Outlines the cavity of the uterus as well as the tubes.
6. Hysteroscope — an instrument for direct vision of the cavity of the uterus.
7. Laparoscope — instrument introduced through a small incision in the navel to visualize the abdominal contents.
8. Luteal phase — that part of the ovarian cycle following ovulation during which the corpus luteum from whence the egg came makes progesterone that creates a favorable nesting place for the newly formed person.
9. pH — hydrogen ion concentration, indicating how acid or alkaline a material is.
10. Vasography — Xray studies of the vas deferens.
11. Peristalsis — progressive wave of contraction and relaxation of a tubular muscular system, by which the contents are forced through the system.

NOTES

1. Speroff, L., Glass, R. W., Kase, N.: *Clinical Gynecologic Endocrinology and Infertility*, The Williams and Wilkins Co., 1975, page 172.
2. Noyes, R. W. and Chapnick, E. M.: "Literature on Psychology and Infertility; A critical Analysis," *Fertil and Steril.*, 15: 543, 1965.
3. Rock, J., Tietze, C. and McLaughlin, H. B.: "Effect of Adoption on Infertility." *Fertil. and Steril.*, 16: 305, 1965.
4. Buxton, C. L. and Herrmann, W. L.: "Effect of Thyroid Therapy on Menstrual Disorders and Sterility," *J. Am. Med. Assoc.*, 155: 1035, 1954.
5. Tyler, E. T.: "The Thyroid Myth in Infertility." *Fertil. and Steril.*, 4: 218, 1953.
6. Spangler, D. B., Jones, G. S. and Jones, H. W., Jr. "Infertility Due to Endometriosis," *Am. J. Obstet. Gynecol.*, 109: 850, 1971.
7. Healy, E. F.: *Medical Ethis*. Loyola Univ. Press, 1956.
8. Kelly, G.: *Medical Moral Problems*. The Cath. Hosp. Assoc. of the U.S. and Canada, 1958, p. 221.
9. Cockett, A. T. and Urry, R. L., eds., *Male Infertility: Workup, Treatment, and Research*, Grune and Stratton, 1976.
10. Niedermeyer, A.: *Compendium of Pastoral Medicine*, Joseph F. Wagner, Inc., 1961, p. 101.
11. Amelar, R. D.: *Infertility in Man*, Philadelphia, F. A. Davis Co., 1966b, p. 27.
12. Gomel, V.: "Microsurgical Reversal of Female Sterilization: A Reappraisal," *Fertil. and Steril.*, 33: 6, 587, June 1980.
13. DeCherney, A. H., and Kase, N.: *Fertil. and Steril.*, 35: 162, Feb. 1981.
14. Silber, S. J., and Cohen, R.: *Fertil. and Steril.*, 33, No. 6, 598, June 1980.

Chapter 15

Technological Aids
for the Infertile Couple

George E. Tagatz, M.D., FACOG

Editorial Preface

Treatment for infertility seldom improves the physical health of the couple. It has a life-giving rather than a health-improving goal. Over a hundred babies have now been born after in vitro *fertilization and embryo transfer. To improve the efficiency of this procedure multiple ovarian follicles are stimulated during a single cycle of the woman. The oocytes are retrieved from the follicle prior to ovulation by laparoscopy. Viable spermatozoa are prepared from the crude semen sample. Fertilization takes place in a Petri dish soon after the sperm are placed in the oocyte incubation medium.*

Approximately 30 hours after fertilization, the cleaving pre-embryos, now at a 2–4 cell stage, are replaced in the mother's uterus. If, following apparent fertilization, some oocytes do not divide or undergo changes in the nucleus or cytoplasm which indicate cell death, they are not placed in the uterus except at the request of the couple.

In artificial insemination homologous (AIH) the physician places the husband's sperm in the cervical canal or the endometrical cavity. However, using this method only 15–20% of couples will eventually achieve a pregnancy.

Artificial insemination utilizing donor semen (AID) led to a 70% pregnancy rate in a program at the University of Minnesota. In these couples where the man has an obvious defect in fertility, nearly ⅔ of the women also had some abnormality which would contribute to infertility. Couples signed informed consent forms accepting the offspring as their own. Donors were screened and were predominantly physicians or medical students.

One of ten marriages will not be blessed with children. At the present time more than half of these couples will benefit from medical consultation for infertility. Both partners and their sexual interaction are evaluated to determine causal factors and to outline a treatment plan. Tests and procedures, basal body temperatures and timed intercourse require tremendous commitment from these couples. Some of the procedures are painful and life patterns can be disrupted. In addition, surgery associated with rare but potentially serious complications is frequently indicated. Treatment seldom improves the physical health of the couple, so decisions regarding therapy have as the medically unique endpoint a life-giving rather than life-sparing goal. These couples weigh risks to themselves against an emotionally compelling desire to achieve the satisfactions of parenthood and the promise of hereditary immortality. Thus it is incumbent upon the physician to protect their welfare by providing an honest, objective assessment of the problem and proposing therapy which weighs medically acceptable and informed risk against potential benefits.

Tubal obstruction occurring as a result of infection or endometriosis of the pelvis continues to be a major cause of infertility. Surgery utilizing the operative microscope provided a significant technological advance for treatment of the problem. However, some tubes are irreparably damaged, and others exhibit abnormalities throughout their length. Removal of apparent obstructions does not restore normal function to the tubes. After microsurgery, intrauterine pregnancies are achieved at the risk of a significant increase in extrauterine or tubal pregnancies. Tubal pregnancies invariably terminate prematurely with rupture of blood vessels and intra-abdominal bleeding. Ruptured ectopic tubal pregnancies remain a leading cause of maternal death.

In vitro fertilization and embryo transfer (IVF-ET) were devised because of obstruction of the fallopian tubes. The birth in 1978 of the first baby conceived outside her mother's body startled both the public and the scientific community. A few biologists were skeptical that in vitro fertilization had indeed been achieved; some philosophers and theologians were alarmed by the apparent intrusion into the sanctity of human reproduction. During the ensuing years, repeated success has refuted scientific disclaimers, but the ethical issues promise to be a continuing subject for reflection.

At the October, 1982, international conference concerning in vitro fertilization and embryo transfer (IVF–ET), the results of the few groups actively performing the procedure were reported. It was estimated that over one hundred babies have been born after conception by IVF and ET. With the exception of one baby with a congenital heart defect, the newborn children have been normal. This compares favorably with the incidence of abnormalities observed in children conceived by sexual intercourse. Collaborative studies have found that 3% of all newborn children have significant congenital anomalies.

With a pregnancy rate of 10–20% per cycle, IVF-ET is currently about as efficient as the natural reproductive process, if one considers only the oocytes which are ovulated. In the natural reproductive process it has been estimated that 80% of the oocytes which are extruded from the ovary at the time of ovulation and fertilized will fail to reach fruition in the birth of a child. The majority of these will be spontaneously aborted after fertilization occurs.

Not only the fittest oocytes fail to survive; in addition, during the natural process of aging, the overwhelming majority of oocytes undergo atresia or die without being released from the ovary. By painstakingly examining serial sections of ovaries obtained after accidental death at various life stages, it has been estimated that approximately seven million (7,000,000) oocytes are present in both ovaries when the female embryo is still developing in the mother's uterus. By the age of 13, when ovulation usually begins, only 400,000 to 1,000,000 oocytes remain in the ovaries of a young woman. When the reproductive life span ceases at menopause (50 ± 7 years), few or no oocytes can be found in the ovary by microscopic examination.

One can assume that the ovulation of more than one oocyte during each cycle is a relatively infrequent occurrence, since natural twinning occurs in only one of 88 births. From the average reproductive life span of forty (40) years and a usual cycle duration of 24–36 days, one can deduce that only 480–500 oocytes (12 × 40) will be extruded from the paired ovaries at the time of ovulation during a women's entire reproductive life span. Thus, during each cycle after puberty, almost 800 oocytes die and are resorbed within the ovary for every oocyte which is exposed by natural processes to potential fertilization. By comparison with this natural attrition of germ plasm, the number of oocytes and pre-embryos which die as a result of failed IVF-ET are relatively few in number.

The actual performance of IVF-ET requires the utilization of several technological advances. To improve the efficiency of IVF–ET, multiple ovarian follicles are stimulated during a single cycle. The natural process of selecting a single dominant follicle for ovulation can be overridden by the administration of either natural or synthetic hormones. The former are two gonadotropins, FSH and LH, which are produced by the body in the pituitary gland. FSH and LH normally stimulate the ovarian follicles to increase the hormonal output of estrogen and progesterone and to mature the oocytes destined for ovulation. Human FSH/LH has been recovered from the urine of postmenopausal women and purified for pharmaceutical application. When these hormones are administered by injection, the number of oocytes ovulated or released from the ovary during each cycle is increased. Couples having sexual intercourse will have twins in 20% of the gonadotropin-stimulated cycles and, rarely, triplets, quadruplets and quintuplets.

As with most therapy, complications attend the administration of gonadotropins. The ovaries are significantly enlarged in 10% of cycles, and in less than 1% of cycles, fluid also leaks from the enlarged ovaries into the abdominal cavity. Together with the accompanying loss of fluid from the blood vessels, the enlarged ovaries and intra-abdominal fluid constitute the "hyperstimulation syndrome" which may lead to decreased blood flow to the kidneys, kidney failure, and death. Throughout the world, four women have died as a result of this complication. In addition, during early clinical trials, two women developed clots in major arteries supplying the head and the legs, and the results were catastrophic; arterial thrombi have not been reported subsequently. The hyperstimulation syndrome is partially avoided by monitoring the ovarian response to FSH/LH. The anatomic response of the ovary is monitored by observing changes in follicle size with ultrasonography.

The hormonal response of the ovary is monitored by serial measurements of the blood levels of estradiol (E_2).

After appropriate ovarian preparation, HCG (human chorionic gonadotropin) is injected to mimic the midcycle surge of LH. LH is the physiological stimulus which produces changes in ovarian hormone secretion and stimulates ovulation at midcycle. During cycles stimulated by gonadotropins, ovulation occurs approximately 36 hours after the administration of HCG.

For IVF-ET, the oocytes are retrieved from the follicle prior to ovulation. Since the ovary is located inside the pelvis, a surgical procedure utilizing the laparoscope is required. The patient is anesthetized with general anesthesia, a needle is inserted into the abdomen, and the abdominal cavity is inflated with carbon dioxide. A long sleeve, which is about one centimeter in diameter, containing a sharply pointed trochar is inserted into the abdomen just below the level of the umbilicus; the trochar is then removed, and the fiber optic laparoscope is introduced. The entire pelvis can be directly viewed with remarkable clarity through the laparoscope. Two sleeves are then similarly inserted into the lower abdomen, utilizing the laparoscope to view their placement. Grasping instruments, suction cannulae, biopsy forceps and cautery probes can be inserted and manipulated through the sleeves under direct visualization through the laparoscope. Oocytes are extracted from the prominent follicles in both ovaries by suction. The recovered oocytes are then placed in a flat dish filled with a nutrient medium and pre-incubated for several hours before exposing them to sperm. Laparoscopy and oocyte recovery are subject to surgical complications which include the risks of anesthesia, occasional penetration of blood vessels and bowel, and rarely death.

Viable spermatozoa are obtained from the crude semen sample by centrifugation in a nutrient medium. After a time, the motile and presumably viable sperm swim from the sperm pellet at the bottom of the tube into the overlying fluid medium. After a second centrifugation and migration, the motile sperm in the medium are counted and an appropriate number are added to the culture fluid containing the incubating oocytes. Only $500,000 - 1,000,000$ sperm are required for successful *in vitro* fertilization. Normal fertility potential in couples utilizing sexual intercourse requires the presence of 20 million motile sperm in the ejaculate. However, only a few of the many sperm deposited in the vagina are capable of reaching the distant site of fertilization in the fallopian tube. The attrition of abnormal spermatozoa in the female reproductive tract was previously thought to be a process of selection which could not be duplicated by centrifugation-migration techniques. This impression has been refuted by the birth of normal offspring after IVF-ET.

Fertilization takes place soon after the sperm are placed in the oocyte incubation medium. Approximately 30 hours after fertilization, the pre-embryo has divided into a two to four cell stage. At this time, without anesthesia, the cleaving pre-embryos are replaced in the mother's uterus. Implantation and further development of the pre-embryo occur in the mother's uterus. In Australia, embryos are being frozen for replacement during subsequent cycles when the maternal hormonal milieu may favor improved rates of implantation. Freezing oocytes for the purpose of delayed utilization also has the potential advantage of reducing the number of laparoscopic surgical procedures required to achieve pregnancy.

Following apparent fertilization, some oocytes do not divide, or they undergo changes in the nucleus or cytoplasm which indicate cell death. We do not plan to place these cells in the uterus unless the couple requests that we do so.

Early pregnancy is diagnosed by changes in estradiol, progesterone, and the appearance of the specific placental hormone, HCG, in the mother's blood. Only two pregnancies have implanted in the fallopian tube after IVF-ET. As pregnancy progresses, the developing fetus can be monitored with ultrasonography and also genetic and biochemical assays performed on the amniotic fluid.

Currently, successful pregnancies are achieved in approximately 20% of couples during each cycle of IVF-ET. The rate of single pregnancies increases when multiple pre-embryos are transferred back to the mother's uterus, but twins are unusual. The group from Australia with the most extensive experience in IVF-ET found that the pregnancy rate did not exceed 30% regardless of the number of pre-embryos replaced in the uterus. They suggest that the intrauterine environment provided by the mother is the rate-limiting factor which determines pregnancy rates. At the present time, when many other methodological variables have not been adequately evaluated, this hypothesis must be considered to be speculative.

The birth of normal offspring after IVF-ET is an achievement which has overshadowed the paucity of available information concerning the basic processes of fertilization and embryonic development in humans. Scientific speculation notwithstanding, it is obvious to students of biology that IVF is not a feat of technology which supersedes the natural reproductive process. Although fertilization takes place outside the body, the oocytes are obtained from the mother and the sperm is donated by the father. The various methodological steps result in merely approximating the environment of the male and female germ cells. Given the appropriate timing and environment, the germ cells proceed with the miracle of fertilization and the beginning of human life.

The remainder of this chapter will present data on the procedures for remedying the infertility which is traced to the male partner in a couple. These are: Artificial Insemination Homologous (AIH) in which the husband's sperm is used in the insemination, and Artificial Insemination Utilizing Donor Semen (AID).

Artificial Insemination Homologous

Artificial insemination homologous (AIH) is performed by placing the husband's sperm into the cervical canal or the endometrial cavity. The primary indications for performing AIH are: (1) poor semen quality due to a reduced sperm concentration or very small semen volume or, (2) reasonably good semen quality, but repeatedly deficient sperm present in the cervical mucus after intercourse. Other indications are relatively rare. For example, on occasion the male has difficulty maintaining an erection during intercourse, but is able to ejaculate with masturbation. Couples may be unable or unwilling to have intercourse with the frequency and timing which is adequate to achieve pregnancy. Sexual problems relating to intercourse such as vaginismus and dyspareunia may persist despite psychotherapy. The physician may also utilize AIH to treat couples in whom sperm antibodies have been demonstrated. Physicians have also used AIH to treat couples with no discernible abnormality after many years of "unexplained infertility."

AIH is performed two or three times at mid-cycle to bracket the time of ovulation. The time of apparent ovulation is projected from the range observed during previous cycles and is monitored during the treatment cycles. The most useful index of apparent ovulation is the basal body temperature which rises $0.5 - 1.0°$ Fahrenheit at about the

401

time of ovulation. Other indices of apparent ovulation include serial changes in the serum concentrations of estrogen (estradiol) and progesterone. Changes in cervical mucus parallel the fluctuations of these hormones. It has recently become possible to visualize growth and collapse of ovarian follicles with ultrasound.

The semen sample is obtained by masturbation into a sterile container. The whole semen sample may be used, or the semen may be "split" by ejaculating into two containers, with the expectation that the first portion of the ejaculate will contain a higher concentration of motile spermatozoa. For reasons which have not been defined, the seminal fluid of men with poor sperm concentration and motility impairs fertility potential. To remove the seminal fluid from AIH couples with oligospermia or apparent sperm antibodies, the semen sample is suspended in a nutrient medium and the mixture is centrifuged; the motile sperm migrate into the nutrient medium; then insemination is performed with a higher percentage of motile sperm in the much lower concentration of seminal fluid. Concentration of sperm by pooling centrifuged, frozen samples has not improved the likelihood of achieving pregnancy.

Insemination is performed by placing the whole semen, or a selected portion of the ejaculate, or the sperm suspended in nutrient medium into the cervical canal or uterine cavity. The sperm is taken up into a polyethylene catheter and syringe and placed at the site selected. Only small volumes are used to prevent expulsion upward through the uterine cavity and fallopian tubes into the peritoneal cavity. Semen which reaches the peritoneal cavity can cause a significant, but usually transient, inflammation of the pelvic lining which is termed chemical peritonitis. On rare occasions the instillation of the husband's semen above the level of the external cervical opening (os), where semen is normally deposited during intercourse, will carry bacteria into the pelvis and produce infection or bacterial peritonitis.

The objective results of AIH do little to recommend it. The exceptions are those infrequent instances in which the couple are unable or unwilling to deposit semen in the vagina with intercourse. The usual indication for performing AIH is poor semen quality. Only 15 to 20% of these couples will eventually achieve pregnancy. The number of couples who ultimately achieve pregnancy with AIH is no greater than is observed with sexual intercourse. However, the rate of pregnancies achieved per cycle is somewhat better for AIH than sexual intercourse, and this may be an important factor for the couple who elect to undergo the procedure.

Artificial Insemination Utilizing Donor Semen[1]

Insemination utilizing donor semen has been enthusiastically accepted as effective treatment for infertility attributed to the male, often in preference to the alternative of adoption. A program for performing AID was instituted at the University of Minnesota in 1971. We initially analyzed the indications for performing the procedure, the techniques utilized, and the results of treatment in 124 couples. The service was subsequently expanded, and presently more than 250 children who were conceived by AID have been delivered.

AID is usually performed for azoospermia and oligospermia. Azoospermia was present in 93 of 124 males. Oligospermia was present in 26 of 124 males; although 6 had recognized causes, 20 were of idiopathic origin. AID is also performed for genetic indications such as blood group incompatibility which has resulted in erythroblastosis fetalis, or other known genetic risk factors which the couple wish to minimize or obviate. AID is contraindicated when pregnancy would entail a significant risk to the mother.

Our goal is to place the child in a physically and psychologically healthy family with parents having a life expectancy of at least twenty years. The initial assessment of the couple desiring AID includes documentation of the deficiency in semen quality. The psychologic status of the couple is assessed during the interview. A comprehensive general medical history is obtained from the woman and she is given a complete physical examination.

Of the initial 124 females, only 48 (39%) had fertility potential which was assessed as being normal. Seventy-six (61%) had one or more defects which would impair fertility potential; 62 exhibited anatomic abnormalities of the cervix, uterus, tubes, or pelvis and 22 women had defects of ovulation. Thus, in the couple referred for the correction of an obvious defect in male fertility potential, nearly two-thirds of the women had some abnormality which would contribute to infertility.

During the initial interview, the couple is informed of the likelihood of success and the potential adverse effects of AID. In the original 124 females, the pregnancy rate was 13% per cycle; of those who continued through six cycles of insemination, 70% achieved pregnancy. The 19% incidence of spontaneous abortion in this group did not differ significantly from the rate reported in the general population. At the present time, more than 250 infants have been delivered. Only one child was reported to have a hereditary or developmental defect.

Potential complications are discussed and enumerated in the informed consent document. The most common adverse effect of AID is salpingitis, chemical or bacterial. Chemical salpingitis is due to direct peritoneal spill of semen resulting from the injection of an excessive volume of semen into the cervical canal; it is characterized by immediate pelvic pain which subsides within minutes to hours. Bacterial salpingitis occurred on two occasions following a total of 1377 inseminations performed during the years prior to 1976. Currently, each donor specimen is cultured for the gonococcus at the time of the insemination, and results are reported within 24 hours. In the 2100 semens utilized since 1976, the gonococcus was cultured from only one semen specimen; the female recipient was asymptomatic prior to initiating antibiotic therapy and did not develop clinical disease.

In addition to enumerating the potential complications, the informed consent outlines the responsibilities of the couple as future parents: "It is further agreed that from the moment of conception the husband hereby accepts the act as his own, and agrees: (a) That such child or children so produced are his own legitimate child or children and are the heirs of his body, and (b) That he hereby completely waives forever any right which he might have to disclaim such child or children as his own, and (c) That such child or children so produced are, and shall be considered to be, in all respects including descent or property, child or children of his body."

The donors have always been predominantly medical students or physicians. These men are preferable as donors because of their: (1) documented above-average intelligence, (2) ability to provide a valid genetic history, and (3) awareness of the need for confidentiality. The quality of the donor semen must be optimal but documentation of fertility is not required. The donor's blood type is obtained and his VDRL is obtained to screen for syphilis. When genetic indications exist, appropriate additional screening is preferred. Recently, we have been requiring the donors to sign a waiver in which they relinquish any claim to or jurisdiction over the offspring which result from artificial insemination. Recipients may request donor characteristics in addition

404

to body-build and skin, hair, and eye color. To respond to these requests, we are now tabulating donor participation in art, music, athletics and religion.

The procedure of donor insemination is performed six days of the week. The couple is advised to discontinue the use of douches and spermicidal lubricants such as KY jelly during the cycles in which AID is performed. The coordinator receives the donor semen at a site located away from the AID clinic. Inseminations are performed by physicians in gynecological specialty training who are supervised by the staff reproductive endocrinologists. The timing of apparent ovulation is deduced from the days of highest frequency in previous cycles, and usually two to four inseminations are planned on alternate days to span this interval. Ovulation-inducing agents such as Clomid are utilized for disorders of ovulation only. In a paired study of AID recipients with regular ovulatory cycles we found that treatment with Clomid did not increase the pregnancy rate.

The results of the AID program have been immensely gratifying. The parents are delighted with their healthy children.

Note

1. This discussion of AID is excerpted from the article, "Artificial Insemination Utilizing Donor Semen," by George E. Tagatz, M.D., Mark Gibson, M.D., Phillip Schiller, M.D., and Theodore Nagel, M.D., *Minnesota Medicine*, July, 1980, 539–541.

Chapter 16

Surrogate Parenting:
The Legal Aspects

The Honorable Carol Los Mansmann

Editorial Preface

AID offers the possibility of pregnancy to a couple by using donor sperm. Surrogate parenting uses artificial insemination to cause pregnancy in a woman who will surrender the child after birth to the sperm donor and his wife. The typical procedure for the latter involves three steps: 1) the execution of a contract prior to insemination, 2) the termination of parental rights by the surrogate mother after birth, and 3) the transfer of the child's custody to the natural father and adoption by his wife.

The contracts cover the terms of the arrangement including fees and expenses and the responsibilities of the parties to the contract. The Kentucky Attorney General has given an opinion that such contracts are illegal and unenforceable. Others feel they are legal but not necessarily enforceable in all provisions. These contracts may give rise to suits for custody of the child, for damages, or for negligence.

Implications arise in surrogate parenting from the constitutional right of due process, protecting the interests of the child, as well as of the mother and the father, and perhaps from equal protection of the law which would treat surrogate parenting on a par with AID. The legitimacy of the surrogate child and its inheritance rights also raise legal issues. It does not appear, however, that the surrogate parenting arrangement is in violation of existing law.

I. Introduction

It has been established that one out of every six couples in the United States cannot have children. This phenomenon exists for various reasons, but primarily because of infertility of the husband or wife. The alternatives for these couples is to have no children, or to adopt, or, as is becoming increasingly popular, artificial insemination.

A. Artificial Insemination by Donor (AID)

The "usual" form of artificial insemination is an arrangement whereby the woman is inseminated with the semen of an unrelated male donor who is usually anonymous. This arrangement is satisfactory where the husband is the individual who is infertile.

What if, however, the *wife* and not the husband is infertile? Studies have estimated that at least 2.5 million couples cannot have children because it is the *wife* who is infertile.[1] In that case, remaining childless or adopting children are obviously still alternatives but the "usual" form of artificial insemination is not.

B. Surrogate Motherhood

Another arrangement is now available. This arrangement is sometimes regarded as the counterpart or corollary to the usual form of artificial insemination. It is called "surrogate parenting" or "surrogate motherhood."

The terms, "surrogate parenting" or "surrogate motherhood," as used in this chapter, are not to be confused with other arrangements, such as foster parenting arrangements, where the courts occasionally use similar or identical terms.

Surrogate motherhood was not totally unheard of in the past. Indeed, the Bible even makes reference to it.

And Sarah said to Abram, "Behold now, the Lord has prevented me from bearing children; go in to my maid; it may be that I shall obtain children by her." And Abram harkened to the voice of Sarah.[2]

Surrogate motherhood uses the concept of artificial insemination but in a different way. In the usual form of artificial insemination by donor (AID), no one relinquishes the baby. All that is given up is the semen which is usually contributed by an anonymous donor, often university or medical students. The natural mother and her husband are the legal parents of the child at birth.

In surrogate motherhood, the husband's semen is injected into a fertile woman who is not his wife. This woman is the "surrogate" mother. The surrogate mother carries the child to term on behalf of the natural father and his wife and relinquishes the child to them upon birth.

In both of the above cases, one of the child's parents is related biologically and one is not. In the former situation, however, the natural mother carries the baby and the baby is the legally recognized offspring of the mother and her husband upon birth. In the latter situation, the baby is carried by someone outside of the marital relationship and relinquished to the natural father and his wife upon birth.

The surrogate mother may be married or single, although preliminary reports in the news media would indicate that the surrogate is usually married.

C. Reasons for Surrogate Parenting Arrangements

There are several reasons why a couple might choose surrogate parenting. Infertility of the wife has already been named. The wife may, while fertile, experience difficulty in successfully carrying a baby to term. Inheritable disease on the wife's side of the family may be another problem. Some have also suggested convenience as a reason. For example, a wife with a successful career may be unwilling to take a hiatus from her work to have a baby.

D. Alternatives to Surrogate Motherhood

Further, the alternatives to surrogate parenting are not particularly attractive to all childless couples. The average waiting period to adopt a child through an approved agency is now anywhere from three to seven years because of the diminishing number of children available for adoption. "Black market" adoptions, namely, those not conducted through an approved agency, are illegal under most state laws. In either case, the adopting couple lacks any biological tie to the child, unlike the situation with artificial insemination or surrogate motherhood.

E. Potential Legal Problems

Surrogate motherhood raises numerous potential legal problems: What if the surrogate mother decides to retain custody of the child after birth? Alternatively, what if the couple refuses to take the child as previously agreed? Does the surrogate mother's husband have rights with respect to the child? What if the natural father dies prior to the child's birth? What if the surrogate mother dies as a result of birth? What happens if the child is born with congenital defects? These questions are a sampling of the myriad legal issues posed by surrogate motherhood.

These questions will arise with greater frequency given the increasing popularity of surrogate parenting arrangements. Indeed, there are several organizations which have been established to match infertile couples with potential surrogate mothers. Among these organizations are Surrogate Parenting Associates, Inc. in Louisville, Kentucky, Surrogate Family Services, Inc. in Dearborn, Michigan, and Surrogate Mothering Ltd. in Philadelphia, Pennsylvania.

F. Typical Procedure

The most typical procedure with a surrogate parenting arrangement involves the execution of a contract prior to insemination, the termination of parental rights by the surrogate mother upon birth or after a waiting period through the execution of various documents, and transfer of custody to the natural father and adoption by the nonbiological mother.

Alternative procedures whereby legal rights may be identified include a notice of intent to claim paternity filed by the natural father during the period of pregnancy. He may also formally acknowledge paternity upon birth. A surrogate mother may formally acknowledge the natural father's paternity upon birth as well. Termination of parental rights by the surrogate mother may require court approval. In some cases, the natural father has joined the nonbiological mother in the adoption proceeding although this method appears more precautionary

409

than legally mandated, particularly where his name is on the birth certificate as the natural father.

II. Surrogate Parenting Contracts

Many of the legal questions and problems can be handled by the contract entered into between the parties. A surrogate motherhood arrangement is considered a contractual arrangement. The contract may be oral or in writing although, increasingly, the contracts are in writing and they are becoming lengthier so as to cover the many questions and contingencies which may arise.

A. Parties to the Contract

The parties who are typically parties to the surrogate motherhood contract are the surrogate mother, the natural father and often the surrogate mother's husband. The wife of the natural father is not generally a party to the contract since she has no legal role in the arrangement at this juncture.

B. Possible Terms

The most important provision in the contract is the agreement of the surrogate mother to bear and conceive the child and to terminate all of her parental rights at birth. Sometimes it is stated that she will not form or attempt to form a parent-child relationship with any child she conceives pursuant to the contract.

Some state statutes, usually those pertaining to adoption, provide for a waiting period before a mother can voluntarily terminate her parental rights. The surrogate and her husband may agree in the contract to execute all necessary documents on the last day of the waiting period. They may also agree to execute affidavits prior to the child's birth in order to have the natural father's name placed on the birth certificate.

The consent of the surrogate's husband to the surrogate arrangement is also generally included. Sometimes the contract will state that the surrogate's husband will not attempt to form any parent-child relationship with the child, that he will terminate any and all parental rights to the child and that he will do all acts necessary to rebut the presumption of paternity provided by most state statutes. The importance of this provision will be discussed below.

410

The payment of fees and expenses is usually provided by the contract. Expenses may include all medical expenses as well as travel and accommodation expenses. Most surrogate contracts also provide for the payment of a fee to the surrogate mother for her services. Such fees can range from $4,000 to $15,000. The legality of these "fee" clauses will also be discussed below.

In the event the surrogate mother miscarries or the child dies subsequent to a specified month of pregnancy, the parties may agree that the surrogate mother receive partial compensation. It may also be agreed that the natural father will pay any costs associated with the child's death.

The contract may require a surrogate mother to undergo certain medical tests at periodic intervals. Likewise, the agreement may restrict the surrogate's diet, activities, or use of drugs, alcohol and cigarettes.

It may be agreed that the child shall not be aborted unless, for example, the pregnancy is life-threatening to the surrogate mother. Given some of the Supreme Court's decisions concerning abortions, the enforceability of this provision is questionable, at least with respect to the first trimester of her pregnancy.[3] (The State cannot constitutionally require the consent of the father or the husband as a condition for abortion.)

The contract may require the natural father to pay the costs of a term life insurance policy payable to a beneficiary named by the surrogate. The contract may stipulate that the surrogate assumes all risks of pregnancy, including the risks of complications and death.

Another risk which the contract may cover is the death of the natural father before birth. The contract in this regard may require the natural father to make appropriate arrangements in his will for the support of the child and possibly make the unborn child a beneficiary of term life insurance payable in trust. It may also be agreed that the child could be offered for adoption, with the nonbiological mother possibly receiving the first option to adopt the child.

The parties may agree that if the child is born with congenital defects, the natural father may not refuse to assume legal responsibility for the child.

The parties may wish to agree that the contract shall be confidential. They may also agree that the surrogate and her husband will not attempt to contact the child or the natural father after custody is transferred.

The above matters are just a sample of the problems and contingencies which can be addressed in the parties' agreement.[4]

III. Legality and Enforceability

The next question, however, is whether a court will enforce a surrogate parenting contract. It is possible that the contracts are severable; that is, that some provisions are enforceable and some are not.

A. Black Market Adoption Laws

One legal barrier to the existence and enforcement of surrogate parenting contracts are state black market adoption laws. There is a basic public policy against the commercialization of adoption. In this regard, there are state laws which restrict or bar the adoption of children other than through a licensed agency.[5]

B. "Baby-Selling" Statutes

Even more pertinent to the surrogate parenting situation are the "baby-selling" statutes which basically prohibit the exchange of money for the adoption of a baby. Not only may these statutes render parts of all of surrogate parenting contracts illegal and/or unenforceable but also they may impose criminal penalties in the form of fines and imprisonment for their violation.[6]

At least one court, the Michigan Court of Appeals in the case of *Doe v. Kelley*,[7] has held that a fee for services could not be paid to a surrogate mother, even though the fee was provided by the parties' agreement. The Michigan court relied for its decision upon a Michigan statute which precludes the exchange of money or other consideration in connection with adoption and related proceedings. The court implied that the surrogate arrangement was otherwise permissible.[8]

The Kentucky Attorney General, however, has said that surrogate parenting contracts are illegal and unenforceable.[9] The Attorney General relied upon several Kentucky statutes and a strong state public policy against "baby-buying" to conclude that contracts between married couples and a surrogate mother for the artificial insemination of the surrogate by the husband, with the understanding that the surrogate will terminate her parental rights shortly after the child's birth, are illegal and unenforceable in Kentucky.

The Opinion of the Kentucky Attorney General has been subject to some criticism, particularly for its failure to distinguish between the legality and the enforceability of surrogate parenting contracts or, in other words, between void and voidable contracts.

An illegal contract is one type of unenforceable contract. Many other unenforceable contracts are merely voidable, which means that they are valid contracts but they can be voided or disavowed by a party prior to some action being taken.

It has been suggested that surrogate parenting contracts should be treated as legal but voidable custody contracts that are ratified, and therefore enforceable, upon entry of a final judgment by a court. That judgment terminates the parental rights of the surrogate mother.[10]

It should be noted that "baby-selling" statutes do not expressly address surrogate parenting arrangements. Therefore, there is an argument that they should not apply to such situations. Further, payment in a surrogate parenting arrangement is not made for adoption, which is the situation addressed by most "baby-selling" statutes, but rather for the services and expenses of the surrogate mother. Indeed, in many cases, the natural father may not be involved in an adoption process at all. It can also be argued that these statutes are constitutionally infirm as they apply to the surrogate parenting situation. The constitutional issues will be discussed below.

C. The Uniform Parentage Act

At least twenty states have statutes concerning the "anonymous donor" form of artificial insemination (AID). The primary purpose of most of these statutes is to legitimate the AID child.[11] Most of the statutes follow the Uniform Parentage Act (UPA) in whole or in part.

The UPA was drafted by a commission as a "model" act whose basic purpose was to eliminate the categorization of children as "legitimate" or "illegitimate" in an attempt to ensure the same rights to all children regardless of the marital status of their parents.

Of particular significance is Section 5 of the UPA which essentially provides that the husband of a woman who is artificially inseminated is treated in law as if he were the natural father. The donor of the semen for the artificial insemination is treated in law as if he were not the natural father.

While Section 5 clearly assists the "usual" AID situation, it creates serious legal problems for the surrogate parenting arrangement.

413

The state of Washington has recognized the potential problems raised by Section 5 and has therefore enacted it with important modifications. The Washington statute states in pertinent part that the donor of the semen is treated in law as if he were not the natural father *unless the donor and the woman agree in writing that the donor shall be the father.*[12]

Nonetheless, a number of states have enacted Section 5 intact or with only minor modifications.[13]

IV. Remedies for Breach of Agreement

A. Equitable Relief

Assuming *arguendo* that surrogate parenting contracts are enforceable, there are limitations to the remedies which may be obtained. For example, the availability of equitable relief, as distinguished from an action at law for damages, is questionable.

A party may wish to sue for specific performance in order to force the other party to perform his or her part of the bargain. The most obvious example would be that the natural father may want to force the surrogate mother to relinquish the child should she refuse after the child is born. A court, however, is unlikely to grant such relief both because of constitutional problems, namely, the Thirteenth Amendment prohibition against involuntary servitude and because of other considerations such as the difficulty of court supervision. The same problems would inhere in other forms of equitable relief such as an injunction. Injunction relief might be desirable to force the surrogate mother to receive adequate care. Again, however, it is unlikely that this remedy would be granted.[14]

B. Custody Suits

Should the surrogate mother refuse to surrender the child, the natural father could sue for custody. The surrogate mother could also institute the same suit if she wished to retrieve the child from the father.

In custody suits, the prevailing consideration in most jurisdictions is that of the child's "best interests."[15] This consideration usually requires an inquiry into the fitness of each parent. While former laws heavily favored the mother in custody suits, this situation is changing and courts will tend now, more than ever, to evaluate each parent equally.

The natural father, as a threshold matter, must prove his paternity. In this regard, the contract itself may be evidence of paternity. Even after custody is determined, other questions common to all custody suits, such as support and visitation rights, will have to be addressed.

C. Contract Actions

Legal remedies in contract and possibly also in tort are available to a party injured by another's breach of the contract. For example, the surrogate mother may sue in contract for her expenses and promised fee. The natural father may sue for restitution of monies paid to the surrogate if she fails to perform.

The contract may contain a liquidated damages clause to provide for the event that either party fails to perform his or her part of the agreement. Liquidated damages is an amount which the parties agree is a reasonable estimation of the damages owing to one in the event of a breach by the other. A liquidated damages clause, however, may not be enforceable if the amount specified in the provision is deemed to be a penalty rather than an accurate reflection of a party's consequential damages.

D. Tort Actions

It is also possible that either party may sue in tort for damages. For instance, the natural father may sue for negligence if the surrogate mother negligently causes harm to the fetus during pregnancy. Alternatively, either party may wish to maintain an action for the intentional infliction of emotional distress in certain circumstances. [16]

V. Constitutional Implications

The constitutional dimensions of the legal issues inherent in the surrogate motherhood situation must not be overlooked. All laws must be scrutinized in light of constitutional protections. Specifically, the due process clauses of the Fifth and Fourteenth Amendments and the equal protection clause of the Fourteenth Amendment are implicated.

A. Due Process

The requirement of substantive due process applies to both the federal and the state governments. Usually, a balancing test is used to determine the constitutionality of a particular governmental restriction. The stringency of the test will depend upon the nature of the right at issue.

At minimum, a government regulation must be rationally related to a constitutionally permissible purpose. [17]

A more stringent showing is required, however, where the regulation infringes on a right which is deemed "fundamental." In that case, the regulation may be justified only by a compelling state interest. Further, the statute must be narrowly drawn to protect only that legitimate state interest. (See, for example, *Roe v. Wade,* involving the right to an abortion). [18]

The right of privacy (or "zones of privacy") is considered to be a fundamental right which is implied in various provisions of the Constitution. [19] Certain personal rights are considered to be included in the right of privacy. These rights include the right of marital privacy, *Loving v. Virginia,* [20] the right of procreation, *Skinner v. Oklahoma,* [21] and the right to bear or not to bear a child, *Eisenstadt v. Baird.* [22] It is the right enunciated by the U.S. Supreme Court in *Eisenstadt* which probably states the strongest case for the constitutional protection of surrogate parenting.

Even with fundamental rights such as the right to bear a child, there is a point at which the government's interests become sufficiently compelling so as to sustain some regulation. *See, e.g., Roe v. Wade,* [18] as revised by *Planned Parenthood of Central Missouri v. Danforth.* [3] (With regard to abortion, the state's interests in the mother's health is sufficiently compelling during even the first trimester of pregnancy to justify reasonable state regulation related to the preservation and protection of maternal health. The state's interest in preserving life is sufficiently compelling at the moment of viability as to permit the state's proscription of abortion during that period, except when necessary to preserve the life or health of the mother).

With surrogate motherhood, there are several governmental interests involved aside from those related to the health of the mother or the life of the unborn child. For example, the government arguably has an interest in protecting the natural mother from coercive pressure to surrender the child. It is an interesting question whether the government also has an interest in protecting the parental rights of the natural father.

An even stronger governmental interest is that of protecting and promoting the "best interests" of the child.

Given the possible state interests involved, there is a strong argument that surrogate parenting is permissible with some governmental regulation in those areas where its interests are compelling. As the converse to that, the government can regulate, without totally prohibiting, surrogate parenting.[23] For instance, the state could arguably mandate a five-day waiting period after birth before the surrogate mother voluntarily terminates her parental rights.

In summary, the fundamental rights of the surrogate mother and those of the couple (or at least the natural father) would be balanced against the interests of the state. The likely result is that of reasonable state regulation which would protect the natural mother and the child, but which would not categorically prohibit surrogate parenting arrangements.

B. Equal Protection

The equal protection clause of the Fourteenth Amendment may also be implicated by surrogate parenting arrangements. The concept of equal protection applies through the Fourteenth Amendment to the states. Under this clause, the states must afford equal treatment to those who are "similarly situated."

Usually the classification employed by the state need only have a rational connection to the objectives of the legislation. Where, however, a "suspect classification" or a "fundamental right" is involved, the state action is examined with "strict scrutiny." In this inquiry, the classification must be necessary to satisfy a compelling state interest.[24] The state must also use the least burdensome means of achieving its interests.[25]

The case law seems to indicate that fundamental rights are indeed implicated in a surrogate parenting arrangement. Therefore, if the "usual" form of artificial insemination, where the husband is infertile, is considered legal, a state prohibition against surrogate parenting, where the wife is infertile, is arguably a denial of equal protection.

417

Again, however, these fundamental rights are not absolute and, as with substantive due process, the state may reasonably regulate where its interests are compelling.

VI. Other Issues

A. Legitimacy

In the discussion of possible contractual terms of a surrogate parenting contract, the consent of the surrogate's husband was mentioned. His consent is important because a presumption of legitimacy generally attaches to children born within the marriage. The child is presumed legitimate as to that couple. The surrogate husband would automatically be responsible legally for the care and support of the child.

This presumption may create problems for surrogate parenting arrangements since the individuals involved theoretically do not wish the surrogate child to be considered legitimate as to the surrogate mother and her husband. This presumption of legitimacy as to the "surrogate couple," however, arguably can be rebutted by the contract between the parties.

As already mentioned, some state statutes extend the presumption of legitimacy to AID children, deeming them in law to be children of the woman who is artificially inseminated and her husband. Indeed, some of the statutes do not seem to create rebuttable presumptions but rather appear to establish conclusive presumptions. Under these circumstances, the contract may not be sufficient to handle the legitimacy problem. Alternatively, however, the statutes may encounter constitutional problems as applied to surrogate parenting situations in light of the discussion above. Assuming that they are applicable to surrogate parenting arrangements, the artificial insemination statutes may at least be unconstitutional to the extent they establish a conclusive presumption of legitimacy as to a surrogate mother and her husband.[26]

B. Inheritance Rights

The presumption of legitimacy is also important in terms of the child's inheritance rights.

A surrogate child has the legal right to inherit from the surrogate mother until the child is adopted by the wife of the natural father. Once

418

that occurs, the child's inheritance rights through its natural mother are extinguished and its inheritance rights exist only through its adoptive mother. The child also has inheritance rights with regard to the husband of the surrogate mother if the presumption of legitimacy as to the surrogate couple is unrebutted.

C. Adultery

Another issue, although probably one with little significance today, is that of adultery. Adultery generally requires some penetration of a female by the male sex organ.

In 1921, a Canadian court held that artificial insemination constituted adultery because reproductive powers and facilities had been voluntarily surrendered to another.[27] A more recent American case, however, probably represents the modern view. In *People v. Sorenson*,[28] the court said that to suggest that artificial insemination involves an illicit affair or the sexual intercourse normally associated with adultery is "patently absurd."

VII. Conclusion

Surrogate motherhood is as controversial an issue as abortion, if not more so. As the practice becomes more prevalent and salient, the involvement of the courts and the legislature will increase.

As with abortion regulation, the states have certain interests at stake which will probably be deemed "compelling" and therefore, subject to constitutional protection. As with abortion, however, the use of a balancing test will require constitutional protection of the rights of all of the individual parties involved: the child, the natural/surrogate mother and her husband and the natural father and his wife, the adoptive mother.

The enforceability of specific provisions in surrogate parenting contracts, or the remedies for the breach thereof, will vary depending upon the provision and the relief sought. To the extent, however, that the constitutional analysis for abortion and other similar issues applies, it appears that the surrogate parenting arrangement, in general, is not violative of existing law.

Notes

1. *Pittsburgh Post-Gazette*, Dec. 13, 1982, pp. 1 & 2.
2. Gen. 16:2 (Revised Standard Version).
3. See *Planned Parenthood of Central Missouri v. Danforth*, 428 U.S. 52, 69 (1976).
4. See Brophy, "A Surrogate Mother Contract to Bear a Child," *Journal of Family Law*, 20, (Jan. 1982) 263–291.
5. See Mady, "Surrogate Mothers: The Legal Issues," *American Journal of Law and Medicine*, 7 (Fall 1981) 323–52.
6. *Ibid.*
7. 106 Mich. App. 169 (1981).
8. See Jabro, "Surrogate Motherhood: The Outer Limits of Protected Conduct," Det. C. L. Rev., Winter, 1981, 1131–46.
9. *Ky. Op. Att'y Gen.*, 81–118 (1981).
10. Phillips and Phillips, "In Defense of Surrogate Parenting," Ky. L. J., 69, (Fall 1980–81), 877–931.
11. Cf. *Conn. Gen. Stat.* Sec. 45–69(f) (Supp. 1981).
12. *Wash. Rev. Code Ann.* Sec. 26–26.050(2).
13. Cf. *Ca. Civ. Code*, Sec. 7005 (West Supp. 1980).
14. Townsend, "Surrogate Mother Agreements: Contemporary Legal Aspects of a Biblical Notion," *U. Rich. L. Rev.*, 16, (Winter, 1982), 467–83; Black, "Legal Problems of Surrogate Motherhood," *New England Law Review*, 16 (Summer, 1981), 373–95.
15. Erickson, "Contracts to Bear a Child," *Cal. L. Rev.*, 66 (1978), 611–22.
16. See references in note 14.
17. *Maher v. Roe*, 432 U.S. 464, 478 (1977).
18. 410 U.S. 113, 155 (1973).
19. *See Stanley v. Georgia*, 394 U.S. 557, 564 (1969) (First Amendment); *Terry v. Ohio*, 392 U.S. 1, 8–9 (1968) (Fourth and Fifth Amendments); *Griswold v. Connecticut*, 381 U.S. 479, 486 (1965) (Ninth Amendment); *Meyer v. Nebraska*, 262 U.S. 390, 399 (1923) (Fourteenth Amendment).
20. 388 U.S. 1 (1967).
21. 316 U.S. 535 (1942).
22. 405 U.S. 438, 453 (1971).
23. See reference in note 18.
24. See *Skinner v. Oklahoma*, 316 U.S. at 535.
25. See *Dunn v. Blumstein*, 405 U.S. 330 (1972).
26. See Van Hoften, "Surrogate Motherhood in California: Legislative Proposals," *San Diego Law Review*, 18 (March, 1981), 341–85.
27. *Oxford v. Oxford*, 58 D. L. R. 251 (1921).
28. 68 Cal. 2d 280, 437 P. 2d495, 66 Cal. Rpts. 7 (1968).

Chapter 17

Christian Marriage and Reproductive Technologies

Francis G. Morrisey, OMI

Editorial Preface

The new Code of Canon Law of the Church provides a fresh perspective from which to evaluate reproductive technologies. It describes marriage as a "covenant" constituting a partnership of the whole of life and ordered to the good of the spouses and the generation and education of children. The phrase "good of the spouses" includes conjugal love and mutual assistance. The couple exchange the right to connatural conjugal acts but do not have a right to children, rather children are the "supreme gift of marriage," according to Vatican II.

To consider the good of the child in marriage morality one begins with the means of having children and the means of avoiding them. Besides the traditional means of having children by birth or adoption, science has now introduced artificial insemination, in vitro fertilization, and embryo transfer.

Magisterial teaching has opposed contraception and sterilization. A Rota decision of 1968 indicates that the intention to avoid children by these means or

421

by abortion renders a marriage null. Pope John Paul II has reiterated Church teaching on birth control and condemned experimental manipulations of the human embryo.

In evaluating new technologies of human reproduction one should begin with the bonum prolis *(the child as a good). Perfecting a technique like surrogate parenthood, which is now occuring, does not prevent the use of such a technique by the rich to exploit the poor or by the State to provide services to the poor. The most basic objection to new reproductive technologies lies in the fact that the child as a good is not considered primarily as a gift, but as the object of a right.*

Applications of the canonical teaching about marriage begin with marriage preparation, followed by a personalist approach to parenthood and openness to children. This new personalist approach as found in the new Code must be used to provide authentic solutions to the new scientific techniques of human reproduction.

The topic "Christian Marriage and Reproductive Technologies"* is indeed a difficult one. It could be approached from many perspectives: that of pure science, that of systematic theology, that of medical ethics, to mention but three aspects of the problem.

However, I will treat of it from a different viewpoint, that of the new law of the Catholic Church. It would be easy to state simply that the new law does not speak of reproductive technologies, although it treats of Christian marriage, and then simply leave the matter at that. But this would, in part, be evading the issue since the new law, an "instrument of grace" to use Paul VI's words, has as one of its purposes "to deepen the work of the Spirit" in the hearts of humanity.[1]

The Spirit guides the Church and guides creation according to a providential plan, the overall details of which are not readily available to us at any given moment. Rather, we are expected to read the "signs of the times" to see in what way human intelligence can be placed at the service of creation. The introductory paragraphs of *Gaudium et Spes* outline this challenge in very descriptive terms: "We must recognize and understand the world in which we live, its expectations, its long-ings, and its often dramatic characteristics . . . Profound and rapid changes are spreading by degrees around the whole world . . . while man extends his power in every direction, he does not always succeed in subjecting it to his own welfare . . . Never before today has man been so keenly aware of freedom, yet at the same time, new forms of social and psychological slavery make their appearance."[2]

These words, written nearly twenty years ago, are even truer today. A reflexion on their consequences leads us to a greater awareness of the responsibilities placed on leaders of the People of God to help humanity find its course and to be for all "a light of the nations."

The revised Code of Canon Law, signed by Pope John Paul II on January 25, 1983, and promulgated by the Apostolic Constitution *Sacrae Disciplinae Leges* should not be expected to provide legal answers to questions which often evade the legal sphere. However, its teaching and insights provide us with a framework within which, from a legal perspective, we can evaluate certain phenomena and practices which the Church has to face.

I have no personal expertise whatever — and regrettably so — in the area of medical ethics, and will have to rely on data and conclusions presented by others in order to put together some type of synthesis between law and science in the area which concerns us. Hopefully, though, the views of people conversant with different disciplines will converge and give the People of God a better opportunity to reflect on data regarding urgent situations facing them.

It is interesting to note at the outset two dimensions in the presentation of the problem of reproductive technologies and Christian marriage: on the one hand, there are those who refuse to procreate, and on the other, those who are desperately trying to have children. Both of these expressions are sides of the same coin which expresses humanity's desire to people the earth and to control creation. Since law is usually not situated in the extremes, but rather tries to steer a middle course, we shall first of all examine the contents of the new legislation on Christian marriage, then proceed to an overview of the ways in which the teaching on the ends of marriage is applied, to come eventually to some practical applications.

I. The Ends of Marriage in the New Canonical Legislation

a. The Nature of Marriage

The Second Vatican Council defined Christian marriage in terms of a "covenant" between two baptized persons.[3] By introducing this notion of covenant into the Church's legislation, Pope John Paul II not

423

only retained the Council's thrust and insight, but also provided canonists with a new and providential means to apply the matrimonial legislation to the needs of the times.

Canon 1055 of the new Code, in paragraph 1, reads as follows:

> The matrimonial covenant, by which a man and a woman constitute between themselves a partnership of the whole of life, ordered by its natural purpose to the good of the spouses and the generation and education of children, has been raised by Christ the Lord to the dignity of a sacrament when it is celebrated between baptized persons.[4]

It is interesting to note that this canon was the object of very serious debate and that the text underwent numerous revisions before it was promulgated in its present form.

We could state immediately that the notion of covenant incorporated into the law has two important legal dimensions: a marriage takes place "in the Lord", and the couple must be capable of fulfilling that which they assumed. Consequently, a Christian marriage must first take into consideration the faith dimension of the act. For Catholics, the faith dimension will be enlightened by the teachings of the Magisterium, although we must recognize that, at times, the teachings of the Church on marriage have little direct import on the decision of the couple and the absence of faith seems even to jeopardize the validity of the covenant.[5]

Then, in addition to being celebrated "in the Lord", a Christian marriage must also be able to express what it is: a sign of the lasting unity between Christ and His Church. Consequently, it is not surprising to note that the new law specifies that a person must be capable of assuming the essential obligations of marriage.

The new Code wisely avoids stating what these obligations are; rather, the matter is left to jurisprudence and canonical practice.[6] However, it has been traditional in the Church to teach that the aptitude for connatural conjugal acts, apt by their nature to provide for the generation of children, is one of the essential elements of marriage. From this, it is easy to deduce the obligation which this element implies.

We have recently seen in the press dramatic examples of cases where marriages were refused (at least temporarily) because of the incapacity of one of the parties to perform the conjugal act.

Among other things, the new canon law provides in canon 1061 that the consummation of marriage — by which one of the essential obligations can be fulfilled — must take place *humano modo*, that is, it must be fully a human act, not simply a series of biological or physical functions. In no way does the law see the unitive act of man and woman as a simple technology. The words *humano modo* were inserted after a special consultation with the bishops of the world[7] and portray the personalist philosophy which pervades so much of the new marriage legislation and which gives us a clue to an answer to the ethical and legal questions raised by new technologies.

After mentioning that marriage is a covenant, canon 1055 states that its object is the establishment of a "partnership of the whole of life". The new law goes far beyond the 1917 legislation which defined the object of matrimonial consent in terms of the "ius in corpus," the exchange of rights over the body for acts apt of their nature for the generation of children. The 1983 legislation, in the light of the conciliar teaching and the guidelines of *Humanae Vitae*, implies that marriage is to be a total gift of self to the other partner, a gift characterized by oblative love which excludes undue self-seeking and personal satisfaction.[8]

This covenant — which begins by a contract, but which goes far beyond a simple human agreement — has a number of purposes or ends. These are radically changed in the new law and merit particular study.

b. The Ends of Marriage

i. The good of the spouses

In the 1917 Code, the ends of marriage were presented in terms of primary and secondary ends. The secondary end was mutual assistance and remedy to concupiscence. But, since the Council took such pains to avoid speaking of primary and secondary ends,[9] the new Code had no choice but to reflect this conciliar thought, and thus no mention is made of a hierarchy of purposes.

However, given the rest of the teaching on marriage as a covenant and the insistence on its personalistic dimensions, it would not have been fitting to continue speaking in terms of "remedy to concupiscence". Many bishops and canonists instead wanted a reference to

425

conjugal love in the text.[10] However, conjugal love is not a juridical element; furthermore, it is not a necessary prerequisite to marriage because in some cultures where marriages are arranged, a young couple marries and then learns to fall in love.

The Code Commission decided that the best way to describe these elements of mutual assistance and conjugal love would be to speak of the "good of the spouses" — the "*bonum coniugum*," an expression used in *Gaudium et Spes*, #48. Thus, in addition to the three traditional goods of marriage — children, fidelity, indissolubility — there is now a fourth "bonum", the good of the spouses. Such a notion is necessarily subjective, and the Code Commission did not wish to elaborate further on it; therefore, it is left to jurisprudence to determine what would constitute the good of the spouses in a given culture.[11]

We will have to be careful in applying this expression to avoid an approach that would be entirely subjective, abstracting from any objective good. Otherwise, some might be inclined to state that whatever constitutes the good of the spouses — here and now — would conform to the nature of Christian marriage. It is evident that such was not the Council's intention, nor that of the Code Commission.

Yet, the words do provide us with a means of evaluating certain developments relating to the good of the spouses. If it can be shown that such are truly for their good as a whole — and not simply for Peter and Mary at this moment — it will be difficult to state that they are contrary to the "*bonum coniugum*" and to the nature of Christian marriage.

In passing, it could be noted that canon 1056 speaks explicitly about the unity and the indissolubility of marriage as two of its essential properties. These elements, along with the two ends of marriage, provide the four aspects or "*bona*" upon which a true Christian marriage is to be evaluated.

ii. The child as a good

The traditional primary end of marriage has been the generation and the education of children. This has also recently been understood in some Church court decisions as even including the right to Catholic education of children.[12]

Pius XII expressed the teaching of the Church in this matter in succinct terms which imply that the right to connatural conjugal acts suffers no interruption in time or space. This, of course, does not imply the uninterrupted use of the right, but refers to its very existence, without which the object of consent would be deficient.[13]

The law itself says nothing about the means taken to provide for the existence of this end. An evaluation of such would have to take place within the context of general Church teaching.

A study of canon 1055 reveals that it is not necessary for both ends of marriage to co-exist in order for it to be a Christian marriage. Otherwise, we would not be able to authorize the union of those who had passed the age of child-bearing. What is important in law is that neither end be excluded by a positive act of the will.[14]

Thus, we cannot speak in terms of a right to children. Those who argue in such terms are not within the scope of Church law. Indeed, Vatican II, in *Gaudium et Spes*, speaks of children as being the "supreme gift of marriage" and there is no right to a gift.

c. Openness to Children and the Validity of Marriage

Many cases have come before the Roman Rota and other courts where the object under discussion was the alleged nullity of marriage because of an intention on the part of one or both parties to exclude the *"bonum prolis"* (the child as a good).

In recent years, jurisprudence has distinguished two aspects of this ground: the right to conjugal acts, the right to the results of the conjugal act.

The right to conjugal acts presupposes that the act between the spouses is performed in a connatural way. There seems to be little in current teaching and jurisprudence which prohibits the use of certain means of artificial insemination to help a couple unite in marriage, provided that both parties perform the act in a normal way and the semen is then "assisted" in its natural course. As Pius XII stated, "One does not necessarily proscribe the use of certain artificial methods intended simply either to facilitate the natural act or enable the natural act, effected in a normal manner, to attain its end."[15]

The cases presented to the Rota were done so in terms of *exclusion* of the good of children, while the techniques we have been asked to consider are generally oriented in the other direction: towards the generation of offspring.

The common jurisprudence is centered on the intentions of the parties at the time of the union. Were they to exclude the *right* to connatural conjugal acts for a certain period — for instance, until a University degree is obtained, or until the down payment on a home is secured — then the validity of the marriage is jeopardized, at least until such time as the parties consent to recognize the existence of the right.

The second aspect of this ground of nullity is the right to the results of the conjugal act. A couple could consent to the exchange of connatural conjugal acts, but could then have recourse to means that would terminate the results of such acts were a pregnancy to occur. Thus, the intention at the time of marriage to terminate any pregnancies by abortion would also exclude the object of consent itself. Consequently, the marriage would be invalid.

As can be seen from this summary overview of the matter, the jurisprudence of the Church and its legislation (both old and new) carries a special interest for children in Christian marriage. Again, there is nothing in the law which states — or could state — that a couple must have children for marriage to be considered valid (although such an attitude, abstracting from an ecclesial context, is said to exist in parts of the world where a marriage is not considered to be such until a child is born). But, if a child is conceived in a natural way (and indeed in a way that is not considered natural), the spouses must have the intention to let it come to term.

There would appear, then, to be four canons in the new Code which have a bearing on the use of new reproductive technologies, but only in an indirect way:
1) canon 1055 on the nature of marriage,
2) canon 1061 on the notion of consummation (*"humano modo"*),
3) canon 1101 on the exclusion of any of the essential properties of marriage,
4) canon 1398 on abortion where the law maintains an excommunication against those who procure such.

It is only through official pronouncements and the jurisprudence of the Church courts that in the years ahead we will be able to ascertain:
1) what constitutes the *"bonum coniugum"* in today's context,
2) what constitutes the *"humano modo"* dimension of marital consummation,
3) what will be necessary for the *"bonum prolis"* in the light of the new legislation,
4) what will constitute an exclusion of the *"bonum prolis"* on the part of the spouses.

II. The Means of Procuring The Child As A Good

Even to consider briefly the various means available to couples to have children implies that we distinguish between the traditional forms and the newer means used to provide for birth. An overview of the more commonly used means would be in order at this time.

a. The Means of Having Children

i. Traditional forms

Three standard forms have been employed by parents who wish to share their love and existence with others. The first and most common one is the natural generation of children.

However, because of the fact that such a natural generation cannot always occur when wanted, either because of impotence, sterility or physical disability on the part of one or both spouses, it is considered necessary to have recourse to other means to provide for children.

At times, a simple surgical procedure can correct a malfunctioning organ and thus remedy the situation. But, rather often, such is not the case. The future parents must then turn elsewhere.

The usual practice is for them to adopt children if they are unable to have any on their own. It is interesting to note that the new law provides for newer situations regarding adoption by having a canon inserted on the manner in which the names of adopted children are to be inscribed in the baptismal registers.[16]

In addition to formal adoption, the use of foster homes is also a means used by some couples to share what they have with others. I am not aware of any canon in the new Code that treats directly of such cases, although many canons speak of "those taking the place of parents" and the situation of foster homes could be included under this heading.

ii. Newer forms

Three major means seem to be acquiring greater acceptance by the general public when it comes to promoting the birth of children, although many of these are still in an experimental stage: artificial insemination, *in vitro* fertilization, surrogate parenthood. The last two means are not readily available to everyone.

Two forms of artificial insemination are generally considered: AIH and AID (depending on whether the semen is supplied by the husband or by a donor.)

Three major techniques are being considered in cases of *in vitro* fertilization: a) fertilization takes place *without* subsequent transfer of the embryo to the uterus of a female (this does not result in birth); b) *in vitro* fertilization followed by embryo transfer; c) embryo transfer following fertilization by mating or artificial insemination. It is the second method which is generally referred to when there is question of having children.

Two situations are generally considered under the heading of surrogate parenthood. The first case is generally understood to mean that the fertilized ovum would be placed for gestation in the womb of another woman. The second, also known as "host motherhood," consists in having a woman impregnated by artificial insemination from a donor not her husband and in her giving the baby to the father and his wife.

Experiments on animals have been successful in the first case; I am not aware that such have been successfully carried out with humans, although it is quite possible that such is the case.

It is easy to see that once the basic techniques have been perfected, there will be many variations on the theme with special emphasis placed on the quality of the child, on physical and intellectual traits, family antecedents, and so forth. Such forms of genetic engineering or manipulation are common today with animals. Even the cloning of humans is on the horizon.

b. The means of avoiding children

It is significant that while certain couples are trying desperately to have a child, others are trying equally desperately to avoid conception or birth. In fact, it would appear that in our countries the latter are in the majority. The Church has already made its mind known on such matters as artificial birth control (by whatever method is used — from onanism to medical and pharmaceutical products). Some methods of regulation of births are considered natural and are encouraged (such as forms of Natural Family Planning). We are all familiar with the literature on both aspects.

In addition, there is the radical "solution" of abortion in its various facets which can terminate the life of a child that has been conceived.

What is important for us from a law perspective is to evaluate the various means used for and against the conception of children in their relationship to ecclesial legislation. We shall do so in the light of official Church teaching and in the perspective of some commonly raised questions.

c. Evaluation of the Means

i. Magisterial pronouncements

Pius XI

It is with Pius XI that we find a particular preoccupation with medico-moral issues. Before that time, the statements of Popes and bishops did not address themselves directly to particular methods and means (with the exception of abortion), but rather remained at a more general level.

In *Casti Connubii*, Pius XI condemned contraception by stating that

> Any use of marriage, whatever, in the exercise of which the act is deprived through human industry of its natural power of procreating life, violates the law of God and of nature, and those who commit anything of this kind are marked with the stain of grave sin. [17]

In the same encyclical, he condemned eugenic methods whereby only well-formed children and those who met certain criteria would be allowed to be born. [18]

Pius XII

In his famous address to Italian midwives in 1951, Pius XII outlined general principles which still form the basis of contemporary Church teaching.

> Matrimony obliges to a state of life, which, while carrying with it certain rights, also imposes the fulfillment of a positive work concerning the state of life itself . . . On partners who make use of matrimony by the specific act of their state, nature and the Creator impose the function of

431

providing for the conservation of the human race. This is the characteristic service from which their state of life derives its peculiar value, the *bonum prolis*.[19]

In an earlier address on September 29, 1949, he condemned forms of artificial insemination, stating that "in marriage, with the use of an active element from a third person, [it] is equally immoral and as such is to be rejected summarily. Only marriage partners have mutual rights over their bodies for the procreation of new life, and these rights are exclusive, non transferable and inalienable."[20]

The Sacred Roman Rota

A celebrated decision by Cardinal Felici, October 22, 1957, recalls the teaching of the Church regarding the openness to children.[21] A person who, at the time of consent, would limit marriage rights to "*si et quando*" — if and when — he felt like it, would be placing a limitation on the right and the marriage would be invalid. The Church courts have retained this expression in subsequent jurisprudence.

A further decision by Bejan, March 30, 1968, spells out the conditions against the *bonum prolis* that would render a marriage null: "If you avoid the generation of a child, provided you kill the child or procure an abortion, on condition that you take potions to prevent generation, provided you use means against fecundation, or, provided that after marriage you undergo an operation to become perpetually sterile."[22]

The Sacred Congregation for the Doctrine of Faith

On March 13, 1975, the Sacred Congregation for the Doctrine of Faith upheld the Church's stand on sterilization: "Sterility intended in itself is not oriented to the integral good of the person as rightly pursued."[23] This teaching was made explicit by the NCCB Administrative Board: "Any sterilization which of itself, that is, of its own nature and condition, has the sole immediate effect of rendering the generative faculty incapable of procreation, is completely forbidden."[24]

On December 29, 1975, the same Sacred Congregation for the Doctrine of Faith issued a further declaration on sexual ethics, reaffirming the enduring validity of the Church's teachings on sexual morality. Based in part on the clear and concise teaching of Vatican II,[25] the document states that the principal criterion of the morality of the sexual act is the following: respect for its finality ensures the moral goodness of the sexual acts.[26] The document also states that "facts do not constitute a criterion for judging the moral value of human acts."[27]

These and similar declarations do not apply directly to the reproductive techniques we are asked to consider, but the principles outlined therein can be readily applied to other moral situations, especially when considered in relation with the law of the Church.

Pope John Paul II

Pope John Paul II has spoken on numerous occasions about the value of human life and its protection. On January 15, 1981, he spoke about natural family planning and artificial birth control. At that time he said: "Perhaps the most urgent need today is to develop an authentic philosophy of life and of the transmission of life, considered precisely as 'pro-creation,' that is, as discovering and collaborating with the design of God the Creator."[28]

This form of "pro-creation" with God is a theme underlying his writings. It takes on different aspects, but usually centers on the human person as a whole.

For instance, in an address to the Pontifical Academy of Science, October 23, 1982, Pope John Paul II outlined the acceptable limits of biological research and stressed the same principle. Speaking first in positive terms of the contribution of science to the development of personal well-being, he stated: "I have no reason to be apprehensive for those experiments in biology that are performed by scientists who, like you, have a profound respect for the human person, since I am sure that they will contribute to the integral well-being of man."[29]

But, then, he immediately draws the line in clear and unambiguous terms: "On the other hand, I condemn in the most explicit and formal way experimental manipulations of the human embryo since the human being, from conception to death, cannot be exploited for any purpose whatsoever."[30]

The Pope does not mention any specific technique in this address, nor does he say what constitutes an "experimental manipulation." However, we must recognize that it is within these parameters that acceptable scientific developments must progress. It is not impossible that in years to come, a certain number of distinctions will be made between "manipulation" and authorized scientific techniques. Indeed, in the same allocution, Pope John Paul notes the progress accomplished by *in vitro* experiments "which have yielded results in the care of diseases related to chromosome defects."

Pius XII had warned that just because something is new, this doesn't mean that it is wrong, but it must be evaluated carefully. The same cautious note is found in another address of the present Holy Father, October 3, 1981, to the same Pontifical Academy of Science: "I have firm confidence in the world scientific community . . . being certain that thanks to them, biological progress and research, as also all other scientific research and its technological application will be accomplished in full respect for the norms of morality, safeguarding the dignity of people and their freedom and equality."[31]

ii. Theological evaluation

In the light of the official teaching of the Church, we can now turn to a number of theological positions and practical applications of the data.

We must be careful to avoid two extremes in evaluating scientific progress: to accept all data and all means as good, or to condemn events as being against "nature" without making necessary distinctions, which is a simplistic approach.

Personally, I am very concerned about the credibility of certain "one-issue" over-simplified statements issued in the name of Catholic teaching on matters relating to science; it is sometimes a simple matter to approve or to condemn, but the reasons given for such an action must be solidly based in true facts.

We must recognize that relations between Church and Science have not always been cordial. The Church even has on occasion made mistakes by the too hasty condemnation of scientific theories or facts, even in the area of medical science. I hope that we remain acutely aware of history as we make new pronouncements, especially if we wish to keep them relevant in the light of true Gospel values.

The various Catholic theological positions outlined in recent works[32] seem to use Pius XII's condemnation of reproductive technologies as a starting point, making a clear distinction between reproduction and procreation. Many writers are still in a state of doubt regarding certain particular applications, but we must remember that "there are moments when a state of grace can still mean a state of doubt."[33]

The *first* point to be considered in an evaluation of new technologies is that of the *child* itself. Why do the parents insist so much on using these techniques? Is it for the good of the child *(bonum prolis)*, or to satisfy a desire? Is it to bring about personal self-fulfillment or to allow another human being to exist? The answer to such questions will provide an insight into the morality of certain acts.

Secondly, we note that in some of the newer situations, we are still at the level of technology or technique. We have not yet been able to go too far in the level of application. If we were only on a therapeutic level, we could recognize the usefulness of such procedures in certain instances. But, we must note that they lead — or could lead — to new forms of generation, of family life, of life in society; we are now far beyond the medical arena. I believe that moral theology and ethics should be raising some very serious questions on this point. The impression is given that some technologies are leading to the determination or organization of an objective; this could be a means of controlling the future, which is generally considered to be beyond man's grasp.

In the area of surrogate parenthood, for instance, there are many serious questions. The practice of supplying "wet nurses" has been recognized and accepted for centuries. But, we are on a different level here. Psychological studies are showing the influence of a mother on her child during the period of pregnancy; the results of this are also found in marriage courts today where instances of affective immaturity are even traced back to this period.[34] Therefore, what remains to be seen is the type of relationship that will be established between a child and the mother. The possibility of surrogate parenthood might even become something "chic" in certain areas, where people would try to experience things for themselves, not for the child. If things proceed in such a fashion, it will not be long before we repeat the same pattern of having the rich who can afford such "services" exploit the poor who need the money this would give them. Then it is only a short step to saying that a person has a right to such extern services and that the State must pay for them.

Thirdly, we should note that the simple fact of pregnancy is not sufficient to give value to the child. It can often happen that, through the child, a person would be seeking for her personal satisfaction. There is a cultural tendency in some areas to seek for those things that give

435

pleasure, to live different experiences. In such instances, the finality of the act is thwarted. The pleasure principle does not justify any means. In passing, I wonder also about the fact that the State sometimes provides unwed mothers — especially if they are quite young — with support when they keep their children. Is this really for the good of the child who is deprived of a "normal" home situation?

Fourthly, we are now in a position to be able to assess a certain number of long-range results that have evolved from a contraceptive mentality. The high divorce rate inevitably flows in part from the fact that many people feel unable to sustain lasting relationships, especially when there is little challenge for them to continue. When a pregnancy is described today as a "contraceptive failure," it is easy to see how we have lost the sense of meaning of human life.

iii. Orientations

From what has been said, we can note that from the perspective of the sacrament of Christian marriage, there are openings towards the good of the spouses; but problems still remain in the case of *in vitro* fertilization and of surrogate parenting. The *bonum coniugum* must not be seen simply in terms of an immediate gain; the union of husband and wife, *humano modo*, does not find its expression when such techniques are used exclusively; the faith dimension of the covenant can be weakened by a simple reliance on human potential; the *bonum prolis* itself is in question if parents refuse to accept a deformed child born of the process, or if life that has been conceived in a laboratory is simply discarded.

There might be possibilities regarding certain forms of artificial insemination, provided it takes place between husband and wife and provided that the principles laid down by Pius XII are observed.

Personally, I feel that the most basic objection to the use of these and similar reproductive technologies for solving a couple's infertility lies in the fact that the good of the child is not primarily considered. Although the new law no longer speaks in terms of primary and secondary ends of marriage, these ends do exist and are to be preserved.

A written statement of November, 1981, by the USCC outlines some major issues underlying *in vitro* fertilization. "Despite the lack of a moral and legal consensus on the advisability of human *in vitro* fertilization experiments, there is consensus on one point: Baby Louise Brown, born in England in 1978, attracted so much publicity because her life as an individual began in a laboratory rather than in her mother's fallopian tubes . . . It is clear that from the moment of fertilization there exists a new individual who requires nothing but a hospital environment in which to direct its own growth and development." It is the life of this individual that merits our particular concern.[35]

III. Applications of the Teaching

a. Marriage Preparation

In the new Code, canon 1063 provides one of the most beautiful pastoral approaches to a long-term solution to some of the difficult pastoral problems we are called upon to solve in the area of Christian marriage. This canon deals with preparation for marriage and stresses four areas in which the ecclesial community must provide the faithful with assistance to preserve the Christian spirit of the matrimonial state and to help it progress toward perfection.

1. *Remote preparation* — on the duties of spouses and Christian parents.
2. *Personal preparation* — on the sanctity and duties of the married state.
3. *Community preparation* — through a fruitful liturgical celebration showing the mystery of unity and fruitful love that exists between Christ and the Church.
4. *Assistance* — so that the couple will be able to keep the conjugal covenant and come with time to a holier and fuller living of family life.

The canon insists on the sanctity and spiritual dimension of marriage. If we limit our preparation solely to the human, material and psychological aspects of marriage, we are heading for a repetition of our present state: what counts is only that which provides immediate and tangible results. If this canon is taken seriously and if we take the time to implement it carefully, we will have on hand an adapted instrument to project values and orientations to give true meaning to conjugal life, a meaning that goes far beyond the immediate.

b. Openness to Children

The new Code, in canon 835, shows how parents, in virtue of their office, share in the Church's mission of sanctification as they lead their conjugal life in a Christian way and provide for the Christian education of their children.

The law does not limit itself to speaking of the generation of children; rather, it is also concerned with the total good of the child — its spiritual, material and physical welfare.

In other words, we see a holistic, personalistic approach permeating the entire text. It is this personalist dimension that appears to be missing in the techniques we have been considering. Once we lose sight of the value of human life in all its dimensions, we lose sight of our own purpose which is entrusted to us as members of the People of God (canon 204).

c. Nuanced Positions

The Church finds itself involved today in new situations that were not foreseen even a generation or so ago. We cannot pour the new wine of these developments into old skins which do not allow for new methods.

Vatican II showed how, at times, our approach must change. When it considered the declaration on freedom of conscience, it showed that the starting point had to be revised if we were to get out of the doctrinal impasse in which we had placed ourselves: instead of approaching the question from the perspective of "error," the question had to be faced from the point of view of the person involved.

The new marriage legislation tries to take the same approach. To see each union simply as a clone of another one, to remove the personal faith dimension, to overlook the personalistic dimension found in the good of the spouses, would be to reduce marriage to a static reality. New situations are simply not to be resolved without taking into account the various personalistic elements of the question.

We will have to continue to approach the problems of reproductive technologies from the aspect of the person — especially the person of the child — both in immediate and in long-term considerations, if we are to make further headway in our understanding of the bearing of such technologies on our world.

Conclusion

The Pastoral Constitution *Gaudium et Spes* spoke eloquently of the place and role of the Church in the modern world. The Church's insistence on human dignity is probably one of the most tangible contributions it can make to the world at this time — even though the world might not want to hear what we have to say.

It is easy to see that we would be heading for a very depersonalized milieu if we were to let ourselves simply be manipulated by those who place their values elsewhere.

The new law of the Church cannot address itself directly to medical and moral problems. But, from this overview, we have been able to see how the legislation stresses the personal dimension of faith in the Lord and membership in the ecclesial community. Thus, the law finds itself in the same line and thrust as we note elsewhere in Church teaching and ministry. The new techniques raise difficult problems; our approach to a solution lies in the fact that we cannot lose sight of the value of a human person whose intelligence is to be put at the service of creation, bestowed upon us by God in His wisdom and love.

Notes

* Paper prepared for presentation at the Bishops' Workshop for 1983, "Pastoral Problems of Nuclear and Reproductive Technologies," Pope John Center (St. Louis, Missouri), Dallas, Texas, January 31–February 4, 1983.
1. Paul VI, Allocution of September 17, 1973, in *Origins*, 3(1973–1974), p. 263 ss.
2. Vatican II, *Gaudium et Spes*, #4 (Abbott translation).
3. *Ibid.*, #48.
4. "Matrimoniale foedus, quo vir et mulier inter se totius vitae consortium constituunt, indole sua naturali ad bonum coniugum atque ad prolis generationem et educationem ordinatum, a Christo Domino ad sacramenti dignitatem inter baptizatos evectum est" (Canon 1055, par. 1).
5. In this regard, see the declaration of the International Theological Commission, in *Origins*, 8(1978–1979), p. 237.
6. *Pontificia Commissio Codici Juris Canonici Recognoscendo, Relatio . . .*, Romae, Typis polyglottis Vaticanis, 1981, pp. 244–245, 258.
7. Cf. *Communicationes*, 9(1977), p. 129.
8. Cf. Paul VI, Encyclical letter, *Humanae Vitae*, #9.
9. Cf. Vatican II, *Gaudium et Spes*, #50.
10. Cf. *Communicationes*, 9(1977), p. 121.
11. Cf. *Relatio . . .*, p. 243.
12. For instance, see Portsmouth Diocesan Tribunal, *c.* O'RYAN, May 29, 1974, in *Studia Canonica*, 8(1974), pp. 433–438.
13. Cf. Pius XII, Allocution of October 29, 1951, in *A.A.S.*, 43(1951), p. 845.
14. See also canon 1101, par. 2, revised Code of Canon Law.
15. As quoted in B. M. Ashley – K. D. O'Rourke, *Health Care Ethics*, St. Louis, The Catholic Hospital Association, Second Edition, 1982, p. 289.
16. See canon 877, revised Code of Canon Law.
17. As quoted in Ashley –O'Rourke, *op. cit.*, p. 259.
18. Cf. *A.A.S.*, 22(1930), pp. 564–565.
19. PIUS XII, Allocution of October 29, 1951, in *A.A.S.*, 43(1951), p. 845; translation Ashley – O'Rourke, *op. cit.*, p. 259.

20. PIUS XII, September 29, 1949, in *A.A.S.*, 41(1949), p. 559; translation Ashley – O'Rourke, *op. cit.*, p. 288.
21. *S.R.R. Decisiones, c.* FELICI, 49(1957), p. 625.
22. In *Monitor Ecclesiasticus*, 93(1968), p. 483.
23. Text in *Origins*, 6(1976–1977), p. 35.
24. Text in *Origins*, 7(1977–1978), p. 399.
25. Cf. *Gaudium et Spes*, #51.
26. Cf. *Origins*, 5(1975–1976), p. 488.
27. Cf. *ibid.*, p. 490.
28. Cf. *Origins*, 10(1980–1981), p. 527.
29. Text in *Origins*, 12(1982–1983), p. 342.
30. *Ibid.*
31. *Ibid.*
32. Cf. Ashley – O'Rourke, *op. cit., passim.* Also David J. ROY, *Technology in Human Reproduction*, Montreal, 1982, Center for Bioethics, 112 pp.
33. Peter NICHOLS, *The Pope's Divisions*, Hammondsworth, England, Penguin Books, 1981, p. 356.
34. For instance, see J. Zusy, "Matrimonial Consent and Immaturity", in *Studia Canonica*, 15(1981), pp. 199–239.
35. Cf. *Origins*, 11(1981–1982), p. 361.

Chapter 18

Pastoral Concerns Regarding Reproductive Technologies

This chapter presents the morning and afternoon plenary discussions between the bishops attending the workshop and the speakers of the day: Dr. Tagatz, Dr. Nabors, Fr. Brinkman, Judge Mansmann, Fr. Morrisey (the authors of chapters thirteen through eighteen); with Fr. Moraczewski and Fr. Ashley as additional panelists. The dialogue has been slightly edited for brevity from tape recordings of the proceedings.

Morning Pleanary Discussion
February 3, 1983

Bishop: Is it possible to bypass a blocked fallopian tube by putting the egg at the lower end of the tube?

Dr. Tagatz: It may become possible, and nobody as yet has tried this, to take the naked oocyte from the ovary and bypass the tube and put it back in the uterus with semen that are already there by virtue of intercourse, and possibly achieve pregnancies. We don't know that yet. Because, you see, all this has happened too fast. It may well be that were that to develop as a technology, it would be acceptable within Catholic principles.

Bishop: If a couple comes to you for artificial insemination and the sperm of the unknown donor impregnates the woman, when the baby is born, whose name appears on the birth certificate as the father?

Dr. Tagatz: The husband. That's not been a problem. I can tell you that we now have somewhere in the neighborhood of 12–16 states in which donor insemination is totally accepted as making the child legal within the marriage.

Dr. Nabors: In the state of Texas, whoever is married to the mother of the child is the legal father. Now, we always know who is the mother of the child, but many times we do not know who the father of the child is, but the husband's name goes on the birth certificate just the same. As a point of law that's been clarified.

Bishop: We understand that the husband is the donor of the semen, and that semen is secured prior to intercourse. So this masturbated semen, that's the number one step and then there's an aspirated ovum — that's the number two step. And then number three step is the fertilization of the ovum by the sperm. Now in that process are there many ova fertilized by sperm? We're not clear on that. One of the reasons for our asking that question is that a reply given about 3–4 years ago by Pope John Paul I when he was Archbishop of Venice was that he was very sympathetic to the couple that wanted to achieve pregnancy and they indeed did achieve it through *in vitro* vertilization, but his objection to the process was that there were many ova fertilized in the dish and then only the better fertilized ovum was inserted into the mother. So at that point of the process where there is the fertilization of the ova by the sperm were there many ova fertilized and some rejected at this point?

Dr. Tagatz: The issue that keeps coming up with the Right-to-Life people who are the most vocal, whether they're Catholic, Protestant or whatever, is that we're setting out to destroy new persons. And I'm perfectly willing to accept personhood as occurring with fertilization from a medical standpoint, in fact I think most doctors would accept it. Now, when we override the normal oocyte mechanism of bringing up one terminal oocyte, we probably

442

cannot bring up more than say from 3–5, that's the maximal number we'll bring up. Those will be at all stages of differing maturation, so that if we were really "scientific" we'd only take the best one, but that's not how we do it. We take them all. Fertilization takes place and possibly takes place in as many as 5 — and I would say that is the usual maximum. Now if fertilization takes place in 5 and then we incubate after division begins to take place in a 2–4 cell stage, we're going to take all of those that appear to be viable with the exception of those cells which are clearly dead. But all forms of so-called abnormalities where you have asymmetrical cleavage so that you're dealing with 5 instead of 8 cells, all of these we thoroughly intend to put back into the uterus and let them take their chances. When you put in 2 or 3 you increase your likelihood of twins, but there's only been one twin that I know of in the world so far.

Bishop: Father Brinkman, you've made in your last sentence or two a conclusion that I suspect you would like to spend a great deal more time working on, specifically relating to the process we're just discussing with *in vitro* fertilization or artificial insemination. You suggest that in view of personhood and the view of the "I" and the "you" and the "we" this kind of medical technology somehow or other disrupts or does a disservice to the "I", the "you" and the "we" in the marriage relationship and in the father-mother relationship. Could you give us a fuller understanding of what your point was as to why this kind of technology somehow or other is not true to the personhood of the father-mother or the husband-wife?

Father Brinkman: Yes, you heard me correctly, and I wish I could put it in a very short manner. In 1956 Pope Pius XII discussed the question of *in vitro* vertilization and he said that it is intrinsically evil. But we don't know exactly what Pius XII understood by *in vitro* fertilization, he may have been thinking of a fetus that was being grown in a kind of a plastic bathtub at the University of Rome. He heard about it and this might be what he understood. The process that we're talking about here he probably only knew in theory. In 1949 he said that artificial insemination between the husband and wife must absolutely be excluded. He did not say it is an intrinsic evil. He continued in 1951, in the fourth part of the address to the midwives, to try to discuss this personal unitive

443

dimension biblically — why does a man leave his mother and father, and unite with a wife — and this makes the in-one-flesh. There was nothing said here of procreation, this is purely the personalist aspect. How is it possible to have two individual beings that intertwine in a unity and share in a unity in this act of intercourse, because this intercourse means both knowing and actually uniting? That form of unity between these two persons is the area specifically being bypassed that would exclude this particular technique.

In 1956 it was brought to Pius XII's attention that he may have been a bit too heavy when he said the use of this technology is like taking the hearth of the home and turning it into a biological laboratory, which is very "valuated" language. So he attempted to once more approach the medical community to say that the Church approves their desires to perfect techniques that would help with fertility, but what is it that the husband and wife are desiring? He says it is not simply the child, but to become mothers and fathers. When we do things, we're always fulfilled. When we talk about the common good it is not that people are like bricks in a building, that each person does a function, but that every person in their own respect is fulfilled in working together with others. This is an aspect that he attempted to address by saying how it is that a person is fulfilled. Pius XII attempted to go through a personalist explanation saying that through this personal communion we are bound to a specific moral structure by which we act. What he was trying to point out was that by acting you are making yourself, you are drawing a significance out for yourself.

In Vatican II it was stated simply, man is the only creature that God made *for himself* and he only finds the significance of himself in a disinterested gift. This is a question of giving, of acting with a person, not in abstraction. One of the problems that we sometimes have is thinking of marriage abstractly. If I want, for example, to learn to play a piano I must play the piano. I must act. And in so doing I become a piano player. If I think about playing a piano, I don't become a piano player. When we start with the question of marriage, we must see the reality of marriage as the reality of persons that is created by the acting and interacting *with* one another. That acting, which is in intercourse, is a single action which is the affirmation of the totality of the person. That totality of the person is experienced as a unity. It is here that the spiritual and corporal domain are unified. When we act towards one another, when we give ourselves as a totality, and when we receive as a totality, it means that those significances are borne out of the action. In acting I am transformed from being simply a husband to becoming a father, not that I produce fatherhood, but in the light of her femininity as realized, I become a father.

This personalist explanation is very difficult to follow. In my lecture I say that most people probably will not be convinced about it because we don't think this way. Let me give you a series of examples. If you take the case of a husband and a wife, most of us are going to say that you cannot have sex unless you have marriage, there's just no two ways about it. We say that there is some kind of moral necessity of marriage in order to let people have sex. I think most people would agree on that. When we look at the person wanting the fulfillment of motherhood in marriage we say we can very well sympathize with her. She wants to fill out a part of her significance in a specific way as mother — fulfillment of the self.

But what is the difference between a woman wanting to be fulfilled as a mother, but not having a husband? She feels, I wish to be a mother but without benefit of marriage, I wish to be artificially inseminated, and I wish to be a mother. We would probably immediately say no, you have no rights to that. But let's make the case a little bit more difficult. What happens if the woman is married, her husband dies in war, but he had before going off deposited his semen, and now that he is dead there is no marriage. Can she be inseminated because she wants to have a child by this man as a father? This is the question. Is the fulfillment to be drawn from simply the biological activity or is it that the human person responds through a moral dimension first that makes us human?

Let me give you an example from anthropology. None of these are convincing unless you think through the process. One of the things that anthropologists try to look at is the differentiation of man from the animals. You can find in the animal world that social animals, the wolves, chimpanzees, and so forth, live in a community because they need each other in some respect to keep themselves in existence — social community is their defense. But when they're eating each one eats alone, they grab the food. But humans don't do that — they bring the food in and it is shared from the community. There is something specifically different that we confront. When you confront a human being, already you have a notion of benevolence. There is something of justice that enters into what we can do to human beings.

Father Moraczewski: I have a comment on *in vitro* fertilization for fear that there may have been a misunderstanding. When 4 or 5 oocytes are collected and put in a Petri dish and fertilized, and the one which shows normal cleavage is replaced into the woman's uterus, there are several problems. Let's say out of the 5 only one is selected and it was decided that the other oocytes are not dividing properly, and therefore may have an abnormality. Nevertheless, if they have been fertilized and the process begun, they could be considered as human beings, human persons, even though they'd become handicapped or disabled in some way during the process of further development. So, in a dish they may have started normally, but during the first few hours of the biological process of division, they, because of the abnormality of their environment, may have undergone an injury. So you might say they died in the embryo, in the plate. Thus, the process of introducing them into the Petri dish has a moral question. So we cannot simply say they died in the dish, therefore there's no problem.

The second problem is that if you introduce three embryos and only one birth results, that means two died along the way, and this is supported by the statistics. Of the embryos replaced, only approximately 10–15% resulted in actual pregnancy and live birth. So there were still a number of human beings whose life had begun, and they had been placed back in the uterus, but then subsequently failed to implant, or after implantation failed to develop successfully to birth. Now granted that in the normal procedure there is a certain loss also; nonetheless, what has happened here is that by free human choice we have placed those embryos back into an environment from which we have taken them out. So the deaths that result are ultimately the result of free, deliberate human action and not merely an accident of biology or circumstance. I think that has to be taken into consideration in making the moral evaluation of *in vitro* fertilization.

Dr. Tagatz: You understood what I was saying and I think that's absolutely the way it is. Obviously we've interjected a different step and there is a loss as a result of that step which is comparable to the loss in a normal situation.

But I tell you, being a fairly simplistic Lutheran, it's very important to me that I understand the Catholic position. It seems to me that for the sanctity of the family and to prevent promiscuity it was originally thought within the Church that all intercourse should be directed toward procreation. Now, if you know your philosophy, you know that means that you draw a circle, all intercourse within marriage toward procreation. That does not exclude procreation within marriage without intercourse. That is a basic philosophical viewpoint. To me, I cannot see how it would be untenable to the Church to accept attempts at procreation within marriage which do not include intercourse.

Bishop: My question is about one of these steps of *in vitro* fertilization. I suppose that the donor is the father of the child to come, and my question is about masturbation in that case. If I don't misstate our moral theology, masturbation usually is not acceptable because it goes against the natural function of the normal erection and ejaculation. Assuming again that the donor is the father, could we consider that the masturbation may, in order to help nature to achieve reproduction, be considered ethically acceptable?

Father Ashley: First, I think we should keep very clearly in mind just how the problem comes before us. There's one thing that has been established in the Church, not certainly by a solemn definition, but by a very solemn process, and that is the principle that is operative in the field we're in. It is the inseparability of the unitive and procreative function of the marital act. That is something of a fixed point, as I see it. Not all theologians accept that, but it is truly a very solidly stated position, and our official position. So, when we look at the various technological proposals, the problem is to try to judge them in view of this principle, and the application is not a very easy one.

What Father Brinkman was doing was an attempt to give the present Pope's personal way of explaining that principle. But the principle, however we explain it, is there. Now Pius XII certainly had that same principle in mind in his various allocutions in which he ruled out masturbation and ruled out artificial insemination. Those pronouncements on his part, though, are of a different order certainly than this principle. Because Pius XII as Pope was still speaking only in allocutions and things of this sort, they don't have the same solemn character as *Humanae Vitae* has, but he was trying to face this technology and apply the principle to it. His allocutions are guides to us, but I don't think we can say that there isn't still much more to be discussed about those issues, and that's what we're trying to do here. So we shouldn't be alarmed that we have not got the two things together yet. It's going to take some time before this is sorted out.

Now, with regard to masturbation, I really don't know what the answer to that is, but I'll say this. We have on the one hand the allocutions of Pius XII, generally supported by the theology that was operating at that time. Then we have the fact that recent theologians have kept silent on this issue. I haven't seen any recent writing on this, but I think that many of them do allow masturbation for the purpose of sterility tests, this would be their opinion. The justification they give for it, though, tends to be based on proportionalism, which does not accept the notion of something being intrinsically evil. I don't think we can go that way, I think we have to say some things are intrinsically evil, and something breaking this principle of the unity of the unitive and procreative ends of sexuality would be intrinsically evil.

In the first edition of the book that I published with Father Kevin O'Rourke, we stated the opinion that in a case like this perhaps the action is not masturbation. We didn't give this as a settled opinion, but we proposed it as a possibility, saying it was an act of self-stimulation, whereas masturbation is ordinarily understood as an act in which an orgasm is produced for the purpose of the pleasure and relief of tension involved in the orgasm. In the second edition we omitted that, out of deference to the statement of Pius XII, and because, after further consideration, we weren't sure that that argument held. I still think that there is something to be said for it. Now, what is a Bishop going to do in this situation? The safe thing, of course, is to follow the direction of Pius XII in the matter. That would be the conservative and safe line to follow. I do think though, that in fact, we are in a situation where this kind of thing is still not so clear, and it perhaps is within the episcopal prudence to make some other decision.

Afternoon Plenary Discussion
February 3, 1983

Bishop: Can a woman volunteer within the law to be a surrogate mother by natural intercourse, or in other words, can adultery be contracted?

Judge Mansmann: There is a challenge to the procedure saying that that is an adulterous situation. Generally, case law has said that where there is an insemination that is not an adulterous situation. However, the motives of the people in entering into the relationship will not prevent an adultery violation of criminal statutes from coming into being. The best motives in the world will not vitiate this in the sense of the intent that the law places on those situations, and indeed adultery may very well be charged in those situations.

Bishop: Would you respond to the statement that a married couple has a right to children and therefore a right of recourse to reproductive technology?

Father Morrisey: The law of the Church is very clear in saying that there can be no right to children. The basic right involved in marriage is the right to acts apt by their nature to the generation of children. But there are many cases of sterility and in that instance the couple cannot claim a right to a child according to Church law. The law just doesn't provide for that type of situation.

Father Ashley: I think it would help with this kind of problem if we thought more about the rights of the child. Now it's a little hard to talk about the rights of a child who might not exist. We're not talking about that. I'm talking about the child who does exist. This child has a right, I believe, to have parents in the ordinary sense of the term, "parents." It seems to me that's an important part of human nature, and that raises a question about some of these artificial modes because it means that we deliberately bring into the world a child who lacks one of the characteristics of being human. I don't say it is of the essence, but it is a part of the integral description of being human, to have parents, to be a part of the human race in the sense that one has parents the way that most people have.

Bishop: Would Judge Mansmann care to speak about the ethical obligations of attorneys?

449

Judge Mansmann: The attorney who serves as an intermediary in these situations in a sense represents the interests of all the parties at one time. The interests of the parties may very well be adverse as they often are when parties contract and ask each other to obligate themselves in a contract. In a sense, it's the lawyer who is representing everybody's interest. And so he has ethical problems, it seems to me, and each of the parties may, for the contract to be validly entered, have to have their own lawyer representing their interests. Now, the big question is this: If there is a main interest here of the rights of the child what lawyer is representing *those* interests at the time that the contract is entered into? Certainly, once the child is born there is the opportunity, if difficulty arises, for the court to appoint counsel to represent the interests of the child, but clearly the lawyer who is representing the surrogate mother and her husband, who may want to keep the child, should not be the same lawyer who is representing the surrogate father and his wife who are struggling over the child, not representing the child. So that is one of the main ethical considerations that lawyers have that is based on the law rather than that which arises from basic principles of morality.

Bishop: Father Morrisey, you made the distinction between wanting to bring a new life into the world as opposed to wanting to satisfy a need. Did you, by making this distinction, imply that a couple or a person who wanted exclusively to satisfy a need might be considered to continue to exclude the *bonum prolis* in a marital covenant?

Father Morrisey: This is one of the questions that is being raised by the new Code as we shift from a law based on structure, on organization, and outward conformity to a law based on the person with the values of the person, the potentiality of the person in a faith community. And it's going to take some time before we're able to see if the good of the spouses as distinguished from the good of the child will be interpreted by the courts as meaning something more than just simply the unity and the indissolubility of the union. And so I've made the distinction because it's in the law. I have no idea yet as to what way the courts are going to go. I'm sure for a while they're just going to keep the interpretation that we've had under the present legislation. But see, we did not have the *bonum coniugum* in the previous law, and so there will be a new body of court decisions interpreting what that will mean. I was delighted to see that it remained in the final text since there was a lot of opposition to it because people were saying we were making the marriage law of the Church too subjective, while before it was perhaps too static; some were saying we were moving too much in the other direction.

Bishop: I would welcome it if you would be kind enough to make some brief comment upon your evaluation of official teaching of the Church on these matters?

Father Morrisey: If we look back at Pius XI, we see there that he had talked in negative terms about contraception and about eugenic methods of providing for a superior race. Those two aspects had been condemned straightforwardly. Pius XII gave us a statement that we still find repeated in a lot of books: marriage obliges to a state of life which, while carrying with it certain rights, also imposes the fulfillment of a positive work concerning the state of life itself on partners who make use of matrimony by the specific act of their state. Nature and the Creator impose the function of providing for the conservation of the human race. This is the characteristic service from which their state of life derives its peculiar value — the *bonum prolis*. And so, insisting on this question of the *bonum prolis*, I think we can see we are already heading in a new direction and this applies to the statements of the Congregation of the Doctrine of the Faith. We have their statement and the NCCB's statement, "any sterilization which of itself, that is of its own nature and condition has the sole immediate effect of rendering the generative faculty incapable of procreation is completely forbidden." You can see that that's a very nuanced statement with all the qualifiers that have been put there. And the Congregation of the Doctrine of Faith says facts do not constitute a criterion for judging the moral value of human acts. Just because it is done, and done frequently, does not necessarily make a thing right.

But what I'm worried about is that just because something is new, and if we continue looking at it from the same starting point, we might find ourselves in the same position that the Council found itself in with freedom of conscience, until such time as it said, let's re-examine the matter totally. I'm just worried about the credibility of our Church statements if we come out categorically

451

when we're not sure of all the facts, and it's in that line that I'm trying to show that there are two tendencies. I know we can quote texts from the Popes and so on, but I think there is an openness that's here and it's at the end of *Gaudium et Spes*, it's the whole openness to the world that the Creator has given us and entrusted to us as stewards. It's a whole question of responsible stewardship of creation.

Father Ashley: Christopher Derrick said very well to us that the basic Christian attitude is one of reverence for the work of the Creator, of seeing our own work, our technology, as cooperation with the work of the Creator. That means, then, that if we *innovate* in technology, a certain kind of sane conservatism is necessary. It isn't dogmatism. We can't say *a priori* that a new proposal is destructive of a natural order, because maybe it isn't. Maybe it's a good thing. On the other hand, we can't simply accept it because it's new and it has immediate pragmatic effects. Rather, I think, we have to have a sane conservatism in the sense that we don't condemn, but we do not approve a departure from the ordinary course of affairs until it has been tested and tried, or thoroughly reflected upon and explored. That's against the modern temperament, which is to try everything out immediately, and put it into effect immediately. But the ecological movement taught us that that has led to a destruction of nature.

In the present matter the thing that is clear, and that we have to keep pointing to, is the principle of inseparability of the unitive and procreative meanings of marriage. That's the point of clarity. When a new technology is proposed we have to ask ourselves: is that in accordance with the principle or does it violate it? We shouldn't be quick to say that it violates it, but until we're sure that it doesn't violate it, I don't see how we can use it as a solution of our problems. You may say that's probabilism in reverse, but it seems to me that in the question of reverence for the natural order of things, we need to have that kind of conservatism. In the present case then, I think that our discussions show that it is not clear that some of these new technologies violate the divine purpose, the divine plan. But we're not sure, and they're suspect because they seem to be a radical intervention in the basic relation between the spouses. So we have to wait until we've found out some more.

Father Morrisey: I agree with Father Ashley, obviously, that the

Church must always be in a critical position regarding the events in the world in which we live, whether it be the field of politics, or models of society, or obviously, in this particular new era and new area of human life and living. What bothers me is that while in the medical field much progress is being made in the processes and techniques whereby human life can be generated, I have yet to hear doctors say that they have allowed themselves to be questioned by or have worked together with experts from other disciplines, such as psychologists, sociologists, philosophers, or even people involved in the field of ethics. I think it could be enriching to them if they allowed themselves not only to be criticized by these people, but sometimes to work in conjunction with them.

When Judge Mansmann presented her two models I was very happy to see that in the second model, where the state might well become involved, someone would represent not only those who were directly involved in the surrogate contracting, but also those indirectly touched by it, and particularly the child and the rights of the child. I was happy, too, that the lawmakers would not only look into the jurisprudence of the past and the purely legal aspects but they would also question other disciplines in order to protect the dignity of the human person. I don't know whether the Judge at this time feels that enough has been done in this field by governments and legislatures to be able to say what is happening. And will the rights of the child be protected as well as those of the other woman?

Judge Mansmann: I don't think that there's any question that very little has been done by legislatures in looking at all the ramifications that are involved here in the relationships of the parties. It has all been piecemeal. The law, and maybe the Church, is playing catch-up ball here. Science seems to be way ahead of us, and the law is trying, whenever a dispute erupts, to stick a finger in the dike here and there with a little bit of legislation or something that can be interpreted by courts.

As far as the best interests of the child are concerned, I think courts, in analagous situations, are saying it doesn't matter what the parties agreed to, or what their intentions were, the child has rights and we're going to look at them. I'm reminded of the case that the Pennsylvania Supreme Court handed down two days ago. It was a situation where a couple were not married, engaged in intercourse, and a child was born of that union. The father of the child maintained that the mother had duped him, that she had told him that she was using contraceptives when she was not. He had no intention to father a child. In fact, he was duped. The lower court would not hear the argument saying, it doesn't matter because first of all, you intend the natural and probable consequences of your acts and, secondly, now that we have a different person involved here, a child who has rights protectable under the law, we will look only to those rights. You are the child's father. The child has the right to support. You have those full obligations. The Pennsylvania Supreme Court adopted that decision, saying that the best interests of the child here prohibit the defense of "I've been duped" under the circumstances. So in analagous situations clearly we are starting to look at the best interests of the child.

Bishop: I have a few remarks to be addressed to Father Morrisey. On the one hand we say that parents have no direct right to having a child. But we can see, on the other hand, the difficulty of people who have lived with the assumption that the primary end of marriage is orientated towards children. On a psychological level most people have lived on the assumption that they not only have a right, they have a duty to children. So it's going to take a long time to switch that mentality around to have them accept the fact that it they're going to be infertile, they'll have to live a different style of marriage without any expectations of having children.

There's also the fact that, if it has taken the Church 50 years to find a new definition of marriage, from 1917 to the Council, it might well take another 50 years to refine the *humano modo* that is expressed in the definition of the sexual act. And in that respect I think that, when you say we're always putting our finger in the dike as Judge Mansmann has said, this is true for civil law but it is also true in the development of doctrine, and in the expression it finds in law. I think that in the mere fact that we're not saying something is absolutely wrong, but are taking a critical stance and forcing others to refine their positions, we're already rendering a service to the overall community.

Father Morrisey: I agree absolutely. The other day one of the reporters that was carrying on an interview regarding the new Code said to me: I know of very few organizations in the world where the chief executive office will call in somebody and say, "I have a very urgent

454

task for you to carry out, in this case to revise the laws of the Church; I want you to do it as soon as you can and report to me in a quarter of a century!" This is what we did in this Code in 24 years to the day, that is almost a quarter century. The biggest advantage of the new code is that it consolidates quite a number of experiments, insights, and avenues of approach that have been taken in the last 18 years since Vatican II ended, and it provides a springboard now for continual renewal in the Church by consolidating the data that we have to date. We see in the marriage canons in particular, the whole consolidation of the psychic incapacities for a marriage, which was perhaps one of the canons we were afraid we were going to lose, but which finds its way into the new Code with a few changes that are even for the better. So most of the canonists are not looking at this law for tangible effects before the turn of the

Bishop: We have given a lot of attention to war and peace and rightly so. It's an overriding issue in our day and certainly civilization could come to an end through the misuse of the power that is in human hands. At the same time it seems that the issues that we have been discussing here at this Workshop are in a sense even more personal, more a matter of concern to the people who are committed to our care. So it seems to me that we should probably give them equal care and equal attention, and have a like committee to investigate these happenings in technology and the moral implications they have for people in their average lives. It seems to be that things happen and they come out in the news and often there's no response, no sort of guidance for our people, because we haven't made the kind of study we are making on peace and war. So I am wondering if what Father Ashley had in mind was whether or not we should have something geared for purposes of this kind in the U.S. Catholic Conference, or whether he had something else in mind.

Father Ashley: Personally I think that the kind of thing we've been talking about today does not involve a large number of people and that some of this will be eliminated by further technology. This *in vitro* fertilization we've just been talking about is primarily done because of women who have an occlusion of the fallopian tubes. Scientists will probably find a solution for that even in these difficult cases that were described. It doesn't seem to be a terribly difficult problem to get that ovum from the ovary into the womb;

it is just a couple of inches that have to be traversed, but I'm sure that technology is going to find a way to do that. I really don't think we should exaggerate the importance of this type of problem. The general issue "where is technology going," is very, very important. But I really don't think that the thing we're dealing with has been one of the major problems facing the Church.

Judge Mansmann: It may very well be that as far as numbers are concerned they are not large. What's happening, however, and we saw it in the abortion area, is that the money for research is then diverted from something like figuring out a way to go four inches in the fallopian tubes, and is placed instead in the *in vitro* fertilization area. What we saw with abortion, is that the emphasis was not placed on trying to do something in the womb with the unborn child that does have a birth defect, or trying to do something that will prevent that. Instead, the money all went to having the abortion procedure as such be made simpler and easier and clear of complications. So, we have to be very careful, you know, even though it's a small number of people right now, the problem may never be resolved because the emphasis is not there to do that.

Father Ashley: I agree very much with that.

Bishop: Father Ashley, my question is in the same line. Father Morrisey urged a certain modesty of judgment and you indicated a need for a tentative conservatism. Yet, I wonder if, as the Judge has said, in the meantime there is a certain built-in momentum as the technology develops, so that by the time we get to the point of judgment we may find ourselves a little bit late? My question is, do you believe that we are effectively engaged at this moment in the dialogue with the medical and the scientific field, in raising the question out of our tradition as it is now? Are we judging in the kind of categories that have been presented in the personalist approach, judging in the kind of categories that do specifically uphold the dignity of the human person, the sacredness of the covenant, and, really questioning, although tentatively, the technology?

Father Ashley: What I was trying to say was that our emphasis should be on teaching the principles which are very clear, and then saying to the medical profession, we don't see off-hand *prima facie*, how what you're doing can possibly be reconciled with these principles. It's up to you to justify what you're doing. You are proposing a thing which on the face of it seems to be very disruptive of family life, and we're not ready to accept that until you show us that it is justified. Now Dr. Tagatz this morning tried to make out a case for what he was doing. A very sincere case and he made some good points. I wasn't convinced that he had made his case, though. I think that's what I would say to him, I still have this difficulty and that difficulty before I would dare to recommend what you're proposing. We shouldn't be on the defensive in this matter. Those who propose it should be on the defensive. They're the ones who are proposing something that is novel, surprising, and effective perhaps in the short range, but in the long range, perhaps destructive of family life.

Bishop: May a contract be declared null if a surrogate mother made it without the consent of her husband?

Judge Mansmann: The difficulty there is establishing what right is being asserted, under the contract. If the right is that of the natural father to the child, the contract will not be considered void because the husband of the surrogate might not have any rights in that situation. He is not the father of the child and he might not have rights that he can assert to make the contract void. We say, the person doesn't have standing in the law to challenge the contract itself. Now in those jurisdictions where the husband of the mother automatically becomes the father of the child, he asserts his own rights and he can say that this child cannot be taken away, because it is mine under the law even though it is not mine biologically. So it depends on the jurisdiction, it depends on what presumption arises as far as paternity. In some situations, yes, it could be, in others he will have no standing to challenge it.

Bishop: Father Morrisey, you listed, as we would expect, one of the ends of marriage as the good of the child. Do you see any violation of that good from a canonical point of view, through artificial insemination by the husband, and secondly, by *in vitro* fertilization?

Father Morrisey: I'm going to wiggle out of that question because you said "from a canonical point of view." I'm not sure if we're ready yet to have a canonical view on that. There's no way in the Church law at the present time that we can declare a marriage null because of an intention to have children. That is where the Canon Law would come in. There would be many moral-ethical questions of a completely different line, but it's very rare that our courts ever

457

have to make a declaration to the effect that a marriage is valid. It can occur in some instances regarding successions in those countries where there are concordats and agreements between the two courts. But most of the time we'll be called upon to judge the nullity of an act. Personally, as a judge, I'd uphold the validity of such a marriage unless there were other elements involved too.

Bishop: Father Morrisey, you made some reference to the importance of adequate preparation for marriage, especially under the new Code, and you made reference to the question of the good of the couple. It seems to me that very soon our parish priests and their various assistants are going to need a lot of help in how they are going to prepare their couples for marriage, especially in view of this new aspect of the *good of the couple*. Would you comment on that please?

Father Morrisey: I think that one of the major applications of the new Code is the shift from the Church identified by the clergy to a Church identified by the faithful, and the faithful have two aspects, the clergy and the laity. And so the responsibilities of the life of the Church are presented now in terms of the faithful, the whole Christian community. It is interesting to note that in six of the Sacraments, there is regretfully an exception in the Sacrament of Ordination, we find the Canon calling on the whole community to provide for the celebration of the Sacrament. We notice the Code has taken the stand that the development of faith and santification is primarily through the Word of God. And the Sacraments are presented as community events. Preparation for marriage is just one of the many aspects coming through. The Canon says that it is up to the pastors to see that their ecclesial community provides such service. It doesn't say that the pastor is to provide the service, physically he could not do it.

I've been doing a lot of talking lately about the necessity of holding a Plenary Council to implement the new Code, where we take 2–3–4 years to reflect upon the various ways in which the Code foresees the Bishops will carry out their office. Then, when we have a Plenary Council, the decisions that pertain to an Episcopal Conference would be taken for the sharing of responsibilities. Only then could the synods be held in the dioceses for the many other decisions that a Bishop has to make. Otherwise, what's going to happen is that these decisions will be taken in each diocese without reference, or with little reference, to the neighboring dioceses or to an overall vision of the shift that the new Code is bringing in. And so the preparation for marriage is but one of many aspects or ways in which all the faithful share in the three missions of teaching, sanctifying and governing. If we expect the priests to do this on their own, it's totally impossible.

Bishop: Judge Mansmann, when you mention about ethical considerations, are ethical considerations also being weighed in these legal discussions?

Judge Mansmann: No, not at all. In fact, since the law itself is not addressing those problems, it quite obviously doesn't take into account any ethical considerations whatever. The parties that appear are free to contract for whatever reason they choose, one may be convenience — I don't want several months of my life being disturbed from my business or my work, my profession or whatever.

Bishop: Then my next question is a general one. Is the scientific method by which all of these things have taken place, without any ethical considerations, going to be the determination of where we go in society? For those who want to look to a further and a much deeper understanding of life, how in the world can we have that kind of consideration when communication is so instantaneous today?

Judge Mansmann: Well, there are two views, almost diametrically opposed, as to what the law is or what the law should be. In one view, the law is seen as responding to society and, in a sense, a stopgap measure to problems that arise. On the other hand, the law is seen as promoting morality or ethics and charging all of us to pursue a greater good. At present all we have is the stopgap kind of legal reasoning or prohibition or whatever. Without question, what we need to do is, stop for a moment, look at all the ethical and moral considerations that interact among all of our different philosophies, and professions, and whatever, and decide what goals, what interests, we want to protect and to translate into the law.

Bishop: Judge Mansmann, with regard to the rights of the husband of the surrogate mother, suppose this man wanted a little room in her womb for his own. Suppose he's a soldier and he's going to be gone for the next months and there's no room. Does he have any rights in this?

Judge Mansmann: The question is not so much what is the quality of the rights he has, but what can the law really protect for him? Can he say to the court, enjoin my wife while I am gone overseas from engaging in any activity that takes her womb for someone else? The law can't respond to those situations, just as the law couldn't for example, enforce the provision of the surrogate mother contract that says that she cannot smoke cigarettes or take drugs, because of the lack of court supervision over something like that. That's the difficulty. He may have a clearly defined right as the husband in the situation, we can translate that into the law, but how do we enforce that? The vast majority of our daily life-span is based upon voluntary compliance with general principles in law and morality of our people. If we don't have that, then the law just does not respond, it can't respond to every possible situation.

460

PART V

Postlude

Chapter 19

"Reprise and Coda"

Sister Margaret John Kelly, D.C.

Just as the program design of this three day workshop provided for
a day's reflections on the concept of "personhood" between scientific
considerations of nuclear energy and reproductive technologies, so the
Holy Father in his opening greeting urged the centrality of "humanity"
within discussions of scientific progress. Repeating his challenge of
Redemptor Hominis, the Pope urged "the priority of ethics over technology, the primacy of persons over things, and the superiority of spirit over
matter."[1] Throughout the three days, the workshop participants were
consistently asked to establish such priorities, to determine what is
specifically human and thus moral, and to evaluate current scientific
knowledge and technology according to its capacity to contribute to the
advancement of the individual, family and society. Those basic prob-
ings led participants through a variety of topics and issues including the
formative influences on the various definitions of "human," the dual
potential for risk and benefit inherent in "scientific advances," the
difficulty of sorting out cultural and economic biases in discussing

"progress," and exploration of the limits on science's efforts to "improve nature."

Because of the unique status of music among the sister arts, the title for this summary presentation "Reprise and Coda" has been drawn from the language of musical composition. Unlike the visual and literary art forms which once produced are frozen in time, music must be vitalized through performance. This translation of notation into the aesthetic experience captures the centrality of the human person, as the means of seeking out the mysteries of nature. The musical reference also subtly points up the potential for harmony and discord present in all intellectual efforts and scientific progress. That human intellectual activity generates both life and death, harmony and cacophony, is documented in a long litany of historical paradigms from the tower of Babel to communications satellites, from Hiroshima to nuclear medicine. With the pace of technological advancement so accelerated in this contemporary era, sensitivity to this dual potential is essential and was frequently cited in the workshop.

The Reprise, the thematic recapitulation of the three days program, then, will focus on the central definitional and evaluative issues in its two sections. The first will include general observations about the climate and context of the workshop; the second will raise three compelling questions which surfaced frequently through the sessions. The Coda, a new theme, will offer three proposals for future consideration and action.

Reprise

I. General Context
"Cosmic Piety" and "Time Awareness"

In the opening presentation, Christopher Derrick set the tone of this workshop when he encouraged the participants to look on their activity as an act of religion. He noted that the truly scientific approach, the exploration of the universe and the discovery of its secrets, is the act of the human seeking God. He suggests that persons should look on all sources of energy and the physical reproductive powers with that "cosmic piety" described by Bertrand Russell, and should resist the "desacralizing" trend of the era. It is this attitude that Chesterton cited when he reflected that "the world will never starve from wonders, but only from want of wonder", or what Carlyle referenced when he said, "The man who cannot wonder is but a pair of spectacles behind which there is no eye".

In addition to their stress on the respect for the Divine which must characterize reflection on scientific advances, all the speakers moved rapidly from the present to the future and back to the past in much of the same way that T. S. Eliot reminded us that "time present and time past are both perhaps present in time future and time future contained in time past."[2] Historical consciousness, as well as awareness of future implications, provided the framework within which the present scientific/technological era was approached by speakers and bishops alike.

To select an image, then, which captures these two basic attitudes of "cosmic piety" and "time awareness" permeating the three days of discussion, we can turn to the literary accounts of the first "cosmic piety" experience: the creation accounts in Genesis. The juxtaposition of these two very distinctive renderings of Creation may strike one occasionally as redundant but more frequently as mysterious and even provocatively symbolic. Reflection on these two versions within the overall context of this workshop can be profitable because the two stories provide insights into what it is to be human: to be *part of* and yet *in control* of the world; to be part of the *historical process* and yet shaping history as part of the *eternal* plan; to be at once a *creator* and a *destroyer*. Early then in Scripture, we see described the essential relationship existing between God the Creator, the Planner and Provider — and man the Creature, the Discoverer and the Inventor. We also recognize the awesome reality that each one is just a small part of human history with obligations to the present but also to the future, to oneself, and also to society. As Shakespeare warned, many years later, persons have their "exits and entrances" on the world's stage.

The first version of creation in Genesis I is very simple, straightforward and logical in its method. Light, the source and symbol of life, was the first step in the process which then worked through the separation of land, the creation of the waters and the sun, and the whole hierarchical biological system from vegetation, fish, birds, cattle. When the eco-system with its food chain was fully in place, God created the human persons. "Male and female he created them." He blessed them and then urged them "to multiply, to fill the earth and to *subdue*

464

it", a term implying conquering and controlling of the earth but not destroying it.

In the second account, the narrative technique appears less straightforward and more symbolic and yes, more "human", more personalistic and existential. The story focuses on the moral challenge presented to Adam and introduces the concept of moral awareness and social responsibility. (It seems significant to note here that it is this moral sense which Dr. Tymieniecka insists is what characterizes the *human* person, the highest demonstration of which is benevolence where one operates primarily out of a desire to do good to others.) In this second version, we also see that God creates man from the dust of the earth (not as in the first account) and only the male of the species is formed at first. Then *for* man, God created the garden but gives him a single prohibition, "Do not eat of the tree of the knowledge of good and evil for on that day you will most surely die". Only after this limitation is established does God create the rest of the universe. It seems significant that the power to name, and thus control, the living creatures was given *after* the prohibition. However, despite his lovely surroundings and the vast menagerie of birds and beasts, and his position of power, Adam is not satisfied. He is so restless, unfilled and yearning that God draws woman from the side of man and Paradise is now completed. It is significant to note that in this second version we have direct reference to the interpersonal unity (spiritual and physical) made possible by sexual differentiation.

This second version, while expressing the human need for interdependence, stresses self-fulfillment and self-determination. So often throughout the three days, the issue of freedom and fulfillment surfaced as speakers searched out definitions of personhood. It was pointed out that the behavioral sciences (and some philosophies and theologies) currently reveal a lack of consensus on these very concepts. Historically, views have vacillated between man as product of his heredity or his environment to the current situation where prenatal existence as well as genetic composition and chemical balance is getting more attention than the *tubula rasa* or environmental approach. This question of human freedom with its extremes of selfish self-actualizing and altruistic social responsibility dominates contemporary thought and is evidenced in various ways: the best seller list; court decisions on the insanity plea; renewed stress on volunteerism as the solution to the economic crunch; and nostalgia for the "America the Beautiful" theme "confirm thy soul in self-control; thy liberty in law." The current interest in this aspect of personhood at both the scholarly and popular level suggests that this era will be significant in relating historical and futuristic concepts of self-determination.

In analyzing the two scriptural accounts, we of course see many similarities, but we also see some dramatic shades of emphasis. In the first account, human physical activity (subduing of the earth) is stressed; whereas in the second account, intellectual judgement, free choice and social responsibility are stressed. The directive God gave to Adam in the second account appears not just to subdue the earth but also to respect special powers or parts of creation. Limitations are established; total control by knowledge is restricted. This may be the earliest record of that quality Russell described as "cosmic piety;" Chesterton as "sense of wonder;" and the poet, W. H. Auden, captured when he declared, "the great vice of Americans is not materialism but a lack of respect for matter."[3]

The parallels between these literary renderings of man's relationship to the world and the expressed consensus of the participants at the workshop are obvious. Consistent with the first version, there is no question that God does intend humanity to master the universe by seeking new knowledge and developing new technologies. But frequently the emphasis of the second version surfaced as participants asked: Is it possible that "advances" can transgress human limitations and cause us to overlook some obligations, creating an imbalance for the present as well as for the future? Throughout the discussions, a sense of global, social responsibility emerged. It was frequently observed that decisions about "progress" must be made within the context of the current inequities existing between and within nations and people. Dr. Tymieniecka captured this in defining the *moral person* as "the custodian of the existential balance within the unity of everything-there-is-alive."

As we stand on the eve of the third milennium within the Christian era and come to the close of this workshop, there is a palapable awareness that this decade of the eighties is extremely crucial. A Victorian poet, Matthew Arnold, poetically described such a period in "Stanzas from the Grand Chartreuse" as "wandering between two worlds, one dead, the other powerless to be born." The workshop discussions seem also to indicate that we are, indeed, between two worlds: one which our genius now makes possible and another which our planning action could assure. Einstein reminded us almost 50 years ago that we had reached a

466

point scientifically of "a perfection of means and a confusion of goals."
Yeats with his complex cyclical theory of history characterized this as
the time when the "rough beast" slouches toward Bethelehem to be
born. Workshop speakers referred to it as the "crisis of culture."

All the descriptors carry the basic theme of imbalance, a lack of due
proportion in the use of power. These workshop discussions heightened
sensitivity to the need to master the macro-and micro-universe but also
to exercise control in a manner that is motivated by a respectful sense of
the Creator's rights and the rights of all inhabitants of the world, those
of today and of tomorrow as well.

While one may run the risk of leaning toward a fundamentalist
interpretation of Genesis, it appears that one can consider these two
versions of creation as reflective of our current scientific/technological
situation and the attitudes expressed in the workshop. We are conscious
of several questions. Is the western industrialized world now at the same
point as that described in the second scriptural account? Are we raising
the *same* unarticulated but basic question as the scriptural Adam and
Eve did as they tested their own human power? "If we are able, why
shouldn't we?" Are we losing our perspective on power? Can we with
our propensity for the predictable and perfect (a drive nurtured by our
technological society but contrary to human experience), be taken in by
the fascination of short time comfort and progress so that we overlook
the long term consequences for all persons? Can an insatiable desire for
knowledge and power upset the physical, moral and social equilibrium?

Information should yield knowledge and knowledge should further wisdom but the chain is often broken. One is reminded of Hawthorne's poignant and pathetic story "The Birthmark" in which the
scientist driven by a desire for total power and total perfection concocts a
chemical treatment to remove a tiny birthmark from his wife's lovely
face, and in so doing, destroys her completely. These sessions have
captured that scriptural reflection and highlighted the fact that one
must relate the *primary* imperative of *human development* with economic
and technological imperatives. The two versions of Scripture then
emerge as a paradigm for the dual directive of mastering the world but
also discovering and then respecting that often elusive line between
human freedom and divinely assigned limitations. This tension is
concretely projected in the El Greco exhibit which, by coincidence or
perhaps by divine design, is also here in Dallas at this time. El Greco's
elongated figures capture that human challenge to seek the transcen-

467

dent, the infinite, while accepting the limitations of earthbound existence and creature-status.

This issue of limits surfaced within another perspective as participants frequently questioned what is legitimate enhancement of human personhood and what is destructive of its essence/existence? This question of limits grows in importance when one recognizes, as was suggested by Dr. Vitz, that scientific investigation over the next two decades will focus very heavily on the boundaries and relationships between the brain and the mind, the organic base and the highest *human* activities — thinking and loving. The "artificial intelligence" of the computer will continue to stimulate research into understanding and controlling its prototype "the human intelligence," and the potential for drugs to alter behavior will raise normative and manipulative issues. On the reproductive issue, Dr. Nabors explained the ways in which sterility in the male and female could be medically and surgically corrected so that children could be conceived, while Dr. Tagatz described the manner in which the natural process of intercourse could be circumvented by "in vitro fertilization" procedures and Judge Mansmann explored the surrogate methodology of reproduction. Each presentation emphasized the pace at which barriers are broken and caused participants to reflect on limitations.

The two versions of creation then serve as the paradigm for the healthy wonder, social responsibility and moral limitative themes which surfaced so frequently in the dialogues. The speakers and bishops frequently cautioned not to evaluate progress in its relation to the present generation or to one political, geographic entity. Because we have truly entered the era of the "global village" and "eternal now," the effects of today's decisions in one nation are experienced by other nations, not only in the present but also into the future. The tree of knowledge of good and evil may then symbolize for us a choice between the logic of life and social responsibility or the logic of "non-centered progress." It is no wonder that the Promethean and Faustian themes have retained their great appeal through the various historical periods and cultures.

II. Recurrent Question: The Hourglass or the Digital?

One basic critical issue pervaded the speakers' presentations as well as the bishops' discussions, "How can one relate the current and

468

emerging findings within the various academic disciplines with traditional teachings?" Within the Magisterial framework, the question emerged: "How can we establish continuity within Church teaching and yet be responsive to the evolutionary cultural/technological process?" The basic underlying question then appears to be, are there some philosophical/theological absolutes, some constants, some essentials that can provide a secure matrix for assessing contemporary technologies? This question, of course, justified placing the issue of personhood between the discussions of technology, because the thread from the prelapsarian era to our own space age is human intelligence and free choice.

While the paragraph above frames the basic question, images can capture more effectively the dilemma facing the bishops who seek to provide leadership and to give answers to questions which have never surfaced before. The basic tension within the discussions was, as it were, that between the digital watch and the hourglass. The central questions raised throughout this workshop focused on the manner in which to relate subjectivity with historicity; universal concepts of person with the individuality and diversity of individual consciousness; preoccupation with the present with respect for and recognition of the inexorable flow of time. So the two images of the hourglass and the digital watch concretize the central question presented by the bishops. Both instruments achieve the same purpose: i.e., recording the duration of change; but their means are dramatically and essentially different. The hourglass with its constant dropping of sand stresses the continuity of the passage of time. The digital stresses the immediate, the now, without regard for what has been or will be. The digital gives us efficiency, immediacy, convenience, precision, while the hourglass gives us a sense of continuity, aesthetic and kinetic satisfaction, relative accuracy and finally, far less convenience because one obviously can't carry an hourglass with the same ease as a digital watch. The digital requires touch control to be put into operation, while the hourglass requires intellectual judgement of sand volumes in addition to the basic sense-perception. In using the hourglass, one sacrifices the accuracy and convenience of the digital for the involvement and fascination of the hourglass. The hourglass is a particularly interesting image in that it is protected, covered and insulated, but its operation is starkly public and patent. The digital gives us the separate, the discrete, the unrelated, the present, but the hourglass gives us past, present and future. In relationship, these two images project for us the true challenge of recognizing what is valuable in the present, rapidly moving technological society and relating that to the valid, relevant and necessary information of the past. The two time pieces then capture the challenge of contemporary society as it reacts to the rapid explosion of knowledge and technology which has collapsed the traditional 20-year generation span to just a few years.

Related to personhood, the basic question then becomes: has the same reality of *human person* responded to that long chain of progress from the wheel to the engine to the microprocessor? Again, is it essentially the same person who presided at the various stages of development from the macrotechnology of the agricultural and industrial eras to the microtechnology of our computer/information era? Is the human person of "Eden" essentially the same human person of the 20th century post-industrialized society? If the answer is affirmative, what is the essential nature and what are the essential principles which govern his/her operation and activities? If the answer is negative, how does one find a grounding upon which to evaluate and judge contemporary scientific advances, particularly those which impinge directly on what in a less complex era we would have referred to and understood as "human nature?" This basic question of relating the old with the new, the past and the present, surfaced in three precise questions which were raised again and again: 1) Are there constants, universals in the definition of what is human or what is the human person? 2) Is it realistic to think that moral/ethical analysis can keep pace with the rate of technological development? 3) How does one determine legitimate risks when benefits and risks are so related in technological developments?

A. Definition of Personhood. Are there constants?

In recent years, it has become increasingly apparent that the most fundamental concepts are generally the most difficult to grasp. All the recent activity, judicially and legislatively, on the issues of life and death point to this and indicate that the core issue of many contemporary controversies is the development of a generally accepted definition of what a human person is. The many faceted approaches to this essential question heighten the difficulty. Father Senior, while admitting that the bible cannot offer clearcut ethical norms for the twentieth century, identified six "anthropological constants" within Holy Scripture's treatment of the human person. Father Himes presented the dilemma of

470

viewing the human person as the product of the historical situation and yet the essential and historical understanding of personhood being located in Jesus. Just as historicity would tend to stress the digital, the changing; the focus on Christology seems to capture the hourglass, "Jesus, yesterday, today and forever," the universal, absolute measure. Dr. Vitz reported that the social and behavior sciences, relative new-comers to the scholarly world, suffer at this point from a lack of consensus in terms of what is human. The current research in these areas, however, would tend to affirm traditional values of family solidarity and the place of self-discipline in achieving happiness and fulfillment, while current therapies raise significant questions as to the propriety and morality of using drugs to alter personality and behavior to bring them to "normative *human* standards." This move from a psychological to a biological interpretation of behavior shifts emphasis from the individual to the universal concept of human person and human behaviors.

As philosophy seeks to respond to this question of what is the human person, one becomes aware not so much of a plurality of views and definitions but more *gradations* of one definition. Father Ashley supports the hour glass approach of continuity of definition and complements Father Senior's five "anthropoligical constants." Father Ashley's recognition of universal essentials within existential variables seems also to be most consistent with the secular science of aesthetics which was not included in these multi-disciplinary presentations, but does provide insights. It is the universal, unchanging within the human person that allows the man or woman of the twentieth century, who can function just as comfortably in a submarine beneath the water or on a jet plane above the earth, to identify with a Sophocles drama, the cave paintings at Dordogne, a Mozart sonata or a Giacometti sculpture.

Participants were introduced to definitions of human person which touched on origin, abilities and performance. The question was asked: Is it sufficient that one is the offspring of "two like beings" to be considered a human person or must one be the product of traditional intercourse, or must one demonstrate certain cognitive or volitional powers to earn the label of human? On the point of origin, Father Brinkman would require the marital embrace as the only proper locus to create a human person while Dr. Tagatz suggests that the scientific assist through in vitro fertilization is eminently consistent with the Christian stress on family, particularly for the 10% of the married

471

couples who are infertile. Their disagreement is quite basic and goes far beyond the moral questions of loss of embryos in the in vitro process. While scientific advances may preclude the loss of zygotes in the future, it will not affect Fr. Brinkman's contention based on Pope John Paul's writings that sexual intercourse is the only human method of begetting humans.

To be *fully human* is, of course, to be another Christ — the source of spiritual energy. This observation supports Father Himes, as well as other speakers' stress on Christology as central to the study of human personhood. Dependent upon whether one is seeking a minimalist or normative definition of person, one will emphasize different elements: origin, external appearance, purpose, abilities or performance. While the scaling approach is philosophically, theologically and psychologically accurate, it creates particularly acute problems in a pluralistic society. As noted earlier, this is as central to the current life/death debates as it was to the slavery debate of the last century. A base line or minimalist definition of human person appears to be necessary if the theory of *human rights* is to have any meaning.

Frequently throughout the workshop discussions, it became very apparent that one of the major problems in discussing this very complex issue of "personhood" is language. The marital relationship was variously described as a "contract," "covenant" and "totality of donation." "Autonomy" was used by some speakers as the positive expression of self-determination, but by other speakers as selfish self-actualization where the individual becomes the measure and center of all things. Quite obviously words like "rights," "values," and "obligations", essential to a clear perception of personhood and dependent on one's mental categories, must be clarified before discussion can be productive. Even the label "Thomistic" conjured up diverse understandings and applications by the participants.

Definitional problems are closely followed by assumption problems. Several times through the discussion it became very apparent that one must disclose the assumptions under which one approaches the issue of personhood and technological developments before dialogue can be engaged in. While some within the group may have accepted the assumption that the technological imperative is accepted by and is good for the western world, *and for all other nations as well*, others did not readily concede that *technological progress* implies *human progress*. Some assumed that a human economy must be a growth economy while others disagreed. While it would be simplistic to dichotomize, the conviction that technology will and should continue to advance is more readily assumed by the United States' highly consumer-oriented society, than by the Third World nations. Efficiency and comfort goals of the western acquisitive culture are not equally motivating in other nations.

Another assumption which conditions one's responses to the reproductive technologies issue, and which was challenged in the discussions, is that a couple by marriage gains the right to have children. Although it was pointed out that marriage also gives the right to those acts appropriate to the begetting of children, some of the arguments for promoting in vitro fertilization and surrogate parenting arise from the unspoken assumption that married couples have this right. The issue is complicated by the fact that by not affirming the right of the couple to have children, one is opening the possibility of the state or any group building a justification for family-limitation, a practice which does exist in totalitarian states.

To respond then to that first question raised by the workshop, "Are there constants?" requires acknowledgement of a plurality of methodologies in seeking the answer. Father Himes spoke directly of *theologies*, but the discussions about "person" indicate that pluralism also exists within psychology, metaphysics, ethics and philosophy in general. Each of the disciplines, as well as each of the methodologies within each of those disciplines, gives part but not the totality of meaning, and thus necessitates inter-disciplinary study such as was presented in this workshop. The bishops considered the findings of psychology, sociology, physics, engineering, chemistry, anthropology, geology, medicine, biology, philosophy, theology and law in these three days. They acknowledged that focusing on just one field of study or one academic discipline creates the risk of confusing the descriptive with the prescriptive. A firm conviction of the necessity for this multi-disciplinary and inter-disciplinary approach was underscored throughout the discussions as a legitimate means to seek out the "constants" of human person.

B. *Time for Response: Is it Realistic?*

How can leaders respond to issues which appear to require answers before there is sufficient time or means to gain objective information and make informed judgements? The validity of this question is easily confirmed when one realizes that everyone participating in this workshop was alive when Sputnik was launched and now less than 30 years later, a shuttle 400 times the mass of Sputnik is in orbit. Most of us have also traced the evolution of the television screen from the fuzzy nine-inch black and white of the fifties to the life-size color of the seventies to the miniature wristwatch version of the eighties. We also are conscious of the evolution which actually brought each of us a personal calculator in the seventies; and will probably bring a personal computer in the eighties; and presumably will bring a personal robot in the nineties. All of us also have witnessed the transition from a "lift the phone and wait for the operator" experience to the current telephone system which by the end of this decade will encompass one billion phones in direct dialing around the world. That such a pace of technological development is a major problem in seeking to develop pastoral responses to scientific advances was frequently cited.

In addition to the rapidity with which technological developments are appearing, the bishops cited the great problem of sorting out information as it is presented through the media. The problems of distortion of fact by either printed propaganda or the brief telegraphic approach of television news-reporting was noted. On the issue of nuclear energy, phobias have developed from the worst-case scenario emphasis; while on the issue of reproductive technologies, stress on parental needs and satisfaction has obscured the essential ethical and legal questions. Dr. Carney strongly urged that persons consider that faith is the only antidote to phobias, and should mark the Christian. Knowledge should cast out fear as faith should fill any void. Several of the speakers recommended the need for ongoing scientific and moral educational programs such as this workshop, and also the need for reliable advisors. Father Himes recommended adoption of the transcendental reflection method of Bernard Lonergan as a thoughtful productive way of responding to the moral questions raised by advancing technology. All speakers seems to concur that an issue-specific approach is not helpful in a rapidly changing environment, but the adoption of a general method of study including research, study and evaluation can be extremely helpful. It was also noted in this regard that no issue today can be addressed from the individual or national perspective only. Consciousness of all humanity's *stewardship* of the earth's resources (food, energy sources, technology and values), must provide the context within which issues are discussed. Awareness of effects on the present as well as on the future must be heightened.

C. Progress or Risk — How does one distinguish legitimate risk from irresponsible risk?

Another question recurred throughout all the discussion, but particularly in regard to the nuclear energy topic: "If every technological advance implies certain risks, how does one determine the benefits and establish criteria for the true measurement of risks both in short term and long term perspectives?" There is implicit in scientific advance, whether it be nuclear energy or technologic parenting, a great tension between cost benefit and ethics benefits: benefits for the collective and benefits for the individual; benefits for the present and benefits for the future. In the energy issue, human safety needs challenge healthy economy needs, neither of which, as Dr. Carney noted, is an absolute value. In the surrogate parenting and in vitro fertilization issues, risk relates the value of "the artificial family" to the potential of fraud, abuse, physical or psychic harm to the offspring, while it also raises the more basic question of the "natural" mode of reproduction within the marriage covenant. All agree that we cannot live in a risk free society, and yet all recognized at the same time the degrees of safety both in terms of the present and the future; the individual and society; economic or comfort advantage and resource depletion. It was agreed that one of the more difficult discriminations to make is what is essential and necessary from what is desirable. To make these determinations on the energy development issue alone, one requires a considerable amount of data on population patterns, resource depletion trends and industrialization standards. Commentaries on the amazingly long life span of both nuclear and chemical waste products pointed up dramatically the need for cautious long-range thinking, while at the same time encouraging exploration of new frontiers of knowledge. Judge Mansmann's concern about serious legal complications arising out of the surrogate parenting issue was superseded by her concern for the potentially destructive effects of the reproductive technologies on individuals, family and society; although Dr. Tagatz presented in vitro as an assist to family life. The scientific/legal discussions by Dr. Nabors, Dr. Tagatz and Judge Mansmann underline the need for greater study of the Christian aspects of marriage and family such as that presented by Fr. Morrissey. Dr. Carney suggested that decisions about risks can be made only after careful analysis of the values, the obligations and the virtues involved in each technology in each historical period and with global, long-term consciousness of effects. The "small but beautiful" and "according to Nature" theories seem to be variously interpreted as desirable goals or outmoded concepts.

Coda

Jesus the Way, the Truth and the Life

Within the *Reprise* the two stories of creation served as the image for the contextual description of the workshop, and the images of the digital and the hourglass captured the recurrent questions. It seems appropriate to select the person of Jesus, the apex of Creation and interpreter of history, as the paradigm for this concluding section, "The Coda", which will present three new issues for further consideration. In his greeting Pope John Paul II asked us to reflect on God's words, "See, I make all things new". Several speakers cited Jesus as the ultimate source of knowledge of the human person. Jesus as "the way, the truth and the life" was several times presented in the homilies at the Eucharists, and in the prayers of the Divine Office.

While all experienced a degree of difficulty in seeking to state definitively the elements contained in the concept of *personhood*, there has been no difficulty in agreeing that one of the most basic human drives is to explore new frontiers of knowledge. There is a Manifest Destiny in the intellectual order as well as in the geographical order. Because of this innate drive, the rate of information and technology will continue to accelerate at phenomenal rates. Given this "human imperative", it is the Gospel of Jesus that promises that the Truth will set us free, and gives us confidence and security despite the unsettling experience of information-obsolescence and the possibility of technological eco-cide and socio-cide. Indeed, Pope John Paul II in speaking to a group of Catholic doctors late in 1982 quoted the documents of Vatican II and exhorted, "Continue to search without giving up, without ever despairing of the truth".[4] Given this general drive of the human mind, the mandate of the Gospel and the challenge of papal directive, three issues call for further consideration and point to Jesus as the model.

A. Futurism: A Church Concern

Frequently during these days of study and reflection, the underlying classical oft-repeated question "Do the times make the men or do the men make the times?" seemed to lie just below the surface of discussion. Can we create the future or will it be determined for us? The new but rapidly expanding science of Futurism is developed on the premise that indeed we can control our destiny. The goal of futurism is not to predict the future as its title might imply, but to decide what the future ought to be and to make it just that.

Knowledge, coupled with creative imagination and a set of Christian values, can allow one not only to predict and form the future, but more importantly to anticipate and encourage the responses that support and strengthen the human person.

It is a well known fact, documented in John Naisbett's book, *Megatrends*, that many secular groups composed of government and corporate leaders have already formed to assure their influence in forming the future. Naisbett observes that in less than 20 years, phenomenal growth patterns have marked the number of academic institutions conferring degrees in futurism, membership in "the world future society" and the number of periodicals and journals dedicated to this subject.[5] Naisbett's comments echo questions raised by Suhard and other ecclesial figures in the pre-Vatican II era, when Gustav Weigel dramatically announced that we had entered "a revolutionary moment," which could change the Church as well as the world.

Does not concern that Christian values be effective in forming the future suggest that we in the Church, indeed need to be futurists as well, deciding what the future ought to be and assuring that it becomes just that? So often historically the Church has been placed in a reactive rather than a proactive position. Research has yielded two findings recently which appear especially relevant here. A study of individuals' religious affiliation showed that Christians represent one-third of the world population; Catholics approximately one-fourth of the United States population; and that those who classify themselves as nonbelievers and atheists will have increased from less than 1% in 1900 to just over 20% of the world population by the year 2000.[6] Several studies have revealed that religious groups and organized religions still have high confidence levels among the populace. Is it then not realistic to assume that our Church will follow the Gospel imperative, imitate our model Jesus, and then make all things new by actively designing the future? It should be remembered that the person who defines the issue generally wins the debate.

B. Church: Center of Intellectual Life

If the Church is to form the future by directing technology in accordance with God's plan and then restore all things in Christ, it is imperative that the Church have in its community a group of scholars who pursue their study with the mind of Christ. Christian thinkers and Christian communities of scholars such as that chartered by the 1967 Land of Lakes committee are needed now more than ever when "multiple options" become the order of the day, and when "reproduction a la carte" or "family cafeteria" (sexual intercourse, adoption, foster homes, AIH, AID, embryo transplant, or surrogate parenting) and other technological innovations move from the pages of science fiction into the everyday world. Moreover, it is a widely circulated experience corroborated by a recent study conducted jointly by the Department of Education and National Science Foundation that Americans are moving toward "virtual scientific and technological illiteracy".[7] Ironically, a recent bill introduced to upgrade science and mathematic teacher education has received mixed reactions by some who fear that "a little knowledge is indeed a dangerous thing", and are calling for a more studied depth response to a very serious national problem which extends to a large part of the teacher corps in the U.S.

Further support for the need of Christian scholars to think through issues, and then to assist others to responsibly think them through, is found in the prediction that much future legislative action in this country will be generated by grass roots efforts such as initiatives and referenda. The need for broad-based public reaction to judicial, legislative or regulatory actions on issues such as abortion, wrongful life, environmental hazards, is obvious. Indicators of the success of such grass roots movements exist in groups on both sides of the life/abortion issue as well as by groups as diverse as MADD, RID, Love Canal and Times Beach activists, Grey Panthers, "anti-nukes." Democracy (the power of the voters) is receiving its greatest impetus at a time when the issues to be decided are most complex and the electorate is not well informed. To find one's way through the maze of options and consequences now open demands leadership and education from knowledgeable, committed Christians within the Church community.

While the Church has always had many scholars among its ranks, and the workshop validates this, we cannot ignore John Tracy Ellis's frequently repeated challenge that in the intellectual order, we may be replacing the work ethic with a new ethic of leisure, or his equally cogent observation that "no informed mind will deny that religion has been one of the prime factors in shaping humanity's cultural background from the earliest recorded history to our own day".[8] We should also be mindful that in recent years a false opposition has been set up between ministry that is pastoral and "hands-on", with that which is academic or administrative. It would appear that today greater value is placed on the personal model of ministry than on that more disciplined, more removed, but yet essential, service model of scholarship. Have the ministry-service aspects of research and teaching been encouraged and praised as strongly as other direct service roles? Do the fields of economics, genetics, nutrition, nuclear engineering, political science, behavioral sciences, medicine, etc. draw a representative number of Christian leaders? These fields must elucidate the justice and peace issues which are the agenda for this Post Vatican II era. A great deal of contemporary thought, as well as significant political and economic behavior, now runs counter to that agenda. The Church must value and encourage Catholic scholars in these areas so that in the spirit of Vatican II we are prepared "to penetrate the secular with the sacred." This penetration depends upon intellectual leadership so that unjust structures, systems and attitudes can be replaced by conviction and action directed to the development of all persons. Secular knowledge shares as surely in divine wisdom and is within the Church purview as surely as this life participates in the *Eschaton*.

The current lack of consensus about the "person" which marks the social sciences today, and "the verbal fog" which clouds many philosophical and theological discussions, as well as the rapid advances in technology, demand immediate, well-grounded responses. While one is awed by the diversity of disciplines included in the study of any issue, one is also conscious of the growing centrality of justice as the core issue in social development. One can optimistically speculate that the proliferation of various fields of knowledge will continue indeed; but that ethics will assert itself and assume the prominent integrating role it had in classical days. If "everything that rises must converge" it will converge in the person of Jesus, the model of right behavior. The Church through its thinkers can point the way.

C. Prudential Judgements

The third and final consideration for the coda relates the first two issues of "Christian futurism" and "Christian intellectual leadership."

Prudence must characterize Church approaches to determining the morality of various scientific advances. Complex issues require serious study because yesterday's answers are not necessarily appropriate to today's questions. It is not always easy to discern the hour glass universal from the digital transients. The title of this workshop included the issue of "pastoral problems"; and the greatest pastoral problem is the challenge to make the proper judgment about the morality of certain trends, directions or technologies. One bishop recognizing the burden of making such judgments posed the very provocative and anguished question to his brothers, "As bishops, do we always need to have answers?" It would appear that in the role of teacher/leader there is always present a degree of ambiguity which does not, however, diminish the responsibility to pursue knowledge, truth and wisdom. The complexity of the issues being raised by contemporary science, as well as the need for almost immediate responses, require great caution and great prudence as well as deep creative study and prayerful reflection. To avoid the necessity for "a rehabilitation of another Galileo", one of the speakers recommended a "tentative conservatism" as the appropriate and responsible episcopal response. Implied in such an approach is a healthy balance of clearly articulated principles of reflection and Christian standards of judgment which will yield practical, intelligent action plans. In judging these complex scientific questions which have equally complex moral implications, Church leaders must indeed merge the prudence of the serpent with the simplicity of the dove, and be truly wise in regard to the things of this world. They must seek out the scholars of the Church to assist them in assessing the rightness as well as the wisdom of various scientific efforts.

Conclusion

Strengthened by a Church tradition strong in both scholarly and moral leadership and motivated by that three-pronged plan of futurism, scholarship and prudence, we conclude this workshop and leave here in hope because Hopkins was right. He concretized poetically the Divine promise to be always with us and captured well the essential Christian virtue of optimism and the regenerative source of Divine Energy.

> And for all this, nature is never
>   spent;
> There lives the dearest freshness
>   deep down things;
> . . . Because the Holy Ghost over the bent
> World broods with warm breast and
>   with ah! bright wings.[9]

Endnotes

1. John Paul II, *Redemptor Hominis* (10) quoted in "January 26, 1983 letter of greetings to participants in Third Bishops; Workshop, Dallas, February, 1983."

2. T. S. Eliot, "Burnt Norton", *Four Quarters*, New York: Harvest/Harcourt Brace Jovanocich, 1943, p. 13.

3. W. H. Auden, *The Dyer's Hand*, London: Faber and Faber, 1963, p. 336.

4. John Paul II, "Address to World Congress of Catholic Doctors," October 3, 1982, "*L'Osservatore Romano*", October 25, 1982.

5. John Naisbitt, "Industrial Society — Information Society," *Megatrends*, New York: Warner Communications, 1982, p. 18.

6. David B. Barrett, *World Christian Encyclopedia*. London: Oxford University Press, 1982. (Data summarized in Time, May 3, 1982, pp. 66–67.)

7. John Naisbitt, p. 31.

8. John Tracy Ellis, "Forward," *American Catholics* (James Hennesey, S.J., New York: Oxford Press, 1981,) pp. vii-viii.

9. Gerard Manley Hopkins, "God's Grandeur," *Poems and Prose of Gerard Manley Hopkins*, (ed. W. H. Gardner), Baltimore: Penquin Books, 1953, p. 27.

Index

Aquinas, Thomas, 155, 322, 323, 332, 345, 346, 365, 380
Argentina, 32, 88, 89, 116
Aristotle, 298, 357
Arnold, M., 155, 466
Artificial insemination, 5, 352, 375, 406, 421, 427, 429, 432
Artificial insemination donor (AID), 396, 401–408, 417, 418, 430
Artificial insemination, homogeneous, 430
Artificial insemination homologous (AIH), 396, 401, 402, 478
Artificial intelligence, 468
Ascetic theology, 11
Ashley, B., ix, 165, 174, 177, 184, 313–333, 334, 347, 350, 439, 441, 447, 449, 452, 455, 456, 471
Asia, 55
Atheists, 476
Atom, 331
Atom smasher, 140
Atomic Energy Commission, 96, 104, 141
Atomic Industrial Forum, 143
Atoms for Peace Program, 33, 43, 150, 160
Atonement, 302
Auden, W., 466, 481
Augustine, 346
Australia, 400
Austria, 88, 89
Authenticity, 288–312
Autonomy, 190, 193, 195, 200, 201, 202, 217, 315, 336, 340, 472
Autoteleology, 361
Averroes, 365
Azoospermia, 403

Baby-selling statutes, 412, 413
Backfits, 58
Bacon, F., 291
Bacteria, 402
Bacterial peritonitis, 402
Baer, R., 194, 210
Balance of trade, 69
Baldwin, 209
Bandura, A., 195, 196, 210
Baptism, 302, 424

Barrett, D., 481
Barth, K., 295
Barthian Interlude, 295
Bartlett, 209
Basal body temperature, 385, 386, 393, 396, 401
Bashar, 262, 263, 267, 269
Becker, E., 205, 210
Behavioral sciences, 465, 479
Behaviorism, 196
Beis, T., 381
Bejan, 432
Belgium, 57, 61, 88, 89, 118, 147
Bellarmine, R., 346
Beneficence, 153, 159, 161
Benevolence, 335, 465
Benevolent sentiment, 244, 245, 247, 249
Bennett, W., 194, 210
Bergin, A., 206, 207, 210
Bergson, H., 231
Berne, L., 194, 210
Beyea, J., 131
Bible, see Scripture,
Binswanger, L., 255, 342
Biochemical psychotherapy, 197
Biological basis, of psychology, 190
Biological determinism, 199, 368
Biological models of man, 200
Biologism, 329
Biology, 199, 208, 473
Biomass, 70, 75, 172, 173
Birth certificate, 442
Birth control, see contraception,
Bishops, 9, 154
Black, 420
Black Market adoption laws, 412
Black people, 383
Blakeslee, T., 198, 210
Blondel, M., 295, 307
Blood (in Scripture), 265
Blood group incompatibility, 403
Bloom, F., 210
Bobgan, D., 210
Bobgan, M., 210
Body, 230, 231, 233, 267, 268
Boethius, A., 357
Bonds, 179
Bone marrow, 137
Bonum coniugum, 426

484

487

Garcia, 391
Gas, 26, 27, 28, 34, 35, 40, 60, 74,
  95, 146, 158, 179
Gasoline, 69, 85
Gaudium et Spes, 364, 365, 371,
  422, 426, 439, 452
General Electric, 139, 140, 141
Genesis, xi, vii, viii, 262, 263, 265,
  269, 270, 275, 277, 280, 281,
  325, 332, 375, 420, 464, 467
Genetic damage, 47
Genetic engineering, 206, 430
Genetic risk factors, 403
Genetics, 190, 465, 479
Geology, 473
Geothermal, 28, 173
Germany, 27, 31, 62, 88, 90, 118,
  167, 169
Germinal epithelium, 387
Giacometti, A., 471
Gibson, M., 405
Gilkey, L., 296, 305, 311, 312
Gilligan, C., 195, 202, 211
Glass, R., 383, 394
Global climate, 27
Global village, 468
God, 4, 164, 258–287, 259, 268,
  270, 271, 274, 281, 302, 314,
  320, 321, 332, 336, 339, 463,
  464, 465, 466
Gomel, V., 384, 389, 391
Gonadotropins, 384, 398, 399
Gonococcus, 404
Good, 465, 468
Good of the spouses, 421, 426
Goodfield, J., 311
Goodwin, D., 211
Gospel, 324, 476
Gottesman, I., 199, 211
Governments, 453
Gow, K., 194, 211
Goy, R., 211
Grace, 302, 320, 321, 434
Gray Panthers, 478
Greece, 90
Greeks, ancient, 357
Greens, 147
Grief, E., 195, 211
Griffith, J. D., 92
Griswold v. Connecticut, 420

Groeschel, B., 207, 211
Gross, M., 210, 211
Growth, 194, 209
Growth economy, 174, 178, 472
Guze, S., 211

Habakkuk, 262
Hadari, 390
Hadler, A., 207, 212
Hafele, W., 92
Hall, C., 255
Halloway, R., 211
Hamburg, B., 211
Happiness, 471
Harding, J., 163
Harris Polls, 127
Harris, T., 194, 211
Hartmann, H., 209, 211
Harvey, W., 291
Hawthorne, N., 467
Hayden, A., 306
Hazard, P., 291, 311
Health effects, 105, 135
Healy, E., 394
Heart, 263, 264, 266, 268
Heat, 72, 140
Heavy-water reactors, 95
Hebrew Union College, 340
Hedonism, 176
Hegel, G., 289, 293, 311, 365
Heidegger, M., 218, 333
Heisenberg, W., 289, 293, 311
Hellenism, 268
Helping professions, 204
Heredity, 465
Hermansen, K., 211
Herrman, W., 383, 394
Hill, W., 332
Himes, M., 288–312, 315, 316, 317,
  332, 334, 345, 346, 347, 348,
  350, 470, 472, 473, 474
Historical consciousness, 288–312,
  289
Historicity, 314, 316, 317, 323, 324,
  328, 329, 469
History, 4, 274, 313, 348
Hogan, R., 195, 204, 211
Holdren, T., 131
Holloway, R., 198
Homer, 19

494

Philosophy, ix, 206, 208, 261, 317, 465, 473
Phobia, 163
Phobias, 474
Photovoltaic, 80, 81,
Photovoltaics, 30
Physics, 293, 473
Piaget, J., 190, 195–196, 209
Pittsburgh, 140
Pituitary, 398
Pituitary-testicular axis, 385
Pituitary tumors, 385
Pius XI, 431, 451
Pius XII, 352, 355, 375, 376, 431, 434, 439, 440, 443, 447, 448
Placental hormone, 400
Planned Parenthood of Central Missouri v. Danforth, 416, 420
Planning, 61, 62, 63
Plenary Councils, 458
Plomin, R., 199, 210
Pluralism, 290, 316, 473
Plutonium, 32, 51, 149
Pneuma (spirit), 266, 267, 268
Poland, 90
Political Liberalism, 191
Political science, 479
Pollution, 2, 24, 35, 37
Polyani, M., 210, 212
Pontifical Academy of Science, 433, 434
Poor, 422
Pope John Center, vii, ix, 330, 439
Popular psychology, 193, 194
Population, 66, 176, 177, 475
Portugal, 90
Postcoital examinations, 386
Poverty, 3, 71, 183
Power, 467
Prayer, 343
Precariousness, 217
Pre-embryos, 395
Preparation for marriage, 458
Price, 79, 85, 86
Privacy, right, 416
Private sector, 139
Probabilism in reverse, 452
Progesterone, 393, 398, 400, 402
Progress, 463, 468, 472, 475
Project independence, 169

Prolactin, 393
Proliferation, 160, 182
Proliferation, nuclear, 32, 33, 115, 116, 149, 150, 161, 175, 177, 178
Prometheus, 468
Proportionalism, 329, 330, 448
Prostate, 387, 388
Protectionism, 36, 39, 78
Proverbs, 262, 264
Psalms, 262, 263, 264, 265, 272, 273, 275, 280, 284
Psyche, 268
Psyche (soul), 266, 268, 344
Psychologic reason, anastomosis, 389
Psychological research, 190
Psychologists, 3
Psychology, ix, 187–212, 189, 191, 206, 313, 328, 337, 342, 473
Psychology paperback best-sellers, 192
Psychopharmacological treatments, 197
Psychotherapy, 193, 401
Public opinion surveys, 101
Puebla, 344
PH of the vagina, 386, 393

Quadruplets, 398
Quintuplets, 398

Radiation, 46, 47, 48, 49, 50, 93, 96, 105, 106, 107, 108, 109, 112, 113, 136, 140, 162
Radiation measurement, 133
Rahner, K., 289, 306, 309, 312
Rain, 2, 29
Rassmussen, N., 92
Rassmussen Report, 42, 112
Raths, L., 194, 212
Rational and analytic left brain, 198
Rational animal, 326
Rationalism, 123, 191, 205, 335
Razis, 272
Reactor safety, 27, 29, 54
Reactor safety study, 53, 112
Reactors, 2, 93
Realism, 360
Re-anastomosis, 385, 389, 390
Reason, 209, 220, 221, 226
Recession, 69, 70
Reciprocity, 368

495

497

498

499

500

"Technological Powers and the Person"
Pope John Center Publications

The Pope John XXIII Medical-Moral Research and Education Center has dedicated itself to approaching current and emerging medical-moral issues from the perspective of Catholic teaching and the Judeo-Christian heritage. Previous publications of the Pope John Center include:

SEX AND GENDER, A Theological and Scientific Inquiry, edited by Mark F. Schwartz, Sc.D., Albert S. Moraczewski, O.P., Ph.D., James A. Monteleone, M.D., 1983, 420 pp., $19.95.

HANDBOOK ON CRITICAL SEXUAL ISSUES, edited by Donald G. McCarthy, Ph.D., and Edward J. Bayer, S.T.D., 1983, 230 pp., $9.95.

GENETIC MEDICINE AND ENGINEERING, Ethical and Social Dimensions, edited by Albert S. Moraczewski, O.P., Ph.D., 1983, 198 pp., $17.50. Co-published by the Pope John Center and the Catholic Health Association.

HANDBOOK ON CRITICAL LIFE ISSUES, edited by Donald G. McCarthy, Ph.D., and Edward J. Bayer, S.T.D., 1982, 230 pp., $9.95.

MORAL RESPONSIBILITY IN PROLONGING LIFE DECISIONS, edited by Donald G. McCarthy and Albert S. Moraczewski, O.P. 1982, 316 pp., $9.95.

HUMAN SEXUALITY AND PERSONHOOD, Proceedings of the Bishops Workshop in Dallas, February, 1981, 254 pp., $9.95.

GENETIC COUNSELING, THE CHURCH AND THE LAW, edited by Albert S. Moraczewski, O.P. and Gary Atkinson, 1980 259 pp., $9.95.

NEW TECHNOLOGIES OF BIRTH AND DEATH: Medical, Legal, and Moral Dimensions. A volume containing lectures presented by 9 scholars at the Workshop for Bishops in Dallas, January, 1980, 196 pp., $8.95.

A MORAL EVALUATION OF CONTRACEPTION AND STERILIZATION, a Dialogical Study, by Gary Atkinson and Albert S. Moraczewski, O.P., 1980, 115 pp., $4.95.

ARTFUL CHILDMAKING, Artificial Insemination in Catholic Teaching, by John C. Wakefield, 1978, 205 pp., $8.95.

AN ETHICAL EVALUATION OF FETAL EXPERIMENTATION, edited by Donald McCarthy and Albert S. Moraczewski, O.P. 1976, 137 pp., $8.95.

These books may be ordered from: The Pope John Center, 4455 Woodson Road, St. Louis, Missouri 63134. Telephone (314) 428-2424. Prepayment is encouraged. Please add $1.00 for shipping and handling for the first book ordered and 25¢ for each additional book.

Subscriptions to the Pope John Center monthly newsletter, *Ethics and Medics,* may be sent to the same address, annual subscriptions are $12.00.